Collective Power

Patterns for a Self-Organized Future

Ted J. Rau

Amherst MA, 2023

Sociocracy For All

120 Pulpit Hill Road, Unit 8
Amherst MA, 01002
United States of America
info@sociocracyforall.org

Published by Sociocracy For All. Sociocracy For All is a project of Institute for Peaceable Communities (IPC), an incorporated 501(c)(3) non-profit organization in Massachusetts, USA.

Rau, Ted J., 2023 Collective Power: Patterns for a Self-Organized Future/Ted J. Rau. Sociocracy For All. ISBN 978-1-949183-24-5

Cover design: Colibrian

"If you are interested in a world where people listen and work collectively to solve problems, Collective Power is for you. Building on years of real-world experience, Ted Rau provides an operation manual for the creation and maintenance of self-governing communities with serious attention to equity."
– Professor Charlie Schweik, President of the International Association for the Study of the Commons

"Our biggest global problems call on us to cooperate more effectively at every level. Ted Rau is not only a global thought leader in thinking about governance and collaboration, he is also an authentic, passionate practitioner – working hard to bring abstract ideas and principles to life through his stories and personal reflections. This book is such a tremendous resource I will be suggesting it as a key reading for our ProSocial training courses."
– Paul Atkins, Co-founder Prosocial World

"I love this insightful sensemaking around our social constructs, hand in hand with candid sharing of the unlearning and relearning process around power and responsibility. A sweet blend of practical tools, pointed sensemaking, and inner ponderings, that help travel to the many complexities of being more collective together."
– Samantha Slade, author of *Going Horizontal*

"Distribution and acceptance of power is at the core of developing truly shared led teams and organizations. Acknowledging the power of power and knowing how to balance it unlocks the door to better, more safe, inclusive and effective teams and organizations. With Collective Power, Ted Rau elegantly explores and explains power dynamics while he offers insight, examples, inspiration and actionable help to manage the discipline of power distribution. This is the kind of book you wish had been published many years ago. It's a must-read for all who are serious about developing more healthy and sustainable formats for addressing the challenges of today – and tomorrow."
– Mette Aagaard, author of *Medledelse - når teamet er chef* (*Shared Leadership - When the team is the boss*)

"For anyone interested in creating a better world considering the different levels: individual, group, societal and planet, this book is a

must. Ted presents the views of collectively distributed power without the struggles of "power over" and" power-under" by using stories, anecdotes and dialogs in a pedagogical and brilliant way."
– Alicia Medina, author of *Teal, Trust, Transparency*

"In Collective Power, Dr. Ted Rau – one of the world's leading sociocracy practitioners – provides us with a gift. Drawing on a decade of experience, along with vulnerable reflection, Rau reveals how governance and agreements can foster systems that support power-with and power-within. While these are far from new topics, it's Rau's experience with and appreciation for the intentional design of collective containers that makes his multi-layered analysis and guidance so deeply relevant for these times."
– Donnie Maclurcan, Executive Director of the Post Growth Institute

"In this engaging and informative book, Ted successfully puts his finger on the pulse of one of the most significant points of leverage that we have to build a better world now by clarifying the underlying rule sets that enable successful self-organization and exploring anecdotally how these work in real life from the small group to our entire globe."
– Cecile M. Green, author of *Collaboration that Works: A Ruthlessly Practical Handbook for a Generative World,* Co-founder of Round Sky Solutions

Contents

1   Individuals in groups   **3**

  1.1   Shadows of the past   8

      1.1.1   Stepping Up   9

      1.1.2   Stepping Down   12

  1.2   Shared Power, Shared Responsibility   17

  1.3   The evolution of groups   21

  1.4   Managing the polarities: governance   26

  1.5   Responsibility   29

      1.5.1   *Power-over* and *power-under*   30

      1.5.2   *Power-within*, and *power-with*   34

      1.5.3   Self-repair: pillars of resilience   36

  1.6   Chapter Summary   42

2   Collective Alignment   **43**

  2.1   Collective agency   44

  2.2   The Common Ground   46

      2.2.1   Collective common ground   49

      2.2.2   Feeding into the collective Common Ground   . . .   51

      2.2.3   Sense-making, salience, and mindsets   52

      2.2.4   Feedback processes   54

  2.3   Topic management   55

      2.3.1   Backlogs and agendas   56

      2.3.2   Addressing topics   60

      2.3.3   Modes   68

  2.4   Decision-making   71

      2.4.1   Making proposals   71

      2.4.2   Selection process of people + roles   74

      2.4.3   Decision-making methods   78

      2.4.4   Doing things as a collective   84

2.5   Pace and time 90
       2.5.1   Good enough . . . for now 91
       2.5.2   'Clear enough' 93
       2.5.3   Explored enough 96
       2.5.4   Enough *is* enough! 97
2.6   Policy and operations 99
       2.6.1   Improving operations with policies 104
       2.6.2   When to make policies 107
       2.6.3   Agreements, roles, workflows 110
       2.6.4   Roles, leadership, and accountability 110
       2.6.5   Infrastructure roles 113
2.7   Governance choices 114
2.8   Chapter summary 120

3   Organizational Alignment   121
3.1   Organization-level agency 121
       3.1.1   Letting go of responsibility 127
       3.1.2   Purpose, aims and domains 130
       3.1.3   Leadership 145
3.2   Missions and values 149
       3.2.1   A little detour into semantics 151
       3.2.2   Back to aims 152
       3.2.3   The relationship between missions and aims 153
       3.2.4   Values 155
3.3   Strategy 158
       3.3.1   Unity 158
       3.3.2   Strategy as bulk prioritization 162
       3.3.3   Strategies and power 163
       3.3.4   Strategies and emergence 165
       3.3.5   Budget 168
       3.3.6   A system of many pulls 178
3.4   Information flow 179
       3.4.1   Being our own PR center 180
       3.4.2   Feedback 183
       3.4.3   Metrics 185
       3.4.4   Performance and accountability 187
       3.4.5   Information flow via a social network 189
       3.4.6   Resolving conflict together 190
3.5   Organizational governance choices 192
       3.5.1   Who decides the governance system? 193

3.5.2	Legitimacy	200
3.5.3	Centralization and decentralization	211
3.5.4	Side-note: Organization-level membership	218
3.5.5	Working with a mix of volunteer/staff members . .	219
3.6	Chapter summary	222

4 Beyond one organization **223**

4.1	Coalitions	224
4.1.1	A coalition of sovereign entities	225
4.1.2	What makes a good coalition?	227
4.1.3	Issues	229
4.2	Interorganizational collaboration	234
4.3	Movements, networks and organizations	238
4.3.1	What movements can do	240
4.3.2	What movements struggle with	241
4.3.3	Movements interfacing with organizations	245
4.4	Chapter summary	246

5 Society and planet **247**

5.1	Society and organizations	247
5.1.1	Economic systems for self-organization	248
5.1.2	Purpose and profit	254
5.1.3	Legal systems for self-governance	257
5.1.4	Education	267
5.2	Government	270
5.2.1	Informing formal government	272
5.2.2	Replacing formal government	276
5.2.3	Governance options	282
5.2.4	A structure for a bioregion	289
5.3	Identities	294
5.3.1	Empowerment patterns	295
5.3.2	Counteracting societal patterns	303
5.3.3	Spotting toxic patterns	305
5.3.4	Collective responsibility for liberation?	306
5.3.5	Reductionism and context	307
5.4	The planet	311
5.4.1	Constraints	311
5.4.2	Planetary boundaries	314
5.5	A story from the future	322

About this book

The systems that guide human behavior in organizations are governance rules – the rules by which we steer decision-making, information flow, task management, and performance. This book aims to help people make choices on their governance to improve how groups strike a balance between autonomy and alignment so they can move forward together.

Currently, governance systems are primarily optimized for selfish behavior and with little regard for the real complexity of the issues. To change that, we need to optimize our systems for more collaboration – without limiting people's choices.

Without seeing systems, we're oblivious. Here's an example. A few years ago, I went to DC with my kids. Coming from a rural town, my kids were shocked at how many people were living on the streets. My daughter, then 11 years old, asked me: How can we let that happen?

She was convinced that people "just don't care enough", and told me that if she were president, she'd address it and fix it! Of course, she's right. And even as president, there's not much she could do.

But is the reason really that people don't care? We all know it is more complicated than that. Everyone I know gets up in the morning and wants to do something positive and meaningful.[1] It's not my experience that there are evil individuals that 'just need to be better people', or be led by 'better' leaders.

Instead of appealing to good intentions, this book looks at the *systemic* conditions that guide human behavior. It shows the underlying patterns of our governance design choices and explores their advantages and disadvantages. If the conditions change, then human behavior changes.

My intention is not to propose a particular governance system. Instead, I argue for a more intentional design of governance systems overall. That

---

[1] And if you don't see enough evidence in your life for people being inherently altruistic or 'good', I recommend reading "Humankind: A Hopeful History" by Rutger Bregman.

requires more governance literacy – which this book is aimed to build.

I have spent about 10 intense years in self-governance; specifically consent-based, circle-/role-based self-governance, better known under *sociocracy*. It was built on ideas from natural systems, cybernetics and Quaker decision-making by Gerard Endenburg the 1970s. Sociocracy, its cousin Holacracy and other self-management systems like Semco have inspired millions who want to democratize workplaces and volunteer places.

So why do we need governance?

> Imagine a ship sailing at sea. The crew is remarkable. They work together flawlessly, support each other, and have great camaraderie. But despite their unity, they struggle to navigate and keep the ship in order. Water leaks into the vessel, gradually filling its hull.
>
> A group of sailors fears that the ship won't survive the next storm. To make it stronger, they add heavy iron rods and shields to the ship. Now the ship is weighed down. It's so fortified they can't even adjust the sails anymore.
>
> How well do you think this ship will handle the next storm?

Governance is like the ship that holds a team together. It keeps the sailors afloat, helps them navigate to their destination, and ensures their safety during storms. Without governance, the sailors are adrift without a ship.

A ship can't sail when it's fortified with concrete. A rigid ship can't handle storms or ride the waves. The same is true for governance. Having no governance is not enough. But having tight or rigid rules doesn't leave enough room.

This book will be most useful for people who have some first-hand experience in self-management and self-governance systems like sociocracy, Holacracy, and other forms of less formalized, home-made distributed governance methods often referred to as 'teal' (a reference to the book Reinventing Organizations by Frederic Laloux that has inspired countless people to experiment with new forms of governance).

My intention is to make the book enjoyable beginners while providing details for practitioners of self-governance. It is written from and for a Western context but extends beyond. I'm well aware that other cultures have a much more collective orientation than the culture that I grew up in. My context certainly affected my approach, focus and language.

Governance matters. As I will show, more governance literacy is a huge leverage to build the better world we want to see.

May this book support all readers in improving and redesigning the systems that surround us, making the world we want to see.

Chapter 1

Individuals in groups

Mana'o wants to tell me about her colleague, Jenny. Mana'o is a soft-spoken woman in her 30's. She chooses her words carefully.

Jenny had joined the worker cooperative in the Northeast of the USA, which Mana'o is a part of. Her organization uses sociocracy, a self-governance framework with shared power among workers.

Jenny, however, came in with a background in private equity in China. Or, in the words of Mana'o: "Jenny comes from full-on corporate culture."

Mana'o tells me: "Jenny often jumps ahead in the meetings, plowing ahead even! She talks a lot. She gets anxious."

In her onboarding to the cooperative, Jenny was trained on the processes of balancing and sharing power, and Mana'o commented dryly, "it was interesting to watch her understand how things work."

Over time, things improved a bit. "After getting acclimated, Jenny is now more able to hold it together. But when there's a lot going on, she still goes back to corporate conditioning, and then we have to bring her back to earth in our General Circle meetings."

Why did Jenny struggle? Was she not a good fit? Was she not a good collaborator? In Jenny's defense, the situation had many layers. Jenny was trying to understand the pecking order – and her place in it – but it was complicated. When she joined, Jenny was the most experienced in the organization in relation to the content of their work, finances. She also was, by age, the oldest person. But she was new, and as a new person in the cooperative, she was an employee but not yet a worker-owner. The governance system made her an equal. She was asked for her opinions just like anyone else, and she was asked for her consent on major decisions.

Mana'o thinks that when Jenny was doing her bulldozer moves, she was trying to prove her worth. Then she'd backtrack and say, "oh, I shouldn't have a voice in this. I am not an owner." Her team members assured her that she did, in fact, have a voice because she was a member of the General Circle.

Yet, the misunderstandings would sometimes pile up – "whenever the facilitator asked her to wait because she was rushing ahead, she'd interpret this as the message of *you don't count because you are not an owner in this business*. Being a worker co-op and sociocratic is confusing to someone with her background – her focus is on shareholders, where managers serve the owners of the company."

Being in less power than she was used to – because she was new – and with more power than usual – because of her consent rights – the whole landscape of power had shifted under Jenny. As a result, she either under-played her power or overpowered others. She didn't know anything else.

Let's compare this story to another in a different organization in the story I'll call *Oblivious Andrew*. (I will name all the stories in this book for future reference. You can also find them in the index at the end of this book.) This story also happens to be a worker-owned co-op but in the UK. They had a similar experience.

> "Andrew came from a command-and-control background." He had been working with Agile Software Development and was familiar with sociocracy on an intellectual level. My informant Emily said he was "not conscious of his privilege" as a white, middle-class man.
>
> "It is jarring! He does most of the talking, and he keeps interrupting others. He prioritizes his voice over everyone."

People from command-and-control cultures, it seems, have a hard time easing into the group. They take up space and seem to be in competition mode.

Are there ways to hold power without those behaviors? To find out, let's contrast the stories of *Corporate Jenny* and *Oblivious Andrew* with a favorite story of mine, *New CEO*.

> Brian had been working for a small production company with a team of 20 people for several years. The company had been founded and led by a charismatic entrepreneur who had recently decided that it was time to retire. Under the founder's leadership, the company had

already adopted a sociocratic management structure, and Brian had been an active and dedicated member of the General Circle – the circle overseeing the overall operations of the company.

As the founder prepared to step down, Brian was selected to become the company's new CEO; his years of experience within the organization and his understanding of the company's sociocratic approach made him an ideal candidate for the role.

Upon Brian's appointment, one of his curious colleagues approached him and asked, "So now that you're the boss, what are you going to change? What's in store for us?"

Unfazed by the question, Brian simply replied, "Nothing."

The response took aback his colleague. Surely, this was Brian's opportunity to assert his leadership and make his mark on the company?

Sensing the confusion, Brian elaborated, "If I had seen things that needed changing, I would have brought them up all along. Our sociocratic approach allows everyone to contribute and address concerns collaboratively. As the new CEO, I don't see the need to make sweeping changes just for the sake of change. We will continue to work together as a team, making decisions and improvements collectively, as we have always done."

People are expected to assert power when they have i. Brian should have changed *something* to assert his power. People are conditioned to fear the powerful when they are not the ones in power. Brian broke with two patterns at once.

There is an absolute hierarchy of people in the *old power-over/power-under* paradigm. Those in power – with the capacity or ability to influence or control resource allocation and distribution- decide. And those without power carry out those decisions. A whole set of behaviors comes with this paradigm, like 'making a mark' when in power and fearing those in power when we're not. It concerns how well we listen to each other and how speaking time is shared or distributed. The old paradigm seems to affect almost every aspect of collaboration.

The *new* paradigm works entirely differently. It's hard to describe without sounding outlandish, overly optimistic, or cliché.

In my experience, people are so used to the old *power-over* and *power-under* paradigm in workplaces that they have a hard time imagining anything outside of that.

Considering the new paradigm, it can be best to think of non-work places where we do things together, like singing in a choir. We used this image in the sociocracy manual title "Many Voices One Song" (2018). The metaphor carries over quite well: in a choir, each person sings their part, and *together*, it makes the music.

We *know* that one singer shouldn't dominate a four-part harmony. It will simply not sound good. To go from a solo to a 4-part harmony, those singing louder need to tone it down. Those who have been holding back need to sing louder so they can be heard. If it's a four-part harmony, it's more beautiful when balanced.

Of course, in music, there isn't only multi-part harmony. There are also solos, a one-person band, and background choirs. We can choose what kind of song we want to sing and shape our teams and roles in a way that brings out the most beautiful way the song can be.

There are many ways to organize. But if the song we want to sing is a multi-part harmony, then it makes no sense to think of the voices in a power-over relationship. What we need is balance and alignment to bring all the different skills and activities together on one shared aim.

Let's look at another story to see the contrast between old and new. I call this story *Open Door*. It is set in a traditionally extremely hierarchical European department- a university. When this story happened, the department was in the early beginnings of switching to being self-managed. As with any transition, people were a little on edge and confused or just disoriented like Jenny was.

In their old, hierarchical management system, the department had a Leadership Team. That Leadership Team typically met without transparency; no one on the outside knew what they were talking about.

It was part of the department's culture that there were conspiracy theories about the Leadership Team and what they did and didn't do. Overall, people lower in the hierarchy were sure that on the Leadership Team, "they don't really care."

As the self-management transformation began, the Leadership Team made an effort to counter those rumors by making the topics of their agenda public. They wanted to be transparent to show what happens on the Leadership Team.

That new transparency was met with curiosity – the veil lifted after years of mystery. But people were still suspicious. Maybe the Leadership Team wasn't *actually* sharing everything? Who knows? Can we trust them?

The organizational transformation continued in many steps; teams were formed and reshaped. The old Leadership Team was turned into a General Circle – a representative team that connected all the operational teams. In the process, the new General Circle now had a creative idea to induce more trust in the department: they decided to keep the door to their meeting room open.

Yet, people were still not quite satisfied. It wasn't enough to break the culture of secrecy and suspicion.

As this was all in process, the Covid pandemic hit. To deal with the new challenges, a Wellbeing Circle was formed. Since Covid-related decisions were high-stakes and had a big scope, this Wellbeing Circle became a second center of power.

Interestingly, despite the fact that the Wellbeing Circle was brandnew and hadn't done anything to deserve suspicion, people were just as suspicious of the Wellbeing Circle as they had been about the Leadership Team. From the people's viewpoint, it made perfect sense: *always* be suspicious of those in power, no matter who they are and why they exist!

Independently, another new circle formed, called the Strategy Group. It was a group of seven people that met every week and evaluated which capabilities the department needed in order to be fit for the future.

The Strategy Group had observed what happened with the Leadership Team and the Wellbeing Circle. They knew they had to lean heavily into proactively sharing of information to avoid complaints about lack of transparency.

So they made a bold move. They held *all* their meetings as open meetings. Observers were welcome, they were simply asked to turn their camera off on the videocall. In addition, the Strategy Group also recorded all their meetings and made the recordings available.

This whole move was accompanied by worries. On the inside, members of the Strategy Circle worried that their words would be taken out of context and used against them. Some of their topics were sensitive and there was a worry that other departments of the university might look at the recordings and "feel awkward."

So how did it go? Did people crowd into the meetings to observe? Did it feed new conspiracy theories? Did it spark a rebellion?

Here is what happened: in the beginning, four to five people consistently observed their meetings. But that number dwindled quickly over time. It's unknown how many people ever watched the recordings. The fear that every word would be micro-analyzed did not manifest.

And here comes the most fun part: the nature of complaints changed. Instead of conspiracy theories, people now say things like "what you talked about in the strategy group is too abstract. You guys go ahead and talk about all that. I will not observe anymore, I have other things to do." The whole topic lost its charge. There was no battle to fight anymore. And with no battle to fight, people just focused on their work.

The sound of good governance is silence. Good governance is invisible. There's no drama, no accusations, no conspiracies. All that happens is people focus on work.

To get to a drama-free culture focused on work, we need new systems of working collaboratively, without dynamics of *power-over* or *power-under*. We need to learn how to hold power together and assign and distribute it intentionally and transparently. Interdependent individuals sharing power is what this book is about.

1.1   Shadows of the past

When I was told the *Open Door* story, my informant added with exasperation: "The comment about things being too abstract was *still* a complaint. Some people will *never* be satisfied and continue complaining. Some people will *always* feel excluded, no matter what we do." I agree – complaining and suspicion are part of the old paradigm. We are so used to that paradigm that we often don't notice when we rehearse it.

Those types of behavior can even show up where power is shared, and no *power-over* situation is present. The shadow of that *power-over* past is within all of us, including myself.

This next story is about my own silly mind getting suspicious of perceived power.

> In the beginning, Sociocracy For All, the organization that Jerry Koch-Gonzalez and I co-founded, was only him and me. We worked hard and made good progress. I enjoyed that freedom a lot. I operate well in places where there's little clarity, and one has to be involved in a lot of different things, like marketing, IT, content creation, and administration. As we grew and included more members, we operated with a General Circle and its department circles, and I was the operational leader of the General Circle.
>
> However, we noticed that we didn't make time to think more strategically, which we knew would harm us.
>
> That's why our General Circle formally proposed forming an advisory board (a Mission Circle).
>
> When that was proposed, something snapped for me. I don't know how it happened exactly, but all of a sudden, I felt awful. I was scared

and somehow angry. You know how we sometimes walk around and have inner monologues because we are all riled up? Well, that was me, I walked around for about 48 hours preparing speeches in my mind, a never-ending loop of self-defense. Why we are doing what we're doing, and why it is the best way forward, why this and that isn't done yet, but there are good reasons for it... and on and on I went, all in my head.

I finally spoke up to my co-founder. I told him that I was scared and very uncomfortable with the plan. I explained how I was worried that we'd put ourselves in chains and that the board would want silly documents and reports from us.

And I remember what he said: "Uhmmm, you know this is a sociocratic board, right? It will operate by consent, and you'll have consent rights. Nothing can be decided against your voice."

Right. I had forgotten! Well, actually not forgotten. I knew in my head that this is how a sociocratic board is formed and what that means. Heck, I teach this stuff all day!

I realized I had been defending myself against a shadow. What I had been fighting was not the real proposal. I had been fighting the power-over paradigm.

Sometimes, even when we're aware of the changes we're making and the principles we're adopting, our minds can still hold onto the old ways of thinking and reacting. We carry them in every moment of our lives. It's under our skin and in our bones. We continue to fight against *power-over*, even when we're no longer subjected to it. It's exhausting and painful. Feeling powerless is one of the most traumatic thing for a person.

The instant my cofounder reminded me, the worry fell away. The worry of not having a say, of not being trusted, of people telling me what to do. Of having to go back into *that* world.

1.1.1 Stepping Up

In a hierarchical paradigm, some have too much power, and others don't have enough. To get to a place of equal power, those in power need to step down and invite others into power. And those who are with less power need to step up. But stepping up is not trivial.

Here's a real-life example from someone in the same university department with the Leadership Team and the Strategy Group. Emil is the former leader who led the department through their transition. We will hear more about him later. Anke is one of his team members.

> Anke: "This is an important topic. We need to do something!"
> Emil: "Yes! Then do something."
> Anke: "But what do you think we should do?"
> Emil: "I think you're the person who has the expertise. What do you *think* we should do?"
> Anke: "I don't have time to decide that."
> Emil: "But if it's important, someone needs to decide it, no?"
> Anke: "Yes, but you should decide this."
> Emil: "But I don't know what to do. What do you think? I think you can decide."
> Anke: "So you don't care."

Do you see how Anke avoids taking the power she has? Why is that? Stepping up is scary because it requires taking responsibility. People aren't taking on power because they have learned to lean back and let others make decisions and exercise power.

When he told me the story, Emil commented: "In this way of working with distributed leadership, when we take a risk, no one is going to protect us either." Of course, *he* knew that. He had been in a hierarchy long enough to know that being in power means one needs to fend for oneself in a constant state of competition. (We will hear him later speak about what it is like to be on the other side of this power dynamic!)

Power is a two-sided story: if someone wants to give up power, others also have to take it on. Stepping up and stepping down are not possible unilaterally or in a vacuum. Our power relationships are *relationships*, and they can only be *changed* from within those relationships.

For now, let's focus a little more on what it's like to step up for people who are not used to that. Here's a story that happened in the same department and the only reason I heard this story from Emil was because, oddly, it was about inviting me to do more training for the department. Let's call it the *Neutral Admin invite* story.

> The change team that was in charge of implementing their form of shared governance was in agreement about bringing me in for training. Someone had suggested it, and the idea found a lot of resonance. Then the group moved to make a decision. In the consent round, one person, Annelies, said: "I am not sure this is a good idea. It feels too soon, and I feel pressured. Can we just postpone the decision?".
>
> Her circle was intrigued. Annelies had never said such a thing or spoken up in this way! The team was curious and faced her to

hear more. Everyone was aware that it was the first time she had ever objected; this seemed special. They asked gentle questions to understand where she was coming from. But even after listening, it seemed unclear how to proceed. They postponed the topic to see what would emerge.

The next day, Annelies called Emil, her former boss, and told him how difficult it had been for her to raise her voice to object. She also appreciated how well she had been listened to. She said she still couldn't, however, put her finger on her inner resistance.

Finally, she blurted out: "You know, when we have this workshop, it's *you* sending out the email invites, and then I feel pressured to show up. Just imagine your director came and invited you. You couldn't really say no, right?!"

As is often the case, once an objection is fully understood, the solution was easy to find.

In the next meeting, after a quick brainstorming session, the team came up with a plan to move the signup process to a neutral admin account that would ping everyone to register instead of sending the invite from Emil's account.

Would this work for Annelies? Her response was: "Yes, happily. Because then it's my choice whether I register or not."

When Emil told me this story, he pointed out how proud he was of the circle. According to him, when Annelies objected, the circle was excited because dealing with an objection was the situation they had all prepared, studied, and practiced for. Now it was time to back it up with action!

Finding pragmatic solutions is the easy part. But it takes a lot of courage to object; even more so when we don't know *why* we object. It also t takes a lot of trust to receive someone's objection with respect even when we don't yet understand what's driving the objection.

I wanted to know from Emil what made this moment different. What had Emil done to support a shift in the culture so people could step up? Was it that he had stepped down more to make room for others?

I asked Emil why Annelies called him after the meeting. Didn't he mention that this behavior was unusual for her?

He knew. "When she objected but didn't know why she objected, I had mentioned in my meeting evaluation that I am thankful to her for bringing her objection and to everyone for listening so well so the minority's wisdom could enrich the majority's thinking." He was sure that this little comment opened the door for her.

But that's not all. The gentleness was new, Emil says. "At the beginning of our self-management explorations, we were too harsh on objections. People had to explain their reasons for objecting in a specific way and it felt like we were putting them on trial. That didn't work well for us. Some people withheld objections because they feared the inquisition that would follow, especially when they didn't have a better solution or couldn't put their finger on the reason for their objection. I guess many people simply need help finding out what they object to. And that's ok."

The team had become confident, welcoming, less dogmatic, and more psychologically safe. The culture had changed towards a context where people's voices were welcome, no matter what. It seems like Annelies was finally ready to step up. But that's not all. The leader had made an invitation to share. The circle had created the safety that allowed Annelies to step up.

And that included Emil, her former boss. He reflected that "I was blind to my own power and how it landed on her when calendar invites came from me. But I can totally live with the solution of sending it from a neutral admin account. It's not a big deal at all."

1.1.2   Stepping Down

We've looked at the dynamic of stepping up. What does stepping *down* look like?

It's time to focus on Emil's story more deeply. To understand what comes next, readers need to know some more context. Emil had been the one to bring the organization towards self-management. When the following story takes place, the department of 45 people was a good 18 months into the journey. Everyone was excited and inspired by self-management. But then again, Emil had been the boss before the transition. How should they relate to him *now*? How should *he* relate to them now?

Shifting the power balance means renegotiating relationships. While the structures and practices were in the process of changing, Emil's position had never been questioned. I'd had several conversations with Emil, and I knew he cared sincerely for the employees and deeply wanted them to be empowered and supported.

We were in an in-person workshop, which was a good time to feel the power dynamics. It can be challenging for a consultant to get a good grip on the existing power relationships, especially when teams have worked together for a long time. I wanted to find out.

There was this one thing that bugged me. Emil wore a black suit and a white dress shirt, while the other team members wore casual clothes. The visual difference was hard to miss. I thought, what a curious clothing choice for a self-management workshop. Was he secretly still holding on to power? Had I been blinded by him talking up a good game of wanting to empower others? What was he really thinking?

He is what people call a 'natural' leader, full of confidence, body language of power, highly educated. I was starting to wonder who he was without power and status. In addition, there was also a clear class difference, the leader with a PhD, the others more working class. I perceived a dash of gender dynamics as well because the only woman in the group was the boss's secretary. At the same time, he was well-liked and respected; his employees talked about him with a lot of affection that seemed genuine.

His suit and his confidence started to upset people. Were the people who have the power traditionally secretly still holding on to power? Or were the people not stepping into power resenting *his* comfort with power?

Just recently, Emil had made a few single-handed decisions that had undermined trust and stirred the pot. That day, the tension came to the surface in full steam. What was the deal with Emil and his power?!

The situation could have easily turned into a rebellion. But a rebellion doesn't *transform* power, it just replaces who is in charge. What happened was much more interesting and meaningful.

Fortunately, I had a hunch that this situation was not only juicy but that they all had what it took to transform the situation. So I asked whether they'd be willing to discuss the question publicly, in a fishbowl with all the other workshop participants witnessing the conversation. I asked for their consent to record. I let Emil explain his position, and that's where the transcript begins, slightly for clarity and context.

> Emil: So here I am, trying to implement sociocracy in our department. But there's this thing that happens. Whenever I have a proposal, often, people don't speak up. And I'd like to have the objections surface, right? And then when people are not speaking up or reacting, it's hard for me. When that happens, I feel it's *me* who is taken hostage. Because I can't do the right thing. If I keep going with that proposal, it is power-over because I'm pushing through. But then again, they're not saying what they're really thinking or what they're afraid of. How am I to know what they think if they don't tell me? In those moments, it feels like somebody else is taking power over me, or over *us*, or *the organization*. Maybe it's that somehow people feel threatened by the transparency of surfacing the objections – because if the objections

surface, everybody can talk about them. If they're not, they can still go around and do what they normally do to stay under the radar.

Employee 1 (male): This is a topic that I'm really concerned about. I'm really burned on this because I'm the greatest supporter of implementing Sociocracy, and also the biggest critic of it. I love the insight that you just shared with us. Because I think this is actually what we need to do.

Emil: What is that?

Employee 1: Taking care of old stories. We all carry old stories with us. And you now demonstrated vulnerability. You put yourself on the line – you as a person. In the past, you were in power. So, this total shift may land that well with everybody. There is also your informal power. And people respond with fear – the old fear of power.

Emil: Our own old stories are coming up. Yes, that's right.

Employee 1: So, in my view, and what I've been trying to advocate for the last couple of weeks is that we once and for all take hold of those old stories. I have old stories, I'm part of some of them. But let's really dig deep and it's going to hurt, it's gonna hurt you, it's gonna hurt me, it's gonna hurt some of our colleagues. But let's do it.

We may even lose some of our colleagues, me, you, whatever. But the goal is, as an organization, to change, so that we could do exactly what you and I agree on. We have to move on and be better to flow like water in the old organization.

Ted: Let's do a round.

Employee 2 (female): I'm the newest one in the group. And I can see that the history is really preventing us from moving forward. Because people keep saying, okay we tried this, and it didn't work, we tried this it, and it didn't work, so why should this work? And there are many small stories around, and people having an opinion about how you [Emil] are, and how you should be. And I agree with [Employee 1] that we need to get rid of the stories. Or maybe not get rid of them, but talk about them, and put a lid on them and say, okay, that was the story, now we look into the future because there's a lot of people holding on to the past, and we don't move forward. So, it's a good place to start.

Employee 3 (male): We have tried a lot of different concepts, and some of them worked better than others. And now we have a sociocratic model. And so we have transformed. And sometimes we transform before we have understood. Communication is important.

Not everyone needs to know everything but if they aren't in the loop, they get scared and those old stories come back. We may need to see what kind of communication we will need for the different groups so that we don't overburden people with unnecessary information.

Emil: So, we all agree there are a lot of stories right? Yes, and they're detrimental, they're not good for going forward. And as you just said before, I really loved that you addressed the informal power, you know as well as I do, I *have* informal power. But let's bring out the bad things about informal power, also for me, can come out in the open and be released. Because right now, if we don't move on. . . You have to think outside the box, because if you need to think outside the box all the time, maybe it is the *box* that is the problem. So, we are moving outside the box because the box was the problem.

So what should I do? Because many stories are directly connected to me, and what I have done, or decisions I pushed, or other kinds of stories. So, what can I do to make it easier?

Should I be totally vulnerable and really putting my heart out because I'm not sure about that. What should I do? Should I just go back and let others do the work?

Employee 2 (female): Pass. I have many things in my head right now. I can't get them out right now. I have to find a way to say it.

Employee 1: We have sociocracy now, and I think we should seize this opportunity for us to rethink. On Tuesday, we have a ABN meeting. I think we should put it out in the open, what we've discussed, what we've learned, straightforward, vulnerable, for all of us. We need to tell them that we found out that this is an issue that we need to address. It's not a topic that *you* need to address, but *we* need to address it. I'll stand right next to you, and do that and be just as vulnerable as you are, so that we can get this out of the way and move forward. I think you do a lot of things to help it, but my impression is that they don't come through.

Employee 4 (male): I should tell those who weren't here that you are actually not the old-fashioned boss. You know there was so much new energy when you encountered self-management. When you are excited, when you burn for something, that's what everybody loves about you.

But maybe that's part of the problem, and it has to be separated from your voice. But when you have this drive, we see Emil as a person – the person, not the boss.

Employee 3 (female): I'm not sure what I have to say but I think it's important to find the way. I'm not sure I have the way yet, I need to think a little bit more before I maybe have a good idea.

I think what you're saying is quite good, but I think we have to find a good way to do this, because there are so many different people in our division. And we have different ways to look at things.

Employee 4 (male): Yeah, definitely. And that's why I'm not ready to say something because we are so different. We have to find a way to embrace everybody in the right way so I'm not sure we will find the solution right now.

There are so many things I love about this story. I love how calmly and thoughtfully everyone spoke. I love how, as soon as they discovered that they were able to step out of the game, they made plans to tell everyone else. But the biggest one is the switch from *you* to *we*. *We* need to change this. Even more, they even want to have this conversation in a wider group in the division because it affects *everyone*.

It's not enough for one person to have a mindset shift. Those rebelling against the ones in power had vilified the leadership and treated everything they did with suspicion, creating a waterproof belief system that made it look like no one was trustworthy once they were in power.

Luckily, their relationships were strong. Emil was only able to be so vulnerable because there was enough *psychological safety* in the system that allowed for him to come forward. Emil was vulnerable about how even if he steps out of the power game, his employees still keep it going by holding back and refusing responsibility. By doing that, they were keeping *him* in the prison of being the boss, and he was tired of it. He was stuck in the role of the boss forever, and there was no way to shake that unilaterally. It had to be a group effort.

It was his vulnerability, showing his humanity, that made it impossible to keep up the *us* vs. *them* story. His team members had to drop their enemy image and see the game for what it was. They call it 'the box'. The box is not attached to a particular person; it's a system that's bigger than all of them. Seeing that made it possible to transcend the dynamic and step out of the power game.

And then, all of a sudden, they are able to see the other side when they realize that it's not personal or based on 'those in power' but that it's a system. Emil said it well: "In those moments, it feels like somebody else is taking power over me, or over *us*, or *the organization*." That *somebody else* that is taking power over everyone is the power game. The whole system needs to be ready for the whole system to transform.

1.2 Shared Power, Shared Responsibility

Lonnie had shared with Emil that she was feeling insecure about her role. Her work was only situated in one team (that they call *circles*). In the implementation process, she saw many new circles form, and she felt "left out".

It took several meetings for her to be able to say that she was worried about asking to join a circle because she wasn't convinced that another circle would *want* her as a member. She didn't feel like she had skills to offer.

Emil asked her whether she was open to considering putting herself out there, including her willingness to learn new skills for a new role. Her fear was that expressing her willingness to learn would shed light on the fact that "I am not good enough and don't have enough work right now." They considered a few options but closed the meeting without a set action plan. Emil trusted her to do what she was ready for. And she did!

After a while, Emil saw a note Lonnie had written on the internal bulletin board advertising herself as open to new roles.

What happened? Did people ignore her and think badly of her?

Quite the opposite! A total of four circles tried to pull her into their work, and she had to choose one. She and her new circle are very happy with their choice. She continues to be eager to learn, the circle is glad to have an extra hand to do the work, and the customers like her.

After she was settled in her new role, Emil checked in with her and asked her what had caused her change of heart. She said, "I get it now. I understand the point of this new system now."

He asked her to explain. She responded: "This way of working teaches me to take responsibility. And if I am brave, I can just do it."

This comment, I think, is spot on. If we only think about power, we miss out on a key ingredient in the mix. The key here is *responsibility*.

In the beginning of their journey of shared power, people are sometimes focused on wanting power, which makes a lot of sense. They want to have a say on everything. Then, over time, they realize that holding power comes with *responsibility*. Power, the authority to make decisions, comes with the responsibility to make those decisions. Responsibility and power are two sides of the same coin. They are inseparable – at least in a well-managed *power-with* paradigm where the powerful cannot pass blame.

Holding responsibility is sometimes more than we asked for. There's a great story I want to tell but to understand it, we'll need a quick overview of how consent decision-making works.

- In consent decision-making, to make a decision about a proposal, each team member is asked for their consent.
- Only if every team member consents can the proposal pass.
- Each team member decides whether they consent or object. They object if they see harm in the proposal. They consent if the proposal is good enough to try.

Just like the children who are excited to have choice, newbies are often excited about their power in shared decision-making. They can say no to anything! No one will push decisions on them anymore!

What they miss is that they are also asked to be *responsible* for every decision they give their consent to.

To understand what that means, let's look at a story of how that failed, *Standing aside in a House Sale*.

> In a cohousing community, a very sticky decision had to be made regarding a house sale – a decision about who could buy into the community. These are high-stakes decisions for a community, mixed with interpersonal dynamics, money, legal, and process issues. This particular situation was extra hairy because of some of the history of the people involved.
>
> The proposal on the table was to offer the house to one particular buyer. Yet, because of some of the special twists in this situation, two circle members felt conflicted about the proposal. They didn't feel like the sticky aspects of the decision had been given enough consideration. The other circle members argued that this was a time-critical decision and needed to be made before the circle could meet again. Since the two hesitant members had nothing concrete to offer, they didn't know what else to do other than to 'stand aside' and abstain from the decision.

Sidenote: Not everyone may be aware that standing aside is a common practice in consensus decision-making but not a choice in consent decision-making; in consent decision-making, each circle member *needs* to object *or* consent, and nothing in between. If they don't object, that means they consent. And the reason for that is in what we will see next. . .

With the two circle members standing aside, the decision about the house sale was approved and the lucky purchaser was contacted that evening.

The next morning, the two abstaining circle members woke up feeling horrible. They knew deep down they had made a choice they regretted. They resented the decision and the way it was made. They had felt pressured and confused in the process. In their perception, they had been coerced into saying yes with no other option than to take themselves out of the decisions. So they called the others on the circle the next morning – but it was too late. Changing the decision on the new buyer would have been very awkward.

Those who stand aside are sometimes righteous – in retrospect, they can always claim, 'I told you so' and avoid taking responsibility. Those who did take responsibility for a decision are then upset that they are being blamed for what is supposed to be a shared decision.

Being allowed to object means *having the responsibility* to discern. Do I *really* think this decision is ok? If not, I would say one is not only allowed to object but is *responsible* for objecting. After all, why would one say yes to something that will harm the group? Yet, for many people, that means stepping up into a responsibility they haven't yet been willing to fill.

How should people know whether they can be co-responsible for a decision? It can be really hard to know when something is 'just' a little discomfort with a proposal and when something is worth objecting to. To explain more, I have two stories of objections that give us a clue about what is important and when.

The first story is my own, called *I Don't Like Your Facilitation Style.*

I participated in a circle meeting where I was the circle secretary and held no other circle roles. We were in a selection process to choose a new facilitator. We entered the nomination round where people could suggest names of people who could serve in this role, and people's nominations were a bit all over the place. Yet, one member, Phil, nominated himself.

Now here's some self-disclosure. I cannot stand Phil's style. I find his way of talking prickly and just overall unpleasant. I was fine with him in a shared circle, though somewhat reluctant. But thinking of him as the facilitator doing much more of the talking seemed like a nightmare to me. Yet, his self-nomination gained traction in the change round. I was in inner turbulence as each person switched their nomination to Phil. Saying yes to him felt wrong and *way* out of integrity. I was the last person to speak in the change round, and it already felt socially awkward not to follow the trend. But now, as Phil was getting proposed for this role, should I object?

The rush didn't make it easy for me. So I turned inwards and just asked myself this one question: *Do I see any way in which he as the facilitator would negatively impact our work as a circle, including my contribution?* And what I came up with was a clear *no*. No, there was no reason outside of my own aversion to his style that would justify an objection. Honestly, I was a little surprised about that. My aversion felt so strong, and yet, there was nothing substantial about it that I could detect. So I decided to consent.

Fast forward. Phil was the circle's facilitator for one year. I admit that his abrasive style actually didn't come through in his facilitation at all. There was a little bit of the whininess that I disliked here and there, but overall, he did a solid job moving our circle along. It wasn't just tolerable – it was *good*!

I never told my circle what had been going on for me. And I don't think I ever will. I was wrong. And I'm embarrassed by how wrong I was and how judgmental. The question *Do I see any way in which he as facilitator would negatively impact our work as a circle* had saved me from making an unjustified move.

The second story is a client story, *Pleasing Pauline*. The client reached out to me with the following situation:

A member of our circle, Pauline, is really motivated to be a good facilitator. We're all about learning so we loved that. Yet, she is not a very organized person. She loses track and forgets what we were talking about. She means well, and she's put in a lot of effort to learn.

She took extra facilitation training with Sociocracy For All and soon, it was time for selections in her circle. In the nomination round, everyone nominated other people, and when it was her turn, she self-nominated. Pauline, reminding people that she had taken the class, expressed a deep desire to be the facilitator. That swayed many people to change their nomination to her, and she ended up being selected with no objection with a 1-year term.

Yet, many circle members had a bad feeling about this. We weren't really convinced that it would work out well. We didn't feel like we could object. Pauline had wanted it so badly. We couldn't burst her bubble!

> And then what we had feared happened. The meetings didn't flow. They felt disjointed and chaotic. But we didn't know what to tell her. And we were only 4 months into her 12-month term. What can we do?

This is so relatable! And yet, they clearly noticed it wasn't a wise choice and needed to change it. A role selection is not a popularity contest or a 'good effort' award. A team needs to be *functional*, and meetings need to support its operations. In this situation, that was not the case, and that's a dealbreaker.

The people who gave their consent to Pauline wanted to avoid a difficult conversation, just like the people who stood aside in the earlier story did so to avoid responsibility. In doing that, they prioritized their own sense of ease over the group's needs. By contrast, in the story *I don't like your facilitation style*, I was able to tune into the group's needs and noticed that there was no issue on that level – therefore, it was best to consent.

Distinguishing the individual and the group level here is enlightening. We often think of responsibility in absolute terms, but really, there is no absolute responsibility – one is always responsible *for* something or someone. Power and responsibility are relational.

Let's understand better what that means.

1.3   The evolution of groups

One Saturday morning a few years ago, it was a weekend alone with my five young kids and I felt sick with a bad cold. Too fried to get off the couch, two days of caretaking and errands seemed like an insurmountable mountain to me. I shared my worry with my children and told them I felt daunted by the weekend and feeling sick.

One of them, maybe nine at the time, asked me, "Ted, where are you?!"

I had no idea what she meant, so I replied, truthfully, "in our living room?" That wasn't the answer she was fishing for, so she prompted me more. "Look around you, outside the window, Ted! Where are you?!"

I guessed, "in a cohousing community?" Apparently, that's what she wanted to hear. She gently scolded me, saying "Ted, you're pretending that you're all alone. But that's not true. You're in the middle of a community. Ask for help!" (And right she was. A send-help-please email later, I had childcare lined up for the day within just a few minutes.)

Where I grew up, we don't ask for help. We learn to be alone and self-sufficient. We live *next to* each other, not *with* each other. Relying on others counts as a weakness.

Of course, we know that hardly any of us could survive on our own. I know for sure I wouldn't. We're not *actually* alone or self-sufficient.

I organized this book into chapters that move from individuals to groups to organizations and beyond. All of those nested levels sustain us.

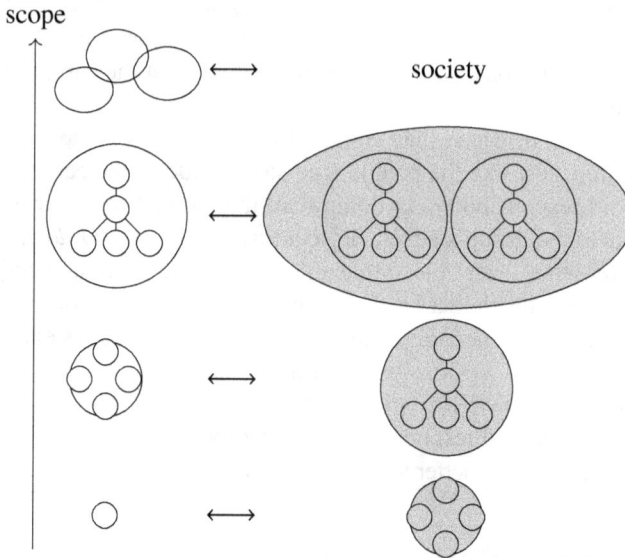

Individual and collective entity on all levels

Each of these levels comes with responsibilities and emergent properties that no other level has, which is more than the sum of its parts. For example, each cell in the body follows instructions encoded in its DNA. But when these cells come together to form tissues and organs, properties emerge not due to individual cells. These properties cannot be predicted by looking at the behavior of each cell in isolation but rather arise from the interactions between cells and the structure of the tissue or organ as a whole. The same is true of groups of people and groups of groups as well as societies.

When we turn a set of individuals into a group, we have two active levels: the individual (their needs, thoughts, opinions, etc.) and the group as a 'being'. Each individual has an identity, and the group has an identity. Each individual has goals, and the group has shared goals that co-exist with the individual goals.

How do these levels interact with each other? One way to understand their relationship is through the concept of *multi-level selection*. The idea of *multi-level selection* is simple but profound. When looking at selection in evolution, there are two poles:

- Each level comes with a competitive side: as an individual, I may prioritize my *individual* needs over the needs of others at the expense of others' needs. In short, that's our selfish side.

  For an organizational context, a more appropriate term is *autonomy*.

- Each level also has a cooperative side: I might be an individual with my own needs but might choose to prioritize the group's needs in some moments. That's our altruistic side.

  For working in organizations, we can think of this side as the side of *alignment*.

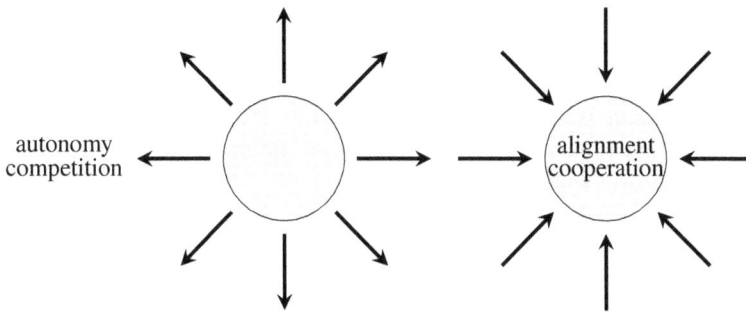

Autonomy and competition are decentralizing forces; alignment and cooperation are centralizing forces.

As an example, imagine two siblings fighting each other – they're in competition mode. As soon as an unfamiliar neighborhood kid threatens the little brother, most likely, siblings will stand together against the 'other' – cooperation mode. That's the basic pattern that happens on *all* levels.

The idea of multi-level selection is that humans compete as individuals within groups and cooperate as groups in competition with other groups. Evolutionary selection happens not only for traits that benefit *individuals* but also for those that benefit *groups*. Humans have evolved with a complex mix of cooperative and competitive tendencies, reflecting the different selective pressures that have shaped our species throughout history.

Our competitive behaviors have been shaped by the pressures of individual survival and reproduction; in some moments, it's smart to be a

Level	Competitive force	Cooperative force
Individual	competing for attention, funds, preference, other personal advantages	collective purpose
Team/group	competing for team funds, attention and direction	team/group purpose
Organization	competing for clients and resources (funding)	organizational purpose
Movement	competing for attention and resources	movement purpose

Selection levels

competitive individual. In other moments, it's wiser to go for the community's well-being.

Competition is not a bad thing – on the contrary, it's a driver for innovation and improvement. Resources are finite, so we need to make choices. A few examples:

- On the individual level, members of a collective might compete for who gets to have extra time on the agenda to have 'their' item talked about or whose project gets extra funding. Having to 'fight' for airtime will make it more likely that people will make an effort to make their point relevant and helpful.
- On the team level, not all departments, circles, or teams might get enough funding. Not having enough revenue to resource all teams fully will mean that teams have to get creative about making the best of the existing funding and how to make their teamwork relevant enough to keep funding in place.
- There is competition between organizations, which will spur innovation in finding niches and added value for clients in new ways.

Markets create competition and innovation and figure out connections that no one would have been able to plan centrally. The *autonomy* opens opportunities.

The cooperative force is the unifier. Team members, individuals, groups, organizations, and movements find common purpose and put aside the competition that is internal to their level. This is where *alignment* is.

Examples:

- When people let go of their personal preferences and give consent to something they can go along with in support of the collective's aim (see consent decision-making in section 2.4), they opt for cooperation for the collective's good. I did that in the story *I Don't Like Your Facilitation Style* when I decided to give consent to Phil as the facilitator.
- While there might be arguments among teams, everyone will focus on the organization's well-being when pitching a new opportunity for the organization.
- Several nonprofits might compete for funding – but if a funder promises a large sum for cooperative projects, the organizations might find a way to work together on a wider-scope umbrella project.

We don't have to answer whether people are competitive *or* cooperative, *good* or *bad*. Humans are simply both because *both* the focus on the individual *and* the focus on the collective are helpful from an evolutionary perspective, and that is what shaped us.

In Dee Hock's words, "[c]ompetition and cooperation are not contraries. They have no opposite meaning. They are complimentary. In every aspect of life, we do both."

Do you need convincing that this is true?

Here's an experiment conducted by poultry geneticist William Muir. (I read about it in the book *Prosocial*[1] that explains many of the concepts in this section.) Muir's experiment aimed to test the effects of individual selection versus group selection on egg-laying productivity. He conducted the study using two different approaches:

1. Individual selection: Muir selected the most productive hens (those that laid the most eggs) from different cages and bred them to create new generations.
2. Group selection: Muir selected the most productive *cages as a whole*, based on their collective egg-laying performance, and bred all the hens from those cages to create a new generation.

After several generations, Muir found that the *group*-selected chickens showed a significant *increase* in egg-laying productivity, whereas the *individually* selected chickens showed *decreased* productivity. Even more, the individually selected chickens were found to be more aggressive, often pecking at each other, leading to injuries and deaths.

---

[1]Wilson, Hayes, Biglan, Embry, (2019)

It's not always about individual success. Groups get better outcomes when they select by groups for more cooperative behavior. After all, the idea of teamwork is to do things that can't be done alone. (And things that can more easily be done alone, *should* be done alone!) In a team, ideally, the weaknesses of individuals are compensated for, and the strengths compound.

Once a group works together, the individual contributions move into the background and it becomes more about their ability to work together. Example: wouldn't one expect that a group performs better if people in it are smarter? Well, turns out that's hardly true. In an experiment[2], people's IQs were tested. They were then assigned to groups for tasks like brainstorming, problem-solving, and decision-making. The study found that the collective intelligence of the groups was only *weakly* correlated with the average intelligence of the individual group members.

For illustration, here's another finding: groups work well if they are *all* either rather active or *all* relatively mellow about the project. What doesn't work so well is if some people are very active and others are less engaged, in other words, if there is a big differential among the involvement of its members.[3] It even goes so far that if we have a group of four people working well together and were in sync about their level of engagement, then adding a fifth person who doesn't match that activity level will drag the group down below their previous level.

If group performance were simply the sum of its parts, we'd expect it to stay the same if we added a less involved person to the mix. But that's not true, showing us that factors governing group behavior differ from those governing individual behavior.

1.4   Managing the polarities: governance

We just saw that humans have a cooperative side and a competitive side. But if we have both, wouldn't the competitive side always win?

Sadly, indeed, many people think a world based on sharing and supporting each other doesn't work because individual interests will always supersede collective interests. This phenomenon is known as the *Tragedy of the Commons*. Even if you don't know the term, you know the effect: if a kind soul stores milk for everyone to use in the shared office fridge, someone will always use more than their share, undermining the trust sys-

---

[2]Woolley et al. (2010).
[3]Pentland, 2012.

tem. Eventually, the kind souls will be fed up, no one buys milk anymore, or each brings their own. The trust system fell apart – because people are just too selfish.

But the concept of the tragedy of the commons is incomplete.[4] It pretends that we're *always* in competition mode, and that's not true. Remember the chickens? They worked together. Humans work together all the time.

But obviously, leaning back and claiming that people have a good core is not enough. The key to making the best of *both* forces – the cooperative and the competitive side – is to *actively manage both sides*, instead of tipping into extremes.

- An organization that overstates collaboration and alignment might struggle to perform and innovate.
- An organization that overemphasizes competition and autonomy might miss its collective goals and unity.

Typically, people in the Western world don't need to be told to be more competitive; it's the cooperative side that people tend to be weak on. To shift the existing system into balance, we need to optimize for cooperative, group-level behavior.

What does it mean to design for cooperative, prosocial behavior? Lucky for us, the conditions of *how* things can in fact work out have been studied extensively by Dr. Elinor Ostrom. Ostrom was an American political scientist who devoted her career to studying the management of common-pool resources like fisheries, forests, or grazing lands. Noticing that the effects described in the tragedy of the commons didn't happen everywhere, Ostrom was curious to understand what traits made *some* commons sustainable and what the success factors were in their management without resorting to privatization or government intervention.

This research earned her the Nobel Prize in Economics. Sadly, her results are incompatible with mainstream economics and its claim that everyone is just looking out for their own personal advantage – so her contribution hasn't been received as much as it should.

Ostrom conducted field research in a variety of settings. Across all of them, she identified a set of eight core design principles that were associated with successful management of common-pool resources (CPR). Later she

---

[4]Good reasons have been brought forward that it might even have been flawed in the first place because the examples to support the theory of the tragedy of the commons are free-for-alls, not commons where the resource is managed together, see Bollier & Helfrich 2019.

and David Sloan Wilson worked together to generalize them to form the eight core design principles (CDPs) for prosocial behavior[5]:

1. *Shared identity and purpose.*   We need to know who we are. Example: if we share a resource like a community building, then we need to be in agreement about what the building is for. We also need to be clear about what belongs to that shared building (is the shed next to it also shared?), as well as being clear on who is a member.

2. *Fair distribution of contributions and benefits.* For example, ensure fair salaries, workload, and budgeting so no one does too little or gets too much. Large pay gaps undermine self-management. High salary differences make it harder to share control and collaborate as equals. (See section 3.3.5.)

3. *Fair and inclusive decision-making.*   Decision-making needs to be inclusive of the people who are affected. There are different decision-making methods that meet this requirement. (See section 2.4.)

4. *Monitoring of agreed behaviors.* If people can just break the rules, the system will deteriorate. If people can't know the rules because notes aren't public, the system won't succeed. (See section 2.6.4)

5. *Graduated responding to helpful and unhelpful behavior.* Example: a system will work best if colleagues give feedback if something worked well for them and also if it didn't work well for them. (See section 2.2.4.)

6. *Fast and fair conflict resolution.* There should be mechanisms in place to resolve conflicts that arise between users of the resource. (See section 3.4.6.)

7. *Authority to self-govern.* It's much harder to self-govern when a group has very little choice on their actions. Examples are units of a larger company where the mother company restricts the unit.

8. *Collaborative relations with other groups.* The more cooperation there is with other groups, the stronger a self-governed entity will be. (See section 4.2.)

In short: the tragedy of the commons is not the end of the story. We're not just after our own personal advantage. We *also* cooperate, and we do that because it benefits the groups we're in. That collective level needs its own attention and caretaking. A well-governed collective will manage the polarity of individuals and the collective needs on all levels: individuals, teams, organizations, and beyond.

---

[5] See www.prosocial.world.

1.5   Responsibility

Earlier, we saw the story of how *responsibility* is a key term in new forms of working when Lonnie said: "This way of working teaches me to take responsibility."

I suspect responsibility is baked into us as a sense of commitment to that cooperative, community-minded level. I might be an individual, but I feel responsible to my group. I might be a team member, but I feel the responsibility to the organization – and so on. Maybe *feeling responsible* is how that evolutionary drive to cooperate *manifests* inside us. If we feel that call, then instead of an "isolated I", we view ourselves as an "isolated I" – as fundamentally socially situated and interdependent with our networks and relationships.[6]

If we think about it that way, it makes perfect sense that, as we saw, power comes with responsibility. Our personal agency is balanced with the commitment to cooperation. Most people who step into power will also feel that responsibility that reminds them of the next-bigger entity.

Level

Individual	Personal responsibility $\rightarrow$	for own actions in the context of the *collective*
Collective	Collective responsibility $\rightarrow$	for collective actions in the context of the *organization*
Organization	System responsibility $\rightarrow$	for organizational actions in the context of the wider *system*

Responsibility as the baked-in feeling of individuals towards the next-wider level

As such, responsibility is a relational term that involves the relationship *between* an individual or group and the expectations, obligations, or duties they are expected to fulfill.

The clearer we are about what responsibility lies where, the more easily we will be able to fulfill that responsibility. That clarity is what *self-responsibility* is: knowing what's mine – a commitment to taking charge of our own actions, decisions, and well-being while recognizing the impact of our decisions.

---

[6]Bollier 2019.

1.5.1 *Power-over* and *power-under*

Hierarchical power is out of balance; it puts absolute decision-making at the top and disregards the well-being of teams and individuals. In general, *power-over* oversteps the responsibility each person has to themselves or their collective; someone decides about something that is not theirs to decide.

The flipside also exists: if an individual (or a collective) doesn't step into their individual power and defers to the others, it's *power-under*. That's when someone doesn't use their power or believes/pretends that they don't have any power. That's when people complain instead of acting, when they cave in or sacrifice themselves.

Power-under and *power-over* are two sides of the same coin and part of a power game that is out of balance.

Here's the *Furnace Story* to illustrate that.

> It was a group of maybe 28 people in one room inside an old factory building in a sociocracy workshop. We had just talked about consent and objections.
>
> To illustrate how consent works, I made a simple practice proposal about heating. It was rather warm in the room where we held the workshop, and street noise was outside. Since I am hard of hearing and background noise makes it harder for me to hear workshop participants, I proposed to keep the windows closed and turn the furnace down.
>
> Since this was just an exercise and I wanted to embody the learning, I defined three imaginary areas in the room: "stand on the left side if this proposal is your preference. Stand on the right side of the room if you object. And stand in the middle if the proposal is acceptable to you." People shuffled around a bit, and a handful of people indicated they preferred the proposal. Most people were standing in the middle. No one objected.
>
> Yet – one middle-aged woman stood somewhere outside of the three areas. I assumed she had not decided yet, or maybe she didn't understand the choices, so I checked in with her. But here's what she said: "I don't really care about the furnace or the window, but I'm standing here outside of the area, so we remember that some people aren't heard, and they're left out."

Now what? Given that I needed a decision about the window and furnace, what were my choices as a facilitator? I could tell her that since she didn't care about the furnace and window issue at hand, she obviously didn't have an objection and just declared the decision made. But clearly, that would have added fuel to her fire because she'd feel confirmed about her voice not being appropriately heard. Her tone made clear that she would not easily return to the exercise. So, should I start a whole conversation about this topic – which takes away from the group's time for learning and practicing (and also keeps the room uncomfortably warm)? That would mean prioritizing her voice above everyone else.

I said the magic words that have saved me in facilitation many times before: *Tell me more.* She explained a little, and I had time to sort my thoughts and understand better where she came from.

But honestly, that wasn't enough. I was still upset. My inner monologue included statements like: you just want attention, you are undermining your own power by 'standing aside' instead of objecting or consenting, that standing aside is a sure strategy to be left out. And that if we wanted to include all voices, as she said, we should get back to learning and practicing instead of making this an artificial meta-conversation. All those thoughts were flashing through my head.

I used my second set of magic words for these situations: do a round. *What do others think?*

Others were reflecting, which bought me more time. Others didn't seem as triggered as I was – a very useful reality check.

After a few minutes of listening to others, I felt the ground under my feet again. I told her I understood she was worried about all the situations in which people's voices are ignored and dismissed. Where we have no agency, we can't say *yes* nor *no* because we're not even asked. I paused. Then, I asked her how she felt about the windows and furnaces. She repeated that she didn't care. I said "great, I'm glad we were able to hear you. Looks like we can go with the proposal and move on to other topics."

What we discussed at that moment wasn't about the furnace or the windows. It wasn't about the proposal at all. It wasn't even about the present – it was a shadow of the past and a projection into the future – just like when I freaked out about the creation of the SoFA board. What was really in question was how I – how *we* – related to all the collective and past experiences of people not having been heard. And while I was presenting a non-oppressive way of making decisions, her mind was reactive, wanting to be assured that her voice would matter.

What's important to see is that *she* gave *her* power away to decide. She had the power to decide about the window and furnace, but she didn't use that power. At the same time, by starting this other topic without the group's consent, she overpowered the group. By giving away her power, she also *over*powered at the same time.

The *power-under* game is elaborate and sophisticated. It's courageously described in the book *Power Under* by Steve Wineman with many examples. Wineman says, "power-under [. . .], is not the absence of power but a particular expression of it. It is the power to manipulate, to maintain control of the victim role, to create a context of guilt and obligation in which others respond to our needs." (Wineman, 2003)

In a power game, everyone loses. As Emil said in our earlier story about what it's like to be put into perceived *power-over*: "When people are not speaking up, it's hard for me. When that happens, I feel it's *me* who is taken hostage. Because I can't do the right thing."

Dragging a group into a power game holds the group hostage for the individual's advantage – the individual defers responsibility, and the group suffers. This insight is also beautifully summarized by Marshall Rosenberg (the founder of Nonviolent Communication) in this quote: "Never give anybody the power to submit or rebel." If people submit, they accept their *power-under* stance and give away their power. If they rebel, they fight *against* their *power-under* stance but still stay within a frame of power imbalance; they are still operating from the assumption that there is an unequal power dynamic at play. Their actions seek to resist or invert the power structure, but they don't fundamentally change the script - there is still a top and a bottom in the relationship. Rebelling may allow someone to gain more autonomy or control in the short term. However, long-term it maintains a worldview of power differences rather than equitable power. The rebel needs the 'authority' to rebel against. Their sense of agency comes from butting up against rather than escaping the dominant power.

Collective power relies on everyone using the power they have. Both *power-under* and *power-over* weakens the collective. The group can operate normally only when all members step into their power again. Remember the *Open Door* story where the Strategy Group decided to record meetings? In that story, staff members suspected secrecy covering illegitimate power (*power over*). When the Strategy Group decided to have observable and recorded meetings, that transparency contradicted the *power-over* story, and the situation cooled off. People lost interest and went back to work. The collective purpose – their work – took a front seat again.

In the words of Cyndi Suarez: "Disrupting relationships of power requires one to redirect one's life energy away from patterns of domination and toward co-creating new, mutual realities."[7]

Another way to describe group dynamics related to power is the Drama Triangle, a social model first described by Stephen Karpman in the 1960s. It portrays three roles that people can unconsciously adopt in conflict situations. These are not attached to specific people – everyone can take on a role and even switch in and out of them.

- The **victim** role is taken by the person in a power-under stance. The person is not stepping into their own agency and trying to get the collective to take on their issue.

- The **persecutor** role is taken by the person blaming the person in the victim role for their issues.

- The **rescuer** is the role takens by someone who seeks to help and protect the victim, often without being asked or considering whether their actions are helpful or necessary.

These roles feed off each other. The victim 'needs' someone to blame them to prove their story that a wrong is being done to them. Persecutors often see themselves as victims who have to hold up the standards for everyone – '*someone* has to hold people accountable here.' They see themselves as victims because they think that they must do the dirty work while everyone else gets to defer accountability. They sacrifice themselves for the cause, and sacrifice introduces a power-under element that inspires everyone else to get into position to keep the drama going. People in rescuer stance are not interested in changing the power dynamic because they feel too good about being the helper. Keeping the unhealthy dynamic going gives the advantage of being a 'good person.'

One can see the roles in the drama triangle as mis-placements of responsibility, connecting the frame of responsibility, *power over/under* and the drama triangle. The whole drama begins as soon as someone either rejects their own responsibility or gets into someone else's business.

Whenever someone denies their responsibility, the system tries to self-correct. But the drama triangle roles are an unhealthy and ineffective attempt to self-correct because we can't blame people *into* agency: The victim denies any responsibility and assigns it to the persecutor. The persecutor blames the victim for not taking responsibility. The rescuer takes on the responsibility *for* the victim, trying to alleviate their problems without addressing the root cause. What are better ways?

---

[7]Suarez 2018, p. 20.

1.5.2   *Power-within*, and *power-with*

What we *can* do is support people in stepping into their own agency and creating systems where power is managed healthily. We support their own sense of well-being and self-responsibility. Then their commitment to the group will likely surface on its own.

I've seen this again and again in raising children. A child that feels frustrated that they are not taken seriously will rebel (or submit), and will not care about the collective's needs. Once they are in balance with themselves – we call that *power-within* – they will happily contribute to the collective again. Contributing to the collective is a basic need, baked into us as responsibility to our collective.

When a system incentivizes prosocial behavior, people can tap into their own agency and responsibility. People know that they matter. They are trusted, connected, and enabled.

Some people can tap into their personal power and self-responsibility easily, even under less-than-ideal circumstances. Others might rely more on their environment to get in touch with that part of themselves. How well we can hold our own agency depends on our mental and emotional health, cultural background, or the social system.

Power-with is the collective agency that builds when a system is well-managed and governance helps people align their strengths to cooperate. *Power-within* is a necessary condition to reach *power-with*, but in addition, *power-with* needs governance and agreements to be balanced and flourish.

too much:	*power-over*
too little:	*power-under*
in balance	*power-within* (individual)
	power-with (collective)

Healthy and unhealthy relationships to power

This is what makes the difference between a hierarchical system and a collective power system. Overriding needs on any level is coercive and abusive. In a hierarchical governance system, the need of the superior or the needs of the collective are put *above* the needs of the individual, effectively overreaching into the individual's responsibility. We serve the organization at the expense of ourselves. That's unbalanced design.

When we manage *collective* needs well, the *individual* needs don't disappear, If we manage an *organization's* needs, the *teams'* needs don't disappear. A good governance system will *balance and integrate* all needs on all the levels.

Here's a story, *This Little Light Of Ours*, to illustrate how taking care of one level can also positively impact all other levels.

> Rebecca got excited about sociocracy when she read that businesses are more profitable when they use more self-management. Good process had been a value held by her throughout her life – she had seen a successful consensus process early in her life. What would more self-management look like in her business of 8 people?
>
> Rebecca admitted that her staff had been criticizing her leadership, saying that they "have ideas on marketing, but you don't listen to our ideas," and they had stopped giving their marketing advice. She decided to turn things around. She invited a consultant to run a process of exploration with picture forming and proposal shaping. She wanted to show that their ideas mattered to her as the owner, so she even shut down the phones for three hours to create space.
>
> What happened next, she called "cathartic." Everything everyone said got written down. All ideas were heard. There was no rush, just listening. Based on all those ideas, Rebecca formed several circles that focused on different parts of the effort. People felt heard, things got implemented, and new ideas and projects got started. Everyone's confidence increased. There was new energy! Rebecca put it this way: "The light shone on each little corner of the business."
>
> Rebecca was looking forward to passing on more responsibility. She was feeling much better and even made a profit-share offer so employees would get a personal benefit from better results in the business.
>
> Another remarkable move was to give the external consultants (graphic design, web development, and UX consultant) a voice in the respective work circles. Now, the consultants felt more part of the team, which gave the teams more benefit because there was more integration and better interfaces with the consultants. For example, when an employee would produce a promo video, the consultants would have consent rights to decide whether the video is good enough to be used and to give feedback. This gave the consultants a whole other level of appreciation – and increased the level of professionalism in the teams overall.

A better governance system had helped not only the business but also the teams and the individuals in it. She shared power with others – being more cooperative on the group level – but she didn't lose anything.

A collective built on unnecessary coercive power, high power differentials or even enemy images will be weaker and more prone to exploitation via the tragedy of the commons and weaken the collective. We saw that unbalanced power dynamics along with drama, suspicion and resentment distract from the shared goals.

Power-within and *power-with* are highly interdependent because we're individuals, group members, and organizations and members of society simultaneously. My family or my team aren't completely separate entities from me as a person. An individual's actions impact their team. We've all seen situations like *Emely's Divorce*:

> A software development company with several teams was working on different projects. One of the teams was responsible for developing a critical feature for a client. One of the developers within the team, Emely, had been struggling with personal issues that affected her mental well-being. Consequently, her productivity and the quality of her work significantly decreased. Since Emely played a crucial role in the project (and she wasn't willing to acknowledge that she wasn't in good shape), her struggles began to impact the team's progress. The team started deteriorating, and people got upset with each other. Someone pointed out that Emely had dropped the ball, making Emely just more defensive. "You have no idea how hard I worked given how many things I have going on! You don't know a thing about me!" There was turmoil in the whole team, and soon, the teams around it got dragged into the situation. The whole organization started to suffer, and they nearly lost the client.

In this example, the individual and the group are not in competition. Individuals are interested in building well-governed teams and organizations, and teams and organizations are interested in keeping their members in good shape. With a *healthier* way of team governance, even the needs of *individuals* are better served. With better *organizational* governance, the *teams* in it are better served.

1.5.3   Self-repair: pillars of resilience

While it's essential to have clarity on who is responsible for what, we should be realistic about the fact that the levels are interdependent. Sometimes, it's impossible to pin responsibility on one location only. Consider this story, *Glenn's Glasses*.

It was a meeting of a brand new circle. That day, the six people in the circle had met each other only for the second time. It was an online meeting on Zoom, and I was the trainer and convener.

My task of the day was to help them select roles so they could launch the project. We ran a standard selection process for the leader role, and Glenn was the candidate with the most support. I formally proposed Glenn as our project leader with a term of 4 months.

I did a consent round, and one of the circle members, Bridget, objected. I asked her what her objection was, and she said: "I object because Glenn touches his glasses so much."

For a split second, I'm sure, I just stared at Bridget's box on Zoom. Maybe I was waiting for her to say it had been a joke.

But no, she seemed serious. I had no idea what else to do, so I used my standard line. I said, "Ok, tell me more."

On the *inside*, I was thinking more something like 'what nonsense! I've never heard such a bogus objection!' But I knew that leaking that attitude to the outside would be detrimental, no matter what would happen next. I have a little mantra for these situations: 'I'm *sure* she has a point, I just don't see it yet.'

Bridget explained that when people fumble with their glasses, she is anxious. And if looking at the leader makes her anxious, how can she work with him?

Now I understood *a bit* where she was coming from. I was impressed because that almost sounded logical. I still didn't buy it. Or, I should say, I believed this was very real for her. I just didn't think it was within our shared responsibility.

Similar to the furnace story, I was in a bind. But it also didn't seem like she was trying to play power games with me.

Quickly and quietly, I assessed my options. It was not the moment to explain to Bridget that her objection was merely a preference. And as these perfect storms go, we only had seven minutes left. I felt the urge to check in with Glenn, but then again, why would Glenn have anything useful to say here? This wasn't his responsibility either.

I also knew that the people didn't know each other well enough to have an established relationship of trust, so doing a round of reactions to examine the objection seemed out of the question because who knows what people would have said? I was sure it would do more harm than good. It could easily turn into a disaster where people would comment on whether Glenn touched his glasses too much or whether Bridget had a right to get anxious in his presence.

I decided to go a different route and take the objection at face value. I didn't argue back; I simply went into objection mode.

Objection integration gives us different options. One option is to modify the proposal. This would have meant asking someone else to be the leader, and I didn't want to do that. Another option would have been to ask him to keep his camera off or stop touching his glasses, but all of that seemed absurd.

So, I went to the two other ways of integrating an objection: shortening the term and tracking (measuring) the concern. In this case, the term had been four months, so I changed the evaluation date to 6 weeks. For measuring the concern, I knew I had to measure her anxiety level (not the number of times he touched his glasses!). So, I proposed to stick with Glenn in the leader role, evaluate in 6 weeks, and see how things are going, and I'd check in with Bridget's anxiety level every week after our meeting. Everyone consented to that. Integrating the objection had taken about two minutes. I breathed a sigh of relief!

I later asked Glenn how the process had landed on him, and he said it was fine. He was a resilient guy. I asked Bridget the same question, and she said she was very happy because I had taken her concern seriously. (Phew! Sometimes, a poker face goes a long way!)

In the next few weeks, I sent a one-sentence email after each meeting asking Bridget how things were going, and she responded each time that all was well. After six weeks, I asked for a 5-minute process to evaluate whether Glenn would be the leader for the rest of the 4-month project. Bridget praised his leadership skills and the calming effect of his competence.

For everyone who, like me, was convinced that Bridget should have kept her thoughts to herself and that her objection was only a preference that had nothing to do with the circle functioning, imagine this: let's assume that Bridget *really* gets anxious when Glenn adjusts his glasses, and let's say she's doing her best to stay calm but can't. Let's further imagine that Bridget's anxiety drives everyone else crazy. It gets so bad that we get all distracted, and our team performance drops. Whose 'fault' is that?

I imagine this dialogue:

"Bridget, you're driving us crazy with your anxiety!"

"Yeah, I know! I'm so sorry! I tried my best but can't shake it off!"

"Ugh, Bridget, why didn't you tell us when we selected Glenn?!"

"Well, I did, but no one believed me!"

Since everything and everyone is interdependent, the lines between individuals' well-being and the group's well-being blur. What does it mean to be self-responsible and only bother the circle with circle matters? Maybe objecting was the most self-responsible thing Bridget could do?

Responsibility and self-responsibility are more clear-cut than one might hope. The story highlights what we can do when things break down. For whatever reason, Bridget couldn't take responsibility for her anxiety. As a result, she leaked it into the group. Now what?

When things break down, we generally have four pillars of resilience:

1. **Skills and Experience:** This refers to the abilities, knowledge, and expertise each member brings to the organization. They are the technical or practical abilities individuals need to perform their roles effectively. Skills can be trained and developed over time. We need them to find innovative solutions that have not been done before, such as a creative process for a new strategy.

2. **Trust and Relationships:** This pillar refers to the interpersonal dynamics and connections within the organization. A strong foundation of trust, respect, and open communication supports a supportive and productive working environment. Relationships are built and nurtured over time through shared experiences and interactions.

3. **Structures and Processes:** Structures make the organization's governance – agreements, contracts, rules, workflows, organizational structures, all of our human-made artifacts, mental models, and enabling constraints we give ourselves. In one word: our governance!

4. **Principles and Values:** These are the fundamental beliefs that guide the behaviors and decision-making within the organization. Principles or values define what we stand for, its purpose, and our culture. They can be implicit – a shared sense of priorities – or explicit and written down.

We always need *some* of each of the pillars of resilience, meaning we can't do without any of them, although the mix for each might vary.

But overall, we need *enough* critical levels on the *sum of all four* of them to make things work. The main idea is that being well-resourced is better than being too lopsided and low. That's true on all levels – the individual, team, organization, and beyond. (Different models of self-governance methods lean into these systems differently; see section 2.7.)

One cannot build an organization on *trust and relationships* alone, at least not beyond a specific group size because it's highly ineffective at

Structures
and Processes

Principles   Trust and
and Values   Relationships

Skills
and Experience

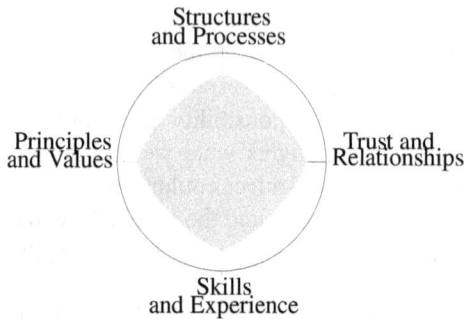

Well-resourced and balanced

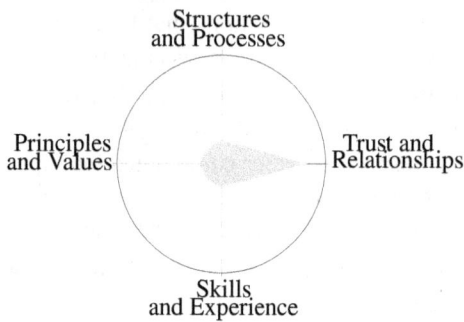

Structures
and Processes

Principles   Trust and
and Values   Relationships

Skills
and Experience

Leaning too much on only one pillar of resilience

scale. With every additional person, the number of relationships increases
exponentially, adding complexity and potential friction.

When there's not enough clarity and structure to hold them, oftentimes,
informal structures and patterns creep back in. (More on that topic in
section 2.6.) Also, what happens if there is conflict? We need a plan B or
a process to hold the space for us during interpersonal tension.

An organization can't run only on *structures and processes* because
they are too fragile. Besides, it's virtually impossible to have a waterproof
system of processes and structures that apply to *all* situations. We will
only sometimes have a process for everything that could happen, and if we
tried, we would become bureaucratic and overbuilt.

Emergence and adaptability might work in the early stages when running an organization solely on *skills and experience*. Re-inventing the
wheel each time we need one is also slower than building systems in places

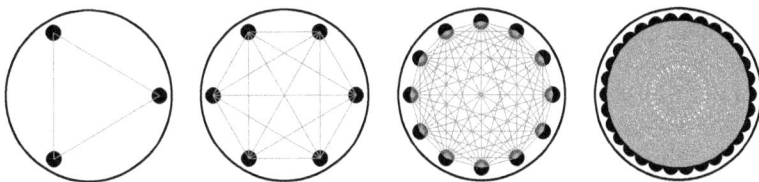

The number of relationships increases exponentially with each additional member

where situations reoccur. If one pillar breaks down (for example, when we're stressed or upset), we need something to fall back on.

Principles and values also just go so far. They can guide our actions in a particularly tricky moment, in *Glenn's Glasses*, for example, I might have acted on my values of kindness that led me to use a gentler approach instead of insisting that "this is not a valid objection."

Bridget might have leaked her anxiety into the group, but it could still be cushioned. The group was new to each other in this second-ever meeting, and bonds weren't strong. People also weren't super clear on processes and the definition of objections because they were new learners. So we fell back onto the last resource we had; in this case, that was my skills in integrating whatever objection-like thing occurred. Honestly, the situation would have escalated in an unhealthy way without that.

Things would have been different in an ongoing team with more experience and more of a track record. For example, if people had known each other well, I would have asked everyone in the group for input. I would have trusted that the group would give loving pushback and say something like – with a smile – "C'mon, Bridget, is this really about Glenn?"

Suppose we had found ourselves in a situation where processes would have been tighter and accepted by everyone. In that case, we might have evaluated the objection and dismissed it as invalid, and we would have solved the situation that way. Bridget may have accepted that.

I think of governance as a garden. A garden needs sunlight, water, and nutrient-rich soil. Asking a gardener the most essential thing for a garden, sun, water, or soil, is pointless because it's all four (and more). If it doesn't rain for a while, the plants may suffer, but they can recover. If all three are missing, the plants will likely suffer too much.

In the best possible world, a garden has the perfect balance of sun, nutrients, and water level. In a perfect world, in an organization, people are always self-responsible and aware. They have all the skills and creativity;

they build the necessary structures and processes. They form solid and caring bonds with each other. But that's unlikely. And that's also okay because their system has resilience.

We will see later that a governance system only needs to be good enough. Even if things aren't perfect, we can make do and get the system running smoothly again. The people in the system don't have to be perfect – and any system that would assume that will be bound to fail.

1.6   Chapter Summary

This chapter discusses the importance of governance in organizations. Just like a ship needs strong structure and systems to sail, organizations need good governance to align people and enable collective agency.

Individuals are both competitive and cooperative. Good governance manages this polarity, balancing individual interests with collective needs. Prosocial Core Design Principles like shared identity, inclusive decision-making, monitoring behaviors, and conflict resolution can help manage this polarity and thus enable prosocial cooperation.

With power comes responsibility. Power and responsibility are two sides of the same coin. Those who hold power must also take responsibility for decisions and actions. How well individual responsibility is held leads to different patterns:

- power-over (hierarchical control)
- power-under (avoiding agency/responsibility)
- power-within (personal agency)
- power-with (collective agency and aligned strengths)

The aim of this book is to examine how governance and agreements can foster systems that support *power-within* and *power-with*.

When systems break down, organizations have four main pillars of resilience: skills/experience, relationships/trust, structures/processes, and principles/values. A balanced mix of all four creates organizational health.

Chapter 2

Collective Alignment

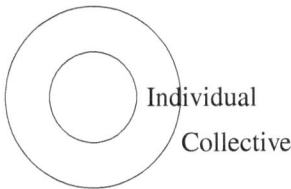

Individual

Collective

Collectives are individuals who come together to contribute to a collective aim that's bigger than what they can do alone. They work when certain preconditions are met.

- **Trust** is crucial in building and maintaining a collective. When individuals trust each other, they are more likely to collaborate, share information, and take risks. When trust exists between group members, they are more likely to make decisions that benefit the group, even if it means sacrificing some individual benefits.
- To bring out the innovative ideas that help the groups adapt, it's vital that individuals can bring whatever ideas they have and be open to disagreements. That requires **psychological safety**. Trust and psychological safety can therefore be seen as supporting forces for both sides, supporting creativity and innovation on for the individual and alignment on the group level.
- **Self-responsibility** is the ability to see clearly what one's individual needs, obligations, and contributions are and what is outside of that – and act accordingly. Self-responsibility is crucial for building and maintaining a collective because it allows individuals to recognize their role in the group and how their actions affect others.

Individual *psychological safety allows innovation*	*self-responsibility to discern*	Collective *trust allows cooperation*

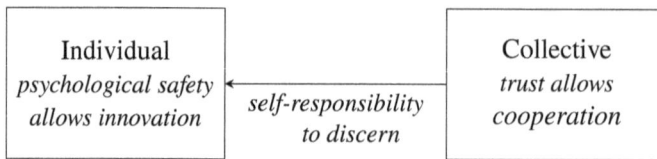

Integration of individual and group needs, aided by psychological safety.

These three ingredients are interdependent. Psychological safety induces trust; trust also supports psychological safety, and so on.

The *collective* depends on individuals holding their boundaries and roles self-responsibly. Those are *necessary conditions* for healthy collectives. There are many methodologies that support personal agency and self-responsibility, such as different forms of communication, coaching and therapy modalities like Nonviolent Communication, clean language, or Acceptance and Commitment Therapy. Some of them serve to get in touch with our personal agency. Others help us hold our own needs, feelings and stories with more healthy perspective. Yet, those are typically for *individuals* as a way to improve the relationship with oneself and one's personal agency.

Yet, just because a number of individuals is acting with self-responsibility, trust, and safety, that doesn't *automatically* mean they will be a healthy collectives. The collective also needs governance to translate individual agency into collective agency.

2.1 Collective agency

What does it mean to have agency? For an individual, having agency means having the power and ability to act and make choices for oneself.

Doing things together is very complex. If I do something alone, many steps are implicit and unnoticeable. Doing things as a group then requires making those steps explicit. Let's take the Four Step Path[1], an old and wise frame to help individual people get clarity for decision-making.

Let's see what each step requires if we take it as a group.

- Be Who You Are. While we typically take for granted our individual identity, a collective self needs to be established and often be made explicit. It's the *aim* that determines the group's identity.

---

[1]Underwood 2000, via Stephanie Nestlerode.

Know who you are	Know where you are	Look around	Decide and do

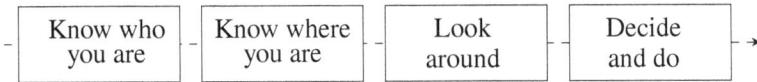

Four-step path

- Be Where You Are. Individuals may consciously or unconsciously understand their circumstances. Establishing the facts *known by a group and as a group* is more complex.

- Look Around. As one person, if I want to look at my options, again, there is often little consciousness of my mind wandering and checking its options. It's often intuitive. As a group, we need to deliberate together. That requires a whole set of processes, like topic management and pacing. (See sections 2.3 and 2.5.) It's not at all trivial to explore possibilities as a group!

- Decide and do. One person alone deciding doesn't require a process. We often don't even notice when we decide. As a group, this is very different. While one person alone 'just decides', a group needs a decision-making method to move forward. This comes with many other artifacts like recording decisions, determining what counts as a valid decision, and many more (see section 2.4).

The first one, being who we are depends on the aim. The be covered more in section 3.1.2). A critical difference between a flock of chickens and a group of people is that the collective will have a aim different from simple survival. The same individuals could meet as either a nonprofit board, a sports team, or a School Faculty. The chickens are always chickens; they don't have functions (as far as we know) that they can add and modify.

More collective species like ants and bees have individuals serving in different roles; foraging, caring for the queen, defending the colony, etc. Yet, these roles are genetically predetermined, and individuals have little variation. In contrast, human groups have far more options and variability due to our more complex culture and technologies.

The aim makes the identity of the group. Ideally, the group knows its aim and also the membership of the group. Knowing who we are is more complex when there are other groups around us, so we will look at aims in more depth in the chapter on organizations in section 2.2.

In the sections in this chapter, I will follow the four-step path beyond Step 1 and see what a group needs to have shared agency in Step 2-4: knowing where you are, what your options are, and picking one.

2.2   The Common Ground

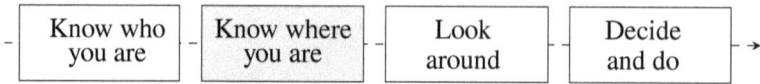

Know who you are	Know where you are	Look around	Decide and do

Four-step path: the common ground determines where we are

I've always been fascinated by how evolution has turned us into synced human individuals – if one person yawns, everyone yawns. If one person eats, everyone gets hungry. One person is throwing up, and we all feel nauseous. One person is laughing; we all laugh. We are tuned into the collective because, as social creatures, working together has served us well.

While our nonverbal cues are good for sleeping, eating, and procreation, they don't extend to when it's time to agree on what we want for dinner tomorrow. That's where symbolic language enables us to discuss more complex topics, like our imagined worlds, future, past or inner life, mental models, and reference points. We can talk about things that aren't or could be here, and things we don't want. Symbolic language is a magic tool that unlocked whole new levels of possibilities for human beings.

In groups, symbolic language helps us review our budget, adjust our 5-year strategy or modify our paid-time-off policy, we need to *talk*. And talking as a group typically means having meetings. (So if you ask yourself after your 5th meeting of the day why on earth we need meetings, here's the answer. Because we want to do things less basic than eating or sleeping, and because we want to do them together.) Words are the way humans mediate and communicate.

Whenever two people talk, they establish what linguists call a *common ground* (cg). The common ground is the set of thoughts (propositions) that we both know and consider true – but only those that we both *know* we know. The common ground is our basis for everything that comes next.

Let's say you and I talk to each other while waiting for the bus. I am telling you I'm going to Northampton to meet my partner, and you say, "oh, that's cool." Now this proposition, *Ted is going to Northampton to visit his partner*, is in our common ground. We know that because if the bus is late and I tell you that I worry that I'll miss my dentist appointment in downtown Amherst in 25 minutes, you'll be surprised. If you cared enough, you would say "wait, didn't you say you were going to Northampton to visit your partner?" It bugs us when our common ground is inconsistent.

Taking care of the common ground in this way is deeply human. Most of the time, humans will play according to the rules and cooperate in respecting how a common ground works. Lying, gaslighting, and contradicting ourselves deeply upset people because they mess with our basic communication rules. If we can't trust that the rules of the common ground are kept, cooperation is compromised.

At that bus stop, you might shrug it off when I'm being inconsistent, but I'm guessing that if you throw out another statement that contradicts what I've said earlier, you'll stop talking to me because you will have decided that I must be crazy and too weird to talk to. Only young children can be illogical or inconsistent without us turning away in suspicion.

How do statements get added to that set of mutually known things, the common ground? If I make an assertion, such as, "my partner is going to pick me up and we'll go have ice cream," you'd just accept that as a new, established fact, because it's compatible with what I've already told you. That new statement presupposes that Northampton has an ice cream shop but that seems in line with what we could expect so that just gets added to the common ground as well. (That's called an accommodation.) We share a larger common ground with people who we know really well because we have more mutually known facts, for example, their family story, their job, where they were born, and so on.

What I find endlessly fascinating is that this common ground only contains what we both *know* we know. What does that mean? Let's say we both happen to know that there was an accident on the bus route and the bus would be late. But we don't know that we both know because we know it from different sources, independently of each other. You checked the bus app before I arrived, and I saw a closed-off road on my way to the bus stop that made it obvious that the bus would have to be late. But we didn't talk about it. I didn't tell you what I knew, and you didn't tell me what you knew. We both know the same fact – the bus is going to be late – but we don't know that we both know.

Let's say we're both standing at the bus stop. It would be awkward if, without further previous comment and before the scheduled bus time, I'd say out of the blue, "ugh, it's a drag that the bus is going to be late." The awkwardness is because I can't refer to something we haven't already established, whether you happen to know it or not. At that bus stop, I would need to say, "yeah, it's a drag, but how do you know the bus will be late? I mean, it will be late, but how do *you* know that?" Another option would be to go with the accommodation and say "yeah, I know." Sometimes, we need to tie ourselves into a knot because we skipped a step and have to backtrack.

The point here is to see that it is not enough that something is *known by you and me separately* and *true*; it also needs to be *known together* by mutual acknowledgment.

In our brains, I imagine the common ground as a box called "common ground that is shared with Person X." I have a box for a partner and one for my neighbor, and one for my kid's teacher. Some people are better at keeping those boxes clean and tidy; I'm not particularly good at it; I frequently have a hard time remembering who I told what. But one of my daughters is impressive and accurately remembers the common ground between herself and each person she knows. A neighbor can tell her in passing that they're going to visit their aunt Mary, and five days later, she'll ask how Aunty Mary is doing in passing. Her management of common grounds with people is top-notch.

For our brains, guessing and tracking who knows what together is a huge cognitive cost. The fact that we do it anyway shows us how important it must be for human collaboration!

Linguistically, only those things that are 'true' that are in the common ground (or easily implied). If I say something and you don't object, it becomes part of the common ground, i.e., a fact. In that way, we spin our self-referential representation of reality collectively. Linguistically, it is *secondary* or even irrelevant whether a statement is a fact out in the real, physical world. People might object to something based on first-hand observation or experience, but beyond that, reality is a whole different story than our language game. To communicate, we have to play according to language game rules, and the language game rule is that a fact is a fact when it's in (or directly follows from) the common ground.

One way to understand the game is by watching children play. Have you ever observed how children around the age of eight or nine seem to argue a lot about their character and special skills and what else is true in that fantasy world they're building? Sometimes, they spend more time building that fantasy world than being in it. That's because they're practicing building common ground worlds. Ultimately, we're all in an imaginary, human-made world of mutually agreed-upon statements. This is important to remember because governance is nothing else but agreements about how we agree on things. It's a convention, a story.

Let's see what happens if we want to deny a statement that has been incorrectly established as a fact. In that case, you'd have to actively object to a fact.

In my work as a linguist, one thing I studied was how people react to incorrect information. My favorite experiment was to show children a picture of a lawn. Just a photo of green grass. I'd show it to them and ask them "what color is the horse in that picture?" There was no horse, and yet the way I asked the question seemed to presuppose that the existence of the horse in that picture was an already established fact, and I was just asking for more information about it. Preschool-age children would just say "brown" because, well, most horses in their minds are brown. Kids around six years old would look at the picture, look at me, look back at the picture. Their body language would show their confusion and discomfort. They didn't know what to do. It just didn't compute. They would often just shrug and say "I don't know." Notice how they weren't able to dispute my sneaky move on the common ground. Finally, children just a little older would look at me, look at the picture, and yell "there is no horse in that picture!"

In the experiment with the nonexistent horse, the most complete response would be to say: "your question seems to assume that there is a horse in the picture, and you're asking me about its color. There is no horse in the picture, so I disagree with your assumption. That makes your question about the color unanswerable." That's complex! It needs skills beyond knowing how to form a sentence to navigate the world of common grounds and the social aspect of language.

On that note, I had a few more complicated scenarios as well where I snuck facts into more complex stories to see how agreeable kids would get when they'd lose track and I'd violate my own presuppositions. As expected, they struggled. But you know what the most shocking finding was? When I compared my findings with adults to create a baseline, I noticed that adults were not much better than kids 8 or 9 years of age. If we add power imbalance to the picture, adults might easily be gaslit into colluding with all kinds of realities. That's why understanding those underlying patterns and mechanisms matters.

2.2.1 Collective common ground

Groups have their own common ground that is *distinct* from the sum of common grounds between individuals. Just like there is a "box" in my brain for the common ground between me and my friend Gina, there is also one for the common ground of the "Fundraising Committee" that contains all the established facts among the members of the Fundraising Committee. This matters because we're trying to answer how one can know something as a collective and not just as 1:1 pairings so we can then base collective agency on our common ground understandings.

The common ground of the Fundraising Committee works like the example of the late bus at the bus stop: it's not enough to know something, it has to be known that it's known. In the case of a collective common ground, the whole group needs to know that everyone in the group knows.

I tell Jane in our Fundraising meeting that our budget is tight and we can't hire a new staff member. Jane now tells Mike that without my knowledge. In my next team meeting with Jane and Mike, I *still* won't be able to refer to that as fact because I don't *know* that Mike knows. We now have to say things like "Mike, I'm not sure whether Jane told you that, but our budget won't actually sustain a new staff member. . . " and *now* we're ready to talk about it because we've established this piece of information as a collective fact. People say things like that all the time – we reference what we think people know or don't know because it's a key thing to track as all processes build on it.

Have you ever been in a position where everyone else knows something, and everyone assumes everyone knows – but you don't? It's very alienating. The reason for that is that the collective common ground is an indicator of our belonging. It's not just that we didn't hear about this new thing – we feel like our belonging to the group is at stake! That's why understanding how we know things as a collective is important.

A collective common ground seems to work in the same way as the common ground for any given two people. But we even seem to track what we know in what kind of *role*.

Let's do a thought experiment on that. Let's imagine we are a governing board. We are all close friends with each other. Now, one of us learns from a friend of a friend outside the organization they saw our CEO making out with the vice president of our competitor. We're a bit amused, a bit alarmed, and a fair bit embarrassed. Since we're all friends, we tell each other because it's juicy gossip, but it never gets said aloud in our meetings. Now let's say the issue gets hairy, and we as board members are now being asked, "did you know that she had that affair?" We'd all look at each other and say "no, the board didn't know." So what we know in a certain *role* as a collective is different from what all the individual members know. Hearing something *officially* has to do with our roles, not just with us as people.

In this case, it can be true that all individuals know and *know* that they all know *but* we know the information as private individuals, not as "the board." That would change if the gossip had been written in an email to TheBoard@TheOrganization.com. In that case, the board would *formally* know because they have been told *in that role*. A collective entity beyond the sum of its members is determined by that collective's role (or aim).

2.2.2 Feeding into the collective Common Ground

Collective common grounds are relevant because shared and mutually acknowledged information is the basis for decision-making, and shared decision-making is the basis for shared agency. A group needs to have enough of a common ground to work together in all kinds of ways. For example, they need to share knowledge about jargon or mental models used in the organization.

A group might choose to do shared sense-making together. From a linguistic perspective, I interpret sense-making as 'trying out' different ways to describe the world to see which descriptions of the world fit. In that way, each of the members of a collective brings the pieces of their individual perspectives to the table, and together, they create a collective narrative that incorporates these different perspectives.

During the sense-making process, group members may disagree, challenge each other's assumptions, and present alternative viewpoints. They may also introduce new information or evidence that leads the collective to revise their individual and collective understanding. Through this process, the collective gradually refines their shared narrative and strengthens their collective common ground.

For groups who take and store meeting minutes, those minutes are an approximation of the collective common ground. Yet, many groups don't have a practice of including communication that happened outside of meetings in their written records, meaning that the minutes will not represent everything that has been established.

Let's say we're on a video call with six people. All video boxes are on, and we assume everyone is looking at each other. We're in the middle of a heated discussion. Twenty minutes late, our seventh team member, Mike, arrives at the meeting in a seventh box. We are continuing our discussion, but our facilitator interrupts for a moment and says, "I just want to acknowledge that Mike is here now."

I used to get a little annoyed by this kind of behavior. I'd like to say, "Why did this need to be said? We all *see* Mike!" And yet, now that I understand, it makes perfect sense to feed information into the collective common ground by saying them out loud (which is the only reason I see why someone would say such a thing); now we not only know that Mike is here, we now also *know* that we all *know* that Mike is here. If it's that, I think it's good stewardship of the collective common ground to do those things. Similarly, information from other sources of knowledge, like feelings, intuition, or other forms of knowing, can also be fed into the common ground by acknowledgment.

A formal report transfers information from someone's personal knowledge into the group's common ground. Only when something has been said and acknowledged can it enter the realm of 'what the collective knows' and can refer to. Sometimes, people report things that every individual in the room knows but that haven't been formally said in the collective. Once it's been said and sufficiently received or noted in the minutes, it becomes collective knowledge. The collection of meeting minutes becomes a written-down common ground for the group. For groups, it often is important enough to put things in writing because the stakes are high, and there's a lot of information.

There are many ways in which we can add information to the common ground of a collective. Reports in meetings only being one of them. We can also email everyone, make a big sign, and send a message on a messaging system. Unlike a meeting where we can see people nod or ask questions and therefore (fairly certainly) know that we all know, that's not necessarily the case in written, asynchronous communication. We can make that assumption, but we all know whether people read their emails is hit or miss. It also depends on the choice of channel. Similar to the gossip example, we know the information as individuals but don't formally connect that with the group-based information.

Suppose we need to be sure that everyone in the group accepts a statement as accurate. In that case, I might make a group-level memorandum of understanding (MOU) that says something like "we accept as true that. . . " and formally approve it in a group decision – more on that in the section on collective speech acts in section 2.4.4.

2.2.3   Sense-making, salience, and mindsets

Agreeing on true assertions in an organization is not only about finding true, observable facts in the organization. It also includes sense-making. Sense-making is a form of feeding the common ground new information by collectively drawing conclusions from already established facts. This can follow a process of choosing what facts are more salient than others.

Let's look at an example. Let's say we are reviewing the undone action items of our team, all 27 of them. Twenty-seven assigned to-do's have not been completed. What does that mean? Do we draw the conclusion that *we're way behind in our work?* If everyone agrees on that interpretation, it becomes a mutually agreed-upon statement in the common ground. We can then build other claims on that fact, like *since we're so behind, we need to hire another person.*

If people don't agree on the conclusion they draw – even though they might agree on each observable fact – then they often disagree on what facts are relevant. There are infinite facts in the world – the sky is blue, remote work is on the rise, and the train to NYC leaves in 5 minutes – and we can't consider them all. Some facts will, therefore, be more salient than others, and the process of choosing what is salient is based on assumptions, experience, belief systems, and bias.

Here's where mindset differences can be challenging because sense-making depends on the 'salience landscape' that drives people's perception (see Vervaeke's work). In those moments, group members aren't able to get to alignment on what is relevant and important because they are in different paradigms of reference points. This book doesn't focus much on mindsets as a lot has been written about them elsewhere, and this book focuses more on structure and governance, but it is clear that mindsets drive our perception and what we consider relevant.

Sense-making is a way to collectivize this experience. In team conversations (synchronous or asynchronous), we 'try on' conclusions by making statements and seeing whether others agree or disagree. In our group process and deliberation, some interpretations will rise to the top of our salient propositions, meaning they will guide our behavior and decisions.

As mentioned above, it can be unclear whether an interpretative statement is a mutually agreed-upon collective or individual statement. If I say my conclusion of *we're so far behind, we should all work more* and no one objects, does that make it a collectively embraced fact? Does the collective common ground and sense-making require active consent (like in an MOU), or is *non-objecting* enough?

The fact that this is unclear can pose an issue when team members have very different perspectives on what they consider a relevant fact and what information they dismiss. For example, if in the above example with 27 undone tasks, the volume of tasks performed every week is 50, I wouldn't be so concerned about 27 undone tasks. The same is true if I consider the undone tasks the 'bottom of the list' that are low on priority and that's why they're not getting done. Let's say we have one anxious team member who keeps pointing out the undone tasks; they are ignoring those contextualizing facts.

Whether objectively true or not, imagine one team member keeps saying *we're so behind!* every meeting. This will set the tone and shape the team's thinking and perception, even if no one actively agrees. They might now perceive all observations that fit into the *we're so behind* narrative as more salient, and that's how the sense-making of the team might shift without an intentional group-level decision or acknowledgment. Understanding the common ground and how statements (whether more observable or more interpretative) shape the common ground of our shared truth is therefore crucial for team-level agency.

2.2.4 Feedback processes

Feedback and performance assessments can be seen as very similar to establishing a common ground. For example, let's return to the story of *Pleasing Pauline*. This was the story where a group selected someone as the facilitator who didn't have the appropriate skills – and everyone but Pauline herself knew that. Since there had not been enough feedback given along the way, there was no common ground on the question of whether Pauline was seen as an organized team member. Pauline and the rest of the team didn't have a shared reality because there was too little acknowledgment of things everyone knew individually.

Assessing someone's performance is, therefore, a particular form of sense-making or filling the collective common ground where more information about the person is agreed-upon. In hierarchical organizations with large power differential, those in power set the narrative and define what the facts are. In a more egalitarian setting, truth is set by mutual consent, which requires a more consensual assessment process.

Speaking self-responsibly is essential and instrumental to holding *power-with* as every piece of communication holds the message content *and* a message about power. If I hold my own needs, feelings, views, and perspectives self-responsibly, then I signal that we have equal power and will hold space for the collective by being clear about what's our own and the group's responsibility.

Many modalities teach exactly that. Nonviolent Communication teaches identifying one's own feelings and needs so we can communicate them while holding our own responsibility for them.

Since people often shy away from feedback, we need to emphasize their participation in that collective process. In the sociocratic performance review process, we ask the focus person to go first (and last) for all process steps to encourage people to acknowledge their strengths and weaknesses. For example, if Pauline had been in a performance review, there's a good chance she might have said something like "I know I'm not the most organized person". That would have made it easier for others to agree with that and therefore treat "Pauline is not the most organized person" as an agreed-upon statement in the collective common ground. That reference point would have made it much easier to object in her selection process because it would not have been the first time that statement would have been made.

That's why an information-rich and feedback-rich environment helps make decisions by increasing the collective common ground. By acknowledging them, we 'pull' things from the unacknowledged space into the collectively held space. Ideally, *all* the information is shared *all* the time. Of course, that is practically impossible. Yet, regular feedback mechanisms (like at the end of each meeting) can help increase the level of shared information in the common ground. That's how we build a stronger foundation for our actions and shared decision-making.

'Groupthink' happens when a collective's common ground becomes too homogeneous or when dissenting opinions are not adequately considered. It's what happens when there is not enough innovation and diversity on the 'friendly competition' side of the collective. Another way to avoid groupthink is by inviting outside voices into the discourse – which will be a topic in section 3.1.2 when we talk about organizations.

For now, let's move to the next step. Now that we have a shared common ground, we can have shared agency if we can direct our *attention* in the same direction.

2.3   Topic management

We've seen how a collective can have a shared common ground – the shared and mutually known information that we accept as reality.

But *knowing* things together is not the same as *doing things* together. To do things, we need to *decide* things. Oftentimes, before we decide things, we need to *talk* about things and weigh our different options.

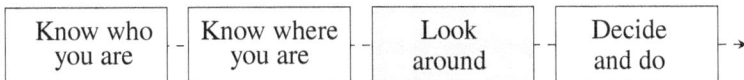

| Know who you are | – | Know where you are | – | Look around | – | Decide and do | → |

Four-step path: when talking, we 'look around' to see our options

While reports and MOUs help build the common ground with what we accept as true facts, explorations are moments when we collectively talk about possible worlds – a possible world in which we start a new Project A, or in which we may cut the budget for Project B. We explore potential actions that would set us on a certain track. These possible worlds are like hot air or a dream. We throw a bunch of them out but most of them just dissipate after the meeting and never enter the common ground or the collective's to do list. They are just ideas, short-lived.

To explore as a group, we need to navigate what we are talking about, like a roadmap, and that means we need to decide together what we talk about in what order. In other words, we need to be able to set an intention or direct our attention to a particular topic.

Every conversation has at least one topic. Let's call that the *Topic on the Table*. In natural flow conversations (outside of meetings), there are different patterns of how we collaboratively establish, maintain, or change the focus or topic of the conversation. We all know this, but we only know it intuitively. For example, a person might say, "I was just about to bring up how I felt about the project but then we changed topics and I missed the moment to speak up." This shows that we are aware of the current topic of a conversation *is*.

The concept of what is *one* topic is squishy. A topic might be narrow or wide, and that's okay. We don't need to be able to pin it down perfectly. We can crack a joke or make a side comment and still be on the same topic as long as we return to the topic. If you are having a discussion on a topic, and someone is making a side comment, and someone else is making a comment about the side comment, and someone adds a joke on top, do you know the kind of tension that we feel when we want to go back to the actual topic? We all have some tolerance in the system, but there are limits.

To establish a topic, we say things like "Oh, that reminds me of this story where...", or "I was also in Italy once, and it was quite funny because I...", or "speaking of weekend plans, I saw an interesting movie last weekend. Have any of you watched The Arrival?"

To make an informal conversation flow, we try to make smooth transitions; it's considered polite and considerate to say things like "slight change of topic, have you heard what happened to Mark?"

2.3.1 Backlogs and agendas

In working together, we want to be intentional about what topics we talk about, and that's why most meetings will have agendas with agenda topics. We don't just have a meeting to hang out but for a certain purpose – that's the difference between a bunch of individuals hanging out and a group that gathers around a certain purpose.

There is a lot of power in choosing what topics we talk about and what topics we don't talk about. In a *power-over* context, the group leader will decide the topics alone. In a context with a lot of *power-under* dynamics, *no one* might decide what we talk about, and we just tiptoe around things we could talk about.

If only one person decides our topics, there is monoculture of perspectives. On the other hand, if we each want attention, then we aren't having a conversation, just a cacophony of personal interests.

How does one *collectively* manage and prioritize topics in a *power-with* fashion? We have topics that we need to talk about. Maybe there is even a 'backlog' or 'parking lot' of topics that group members request to discuss, like a shared to-do list for the collective. There are many ways to store that information – some groups simply retain that information in their collective memory ("we had said we'd talk about hiring a new person in April"). Groups that want to increase their intentionality and accountability will write and maintain a list, like in a cloud-based document, other IT tools, or a paper list in an accessible place. Individuals add their ideas and can funnel individual requests into the collective process.[2]

This parking lot as the shared to-do list can be used to plan agendas. From all possible requests, verbal or written down, old and new, the group needs to figure out what they want to discuss in a given meeting. Since 'the group' can't do such a complex task easily, it can be easiest for one person to put an agenda proposal together. In consent-based systems like sociocracy that agenda proposal is approved by consent, thus sharing the responsibility of choosing topics; then topics that individuals requested become collective 'property'.

We find again the constructive tension between competition and cooperation. Each group member might favor a particular topic that they need to move forward for their *individual* work – that's the side of autonomy. Thanks to governance processes, a collective can balance the individuals' needs with the collective's needs by vetting an agenda via an alignment process. We need to achieve alignment because we manage the shared resource of our meeting time, our attention, and energy. Here's a little story to show what I mean.

> I was in a work meeting where the last agenda item was a short but important and urgent item where I needed approval for a larger budget to continue working on a project. It was important to me because I had

---

[2]Depending on how the backlog is used, it can include unvetted topics, which means it includes individuals' topics, not those accepted by the collective.

> promised outputs to a client. In short, I *really* wanted that topic to be talked about at that meeting. Yet, the other topics dragged along and somehow, we lost ten or fifteen minutes. I got increasingly anxious, but the facilitator seemed relaxed about it. I tried to get his attention politely in the chat on the video platform, but he didn't see it.
>
> I finally said "it's 2.20, and we only have ten minutes left and one more item to go." The facilitator then asserted that "the last agenda item will just have to be moved to the next meeting."
>
> I turned my microphone on and said "excuse me, but I consented to this agenda, assuming we'd do what we consented to. We can't postpone the agenda item; I need to talk about it today."

This could have been avoided if the group had stayed closer to the agenda *or* if a change had been made in the same way the original agreement was made: together. (Once begun, the agenda can still change, but, in sociocratic systems, that requires circle consent again.) We manage the time together, meaning the group's needs need to consider the critical parts.

It's common in meetings to defer to the facilitator (or timekeeper) and make it the facilitator's responsibility to keep the meeting on track. That's an individual-level view of how responsibility is held. A *collective* way of holding the responsibility is by asking all individuals to keep the agreed-upon agenda in mind and be accountable to it. Making agreements together about how meeting time is spent – and changing them together – is a good way to remind groups of their individual responsibility to the collective level. Otherwise, we have the tragedy of the commons and people just using resources (meeting time) without considering the collective.

Meeting time fulfills all the criteria Ostrom discusses for a shared resource. It's not owned by an individual, and it's "rivalous" because when I take up air time, you can't speak. That means Prosocial's core design principles apply, and we need to pay attention to our purpose, fair distribution of costs and benefits, fair and inclusive decision-making about meeting time, and monitoring of agreed-upon behaviors. On that note, in a meeting without a clear process or structure, it's harder to monitor behaviors and to hold people accountable.

The Aristotle Project[3], a study conducted by Google, found that one of the key factors in effective group communication was ensuring that all members had more or less equal speaking time, with conversation turn-taking being distributed evenly among members. That helps create an environment where everyone feels heard and valued and diverse perspec-

---

[3]Find more info https://rework.withgoogle.com/print/guides/5721312655835136

tives and ideas can be shared and considered.

I learned that the hard way, in an embarrassing (to me) and formative moment. If you've met me in person, you know that I have no issues talking in a group. As a child, I was shy and quiet, but I began to feel comfortable talking in groups as a teenager. Trained in Academia, I felt good about my ability to take information in and put it out again. In short, I found myself smart and my contributions necessary.

In the past, meetings had often gone too slow for me – people needed to get to the point, and things were not moving forward. As I entered a circle in my community, I encountered rounds – the sociocratic habit of speaking one by one in a round-robin where everyone speaks once before someone speaks a second time.

> The circle had a lot of work around general community policy, so it was a word-heavy circle. Each round took a while, even with everyone on their best behavior.
>
> Since rounds prevented me from interrupting and injecting my ideas, I started to write my ideas down on a piece of paper. I distinctly remember a moment where I had particularly many ideas and comments. My turn was late in the round, so I wrote a whole sheet of notes full of ideas. When it was *finally* my turn to speak, I was ready to go down the list of comments and lay it all out.
>
> As I looked at the first items on my list, I noticed that most of the points had already been brought by others. Some of my notes became irrelevant because they were tangents and not on topic. I couldn't even read some of my notes or recall their content. There was only one point worth bringing to the group in my turn of the round.

Prior to that experience, I had been that free rider that took up meeting time. At that moment, I learned three big lessons.

1. Not all ideas have to be shared with others. Our 'monkey mind' always produces ideas but can lack discernment. We need to ask ourselves whether they are worth the collective's attention. I learned self-responsibility.
2. The second lesson was even more significant to me: I didn't *have* to have all the ideas; others will have ideas too. I'm not responsible alone.
3. My third learning was that when I was planning my contributions while others were talking, I wasn't actually listening to them because I was so busy listening to myself in my own head. I learned co-creation.

2.3.2 Addressing topics

In informal conversations, there often is no aim besides connection between individuals. But a group with a shared aim needs more process to achieve that aim. Finding our way through the maze of going from problem to solution is challenging and even harder as a group.

We can't talk about five topics at once; we need to take them one after the other – it's the only way for a collective to step into collective agency. Multitasking might *feel* efficient, but if our attention switches all the time, it takes up time and drains our energy. The more people are involved, the easier it is to get distracted.

That's why there should only be *one* topic on the table. The facilitator helps us choose the topic and stay on track.

If the group doesn't know what the Topic on the Table is, they will likely meander aimlessly through the meeting. And even if they know it, they might get off track and tripped off by the following patterns:

(1) **Topic drift:** getting off-topic
(2) **Fork:** two topics are on the table, and we have to choose one to continue effectively
(3) **Dependency:** the solution for a topic depends on another topic
(4) **Circular dependency:** two topics depend on each other

Let's look at each of these patterns in more detail.

Topic drifts

Topic drifts are very common; it's the simple pattern of going off-topic. A

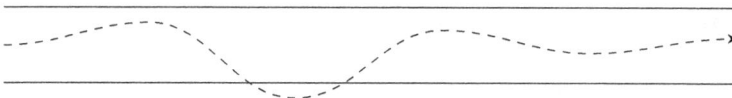

The group catches a topic drift and redirects back to the topic

competing topic can also be another topic but also someone's feelings. For example, if someone gets upset about something, a group might get drawn into caretaking. Using the distinction between *individual* and *collective* needs, caretaking of someone's personal feelings means getting steered away from the collective's needs, just like Bridget's example and her anxiety. (Note that I'm not saying that a collective should never take time to do care-taking of individuals – that can be useful and imperative for the collective's well-being because of the interdependence of individuals and collectives – but it's a common example of how there might be competition between attention on individuals and attention on the collective's work.)

What can the facilitator do in a topic drift? A simple facilitation strategy is to ask to get back on topic. Alternatively, we can park the side topic for later. Even for an emotional moment, if the distraction is minor, we can acknowledge the needs of the individual, give a moment of caring attention so all individuals are ready to show up for the group again and get back to work.

Forks

Forks frequently happen when there is an original topic on our agenda, and a competing topic sneaks in – it might be a new, competing proposal or idea or an emotional issue. In those situations, we can decide whether to stay on the original topic *or* look at the new, competing topic.

This can be hard to decide. After all, new ideas are welcome. Still, they also divert from the collective alignment and forward motion. It's one of those moments where the tensions between emergence and coherence, autonomy and alignment become palpable.

Since we cannot talk about two things at once, a fork requires a choice. A topic drift can *escalate* into a fork when a new side idea gets so much

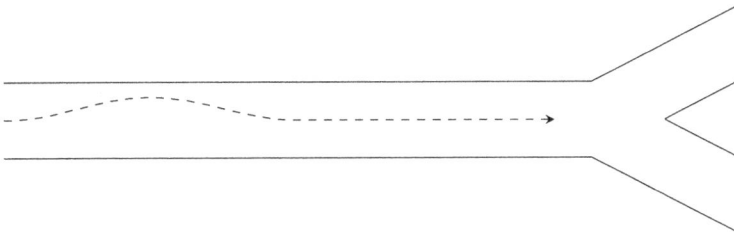

A fork – what should be the topic on the table?

attention that some people want to abandon the Topic on the Table and talk about the new idea. The additional problem with forks is that people often want to dive into the topics (like the new topic), but that's counterproductive with a fork. We need to switch the Topic on the Table from our topic(s) to answering the question '*which* topic shall we talk about?'.

Similar to topic drifts, an emotional issue can become a fork if it escalates. If someone is upset and isn't ready to get back to the group's topic, we now have two competing topics: address the upset *or* continue on the original topic.

Furthermore, a fork is hard to manage when emotions are high. Facilitators are then in a tricky situation of having to ask the group to solve the *fork question* and decide which way to go *while* being stimulated.

When people are stimulated – and that can simply mean excited – they are more likely to prioritize their individual needs over the group's needs. That makes it hard to steer a group in those moments. *Power-over* and *power-under* stances are often played out over topic management, for example, if someone gets really excited about a new idea and then is reluctant when asked to let it go for the sake of the group's progress.

A Fork In The Road is a story of how useful it can be to let the group decide what topics to discuss to avoid resentment of fragmentation.

> Ella, a nonprofit program director, says about herself "I have always worked by myself, and I always wanted to do things my way, my own thing. I always operated thinking that my opinion is the best one."
>
> But over the years, as she learned more collaborative ways of working, she noticed how much she had missed out on what she calls the "beauty and relationships." She noticed that there was a whole universe out there of people who value those things, and it drew her in because it "hit home on an emotional level."
>
> One day, she facilitated a meeting when things went off the rails. One of the members, Susan, was new to the organization. Their organization membership policy said that new people would not have consent/objection rights until they became full members. When learning about this policy, Susan had a strong negative reaction. She asked, "why would I participate if, as a prospective member, I don't even have consent rights?"
>
> Ella, the facilitator, wondered how to 'control the outbreak.' How could she get rid of this problem quickly and get back to the meeting? Or would she have to change the agenda to accommodate this new topic? She remembered their agreement that agendas could only be changed by the circle's consent. She decided to ask the group.
>
> "Should we drop our agenda and make room for this?"

Ella told me that just asking this question was a personal breakthrough for her. She remembered to ask instead of relying on her judgment, which was new behavior for her. She learned to work with collective responsibility.

Ella asked everyone to take a moment to reflect on how important this topic was to them. Then she started a reaction round, and many helpful thoughts surfaced. And by the end of the round, "we were tight again". They decided to continue with their agenda but to have a separate meeting with the new member for more listening.

The new member, Susan, confirmed in the meeting evaluation that she appreciated the process when she said, "it was helpful to have the guideline of a process; appreciated being taken seriously."

Ella successfully supported the group in making a collective choice.

Dependencies and circular dependencies

Dependencies are situations where we *can't* answer A *before* answering B. While in a fork, we can choose either path, with a dependency, we need to answer them both.

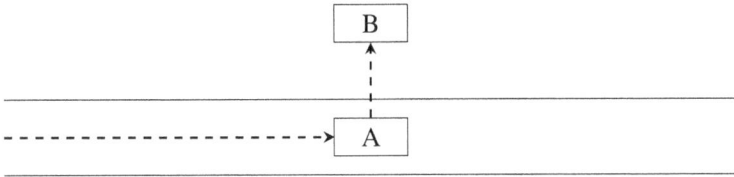

A dependency: A depends on B

Dependencies aren't particularly hard to solve. If we notice that Topic A depends on another, Topic B, we need to pause on Topic A and address Topic B.

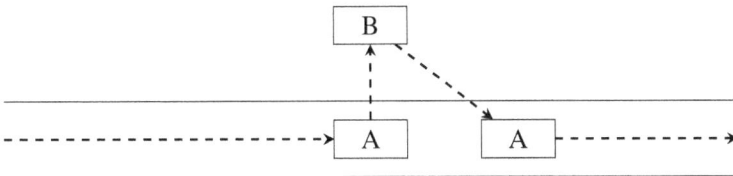

Solving a simple dependency by addressing B before going back to A

Dependencies can happen when a value or strategy is undefined. For example, we want to redefine our certification system because there are concerns that the certification system needs to support low-income applicants more. Yet, supporting low-income applications probably means less revenue, impacting other program areas. Someone flags that it has to be clarified whether affordability was a higher value than other things in the organization. Does this mean the certification system cannot be redefined until the strategy discussion about affordability is complete?

A more complex pattern is a *circular* dependency is when the reverse is also true: Topic *A* depends on Topic *B and* Topic *B* depends on Topic *A*.

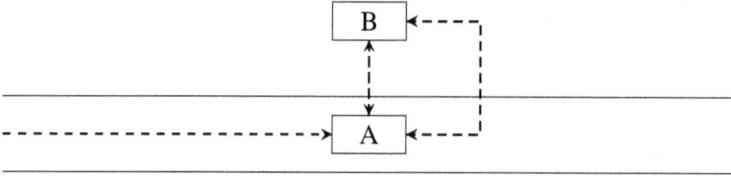

A circular dependency: A depends on B, and B on A

Circular dependencies are common in complex situations (in the sense of the Cynefin framework[4]) where cause-and-effect relationships are unclear, and groups find themselves stuck in a web of dependencies where no linear way seems to offer a viable path.

For illustration, see this next story, *Do I Stay Or Do I Leave?*

A team had been in crisis with interpersonal conflicts, and several people wanted to leave because they were fed up with the dynamics. In an emergency meeting with an external facilitator, a plan was developed to come up with ideas of things the team could work on that would unify them again. Yet, one member objected to that plan because he wanted to know first which team members are staying on the team because it makes less sense to make plans with people who will leave.

The team members argued that they couldn't predict whether they were staying or leaving the team because it depended on the action steps. If brainstormed action steps looked interesting, they might consider staying.

What can we do with a dependency or circular dependency?

- A simple dependency can be solved by addressing B first before going back to A.

- More often than expected, a group might not have to solve everything right away. It might *feel* like we absolutely *need* to make the second

---

[4]Snowden & Boone 2007

decision, but maybe we can put it off and hope that things just clarify over time.

- It's usually possible to follow a both-and approach.

    - Split the time: We can spend half of our allotted time talking about one topic and the other half on the other.

    - Work in parallel: An easier solution might be to put a working group in place to work on one topic while the main group continues on the other.

- Incremental approaches can allow for experimentation, like breaking one complex decision into smaller decisions, or making provisional decisions, making short-term decisions and revising or modifying them later.

See this example of provisional consent.

> In our organization, we approved a Conflict Resolution Policy. We reviewed the 3-page document paragraph by paragraph, asking for consent on what was written in that one paragraph each time. The paragraphs depended on each other, so the facilitator used provisional consent. One can't say yes to a statement like "conflicts should be resolved through dialogue" if the document only defines later what conflict is.
>
> Instead of asking for full consent on each paragraph before moving on, the facilitator asked for provisional consent. The group agreed to move forward *with the understanding* that they may revisit previous decisions if new information or concerns arose. Ultimately, the whole document was approved in a full consent process.

With these strategies, it's possible to solve most dependencies that paralyze organizations everywhere. Can we move forward with our operations, although we haven't fully decolonized our internal systems? Yes. Just do both, not either. Can we move forward with this policy, although we haven't yet written our value statement that might inform it? Yes, move forward with the policy and revise it once you have the value statement. Can we implement a governance system now as a forming group, although we'll have more members later? Yes, approve a system and amend it later. Incremental working is a good answer for many of these issues.

Cul-the-sac

Sometimes, a group might reach a cul-de-sac – when we can't progress on our topic using the same methods we've used before. Now, we need to shift our strategy completely. It's when our ship hits a sandbank and gets stuck.

Let's look at three options when we're facing a cul-de-sac.

Zoom out   The first option is to focus on the situation at hand from a wider perspective. A simple way to do that is to ask, instead of "what should we do about xyz?", the meta-question: "*why* do you think we have a hard time solving the issue?"

In the story *Licensing Is Boring*, the group needed to zoom out.

> We were trying to decide legal matters of licensing. But we were stuck. No proposal was emerging, no questions were asked or answered, and our reactions were all over the place.
>
> So I asked, "*Why* do you think we can't solve this?", and people shared willingly. We felt we needed more information. The topic seemed boring and high-stakes at the same time. The topic should have been prepared better. We agreed that we were all underprepared and were scared to make a wrong decision while at the same time not caring enough to do much about it.
>
> After noticing those reasons, we collectively decided to put one person on the task of writing up what we knew so far and finding out what information we lacked. That seemed like a doable task, not too much work and not too much commitment, but a step forward.

Moving the Topic on the Table one level up by stepping back and looking at our situation can also surface patterns (topic drift, fork, dependencies). For example, needing more information is a dependency: we first have to decide how to get more information before deciding on the matter.

Zoom in   Sometimes, instead of zooming out, the opposite works – going deeper into the details to get better context and backstory. This may involve listening more and more deeply, seeking additional external feedback, or even engaging in an experiment that yields more information. *Building Trust With A Cis Guy* illustrates this.

> A new group promoting communication skills had formed. As they started organizing their activities, the group realized they needed

> to select a leader. The situation was somewhat delicate since John, the only man among the five members, had called the group together. The idea of having him as the leader made some of the members uneasy, not wanting to contribute to patterns of male dominance.
>
> Nevertheless, John had demonstrated the necessary skills, knowledge, and commitment to the feminist movement. Recognizing this, the group approached the situation with an open mind and agreed to an experimental solution. They appointed John as the leader for four weeks to see how it would work out.

In this example, there wouldn't have been a way to decide only based on their knowledge then. No further exploration or information would have been able to give them what they needed: more trust based on more shared *lived experience* with each other. Not everything can be solved with more thinking and reflection.

Abandoning a proposal   Another way out of a cul-de-sac is to decide *not* to decide. While that's so obvious, I think it needs to be said! Not every topic that we talk about also needs to be acted on. (A little cop-out is to postpone a topic for a long time, like a year.)

> In my community, we noticed that in our circle structure, there was a significant gender imbalance. The Buildings and Grounds Circle had mostly men, and Common House Circle had mostly women, while all other circles were mixed.
>
> It wasn't too surprising; the Buildings and Grounds Circle was more oriented toward construction and building maintenance, while Common House Circle was more about interior design. And yet, we were embarrassed when we noticed it. We bounced around a little in the meeting, wondering if anything could and should be done about this pattern.
>
> But there was little we could do. Encourage a few people to switch? Recruit new members? Mostly, we were also aware of how that would have been the circles' choice. In short, we didn't see a lot of possible solutions, and we weren't even sure there was a problem. So, instead of action, we simply acknowledged the gender balance without further action.

In the case of intentionally abandoning or postponing topics, getting out of a cul-de-sac is not only a way to maintain agency but a good example of why competition for our resources forces us to pick only the most important issues – it can be healthy to reduce the clutter in our system!

2.3.3 Modes

Once we have a clear understanding of what our topic is, we need to have alignment on what we're trying to do with that topic. There are three different modes we might be in: understand, explore, or decide mode.

Understanding (reports). That's what we do when one or more people have information on the topic, and they want to make that information enter the collective common ground. This can happen by sharing information, for example, in a report or in answering questions about a piece of information.

Sometimes, reporting is all that's needed. We want to increase the common ground and create more shared reality. In other situations, this phase is the foundation for other steps.

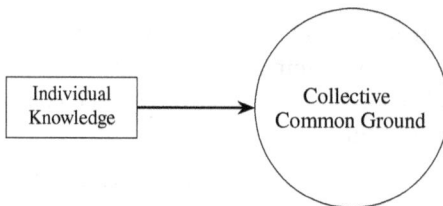

Understand: sharing information into the collective common ground

Exploration – In an exploration, group members share ideas on a topic. It goes beyond establishing the common ground; it's generative.

Individuals each offer ideas, inspiring each other. Through multiple perspectives and diverse viewpoints, we get innovation. In those moments, it's not about alignment but about diversity of thought.

An exploration might be brainstorming, feedback, or advice. Sometimes that's all that's needed. Explorations can also be a part of decision-making, often generating a proposal.

Unlike reports, we don't accept those ideas into the collective common ground. Brainstorming means naming things we *could* do or perspectives on how we *could* describe things, not stating that this is the way things are. Also, those things don't feed onto a to-do list because we haven't committed to those possible actions. Their half-life is short, only until a specific path is chosen.

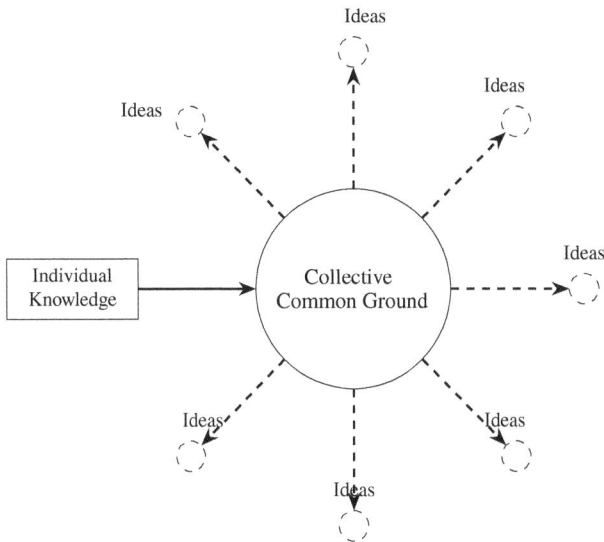

Explore: looking around and generating possible paths

Decision (choosing) is to pick one of the options we've gathered, either because someone suggested it or because we brainstormed options and identified a suitable choice. It can also mean to synthesize options into one choice. This step is about alignment.

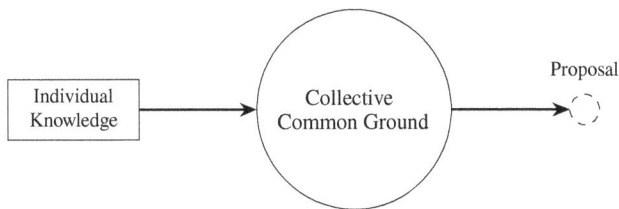

Decide: Picking one option and committing

Asking for time on the agenda requires putting in the work to be clear on *why* we request collective resources. The requests of the group are very different, and it's very helpful if individuals who bring a topic are clear about what their request is. Here's an example of how the waters get muddy if someone doesn't provide that clarity.

> At a biweekly marketing team meeting, Claire, the marketing man-
> ager, introduced a topic related to the performance of their recent social
> media campaign. However, she did not specify whether she wanted
> the team to merely report on the results, explore possible reasons for
> the campaign's performance, or make a decision on future campaigns.
>
> As the discussion unfolded, some team members began sharing
> data and opinions, assuming that Claire was asking for a report on the
> campaign's results. Meanwhile, others started analyzing the reasons
> for the campaign's success or failure, believing that the purpose of the
> discussion was to explore potential improvements. Yet another group
> of team members, under the impression that Claire wanted to make a
> decision, started suggesting new tactics for future campaigns.
>
> The meeting quickly became chaotic, as team members were miss-
> ing each other, and Claire grew increasingly frustrated. Claire had
> wanted only to report, but others were derailing the meeting with their
> new ideas that were entirely beside the point to her.

Clarity on the desired mode can help reduce these frustrations and help the
group move forward as a team.

Sequencing   The steps in the Four-Step Path – know who you are, where
you are, look around, choose, and decide – are not in a random order. It
makes little sense to decide first and then look around second. We can't
explore our options if we don't know who we are. In the same way, how
we go about topics has an inherent sequence to it.

The overall trajectory is to go from what is (*understand*) to what could
be (*exploration*) to then narrow down into one choice and approve it as
a specific way forward (*decide*). (See also the diamond of participatory
decision-making, Kaner 1998.)

Many readers will already know this sequence under a different name:
the *consent process* or *integrated decision-making (IDM)*. In the consent
process, we make sure everyone *understands* a proposal by presenting it
and answering any questions people might have. In the second phase,
people can share their thoughts and feelings – an exploration. Then comes
the consent round – a decision moment.

So a decision *entails* understanding and shared exploration; it shows
up as *understand–explore–decide*. In a parallel manner, explorations nest
because they entail understanding: we need to have shared understanding
before giving reactions. So an exploration doesn't typically come alone –
it's always *understand–explore*.

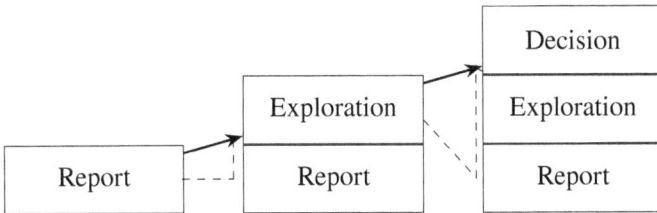

An exploration entails understanding, a decision understanding and exploring

There are a lot of different formats to facilitate a report, exploration, or decision as well, as the feedback (exploration) processes along the way, like liberating structures (https://www.liberatingstructures.com/).

2.4   Decision-making

Decision-making alone is easy. We think for a moment and then decide. As a group, it is more complicated; we can only commit to a certain action together when we've legitimately chosen together. This section looks at what it means to decide together.

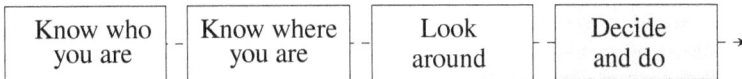

Four-step path: Deciding and doing together

But before we're ready to decide, we need to answer the question of where proposals come from in the first place.

2.4.1   Making proposals

There are two basic approaches to making proposals. We might write a proposal as a group, or we can write it alone.

Proposals made with a broad basis of participation are of better quality because they include more diversity of thought from the beginning, leading to better results in the long run. Yet, preparing proposals can take time.

Many groups struggle with forward motion because they don't know the difference between a suggestion and a proposal. A suggestion is a fleeting idea, a potentiality. A proposal is a request to the group to commit to an action.

When there are many suggestions, picking *one* suggestion can be hard. Someone even called it, "we often get bogged down by brainstorming." That transition from exploration to decision is tender. One reason for that is that the group members' ideas are in direct competition. I like my idea, and you like yours, and we can only do one of them. Now what? An oversupply of ideas leads to (more) competition for attention, which makes alignment harder.

It's also much easier to stay in the stage of wishful thinking. Only rarely are groups short on ideas; more often, they are short on bandwidth for action, so the transition from ideas to decision is the painful bottleneck.

The other reason is that the different ideas in an exploration are often attached to individual preferences. People fall in love with their ideas and attach their egos to them. In that way, it's a moment where the *individual* interests can easily override the *group*'s well-being. For the sake of the group, individuals have to let go of personal preferences for collective action to happen.

Moving through the process together in small cycles of convergence-divergence-convergence can be helpful. The entire process of examining an issue, exploring solutions, and committing to one action consists of sets of nested steps. For example, an exploration falls into understanding (= understanding what we're trying to address), exploration (= brainstorming potential solutions), and then settling on a proposal to send into the decision process. See the list below, and for more information, please see the handbook *Many Voices One Song* (2018).

1. **Understand phase:** understand the issue

   1.1 Understand: gather the information available.
   1.2 Explore the deeper causes – what may *really* be going on?
   1.3 Choose a *shared* description of the situation/issue.

2. **Explore phase:** work up a proposal to address the issue

   2.1 Understand criteria/dimensions of possible solutions
   2.2 Explore proposal ideas: brainstorm solutions
   2.3 Decide: choosing/merging into one proposal

3. **Decide phase:** approve the proposal! (aka consent process)

   3.1 Understand the proposal
   3.2 Explore variety of reactions
   3.3 Decide: approve the proposal

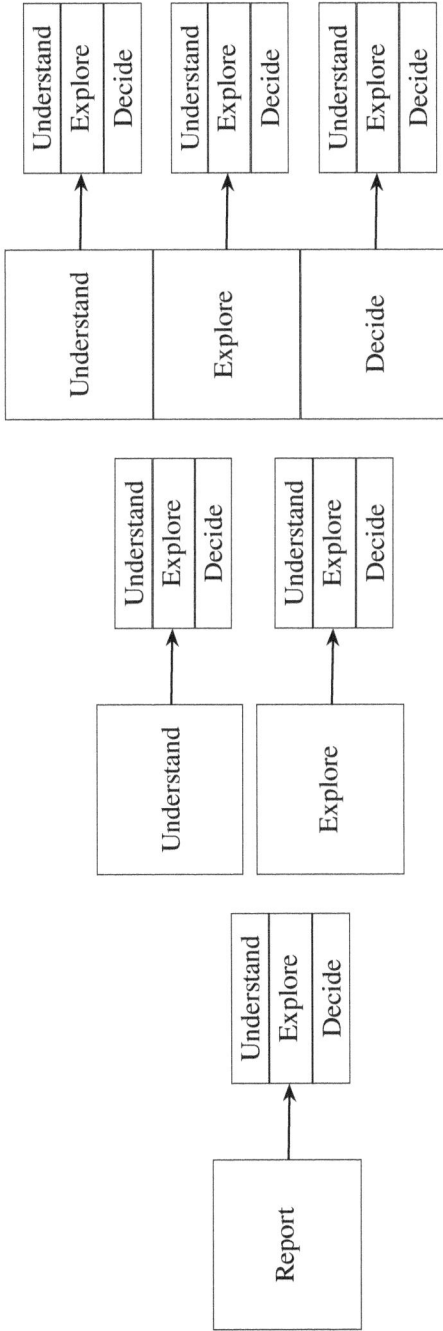

Understand–explore–decide cycles nest and build on each other.

I've enjoyed dividing complex topics into three meetings.

- Meeting 1: Just try to understand the issue.
- Meeting 2: Come up with proposal ideas and pick one.
- Meeting 3: Approve the proposal.

The advantage of spreading it out is that people have time to think between the meetings, and it's a gentle, human-friendly pace. They can also get feedback from people outside the team. In addition, it's practical that the wordsmithing on the 'outputs' of phases one and two (a shared description of the situation, and a spelled-out proposal for decision-making) can be finalized outside of a meeting by one or two people, making optimal use of meeting time.

2.4.2   Selection process of people + roles

I want to show how this basic pattern of *understand – explore – decide* is also expressed in other decision-making patterns, like the selection process. The specifics of the selection process are described in other places (like in *Many Voices One Song, 2018*, or read up on the Holacracy® Election Process), but I'd like to point out how the selection process also follows the same steps.

The basic pattern is to first understand what we're looking for, including role definition and qualifications. Then we make suggestions (in the form of two rounds of nominations), and then a proposal gets picked and approved or modified until there's consent.

Phases	
Understand	Define role and qualifications
Explore	Explore possible candidates in nominations
Decide	Pick a candidate and decide

Phases of a selection process

In common practice, the middle phase of nominations has two parts:

- Individuals think for themselves and just silently pick a candidate they want to nominate. In an autonomy/alignment frame, it's important to have a variety of thoughts and perspectives.

- In the second round (called the change round), people can change their nomination based on what they heard others say. This is where mutual inspiration and possibly some alignment with each other.

That still isn't enough. We still need to find alignment with the collective aim to make sure the proposal is good enough. Here's a story, *Hard-of-Hearing Note-taker*, that comes to mind to illustrate that.

> The group was in a selection process for the nominations. They selected multiple roles at once, but this was about the note-taker. They had gathered qualifications to clarify what they were looking for and what the role required – the notetaker was supposed to take notes and upload them into the digital cloud once ready, as was standard practice in this volunteer organization.
>
> Almost everyone had already shared their nominations – nominating the most tech-y people who brought their laptops to the meetings anyway.
>
> Then the last person in the round spoke, Barbara. She nominated Janet as the note-taker for the following reason:
>
> "I nominate Janet for note-taker because she is hard of hearing. If we can have meetings where Janet can take notes, we've ensured everyone heard everything and that we're on the same page."
>
> This creative reasoning swayed everyone, so everyone changed their nomination to Janet in the change round. The facilitator formally proposed Janet, and everyone gave consent, including Janet.

So far, so good! A great example of a creative idea emerging. Yet, the story is not over yet.

> Five months later, someone noticed that no one was putting meeting minutes in Google Drive. Had Janet not been taking notes? Where were they?
>
> What went wrong?
>
> Upon asking, they discovered that Janet needed to become more familiar with their cloud document storage, had put things into different places, and wasn't comfortable managing the cloud documents.

In all the excitement about the unusual nomination idea, the question of alignment with the needs of the collective had fallen off the radar.

Here, the group had gone for innovation and creativity and even alignment with each other, but not for alignment with their aim. But both are needed in healthy balance to make a good decision.

The pattern of *understand criteria – first round of ideas (– second round of ideas) – alignment with the aim* can be used creatively in many different ways, and depending on the use, different steps seem to move to the foreground. An example is this story, *Which Kid Gets Which Room?*, where I used the process and frontloaded by being thorough when gathering the criteria.

I had moved into a new house with my kids. We had five rooms, five children, and two adults. Who should get what room? The question could easily lead to fighting.

We made a list of all the rooms. We made a list of criteria or considerations (in a way, these are qualifications for child-room pairs). Our list was something like:

- size of the room
- closeness to grownups (for kids who are scared at night)
- closeness to bathrooms
- who has to get up when? Who goes to bed when?
- noise (like hearing loud music at night)
- gender and privacy
- who can/wants to share a room, who wants to be alone

Everyone agreed that those were the criteria.

In the next step, we asked to nominate people into rooms, which sounded like this: 'I think XY and YZ' should share room 1 because they're scared at night.' We went through all the people, and, to my surprise, we found a solution that satisfied *all* the constraints. I am not sure how many more possible solutions to our riddle there would have been, but our plan was to find *one* that works, not *all* that exist.

We asked for consent, and the decision was made.

Ever since needs have changed, and people have traded rooms, but it has never been an area of contention.

I used a quicker process at my daughter's 6th birthday party. Here, it was more the act of shared process that was the most important.

She wanted a piñata – for those in other cultures, that's a decorated papermaché box filled with candy that children hit with sticks until it bursts. Then all children run to stuff their pockets with candy, and that's the game.

I told my daughter I didn't want to do it because I never liked the competitiveness of grabbing the candy. I told her I *could* be swayed if we could distribute the candy in a fair way. My daughter – being more interested in having candy than in the competition – agreed.

When piñata time came around, I told the kids that all candy had to be put on the table, and we'd divide it. They could only eat it when the distribution was okay with everyone. I didn't see anyone too surprised by that.

When the piñata burst, everyone helped pick up the candy within under four seconds. I sat them around the table, with a pile of candy in the middle.

I asked them whether there were things on there that they didn't like or were allergic to. A kid or two shared something for all to hear. One didn't like peanuts, and the other couldn't eat sticky candy because of her braces.

That was a quick check on criteria!

I did a quick estimate and saw that each kid could have at least three items, so I told them to take three things they liked. A few more things were left, so I asked them to choose one more thing and put it on the pile in front of them.

Then we had fewer candy pieces left than there were kids. I got nervous because I was wondering whether there would now be arguments about what's fair. So I tried to say as calmly as possible, "ok, if you have enough, that's fine, or take something else."

Magically, as many hands picked an item as there were items. Some kids didn't and seemed content.

That completed the nomination round – exploration.

Then, I asked them to look around and see if they wanted to trade. No one wanted to trade. I asked, ok, show me your thumbs up if you're ok with what you have.

Change round! And consent!

Everyone showed their thumbs, and off they went to eat.

While this might sound long, it was really an event of under 4 minutes. I was very content with the process, and even more with the kids because they seemed so calm and pleased.

I was proud of myself because I had found a way to reign in competition so the bigger kids wouldn't push the little kids away to get all the candy.

2.4.3   Decision-making methods

Recall the story *Standing Aside In A House Sale* earlier (on page 18) where two members didn't feel comfortable with a house sale decision and stood aside. They didn't object but instead encouraged the rest of the group to decide on the house sale without them.

In this case, if we think about collective decision-making, would you say that the group decided *together*? I would say two individuals unilaterally decided to relinquish their power (which is a *power-under* move) and deferred the decision to the other members. Those then consented, and the decision moved forward. (I commented earlier about how it is not an option to abstain from a decision in consent decision-making.)

Knowing what we know now, I would say that one can only make a decision *together* if *all* individual members of the group participated. Co-responsibility and collective decision-making require the individuals' willingness to be responsible.

'Participate' is a vague term here. One could argue that they participated in the decision *by* choosing to stand aside and therefore participated. I often have these discussions with clients who say things like "everyone should be involved" or "everyone should be allowed to weigh in or have a say." What's our threshold for that? That they are part of the decision somehow, or that they can say no? I recently asked a group of teenagers in a class whether they considered the majority vote 'fair'. One of them, Sebastián, said, "even if you're in the minority and don't get what you wanted, it's still fair because you still participated in the decision."

Ultimately, what is considered 'fair' depends on the group's expectations and the level of trust among its members. The depth and level of participation is a spectrum.

What decision-making methods are most suitable for *shared power* and *shared responsibility* on the collective level? Or, if one person decides alone for the whole collective, under what circumstances would the rest of the collective accept responsibility for that decision? And under what conditions would it be in the best interest of the *collective*?

Given competition within groups, individuals want what they want because it's the best for themselves, or maybe also because they *personally* think it's the best for the group. The other side of the polarity is unity and alignment in meeting the group's needs that transcend beyond the needs of individuals. By what decision-making method(s) can we best decide on that collective level?

Decisions made by one person   The advantage of autocratic decision-making is that it's fast and pragmatic. If a quick decision is needed, having one person decide avoids many of the issues of collaboration. Conversely, unilateral decisions are the least participatory and, therefore, can lack sufficient context.

A few years back, I experienced a situation that showed the advantage of unilateral decision-making.

> We were running late in a meeting because of unforeseen tricky questions. As a result, we only had a few minutes to make a decision on a time-critical matter. The General Circle did one round of input when the first people announced they had to leave on time. It was clear that a decision needed to be taken, but no proposal had surfaced.
>
> That's when a group member suggested to hand over the decision to me. The facilitator concurred and formally proposed that on this question, 'Ted decides.' Everyone showed their thumbs to indicate their consent, and the meeting ended.
>
> Empowering one person saves time and keeps things simple.

One important distinction is how the person got empowered to make the decision alone.

- One side of the polarity is autocratic decision-making. The autocrat typically self-empowers based on position and status. Authority is often inherited, seized or granted by a small ruling body.
- A person can be empowered *by another individual or by a group* (by whatever decision-making method) to make decisions on behalf of the group, for example, operational decisions made by one person in a role.

From a multi-level selection point of view, a decision made by one person is a gamble – this person might or might *not* decide in the interest of the collective. That's why people have different accounts of whether leadership is 'good' or 'bad.' If the leader makes decisions for the sake of the group, then it can be wonderful. But there are few ways to prevent a leader from prioritizing their personal interest over the collective's.

Another question is legitimacy; an autocratic, benevolent leader might be seen as the best strategy to meet the needs of the collective if, for example, everyone agrees that the person is the only one with the skills to do it. For example, gurus are often benevolent leaders and seen as the most qualified or enlightened person to make decisions *on behalf of* and *for* the collective. (See more on legitimacy in section 3.5.2.)

Majority vote   Voting is a decision-making method where the majority decides, and the minority needs to follow.

To those who see it the way 17-year-old Sebastián saw it, participating in a majority vote seems enough to say "I was part of making that decision, and I'm willing to be co-responsible for the result and outcomes." Majority vote is relatively easy and quick.

One detrimental effect of a majority vote is that the choice-making is reduced to the different options we can vote for – we can't say "I vote for Option A but with this one aspect of Option C." All of those factors lead to a situation where the resulting decision can represent too few voices and perspectives up to a point where, if enough people are unhappy with the outcomes, the sense of legitimacy of a decision made by majority vote will fade and it's no longer perceived as collective decision-making.[5]

If we strictly stay on group level (not on nation-states), a group of around 12 people might decide, with seven in favor and five against it, and the decision moves forward. Even Sebastián might struggle with the decision as 'unfair' if it's unclear whether the minority has been appropriately heard. The problem is that a majority vote doesn't create a collective mind – it's just a set of individual votes. Most people might not even think about the collective need but simply cast a ballot based on their preference.

In addition, there is a significant and unexpected disadvantage of majority vote compared to unanimous decision-making. There is evidence that decision-making methods change the outcome of decisions at the end and the nature of the conversation *leading up to the decision*. If a decision-making method requires a unanimous decision (consensus or consent), people are more likely to shift their views than under a majority vote.[6] This means that the merging of individual opinions into a collective understanding is more likely to occur when decision-making is based on everyone's voice, supporting all individuals and fostering a more cohesive collective. Moreover, under unanimous decision-making, minority members in a group are more likely to speak up. For example, if women are underrepresented in a group, they will have less air time under majority vote conditions than under unanimous decision-making[7].

It dramatically affects the level of shared reality – the collective common ground. If voices are missing early on, the foundation on which decisions are based is weak. The more people understand each other, and the more shared knowledge on the topic at hand is shared knowledge, the

---

[5]Kameda 1991; Kaplan and Miller 1987; Nemeth 1977
[6]Hastie et al. 1983
[7]Karpowitz (2012)

easier it will be to move forward, and the more likely it will be that all information relevant to the collective's well-being will surface and a quality decision will be made.

Since a majority vote mostly entails the principle of 'the winner takes it all', voting often leads people to form factions. That's because they need to win the vote to get their individual preference, which means they have to win over as many voters as possible. It's a highly competitive measure to govern the collective need – from the perspective of balancing individual and collective needs, majority vote has exactly the *opposite* features of a system we would need to design to make collectively-oriented decisions on the collective level; In our systems that are based on majority vote, our society has been breeding for the most successful chicken in the cage – and the result is psychopathic chickens. Peter Turchin, in the book 'Ultrasociety,' makes a compelling point when he points out that in Enron, the company culture actively promoted competition and individualism, ultimately leading to unethical behaviors, fraudulent practices, and the company's collapse. In addition, there is very little room to vote 'strategically' because voters hardly have the infrastructure to coordinate much.

In addition, those who are opposing a vote might have essential reasons that affect the collective. If I vote *no* in a vote, it might be that I'm voting *no* because I'd have *personal* disadvantages if the proposal were implemented. But it might also be that I see a reason for how the *collective* would be at a disadvantage if the proposal were implemented.

Many argue that collective wisdom arises from individual votes, but this has been disputed quite a bit because that is only true in processes without distortion where the individual voters are not influenced. That's hardly ever the case. So a majority vote as a mechanism is hit or miss, and its success depends on many other factors, like the perceived legitimacy, quality of deliberation beforehand, and the level of influence on voters.

Ideally, since on the collective level, we need to make a decision for the good of the collective, a decision-making method would need to 'filter out' the *no* votes that are purely based on individual preferences. But highlight the *no* votes that give us more information on dangers to the collective good. That is exactly what consent tries to accomplish.

Consent   In consent decision-making, any member can say no to a proposal by objecting to a proposal; any given proposal only passes if there is no objection. However, objections are not individual *no* votes. Objections are defined as having a *reason to believe that this proposal harms the shared aim.*

The *aim* defines the collective purpose and, therefore, determines the needs of the collective. For example, if a group exists to develop and build a particular tool, then that's the collective's purpose; all actions need to be evaluated on whether they serve this shared aim or not.

In reactions, members of the collective might speak to their individual preferences. In the moment of decision-making, members don't evaluate a given proposal based on their *individual* needs but on how well it might fulfill the aim.

Of course, if a person's personal work contributing to that aim – like in an operational role – is negatively affected by a proposal, then the collective functioning would be affected. This would also be a legitimate objection in relation to the collective's aim. That's because the individual role contributions are integral to the collective work that builds on them. In a way, it's not the individual speaking but the individual's *function* in the collective operations.[8]

That's different for personal preferences that have nothing to do with the collective aim. Remember that the aim of a collective *is* the raison d'être of the collective – it creates the backdrop against which to evaluate any proposal. Because of that, I consider consent the most collectively minded decision-making method, or even the *only* collectively minded decision-making method because it *only* allows objections based on the collective purpose instead of focussing on any number of personal preferences.

Cloud Password System is my favorite story about this:

> A few years back, I was in a circle of three people. I was the note-taker, and a person we'll call Alex was the facilitator. Alex had brought a proposal that stated that we'd move all our passwords for IT tools and cloud-based services to a shared online password manager. The proposal came when everyone on that team of three felt stretched thin. We had just expanded our team, and we had a lot of loose ends and a lack of clarity around who does what. When I read the proposal before the meeting, I was concerned. I wondered if this was the right moment to deal with all of our passwords. My mind went to this whole worry thing where passwords I saved in my local password manager would get overwritten by someone else, and chaos would ensue. I knew I needed at least ten logins daily, and running after updated passwords didn't sound appealing.
>
> In the meeting, we went through the standard consent process. The

---

[8]Hence the very fitting slogan in Holacracy that it's about 'role, not soul'.

first step was questions – no one had questions. The second step was reactions. My team members spoke first, then it was my turn. My turn was not even what would count as a 'quick reaction'. It was more like a three-minute rant about how I'm worried and overworked and how it would upset me off if I had to run after people updating passwords in the cloud. The facilitator (and proposer) listened and, a little shaken, moved to the next step in the process, the consent round. My colleague consented, the proposer consented, and then it was my turn. I knew all along that I'd consent. But I swear, when I consented, the facilitator jumped off his chair in surprise!

He asked me, "Ted, I don't understand, I thought you hated the proposal!" And I said, "Yes, I do. But I also know it's necessary."

I knew there was never a good moment to mess with all your passwords. So this moment was as good or bad as any other.

And I also knew that the proposed action plan was helpful in the long run. While there might be a little blip here and there, I didn't have any reason to believe that there would be significant harm in the short run. Instead, I knew that there would be many benefits in the long run. The situation would have been different had this been two weeks before a big online event or something like that. I would have objected then. But in this case, it was fine. That's why I consented.

This story shows that our reaction and consent answer two different questions. Our reactions are our opinions, fears, and excitement on an individual level. That's all useful information, but the question of *do you consent* is different, bringing our attention from our personal level to the collective level.

I also don't allow too many nuances of *love it, like it, no objection, I'm concerned but it's ok* kind of systems. Ultimately, we're either making a decision together or not. Imagine if you wanted to drive a car, and the alarm indicator for the oil was going off and on as if it couldn't decide whether it was doing its job. That's someone refusing to decide from the point of view of the collective aim. Either we talk more – because the 'machine' isn't working and the oil alarm light is still on, or we get into the car and drive (meaning we move on to implementing the decision).

Consensus Unanimous decisions by consensus (not consent) are interesting. In consensus decision-making, each individual needs to agree. Yet, it is not always clear on what basis that gets decided. It can be on the individual or collective levels – most often and in practice, it's a mix of both.

Considering that, it makes perfect sense that, in my experience, consensus works well in two situations:

- One, in groups that are *highly* committed to their collective aim. In those cases, we can expect that individuals prioritize the collective's needs above their individual needs, and blocks would predominantly be based on concern for the collective level. This can be the case in religious groups. For example, Quakers might find alignment through saying *I yield to the wisdom of the whole*.

- In situations where the collective aim is secondary; in those cases, we cannot strip the function from the individual. Families are like that, for example. It's not so easy to fire me as a parent and onboard a new person to filling my function and keep the collective running. Groups of friends are similar. If you replace all members of a friend group, it's a different group because the group is primarily defined by their individual members, not their function or aim. That's different for a PR team. It's still the PR team even after everyone has been replaced; its primary function didn't change. Of course, one could argue that a friend group also just fills a function, but that leads too far away from the topic.

There are costs to replacing group members. That's why some decisions might cater to an individual preference to keep them engaged in the group. Losing them would have too high of a cost for the group. We've already seen an example of that: Bridget was anxious around Glenn's glasses. In a cost-benefit analysis, giving her what she needed as an individual was less costly than insisting on a strict separation between personal and collective needs and potentially lose her in the process.

As we can see, a perspective of individual-collective gives us valuable insights about the advantages and disadvantages of different methods of decision-making.

2.4.4   Doing things as a collective

In the Four-Step Path, the fourth step is to *decide and do*. After a decision is made, how does a group *do* something?

To understand what a group can even do, let's first look at what a group can do *without* coordination. Without coordination, groups can really only do simple, repetitive, or instinctive behaviors that do not require complex decision-making or negotiation. We can clap, cheer, dance, and sing as a group. Doing a wave in a soccer stadium *hardly* needs any coordination.

There are other things, like running away from a fire, but I'd say we are actually running as a set of individuals, not as a group, because our actions don't depend on each other.

The cultural norms around forming waiting lines help us do that without coordination, just like traffic works because of rules that are set for us. We can stand in line without coordination, for example, when we stand in line to get food. But have you ever stood in line in a store and then noticed there were two lines and you didn't know which line was the 'official' one? All of a sudden, we *do* have to talk to coordinate.

In general, as soon as things get just a little bit more complicated than a simple activity, coordination becomes necessary.

Talking *about* the work to coordinate the work is the *collective's contribution* to *doing* things. Collectives talk so individuals can do things. (This insight will come back later when we talk about policy and operations in section 2.6.) So what kinds of *doing* are done by *talking*?

Speech acts

This brings us right to linguistics with a classic, influential paper by language philosopher J. L. Austin called 'How to do things with words.' It introduced the concept of 'speech acts', later refined by John Searle and now taught in every linguistics 101 class.

A speech act is an *action* that is done *by speaking*. Those are not special at all. In fact, everything we say is a speech act. We use them all the time without noticing. There are several kinds of speech acts.

- Assertive: share information or beliefs or describe the world.
  Examples: giving a report or explaining a concept to someone.
- Directive: guide or influence the behavior of others.
  Examples: giving instructions, making requests/demands.
- Commissive: commits one to a future course of action.
  Examples: promises, offering guarantees, accepting an invitation.
- Expressive: communicate emotions, attitudes, or feelings.
  Examples: congratulating, expressing gratitude, or apologizing.
- Declarative: bring about a change in the world by virtue of the speaker's authority or institutional role.
  Examples: announcing a decision, performing a marriage ceremony, or declaring a state of emergency.

We will see that while each of those can be done *individually*, they can also be done *as a collective*, and governance is needed to do so.

Assertives Let's look at the simplest version: an assertion. When I make an assertion, I offer a statement (proposition) about the world and offer it to others in a statement.

We make assertive statements all day. We feed assertive statements into the common ground and build the common ground.

What I want to look at now is: how can a *collective* make an assertive?

Let's think about this with an example. Let's say a team wants to communicate that they have completed a project successfully and on time. The assertive is a longer version of 'we have done xyx successfully.' They do that to make it general knowledge in the next-bigger collective – the organization. Instead of an individual talking to a group, this is a group communicating to the organization. How do they do that?

- Collective statement: The team can create and deliver a presentation or report. They'd have to all be there to report, or all sign the document.

- Designated spokesperson: The group can appoint a spokesperson who represents the collective and communicates the assertive on behalf of the group.

Interestingly, either one of these involves governance: either to coordinate who does what, a process so each member can endorse and approve the statement, or a process to select a spokesperson. Without a process, there will be drama when someone just speaks on behalf of the group in a self-appointed way.

That means that without governance, there is no legitimate collective speech act. As soon as we are 'speaking as one,' we need a process to do that, and as soon as someone is speaking on behalf of a collective (or group), that person needs to be chosen by the collective.

Let's look at the other speech acts. You will see that the pattern is the same each time.

Directives and Commissives A directive is when someone tells others what to do. For individual speech acts, the way this works, for example, is that if I tell my daughter, 'get your laundry out of the washing machine,' and she doesn't object but somehow (even nonverbally) accepts the task, it enters her *to-do-list*. Just like we have a shared common ground, we also seem to have something like a mental *to-do-list* of tasks we have committed to doing. (There's a lot more to say here about when that happens successfully – just think about how many arguments there are of the kind 'I've never said that I would do it, you just said that I had to, but I never agreed to that!')

What's the collective version of that? How can a collective make a request of others or demand something? For example, how could a group in an organization, as a *collective*, request that people fill out their timesheets on time? The options are similar to the ones in the assertion. The group in charge of timesheets can collectively show up in the company lobby and together yell, 'fill out your timesheets, people!' but that's typically impractical. Another option is to write and endorse something like an open letter that makes that demand. The other one would be to elect a spokesperson who then goes to the other groups and says on behalf of the whole group, 'on behalf of the timesheet group, I ask you to fill out your timesheets.'

(A last version – and we'll get back to that – is to make a policy that timesheets have to be filled out on time.)

Commissives are very similar. Instead of making a request of someone else, we make it of ourselves by committing to something. For example, a person might promise to fill out the timesheet on time by saying, 'I promise that I will fill out the timesheet.' They have now committed to that being on their own mental *to-do-list*.

For the collective version, we can use our spokespeople to communicate among teams. For example, Susan from the Budgeting Team notices that one team hasn't submitted their team budget yet. Susan contacts the leader of the project team, Hiroshi, and asks them to get their budget ready and send it over so the financial projection can be completed. Hiroshi, accepting the commitment, puts it on the agenda for the next meeting because it needs to be talked about first.

Each of these ways of making a collective speech act requires a group process to get to the point to legitimately make the speech act on behalf of the group.

Expressives Expressives are speech acts where we don't say much to transfer information but more to convey a sentiment. An expressive is when I say 'phew!' when someone tells me that they almost missed the bus to arrive on time for our annual meeting.

Another example is 'wow!', 'great job!', or 'ouch!' An utterance like 'good morning!', They carry information about relationships but no descriptive (propositional) content.

(Some words can be either. An illustrative example of that is that I can say 'go put your bloody shirt into the laundry!', it might be that I am describing a shirt that has blood stains. Or 'bloody' might merely express my anger; in this case, it might have nothing to do with blood stains – the propositional content fades as the emotional content takes a front seat.)

The collective version of expressives is interesting. A sweet example of making an expressive together is when a group signs a birthday card for someone, where each group member signs their name on the card. Singing happy birthdays together is a simple expressive that a group can make together, mediated by cultural norms because everyone knows the song. (If we want to sing a less-known song, we'll have to use words to coordinate again to figure out which one.)

How does a group say 'ouch' together? Parallel to the other speech acts, they can write a joint letter saying 'we hereby express our sadness' or other expressions like appreciation and condolences. The same can be done by having a spokesperson that delivers a message like 'the board is shocked to learn. . . ' Either way, an internal process is needed for the group to agree on making that speech act.

Declarations   Declarations fascinate me. I was studied declarative speech acts in my linguistic career and got very excited when I noticed that decision-making – my second career – is the collective version of that. Let's dive into them!

Most words describe the world we're in (or the world we want). But a declarative speech act builds on the insight that some words *directly change* the world.

An example of a declarative speech act is to resign. Let's say I am upset with my team members, and I say the words "I hereby resign from this role as of now." If I have the authority to resign, the moment I've said those words, I am no longer in the role. Therefore, reality – the world of mental models and who is responsible for what – has changed.

There are special verbs like *fire* and *hire* that have this 'doing' layer to them. We can hereby declare things something, we can hereby name things, or hereby marry or divorce people by saying magic words.

"I hereby cook these potatoes" doesn't work, neither does "I hereby fix this chair"; only certain mental constructs like naming conventions work that way. Those are the things someone can *do* by speaking.

Observant readers might have noticed that, almost in passing, I also mentioned another necessary condition for this to work: in order to use the magic, I need to be empowered to do so. If I'm not an official, then I can say "I hereby declare you husband and husband" as often as I want to, but they will not be officially married. If I'm your coworker, saying "I hereby fire you" doesn't have the desired effect. In linguistic jargon, that is one of the felicity conditions: for a declarative speech act, the person making it also needs to have the authority to make it.

There are felicity conditions for other speech acts, like demands. If my 10-year-old tells me to clean up my room, that doesn't mean it's now on my committed-to-do list. Conversely, if I, as his parent, tell him to, it might well be, but only if I have autocratic power. That might be the case with a younger child and an authoritative parenting style. The kinds of speech acts we make reflect our assumptions about our governance system and power relationships.[9]

Just like in the individual version, declaratives made by a *group* require the authority to make that speech act. In circle-based distributed governance systems, that's what a decision-making domain of responsibility defines: anything within that domain can be changed via a group declarative. That's what governance *is* – a pattern language of deciding who can decide what. And acts of governance are often declarative speech acts that talk a new policy or authority into being reality.

A membership circle, for example, can hereby set the membership fee to be $100, and it can be effective instantly if they so choose. Once they decide that, the membership fee *is* $100. We can hereby elect a leader, we can hereby initiate a project or fold it. We can declare a certain behavior forbidden or outlaw a particular practice.

Let's say a whole team resigns. They would probably talk it out and draft a statement. They would approve the decision to issue the statement which then is the collective speech act: "we hereby resign."

All collective speech acts follow the same pattern. Governance determines the authority a collective has to assert, express or declare, and it is needed to make the speech act collectively with legitimacy.

Indirect speechacts

Some speech acts are indirect speech acts. An indirect speech act is when I say something that sounds like a particular speech act, but it's another. Indirect speech acts are confusing, but we use them all the time, and most of the time, we are good at interpreting them. For example, I might say "if I were you, I'd apologize." This sounds like me making an assertive speech act describing what I'd do if I were you, many would interpret it as a directive, *telling* the other person to apologize.

---

[9]An interesting exploration here is the Power Manual by Suarez 2018.

We often try to avoid explicit directives and use other speech acts, and give indirect hints, like "you might want to reconsider swimming on a cold day like today", or "do you think it's warm enough to swim?", or "phew, that's cold!" when we mean "do not go swimming!"

Some speech acts are declarations that look like assertives. For example, a Safety Committee approves and communicates the sentence, "To maintain a safe and healthy work environment, all employees are required to wear appropriate personal protective equipment (PPE) when working in hazardous areas." Are they giving us information, or are they telling us to do something? It could simply be reporting on a policy that exists, like in a handbook, so it's assertive - it states an existing reality. If it's new, however, it's probably more likely a directive *telling* us to wear PPE.

A group can't really walk around telling people to do things. Imagine a work safety committee walking around and yelling "'wear PPE when working in hazardous areas!" in unison at individual workers. Performing a collectively uttered directive is cumbersome. That's why policies are indirect speech acts where something is stated in a collectively approved text, and we know it's a directive that tells us to do or refrain from doing something. It's the only practical way of making it work in a group.

2.5   Pace and time

I often wish we lived in a world where we could make perfect decisions. But that is unachievable.

We can't consider *everything* in *all* of our decisions. Human brains have a limited bandwidth, and groups (and organizations) only have limited resources. We only have limited time, knowledge, and access. Constraints are a universal feature of *all* systems, whether we like it or not.

Constraints aren't bad. Constraints are what unleashes creativity. Without any limitation of resources, there would be no need to find a better solution or to make a choice and evaluate choices. Without constraints, there would be no evolution.

In our group processes, we must balance our striving for perfection and our use of resources. That's already hard enough, but another factor makes it more challenging. Every decision comes with uncertainty. That means we're not only balancing our desire for perfection and resource constraints, but we also have to make *guesses* about how that might be best.

Let's say I made a decision alone. I am walking to the bus stop to catch a bus, but then I see the bus coming a minute early. Should I run for the bus or wait for the next one? My mind and intuition will process lots of information within split seconds to make that judgment call. I weigh the likelihood of another bus coming soon with the sore muscles in my legs. I consider the distance to the bus stop and the traffic between me and the bus stop. How comfortable am I to ignore the red traffic light?

As a group, as always, everything is more complicated. As a group, we need to talk about the risks we're taking the resources we're using. We need to discern what information matters enough to be considered. Deciding together means drawing the line somewhere *together*. But where?

2.5.1 Good enough ... for now

Many in the self-management and self-governance movement use the slogan *good enough for now, safe enough to try*, particularly when referring to consent decision-making. It's a great slogan expressing that decisions don't have to be perfect or fully aligned with our preferences. They just need to be good enough to reach the group's collective aim.

Yet, a big question now becomes, how do we know what's *good enough*? *Good enough* relates to the collective agency. Something is not good enough when we can't do what our collective is supposed to do. If so, we've failed to serve the collective aim.

For a collective's success, the measuring stick is its progress towards realizing its aim. A machine, for example, is a system of consenting (= working) parts. The whole chain of parts in the system needs to work for a machine to work. If one of them breaks down, it tells us that something is wrong and the machine no longer works.

What does it look like if something 'breaks' in an organization? In the present, we find out something isn't working. In the future, we ask for appropriate feedback and/or ask for consent.

In this light, it's clear why asking as many people as possible – all with consent rights in a group or via an advice process – can prevent or help us fix mistakes. It can include people with knowledge about the decision and whether they see any potential issue. If they don't, we will go ahead with the decision and see what happens. The bottom line is: if it's working, then it's good enough.

The topic of self-responsibility comes back here. Each part needs to 'know' whether it's working to determine whether the next-broader system is working. Imagine you see a flat tire, but you notice that the tire air pressure alarm lamp isn't on. Would you ignore your evidence and drive anyway? We still wouldn't drive, right? That's the mindset needed here –

a real interest in whether things are working, not just a superficial interest in the warning signals.

Here are two examples of that from a meeting. The first I name *Objections Can Take a While*:

> The team had to make a tricky decision. We wanted to hire a new person, and there were two candidates. One had a lot of support and skills, but the other fit our overall trajectory better. We felt torn but ended up settling on the well-supported choice.
>
> Yet, I was the facilitator and sensed that one of the circle members wasn't *in*. Knowing her, I knew she'd consent to conform with the group because she didn't want to 'be complicated.'
>
> I wanted to leave her a choice, but I didn't want to postpone the decision. So I suggested we make a decision but that we would not let either candidate know our decision for 48 hours in case someone changed their mind.
>
> And that's precisely what happened. She came back the following day with regret and a clearly phrased objection.

Humans aren't machines, so sometimes we need time to determine what's *good enough*. In this next story, *Just Give Me A Minute*, the outcome is consent, and it only took a few extra seconds to decide.

> I was asked for consent on a proposal that I had mixed feelings about because it meant extra work for me when I felt stretched too thin. In the consent round, I hesitated in how I said the words *I consent*. The facilitator reflected back to me, *wait, you said the words, but that didn't sound like consent*.
>
> I searched for myself where the hesitation was coming from. I was able to put my finger on it and shared a piece of resentment I was still holding connected to the topic. I acknowledged that I still had some leftover feelings from our previous project. With my words heard and received, I was complete. I was able to breathe and said firmly *NOW I consent*.
>
> Without the facilitator's help, I might not have noticed that I was only going through the motions of saying the magic word 'consent.'

Everyone needs to learn to recognize the signs in themselves and in others. That's one of the many reasons why learning is an essential factor for the resilience of an organization.

> "Learning organizations are organizations where people con-
> tinually expand their capacity to create the results they truly

> desire, where new and expansive patterns of thinking are nur-
> tured, where collective aspiration is set free, and where people
> are continually learning to see the whole together." (Senge,
> 1990, p. 3)

This quote highlights that a learning organization is not just about individual learning but also collective learning that drives the organization toward its shared vision and purpose.

How do we learn as a collective? One way is to evaluate and create a collective common ground on what's working and what isn't so we can adjust our course and review again. Yet, of course, reviews in a group are highly demanding for resources like time, energy, and attention. While an individual can learn ongoingly (if they take a moment to reflect), it's more complicated for a group because, ideally, we'd call everyone in to share their learnings. While one mind can learn at any time, a collective 'mind' must pick feedback cycles to make it practical. While in a perfect world, we would review all our decisions all the time, our limited attention and resources don't allow for that.

Frequently overlooked, the slogan for consent is not just *good enough* but also includes the part *for now*. The *for now* component implies that the proposal will not be in effect forever but will be reviewed and poten- tially improved later. *Good enough* as a single strategy is, in fact, *not* good enough without reviews and improvement over time. Learning and improvement are part of the game.

2.5.2 'Clear enough'

There are other reasons why a decision might not be ready to be carried out: when things aren't *clear enough*. That might be either because a decision wasn't unclear, the information wasn't absorbed completely, or misunderstood or not *specific enough*. As we saw earlier, the collective common ground is the basis for our actions in a group. People often don't feel ready to act if that common ground is inconsistent or simply doesn't provide guidance.

This story *From Secretary to Colleague* illustrates how unclear or specific things can reduce agency.

> The leader in a workplace shared his frustration with me that the office manager (his former secretary) wouldn't step up into power. She'd always ask for permission on everything, even after so many

self-management aspects had been introduced. He had talked about it and talked about it, explained and explained, but she still simply would not take any chances or take responsibility.

I encouraged the leader to take an hour to sit down and write her role down together. I was confident that the former secretary was capable of stepping up into a more self-responsible role but that she didn't want to make mistakes. I also knew she had great admiration for the leader, so it wasn't out of fear of him that she didn't take responsibility but simply because she wanted to serve him to the best of her abilities. But that's not the relationship he wanted. He wanted her to lead with her expertise in her own responsibility.

He later reported back to me that they had a terrific conversation. They defined her role and talked about decisions she could take alone. Afterward, everything changed. She was clear on how to confidently fill her role and even developed a playful but firm assertiveness. She had arrived. In her case, getting clarity and a more explicit sense of permission was the missing piece – as soon as her role was defined within the new framework, she stepped right into her role and grew as a person and co-worker.

The leader might have assumed that the office manager role was clear enough. She didn't seem to think so. They needed to sit down and discuss the new office manager role until it was *clear enough*.

There is no absolute clarity. That issue of *clear enough* also shows up in the consent process. If asked for consent on a proposal, one needs to understand the proposal first. But how can one be 100% sure that one understands the proposal the way it was meant? Written proposals lower the risk of diverging interpretations, but they can never eliminate the risk of misunderstandings. While self-awareness and self-responsibility can help people to get a sense of whether they understand something, it will always be limited. A common ground between two people is always a bit of an approximation; if my partner tells me a story, I don't ask questions until I get every detail *exactly* right. We operate on assumptions and a gap here and there all the time. The problem is that all those little gaps here and there add up and compound in groups.

Aiming for 100% clarity is pointless. To bring a drastic example, we don't look up each word in a proposal in a dictionary to see if we all mean *exactly* the same thing. Instead, group members read the proposal, get a sense of it, and decide whether they are likely to have the same shared understanding. Sometimes, a question jumps out at someone – and then they ask it and hopefully get an answer.

Making things *too clear* leads to bureaucracy, and that's why not *all* questions need to be answered. Maybe nobody knows the answers, or maybe they simply don't have to be answered yet, but we're confident that it will be easy to answer them later.

Here's a simple story, *Membership Hypotheticals*.

> We were deciding about a membership policy. The membership policy spelled out what it meant to be a member, how one becomes a member, and how one loses organization membership. It seemed pretty complete, but then someone asked a clarifying question about the membership process that no one had an answer to: Would someone get reimbursed for their membership fee if they lost membership status in the middle of their membership year? No one had thought about it, and I, as the facilitator, was a little antsy because I judged that it was a small detail question in a hypothetical scenario. After all, we didn't kick out members regularly! I decided to risk it and simply ask for consent anyway. And amazingly, everyone consented!

I'm confident that if I had been a dutiful facilitator who tried to answer all questions and if I had asked all members what we could do about the reimbursements, we would have never made a decision that day (or any time soon). Sometimes, it's best to move on and see if an unanswered question triggers an objection of 'this is not clear enough.'

In summary, while the collective common ground is essential, there's also a fair bit of uncertainty, and we will negotiate how much lack of clarity we can work with.

We already have the tools to negotiate them because 'not clear enough' is a classic example of a dependency in section 2.3.2 where group members say that they can't say *yes* or *no* or carry out a proposal until it is defined better. Here are a few ideas.

- Risk it and make a vague decision (and cross our fingers).
- Make incremental decisions (accepting something in general and commit to specifying it in the future).
- Say yes to a proposal for now but only let it be effective once it's clarified. Sometimes, that's still progress.
- Approve the part that's clear and leave the unclear part for a future meeting.
- Approve the vague statement for a short term to review it once more clarity is created.

In a world with more uncertainty, skills of decision-making with incomplete clarity are necessary to operate.

2.5.3   Explored enough

Remember, an exploration phase is the moment when a group considers possible alternatives. But when have we explored enough?

How many ideas do we need to brainstorm before we are ready to choose one? When has everyone spoken once? When we run out of ideas? While there are studies showing that gathering more ideas leads to better ideas[10], there's, of course, a balance needed.

I have spent a lot of time observing meetings as a participant or external witness. Many groups struggle when some people want to do *more* exploration, and others think it's enough and we should just get on with it.

This is common in the reaction rounds of the consent process or, more generally, during open discussions of proposals. Some people want to add a whole wish list of amendments to proposals that were already good enough. Things can *always* be improved, but at what cost? The topic management patterns come to mind here – how much do we engage in a topic drift, and how many rabbit holes do we go down before doing something? Sometimes, it seems people are trying to avoid having to do something and open up new brainstorms and new side topics because they hope for an 'ideal' proposal.

I once sat through 10 minutes of listening to a group trying schedule their next meeting. See this story, *Playing Scheduling Riddle*:

> The group had no set meeting frequency, so the first person to speak on the topic asked the group how soon they'd like to meet. Some people now spoke to the meeting frequency, while others named specific dates and times.
> "I think we should meet in 3 weeks."
> "I can't meet on Thursday in 3 weeks; I'll be out of town."
> "Thursdays are generally bad for me, but I could do Wednesday."
> "How about Sunday evenings? How's that for people?"
> "Weekends are generally okay, but only in the morning."
> "Three weeks is not enough time to prepare for the April event."
> "Yeah, I think three or even two weeks seems right."
> "So what about the Sunday evening before that?"

---

[10]One classic study on this topic is the Mednick Remote Associates Test (RAT), developed by psychologist Sarnoff Mednick in the 1960s. The RAT presents participants with three words and asks them to generate a fourth word that is associated with all three. Mednick found that participants who generated more ideas in response to the RAT tended to produce more creative and unique answers than those who generated fewer ideas. Smith & Jones 2015.

They sounded like one of those riddles where you have to find the one possible solution to a random set of constraints, like *Tommy has four sisters, and each sister has a brother. Each sibling has a different hair color: Tommy has red hair, two sisters have blonde hair, one sister has brown hair, and one sister has black hair. How many siblings are in Tommy's family?* Except they didn't try to solve the puzzle; they made it more complex with each suggestion! This is what non-constructive autonomy looks like when there's not enough container to hold it: cacophony. Every counter-proposal adds a new potential fork, and it's unclear what the actual proposal on the table might be.

This is a frequent point of tension for groups. Individuals get their extra exploration time, others get impatient, or too little is explored, and progress toward the collective aim suffers.

Facilitators are in a key position to move from the explore phase to the decide phase. But that requires determining when we have explored *enough*. *Explored enough* is a guess – maybe ten more minutes would bring up a much more promising idea?

Given the uncertainty, there is no magic solution. Because it *is* true that ten more minutes might improve the proposal, and how much time a group is willing to give to exploration depends on a number of factors, including their sense of hope that a better solution is achievable.

Awareness of 'explored enough' can at least create shared language so people see the patterns they need to navigate together.

2.5.4 Enough *is* enough!

There are countless microdecisions and prioritizations that touch on *clear enough*, *explored enough*, and *good enough*. Are we okay with quick-and-dirty in terms of clarity, depth, and quality of our proposals?

Our comfort level or style will affect how fast we can make decisions, experiment, learn, and improve. We can go fast if we go for barely good enough, barely clear enough, and hardly spend time exploring.

- clarity/specificity (*clear enough*)
- depth of explorations (*explored enough*)
- effectiveness (*good enough*)

Too much variety between people's comfort levels makes it hard to function. On the other hand, variety and diversity in organizations are helpful because they make a group more resilient and innovative. If the 'outliers' don't speak up, the group is much more likely to go down the path of groupthink.

The answer, of course, is balance. Achieving balance requires appropriate governance and participation to determine a level that works for the group. Easier said than done, but the collective needs to be able to operate together. The measuring stick for that is the collective aim. When making a decision, the individuals take the perspective of the collective and ask themselves: Do I think this is good enough? Do I think this is clear enough? Do I think we've explored enough alternatives?

The responsibility for the collective aim can only be held when each group member takes responsibility for their respective part. For *good enough*, if a proposal might cause harm, then responsibility lies within the individual members to gauge how much likelihood for what level of harm a collective is willing to accept. The same is true for *clear enough*. The individuals decide on their level of comfort. If they feel like a gap in understanding keeps them from being able to implement a proposal, or if they think the lack of clarity might create harm, they should ask. If they can live with some uncertainty, they may let it go.

I imagine the principle of 'enough *is* enough' by imagining a river where our ship sails somewhere in the middle of the river. We bump into the river bank if we go too far to one side. What we need to learn to navigate is not how to stay exactly in the 'perfect' zone – that would be impossible and rigid; we can't sail in a perfectly straight line. Instead, we need to learn to 'navigate by red flags' and read the symptoms of the river banks. What does not enough clarity look like and feel like? What things do people say when they feel like we haven't explored enough? How do we recognize signs of not being effective enough? (I wouldn't use those as absolute since organizations aren't in place to be 'good.') Instead, they exist to achieve an aim, just like a ship sails to reach a destination.

An imminent threat, a quick opportunity, all of those require fast action, and different decision-making methods balance exploration (or consideration or deliberation) with efficiency in different ways. What's *enough* also depends on the context.

- The fastest decision-making is the autocratic decision. Yet, it comes with minimal participation and deliberation.

- The second-fastest might be the majority vote. Participation and deliberation depend.

- Consensus takes the longest. In most contexts, consent will be faster than consensus but it depends on the level of alignment of the group.

How can one strike a balance between small and fast decisions on one side and more considerate, well-founded decisions with more participation?

2.6 Policy and operations

In this section, we will touch on the rules and norms that collectives or groups give themselves to make their division of labor clear enough, good enough, and aligned enough. I will show how a better concept of policy vs. operations can help us build organizations that follow the principle of *everything is allowed until it's not*.

The starting point is the assumption that operations happen in an organization – everything starts with work. With lots of work happening within a system, self-organization will happen. Operations will cluster and develop routines, becoming specialized and forming feedback loops. There will be patterns – there may be invisible or unacknowledged patterns or acknowledged human-made patterns.

When Jerry Koch-Gonzalez and I founded *Sociocracy For All*, I don't think we ever had a formal meeting for the first year – we were running on trust, grit, and courage. It was just the two of us. When I had an idea and wanted to make it happen, I either just did it, or we had a quick chat between the two of us to get on the same page. It was easy because Jerry and I could operate on trust only because we were close as people, we were geographically close, and our work wasn't very complex. As is common with forming organizations, there was a lot of uncertainty and ambiguity about roles and responsibilities.

This is the primordial soup of self-organization where the organization just consists of doing, and that's all there is.

Then we hired an additional person for our information systems. Let's call him Alex. While in the early stages of our organization, I, as co-founder, built everything tech myself in whatever way I wanted, I now had to coordinate with Alex. I wanted to add a plug-in to our website software. I had always just done things, and it hadn't occurred to me that it wouldn't always be that way. And then my new plug-in broke our website. When Alex and I talked, we made an arrangement that, from now on, I would need to ask before installing a plug-in.

This was the first organizational guardrail that we put on me.

Now let's think about this – why would I agree to a rule that limits what I'm allowed to do? The answer is simple: I happily obeyed this rule because I was more interested in the organization's well-being than in my freedom. I whole-heartedly consented to it.

By adding Alex to the mix, we introduced a more formal division of labor for the first time. Jerry and I had just done whatever was needed; now, there was the need to codify more. Many readers will be familiar with the group development model of *forming, storming, norming, and performing*.[11] While I feel a little mixed about the model, you can see a quick moment of storming here – that's me installing the plug-in. When a group doesn't have a lot of awareness of governance, it can stay in the storming phase for a long time, but normalizing is a good idea to settle those blips and work together better. Ideally, the patterns of *storming*, *norming* and *performing* continue to occur – storming to create variation and new, creative solutions, norming to align them with the collective aim and achieve a higher level of performance as things adjust and adapt.

The point of this story is that policies aren't bad. They are necessary to do good work effectively. Without this rule about plug-ins, the quality of our website would have been low because it would have been in a constant state of disarray and malfunction.

People sometimes have an adverse reaction to policies because they have only experienced policies in coercive contexts and never a policy that they could choose themselves deliberately to improve their work.

When exposed to policies, many people instantly go into rebellion mode. There's a rule, and they want to break it. This is a *power-under* reflex that comes from moments in their past when rules were made that left them feeling powerless. Instead of creating agency around the collective aim (for example, by questioning a particular policy with those who made it or withdrawing consent to the role), they start a power battle.

For some, policies seem to trigger emotional reactions, so let's look at the most common misconceptions first.

Misconception #1: Efficiency reduces connection

People often see 'efficiency' and 'interpersonal connection' as a binary, and it's a false binary. To them, the world of policies, procedures, and governance is a rule set to increase efficiency in organizations. That's not wrong – but it's incomplete. Policies and procedures can *also* improve interpersonal connection.

To see this, let's look at the *Runs And Swims* story.

It was a small work circle with lots of work, a lot to figure out, and a weekly circle meeting. As a regular practice, we did a selection process for different roles, including the leader role. In the nominations, a clear pattern emerged of my colleague Jerry being favored by many for the leader role, leading to the proposal

---

[11] Tuckman, 1965

that he serve as leader of the circle. Yet, Jerry objected to it, saying he'd be overwhelmed with too much on his plate.

This conversation could have gone in many directions, mostly unhealthy ones. We could have pressured him into taking on the role – because who else should do it? We could have also switched to a different candidate, losing his expertise for the role. We could have also discussed whether his workload was in fact higher than everyone else's, invalidating his worry and self-care. I'm sure there are other unhealthy outcomes that I didn't think of!

Luckily, the circle facilitator didn't do any of that. Instead, he asked a promising question: "When you are overwhelmed, what does that look like?" Jerry thought about it briefly and then answered that he skips his regular exercise routine of runs and swims when he gets too busy, and then doesn't feel well.

The facilitator then amended the proposal most elegantly: "Would it work for you if you're accepting the leader role for one year, and we ask each week in our meeting whether you've gone on runs and swims? If we notice it's not working for you, we will revisit and make a new plan." Jerry consented to that plan, and asking him about his runs and swims from the past 7 days became a beloved ritual in every meeting. We even made it a habit to check in with our running and swimming counterparts for some time. We had turned a situation from potentially toxic into sweet, co-responsible, and caring.

In this example, while, of course, everyone individually wanted to support Jerry in his work-life balance, it was not until we made an intentional plan of *how* we would take care of him on an ongoing basis that we gelled into reliable, collective caretaking. Honestly, had we not *instituted* the care, I don't think it would have happened. *I* certainly would have forgotten, which means we would have dumped the responsibility to watch out for his own well-being onto Jerry.

The main point of this action plan was to manifest interpersonal care. Just because we codify it as a policy doesn't mean it's less effective in the integration of efficiency and caring – on the contrary, policies can be *more* caring if they put measures in place.

People who see governance as something cold and efficiency-oriented most typically also think that if we are *more* efficient (or effective), we are also *less* caring. They perceive efficiency and interpersonal connection as two competing priorities, impossible to balance.

Our learnings from multi-level selection will help us understand this better. Interpersonal connection is a need on the individual level (with positive side effects on the collective level). Effectiveness and efficiency are needed on the collective level to make good use of shared resources. In a system where the collective needs are prioritized at the *cost* of the individual level – a *power-over* situation where policies and procedures rule and the needs of the individuals are dismissed – we are playing a zero-sum game where increasing one reduces the other. But that isn't accurate in a system that successfully manages and integrates both levels.

Once we hold the individual and the collective needs in a healthy balance of *power-with*, this dichotomy vanishes. My need as a group member is not just the interpersonal connection or fun. My need is also to contribute to the collective purpose. Therefore, policies that improve the collective level are in my interest as a group member.

Misconception #2: Leadership decides, workers work

When we ask people about the difference between operational and policy decisions, they will say things like 'operational decisions are lower level,' and policy decisions are 'higher-level'. Operational decisions, people often say, are made by staff, and the leadership, managers, or the board makes policy decisions. This definition is inherently hierarchical. It assumes that leaders or managers are better thinkers than workers. Some people are cut out to decide things, and others are only good at doing what others have decided.

That is inaccurate and entrenched in old, elitist thinking patterns. In this section, I want to lay out a definition and practice of policy and operations that is more accurate and more appropriate for self-management. The definition of policy and operations can be hierarchy-free and comes from an understanding of a *leaderful* organization where workers both do things *and* make decisions.

Misconception #3: Bureaucracy is bad, trust is good Another misconception is that bureaucracy is bad. Bureaucracy is often perceived as bad because of its association with inefficiency, red tape, and rigid rules and procedures. Bureaucratic systems can be slow to adapt to changing circumstances, and they may prioritize compliance with rules and regulations over innovation and creativity. In addition, bureaucratic systems can be perceived as unjust – particularly when they are seen as favoring those in positions of power or authority.

But bureaucracy isn't automatically bad. It can have both positive and negative effects depending on the context and how it is implemented. A formalized structure and procedure set can ensure consistency, fairness, and alignment in decision-making. For example, bureaucracy and explicit rules can *support* minorities and people with less privilege by establishing formal procedures and regulations that promote equity and reduce discrimination. Sure, bureaucracies can't undo power imbalances completely, and they routinely underperform compared to their intention.

On the topic of trust, people who say things like "let's not have policies, let's just trust each other". The problem is that the collective aim and commitment need management and care beyond an unexamined assumption of trust. A system based purely on trust will play into the hands of free riders. Autonomy is only one side of the equation, and trust-only systems are frequently unbalanced.

There is one more subtle but significant problem with the trust-over-governance approach: I can only be considerate of things I know. But I can't know what I don't know. Of course, in small groups, we could ask everyone to disclose what we need to know about them so we can consider their needs and then try really, really hard to remember it over the next few years. That might be possible, though I am personally sure I would forget those things. But now think of a group of a hundred people working on different topics that all connect somehow. You would not even know what things you could screw up. If you mess something up that another group was working on, you'd likely be blissfully unaware. So not only is the strategy of "love, trust and consideration" inefficient and hard to scale, but it's also risky because it doesn't factor in the unknown unknowns of individuals. A policy can't eradicate all unknowns unknowns but as it's often made with wider input than an isolated, individual decision, more parameters can be considered.

There's a thought-provoking team game: the broomstick game. Take a team of 6 or so people and ask them to line up in two parallel lines. Ask them all to stick out one finger towards the other line in a way so you can place a broomstick on top of their fingers. The broomstick is just resting on their fingers. No one person is holding the broomstick alone. Standing still is mostly doable. But now, ask them to lower the broomstick to the ground without letting it drop and without ever losing touch with the stick. To succeed in the game, the team needs to lower their fingers in a coordinated manner. If two people just lower their fingers, the broomstick falls. Now, this sounds hard, but it gets even harder. It seems like unexplainable magic, but inadvertently, the broomstick rises on their fingers. Since every person needs to touch the broomstick, there is only a small margin or error. If only one person lifts the stick slightly, everyone else's fingers need to follow upwards to stay connected. The effect compounds and groups get very frustrated by how the stick moves upward when you ask them to lower it.

It can be painful to watch the group struggle with the broomstick moving upwards while figuring out who to put in charge. But it *is* possible to lower it. Some successful strategies are putting one person in charge who gives orders '3-2-1, move down!'. It also works to breathe in the same rhythm and lower it on breathing out. Singing works, too.

What *doesn't* work is to pick a group of people who trust each other and assume it'll now just be fixed. Friends will struggle with the broomstick game just like any other group. The one way I can see trust helping is that we might forgive someone who takes initiative and says ok, Follow me, 1-2-3!' because we trust them. But the reason we got the task done wasn't because of trust but because of coordination. Trust made it possible to short-cut into coordination because we decide to follow someone even if they have empowered themselves autocratically.

I've discussed this effect earlier in section 1.5.3 – a lack of structure can be cushioned by relationships and experience but not replaced. I can't tell you how many groups I've seen where everyone dearly loved and trusted each other, but work still didn't progress. Typically, what happens is that because the work doesn't progress, relationships get strained.

The broom exercise shows that you can't change things just by wanting them to change. And if everyone in the organization wants the same thing, that *still* doesn't mean it'll happen. Shared purpose without systems is not enough. A group needs to develop collective agency and create systems and policies that support that agency.

2.6.1   Improving operations with policies

Let's go back to what it was like for me and my colleague to start our organization. Here's an example that shows how policies can improve and simplify our work.

> In the beginning, we created a lot of content, like videos and articles. At some point, the question came up whether to give content away for free or to create paywalls. We knew we wanted to support

the movement's growth and keep access as open as possible. We put the Creative Commons license onto some of our articles online, indicating that people could use them as they pleased. Yet, we needed to be more consistent. We charged money for some content, and for others, we didn't. Each time we created content, we had to decide (and remember!) anew whether it would be free or paid content. We tended to be inconsistent, so at some point, the question came up, "ok, how do we handle this *in general*? What's open access and what isn't?" We wanted to agree so we wouldn't have to decide each time.

That's when *operational decisions* shift into *policy decisions*. What's the difference?

- Operational decisions are decisions that only affect the specific situation we're working with at that moment; our decision only applies to that instance. In this case, it's about whether or not to give this one article a Creative Commons license.

- Policy decisions apply in general, not only for one case. In this example, a policy decision is a general agreement about all content of a certain kind – not just one webinar recording.

Here's another example of how operational decisions can lack consistency.

This was a newly formed consumer cooperative where volunteers buy food in bulk, package it, and sell it to members. It was Chelsea's role to schedule volunteers to do the packaging. When Chelsea opened her co-op laptop in the morning, two people, Mike and Mark, had offered to take on a shift that needed to be filled. Chelsea didn't know who to choose, Mike or Mark.

In the 'everything is allowed' stage, Chelsea might simply pick one of them based on her own judgment call. For example, Mike emailed first, and that's that. Or she might be aware that Mark needs volunteer hours because he's short on hours, so she'd choose Mark. Without other constraints, Chelsea could do whatever she thinks is best. Next time, when Martha and Maria email at the same time in the same situation, she might give preference to Maria for a different reason than when she chose Mike.

This practice might go on forever, and many operational decisions will go on like that. That's totally fine if it works and everyone is happy with it. Governance does *not* mean to build as much structure and procedures as possible. Instead, governance means creating conditions so groups can *do* things with minimal effort and maximum clarity.

People must learn to *discern* when structures are more helpful than harmful. That's not on governance as a system; that's on people making those choices. The point of this book is to advocate for more governance literacy so people can make better choices for their purposes.

Let's say this practice of first-come-first-serve *does* create issues.

> Chelsea's first-come-first-serve strategy made it harder for busy people to get their hours in, and three members left the co-op because they were upset with how the schedule was managed.
>
> The struggle continued. Eventually, someone brought up the topic, and the board developed a policy that guided how these situations are handled. The board asked Chelsea to follow a general rule and apply it each time: whenever two people email about shifts, check their hour budget and give the extra shift to the member with the least hours.

In this way, operational decisions are case-by-case or single-instance decisions that we make on the fly as we do our work. Policy decisions are made that change the set of constraints that guide our work. Policy decisions intentionally create a pattern.

This might be the first time you hear this definition of policy and operational decisions. However, my definition is helpful and intuitive. For example, if my daughter asks me on a Saturday evening whether she can stay out until midnight, and I say yes, then it's apparent that I have only given permission for today. I have not established a rule that staying out until midnight every Saturday (or even every day) is okay without asking. Every child knows the difference!

Why aren't policies high-level? Because they can occur on *any* level of an organization. In my definition, *each* level has policy and operational decisions. Since work and decision-making are connected in self-governance, those working in a group also make both operational and policy decisions in that group's domain of responsibility. The 'higher' in the organization, the less tangible operations often are, and policies will often have a wider scope, but that's due to their position, not inherent in the difference of policy and operational decisions. (The areas of responsibility will be addressed in section 3.1.2.)

2.6.2   When to make policies

Policy decisions require and introduce infrastructure. Policies should only be added when they are worth doing – holding a lean approach to governance. Some decisions are best made by someone alone. Operational decisions and feedback have less overhead, so they should be prioritized.

Making operational decisions can be hard for people who aren't used to making decisions alone. Here's a story on this point: *The $10 Puzzle*. Emil's department (we've already heard about them throughout this book) was planning a one-week *hackathon* where they wanted to spend time on self-chosen projects and just spend time together to get to know each other more.

> One member, let's call her Annie, had the idea of buying a jigsaw puzzle. Her idea was to set it up in a place; it would draw people's attention and gather them, like forming an "unofficial gathering point."
>
> Yet, Annie wanted the leadership to decide on this puzzle. Even more, she thought two 1-hour meetings would be appropriate, which, according to Emil, "was crazy." Emil asked her whether she would be up for making this decision in a more self-organizing way.
>
> Emil: "You could use the advice process. Present your proposal and ask everyone who has expertise or is affected. So who would you ask?"
>
> Annie: "I'd ask Peggy."
>
> Emil: "Why Peggy?"
>
> Annie: "She sits in my office, and I think she'll support it."
>
> Emil: "How will you know whether someone doesn't like it?"
>
> Annie: "I don't know! "
>
> Emil: "How could you find out?"
>
> Annie: "How many people do I have to ask?"
>
> Emil: "When you feel comfortable enough that you've asked enough people so you'd know."
>
> Knowing Annie well from years of working together, Emil suspects that Annie now wants to ask all 45 people in the department.
>
> Emil: "Asking everyone in the department will take a lot of time."
>
> Annie: "Then how can I find out what people really think?!"
>
> Emil told me that he just left it there. He did not follow up but simply waited to see what would happen. Annie didn't reach out again.
>
> Yet, to Emil's delight, at the hackathon, there was a puzzle table! It became a popular spot, a well-received place of connection, and even a lasting tradition – total success! Everyone praised Annie for her idea and for taking action.

Individual action is excellent. Recurring individual action is also great. The creative, innovative activity like buying a puzzle – or bigger things! – is what happens in less regimented places, where people are free to act. That can be scary for those who are used to waiting for permission, like Annie. And yet, a formal decision would have blown this decision out of proportion. This is not a place for policy but a place for self-guided action! Individual action is a manifestation of healthy autonomy.

An organization implementing too much red tape hampers creative innovation. One misconception of role/circle-based governance systems is that a role or mandate must be created before someone can act. Organizations can harness individual autonomy if they follow an 'everything is allowed until it's not' approach. If there's no policy on this topic and it's in support of the aim, it should be allowed.

On the other hand, some rules set constraints, so we have alignment. As I've said when discussing multi-level selection, good governance is about finding the right balance or combination between those polarities.

So when *is* it useful to make a formal policy and to 'reign in' autonomy to create alignment?

- When it's less work to make and follow a policy than to make an operational decision each time.
- When making a policy increases the quality of our work.
- When people's judgment is not enough to inform a considerate operational decision.
- When we want to mitigate risk.

Let's imagine a situation like my cohousing community. Around seventy people share a community building, and the houses are arranged around the community building. People can reserve the community building for their personal parties. Let's imagine I want to have a birthday party there, and I anticipate it to go on until late on a Sunday evening, with loud music. Let's say this is the first time someone has a party, and there is no policy. I want to celebrate as long into the night as possible, but I want to be a considerate neighbor. What should I do?

One option is to knock on every neighbor's door and have a little conversation. One neighbor might say, please stop music at midnight. Another one might say, turn the music down at 10 but celebrate until whenever. Another might say, keep things quiet until the kids are asleep, and then it doesn't matter anymore. Now, what do I do? What's the solution that expresses 'love and trust' the best? This is hard to answer, and operating on individual case-by-case decisions only means different people will make different decisions. While this is fine, it does shift the responsibility of the relationship between individuals and the community at large onto the individual.

Operating just on trust, love, and good intentions could be more efficient. Because one month later, my neighbor wanted to have a party, too. Should they now also talk to 69 neighbors? Should everyone ask for permission before doing things outside the ordinary? Operating on trust works in a small group, but in a larger group, it's not feasible, and it can contribute to conservative decisions where people avoid doing new things because it's too tedious.

We arrive back at the same point again and again: in the absence of enough governance structure, undesired consequences flourish: *power-under* – deciding to forgo the party we wanted – and *power-over* – having the party with no consideration of the impact.

Earlier in section 2.5.4, we saw that autocratic decisions are the fastest. There are other ways to hold the balance between autonomy and alignment. In systems like sociocracy, policies require circle consent while people in roles make operational decisions independently. Other organizations use the advice process where individuals can decide how much feedback to ask, and some organizations codify how many people need to be asked for advice.

In my cohousing community's case, the circle responsible for the community building could set a policy that quiet hours begin at 10 pm but exceptions would be granted on a case-by-case basis guided by consented-to criteria.

The difference between policy and operational decisions reminds me of the difference between two modes of thinking, like in the psychologist Daniel Kahnemann's book *Thinking Fast and Slow*: "System 1" is fast, intuitive, and emotional thinking. "System 2" is slower, more deliberative and logical. While System 1 is useful because it would be impossible to make all decisions in a deliberative manner, but it also comes with biases where more thorough thinking would have been useful. The difference between quick operational decisions and process-heavy but considerate policy decisions seems like the *collective* counterpart to those two ways of thinking. Operational decisions is how 'a collective' thinks fast, and policy decisions is how 'the collective' thinks fast. Both are needed! We often try to wing things first and then ramp up our thinking when we realize we need more attention on the issue. The same is true in organizations – operational decisions typically come first and then get guided by policy decisions over time.

2.6.3 Agreements, roles, workflows

Making agreements in a formalized and participatory way creates alignment that is situated on the opposite side of innovation and individual action. We decide that it's worth sitting down and defining things.

There are three kinds of policies:

- **Agreements** are general rules that make cooperating more straightforward, for example, HR policies, noise policies, and safety rules.

- **Workflows** are decisions where a group defines how to perform a task; examples are HR workflows for onboarding a new staff member, how to book a meeting room in the office, and how to organize a conference.

- **Defining roles** is another sanity-preservation method. Webinar host, book sales manager, truck steward, SEO wizard – whatever role is useful can be created, defined, and filled.

How thoroughly roles are defined in a role description is a matter of choice – along the lines of *clear/specific enough*. I've acted in many roles that were undefined, and it worked great. Often, defining them comes into play once we pass them on in order to transmit knowledge. Other roles were more defined because there was a need for clarity about who does what in a multi-person workflow.

Roles are an easy way to create alignment via role description while unleashing autonomy and choice within the role. In that way, roles are beneficial to shift collectively held items, at least temporarily, out of the collective realm to free up capacity, simplify, and support a bias towards action.

2.6.4 Roles, leadership, and accountability

How does accountability work in a consent-based organization where circles decide what roles should exist? Who says that someone has to do better or that they should do something differently? In short, how does accountability work without a boss?

Accountability and leadership are two of the most misunderstood topics in self-management. People think there is no accountability in an organization without *power-over*. On the contrary, there is just as much accountability as in any other type of organization. Accountability still works the same way – a person in a role is accountable to the entity that holds the role in its domain. Any person in a role is accountable to the role's and the group's aims.

As Ostrom showed through her research on management of the commons, shared management is only possible with accountability and feedback. There must be consequences if someone is not following policies or other agreements. Self-managed organizations can be weak in how its members hold each other accountable. They either don't clearly define responsibilities in the first place, or they don't follow up when responsibilities aren't met. While feedback is built into many systems, its effectiveness depends entirely on people's willingness and ability to define clear responsibilities and *give* feedback. Self-managed organizations must be aware of how essential accountability is to the success of the whole organization. Just like an immune system protects an organism in many different ways, an organization should respond if its structures and foundations are violated.

Increased transparency can help here, but ultimately, it requires direct follow-through and action. But where does the action come from?

Earlier, I said that a collective can't *do* much. As such, a collective can't 'check in on the progress' or 'give feedback on lack of accountability' in the same way an individual can.

If the collective wants to check on the progress, it would require a report, then a group exploration to give feedback, and possibly a shared assessment statement that states whether we declare something on track and what possible consequences might be. For less time-critical feedback, the group might make a collective speech act condemning a certain action or, demanding a behavior change, or repairing a violation.

For more time-critical things, acting might be more effective, for example, if a violation requires an immediate response. Since it can be challenging for a collective to react in a timely and targeted manner, some systems see the leader as the 'spokesperson' that acts *on behalf* of the collective. Leaders only hold people accountable for the responsibilities set by the group, including the aim and all other agreements. In a way, they are the enforcers of the group's decisions. For example, if the group decides that a webinar role has to organize one webinar per week, then the leader will hold the person in that role accountable. What's worth noting here is that the frame is set by the group – the definition of the role and choosing who holds it. That way, there is no *power-over* situation.

In practice, this can mean that the group leader touches base with the people in roles to check on their work's progress and only flags topics to talk about as a whole group if there is more to say.

How much authority is given to the leader to determine performance quality depends on the system and the agreements made in the organization. Most self-managed systems encourage individual agency and rely more on feedback than pressure or consequences to evaluate performance.

In some systems, the leader is the person who takes on most of the operations by default and who then needs to make an effort to intentionally 'package' those operations into a role so they can be taken off the leader's to-do list and intentionally given to another role on the group. Just like any other member – and even more so –, leaders are expected to notice unclaimed operations and make sure they get funneled into a role or a task that can be assigned. The leader acts on behalf of the collective by surfacing tasks and topics that require clarity or discussion to ensure operations can be carried out effectively. The leader also holds people accountable for carrying out assigned tasks. While assigning tasks may happen by the collective or an authorized individual, an assigned task is a commitment (like a promise) to the collective. The leader acts as the spokesperson for the collective level to make sure the tasks get done.

This way of leadership is a *function* more than a special leadership character trait. Because of the *power-with* frame, this kind of leadership is incompatible with leadership theories that emphasize the 'specialness' of some over others. In my experience, it's even counterproductive if that dynamic is present because it typically means that other group members defer to the leader in a *power-under* stance, weakening the group's ability to have agency as a collective.

What kinds of leadership does this form of *power-with* need? Leaders in this system focus on tasks, goals, or a (gentle) inspiration, hold up the collective's aim and purpose, and inspire people to learn, grow, and contribute. They are equals, self-responsible and focused on balance and integration of everyone's individual needs with the collective needs. A servant leadership model, on the other hand, can sometimes glorify sacrifice or *power-under* where the leaders ignore their own needs.

Many people struggle with a healthy sense of their power and power relationships with others, leading to energy tied up in power dynamics. Leadership figures can trigger this behavior. Once people have mentally arrived in a choice-based system based on *power-with*, leadership and accountability become a question of logistics, not of principle.

The leadership role includes the care and stewardship of the shared aim and the group's ability to work towards the aim. Whatever is needed to support the group and its operations will be the leader's catch-all responsibility by default unless it's specified and distributed within a role, for example, if there is a role of emotional support.

Good followership is an essential component of effective leadership. Followership involves actively engaging with the leadership, supporting the shared aim of the organization, and being accountable for one's role and responsibilities within the organization.

In consent-based/role-based systems, good followership is characterized by a willingness to participate in decision-making and a commitment to the shared aim of the organization. It involves actively contributing to the circles and domains one is involved in and providing constructive feedback to leadership and peers when necessary.

Good followership also requires a certain level of trust in leadership and in the system as a whole. Followers must trust that the leadership is acting in the organization's best interests and that the system supports their participation and contributions. If leadership is met with unnecessary rebellion, it will create friction and slow down the group. If a circle member who is not the leader sees a gap that needs to be filled, it's their responsibility to help fill that gap by alerting the circle to it.

2.6.5   Infrastructure roles

Just like leadership is a function that gives a collective a way to have agency, there are other functions that individuals with direct, individual agency best take on. How those functions are distributed into roles is a choice that each specific governance system can set.

The leader has the function of supporting accountability around operations. Other functions can be clustered into roles:

- being a spokesperson to the outside (representative function)
- information flow to the wider organization
- information flow within the group (e.g., meeting minutes)
- Information storage (e.g., policy manuals, list of role descriptions)
- facilitation of meetings; time-keeping
- tending to social-emotional needs ('vibes' or conflict resolution)
- financial admin, or resource distribution in general
- circle membership manager
- holder of the purpose

Each of these functions plays a vital role in a group's smooth functioning and overall success. By distributing these responsibilities among individuals with the necessary skills and aptitudes, the group can ensure that all aspects of its infrastructure are well-managed.

In a self-governed context, those functions are held by group members. That means that, for example, a facilitator and all other roles need to be able to hold the particular function of the role while also being an individual group member with their particular interests or ideas.

These roles can be distributed in various ways, depending on the specific governance system. The governance system requires a particular clustering of roles, or they are defined on the organizational or group level.

Often, groups will cluster some of those functions in a handful of roles by identifying generic roles to support the functioning of the group:

Role	Responsibilities
Leader	spokesperson (representative function); membership manager; financial admin
Facilitator	meeting facilitation; time-keeping
Secretary/ admin	information flow within the group; management of knowledgebase and official records
Delegate	information flow to the wider organization
As needed/ unassigned	tending to social-emotional needs ('vibes' or conflict resolution); holder of the purpose; learning manager

Example of a definition of standard roles

Which set of roles makes the most sense will depend on the organization; my overall point here is to emphasize the choices that self-organized groups have in defining roles that fit their needs.

2.7 Governance choices

I think of governance around decision-making as three basic agreements:

- How we decide
- Who decides what
- How to change past decisions on the rule set

Governance choices are unlike any other choices because they are fundamental. They are the patterns and practices by which all the rules are made like a constitution determines how laws are made.

Imagine a group that debates their decision-making method each time they need to decide. How shall we make the decision today? By consent, consensus, or majority vote? That might work – but what if it doesn't? How will we decide how to decide?

It's also simply a matter of efficiency. Policies help us in being faster with our collaboration because not each decision needs to be made as "a one-off". It's helpful to make governance choices and formalize processes. We don't reinvent our car every time we use it either – we want just to use it to get somewhere. Governance is a way to get us to a shared decision with a good balance between participation and efficiency.

There is quite a variety among self-organized teams. Of course, variety is great for experimentation and innovation – yet, on a group level, having agreed-upon patterns and practices is also good so we have some consistency and efficiency in our decision-making.

Among the varieties that I'm aware of are the big decision-making methods: autocratic decision-making, majority vote, consensus, consent, and their respective variations like quadratic voting, *systemisches Konsensieren*, modified consensus, and many more. And then there are full governance systems, or frameworks like 'teal' (based on the book Reinventing Organizations by Frederic Laloux) or Semco-style organizing that emphasize more the values and principles of shared responsibility, trust, and empowerment than the nuts and bolts of how to make decisions and leave a lot of the specificity to the organizations using it. Systems like Sociocracy 3.0 – a flavor of sociocracy that emphasizes how sociocracy's patterns and practices can be mixed and matched as desired – are even more permissive than more original versions.

But even within the same governance family, there are finer differences in the processes that determine what's *clear enough*, *explored enough*, or *good enough*. It's like there are dialects in a language. A few examples:

- *Good enough* has a tighter definition in Holacracy than it does in sociocracy. In Holacracy, one cannot object based on a potentially negative impact in the *future* (as opposed to the present), while in sociocracy, that's ok.
- Even within sociocracy, there are sub-dialects. In some practices, people do two reaction rounds in the consent process; in others, only one is standard. How a proposal is co-created might differ from what's considered a complete meeting format.
- There is a variety among organizations practicing the same system, for example, traditions around meeting formats or check-ins.

Any governance system, no matter the dialect, will say something on what's *clear*, *explored* and *good enough* in terms of governance.

The easiest way to understand that is through this story, *Objecting 11 Months Later*. The one that comes to mind is from an organization cutting a bunch of corners in their use of sociocratic governance – you will see what I mean in just a moment. So here's what had happened.

> A member of the Garden Circle sent me a slightly panicky email saying that they had made a decision 11 months ago to apply for a specific grant to reduce the spread of invasive plants (plants that aren't native to the area and have the tendency to destabilize ecosystems by taking over). Their grant application had been accepted according to specific terms and based on the project plan.
>
> The circle had since started the work and spent part of the money. The work included the use of Glyphosate, which comes with controversy and debate over its potential health and environmental impacts. The use of Glyphosate had been in the original proposal, which had been consented to by the Garden Circle.
>
> A circle member had missed the meeting where that decision was made and had recently heard about the Glyphosate part. He had emailed the Garden Circle saying he objected to the decision to use Glyphosate. The circle member who had sent me the email asked me: is he allowed to do that?!

According to the existing governance agreement, any circle member could object. Consequently, my first question was whether he was a member of the circle. If he's a member of the circle, he can object. I admit that it's hard to tell whether one can object nine months after a decision was made, but that's a slightly different story. (The purist in me says that any circle member needs to be able to object to any past decision at any time if new information comes up. But then that circle member needs to work with the circle in assessing the situation; in this case, the full grant would be lost if the project got aborted, and the circle had already spent half of the money, meaning around $5000 would be lost.)

So, was he a circle member?

> Her response wasn't so clear. When I asked her to unpack that, she shared that he had never formally left the circle but that he had missed 9 out of the past ten meetings.
>
> So is one a circle member if one misses 9 out of 10 meetings? To find out, I looked up the governance agreement, and there was

no mention of what would happen if someone didn't show up for meetings, and not even anything close to that. There was no mention of requirements for circle membership (like participation).

I told her there was no solution for her on the governance side of things and that the only chance I saw was in taking the interpersonal route, inviting for conversation and hoping a resolution would be found.

Is a governance agreement that doesn't specify the requirements for circle membership a *clear enough* governance rule set? Let's go back to the pillars of resilience from section 1.5.3 where I said that collaboration works if we have enough of. . .

- structure and processes to have a defined way of how things work,
- trust and relationships to work things out outside of governance just because we trust each other as human beings,
- skills and experience to innovate new solutions,
- principles and values to guide our behavior in the absence of defined rules.

Luckily, this story didn't escalate, meaning the situation must have been cushioned without relying on a defined process in the governance agreement. I'm not sure how it was resolved, but I imagine it was due to interpersonal trust and the value of working things out together.

So if questions like losing circle membership *don't* get defined with more specificity, then the circle needs to either be more alert so these situations don't come up (using their skills and experience), *or* the circle needs to be willing to deal with situations like the one at hand on the interpersonal level. The resilience has to come from somewhere.

What we lean on more is our choice when designing and adjusting our governance system. Between structures & processes, skills & experience, trust & relationships, and principles & values, we need *enough* of each to make the system work, and an organization needs to find the right fit for its culture, style, comfort, and skill level.

- For example, imagine a perfect rule-based system where every governance step we take is specified and spelled out. That would be a fool-proof system, yet with no flexibility or leeway for individual innovation.
- We could also imagine a perfect system based on principles and values where every member has to be carefully chosen based on their commitment to said principles, or they would have to be trained on the principles, with reminders. Could such a system work? A

mindset or principle-based system that is very strong and coherent might be able to do that, for example, a religious or a family system. But would it be able to run without rules, just based on being good members? I doubt it.

- A system could also run on perfect conflict relationships with angel-like, mind-reading people who all have much time to listen to each other. People who want to replace governance processes with 'just be nice to each other' are often convinced that this would work, but my experience says differently.

- Running entirely on skills and experience might be possible in many environments but as a governance system, it's weak in scaling because we can't assume that everyone will be skilled enough.

Every single source of group resilience falls short on its own, so every system needs to *combine all four of them* in some proportion. For example, Holacracy puts more credit on rules, Sociocracy 3.0 emphasizes mindset and principles, and in our practice in Sociocracy For All, we try a mix that includes a good dash of skills and interpersonal connection. More loosely organized Teal organizations put more emphasis on principles and values, for example, in Semco-style self-management.

They all have their raison d'être because situations and conditions can differ. For example, I wouldn't want to use principle/value-based governance when I can't trust that there's enough social cohesion and ability to adapt. In a situation where I am not sure whether people have skills, connection, or shared values, I might tighten structures and processes. Whatever it takes, it will need, between the combination of all four pillars, enough coherence to function.

We look to relationships if there are no rules (or they aren't kept). Our relationships and trust typically deteriorate as soon as things get hard, which only leaves us skills and principles. It's hard to hold onto principles when we're upset.

It's essential to see what happens next. All the pillars of resilience hold the group together and allow us to manage that polarity of autonomy and alignment healthily. Let's say all pillars of resilience break down on the collective level. With no process to hold it together, it breaks apart and the collective level disintegrates. When that happens, the *individual* interests take over, and unity is lost.

The only other way to rescue the shared aim for the sake of the group is to step in and make unilateral decisions – that's when, in structurelessness, *power-over* and *power-under* creep back in.

I used the word 'rescue' intentionally here because it is precisely the behavior from the drama triangle that kicks in at those moments. In a healthy collective, the aim is held and carried out collectively. But with a lack of governance and pillars of resilience, the collective no longer has enough agency to take responsibility. Just like the drama triangle roles surface when people reject or overstep responsibility; the same happens on a group level.

Think of times in your organizations when someone rescued a group or organization by stepping in. What was the vacuum that led to the need for someone else to rescue it? And in what pillar of resilience was it well-resourced, and which were lacking?

Just like the 'right' level of specificity might change over time in our group decisions, our choices might change over time when it comes to designing and redesigning our governance system. A business with a big influx of new members less familiar with the company values and processes might have to add either more rules or more training. An organization where, over time, members got the hang of the system could cut more corners and reduce rules. In trustful times, we might rely on rules less, only to increase our reliance on rules and processes when trust is disturbed.

To float in the healthy middle of a river; we need to learn how not to bump into the riverbank on either side. On the governance level, groups must learn how to read the signs of 'governance blips' to make changes. We need to pay attention when people start complaining or stop moving forward because they lack the clarity to continue. Good governance is silent and almost invisible. Tensions are picked up and processed constructively. All we see is the *absence* of drama, meaning we're in *power-with* mode.

Over time, we will get better and better at navigating design choices for systems and local adaptations based on experiences and the impacts we see. A vision that excites me is the idea that in another few years, almost everyone will have been a part of a consent-based, distributed organization and that all dialects or even different languages will grow closer while offering more choices for people to use. My vision of the future of organizations is to enable people to find their way in a pluralism of choices rather than finding the perfect cookie-cutter system. Imagine that in five years, everyone will have had experience being part of a distributed team, either at work or as a volunteer. That may result in a situation where people who are multi-"lingual" in terms of different systems and approaches will be able to switch between them seamlessly, bring their experiences and good practices from one place to another, and make adjustments as needed, as good stewards of their own systems.

2.8 Chapter summary

A collective is a group that exhibits shared agency and unity of purpose. Governance helps balance individual and collective needs.

To hold authority and responsibility *together*, a group needs to move through all the steps of action together or with as much participation as possible to create a healthy sense of collective agency and responsibility – collective power. Without coordination, groups are limited to simple activities. Complex collective action requires governance processes.

- Shared reality – conceptualized in the *common ground* – matters for decision making. Not what is known *individually* but what is *known together*, provides a foundation for collective decisions. Groups establish facts through acknowledgment and agreement.

- Having shared agency means managing what we talk about. Managing topics and agendas helps focus collective attention and exploration. Patterns like drifts, forks, and dependencies require facilitation, so a group talks about the same topic.

- Decisions represent a convergence of perspectives into alignment. After a decision, a group can 'speak as one'. Unlike individuals making decisions, legitimate collective speech and action rely on governance to confer authority and coordinate.

- Consent prioritizes alignment with collective aims over individual preferences.

- Governance helps groups manage tradeoffs between perfection vs. constraints. That requires (enough) alignment on the pace, depth, and willingness to take risks. Besides *good enough*, there are also *clear* and *explored enough*.

- Constraints and division of labor (agreements, roles, workflows) help do the work. Policies create alignment and quality through consistent rules, while operational decisions allow autonomy. Roles distribute responsibilities for accountability and leadership.

- A leaders' function it to act as spokesperson for collective aims so it can act. Infrastructure roles support group functions.

- Governance choices like decision-making methods are agreements on how to decide and change the rules. They create consistency and alignment on fundamentals so collectives can have agency.

Chapter 3

Organizational Alignment

Groups are different from individuals. Organizations – groups of groups – are yet another step towards more complexity.

They too have emergent properties that groups don't have which we will look at. The biggest difference is that a group can explore or decide together but a group of groups typically cannot. In a group of groups, difficulties arise for lack of alignment – and that alignment is necessary for organizational agency.

How can a collective of collectives act as one?

3.1 Organization-level agency

A 280-people company in software engineering had just started to transform their company from a classical hierarchical organization to what they call 'co-leadership.'

They didn't want to create anything resembling a hierarchical structure, so they had a very flat hierarchy and rejected any other structure. They had a formal CEO – the founder – and about fifty self-organized teams working well on their respective projects.

Yet, they had a sense that they needed more. While the work was done, they worried about a lack of strategy and direction. They only did what was right before them, but coordination across the teams seemed hard and a little hit or miss.

When I listened to them, I was amazed. I got that there were issues around strategy – which wasn't surprising – but I was astonished to hear how smoothly they had transitioned towards a shared leadership model. In the beginning, I was impressed. They made the transition to self-management sound like a walk in the park. No power issues, just happy teams?

But the more I heard, the more I became suspicious. Either there was some invisible magic at work that I needed to learn about, or they didn't tell me everything. How did they run at all?

I began to inquire. Was there really no central management? What about financial decisions? How were they made?

> It turned out that the former CEO and the CFO in fact, made the financial decisions, and it wasn't transparent to teams *how* they were made. There had been thoughts about distributing financial responsibility to a group, but that seemed far beyond what was possible.

Even knowing that, the dots still didn't connect. What was the CEO doing all day? How does one distribute all the power and only make a financial decision here and there? I inquired more.

My informants told me that the CEO was very active in visiting teams and writing emails to teams in an anxious effort to guide and steer them. Now, an image was forming inside my head. And with that, my heart went out to that very CEO! I imagined the situation: he built a successful business that grew and flourished. Then, he wanted to do the right thing and transform the organization into trust and co-leadership. The teams formed, and suddenly, much of his former power was distributed into small teams that all did their own thing. Some decisions didn't get made, but he tried hard to let people figure things out in the spirit of 'co-leadership.' The CEO and the CFO were stuck with the financial responsibility for everything and didn't have a say in any of the work. No wonder he was anxious and lonely!

When I shared that with my informants, they all got very quiet. They said what I had shared with them made sense. "We never looked at it from *his* side. What you said explains a lot about his behavior."

The organization had become like a bagel where the center was mostly empty. But empty spaces don't stay empty. Power is like water; it doesn't just hang out in mid-air. When there's a hole in the ship, it will flow in (or out). It always flows somewhere. If we don't make a deliberate effort to collect and funnel the water, it just flows and then collects wherever it gets caught. In this case, the power that hadn't been distributed intentionally just stayed with the CEO (and CFO). It sounded like the CEO didn't want that power because it was supposed to be co-leadership. It became a lonely double bind.

There are a lot of parallels between the bagel-shaped company in *Ship*

With No Mast and Emil from the story *Fishbowl to break the power game* in our previous chapter. Emil had shared with his team how lonely he felt when they treated him as different and blamed him for the power he had without actually taking on that power themselves.

This was a much bigger organization than Emil's. Instead of a few teams looking to the boss, fifty teams were looking to the boss who wasn't the boss anymore. Unlike Emil's department, this wasn't a situation where everyone could still fit into one room and figure things out. Emil could connect with his colleagues via vulnerability and empathic connection, which helped them connect as peers and step out of the story of the *power-over* paradigm. But in an organization with 280 people, the situation is very different. One can't 'outlove' a lack of structure.

Let's find out what the software company was missing. In order to do that, let's compare it with another story.

> An intentional community was run by large-group consensus. They had a few loosely connected committees that prepared proposals to approve in the all-member meeting. That means the committees didn't have any power to make decisions themselves. That made it hard for committees to act on ideas they had. They knew their governance system was slow and tedious.
>
> One person, Rachel, complained that it was often so loud during social community events that she, as a person who is hard of hearing, couldn't participate. She said: "I've said for years that it's too loud, and the community never did anything about that. Nothing has happened. It's just so clear that no one cares enough. If it's true that you don't care about me, then just tell me!"
>
> Her neighbors assured her that they did care. They offered to sit down with her and strategize. Or could an outside facilitator help fix the governance issues?
>
> Rachel acknowledged the efforts to help but also seemed hesitant. But none of the suggestions touched on their fundamental issue. She said she didn't believe any of those ideas would help.

It was sad to listen to her pain. It was easy to assume that everyone *did* care about Rachel and her ability to participate. She was longing for it, and her neighbors were very willing. And still, it didn't come together. The wiring between people was missing: governance.

It was clear to me in hearing it that governance was invisible to the people in the room. While I saw what was missing, they only saw their interpersonal connections. And they couldn't understand why caring for

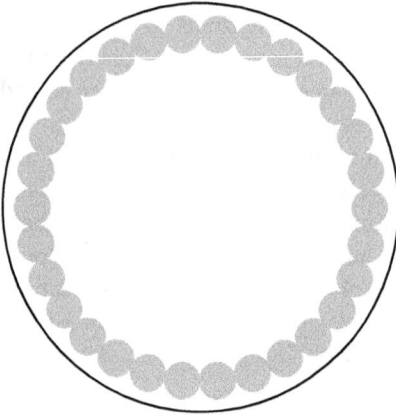

A 'bagel' – limited central   A 'blob' – limited structure,
alignment, limited agency   limited agency

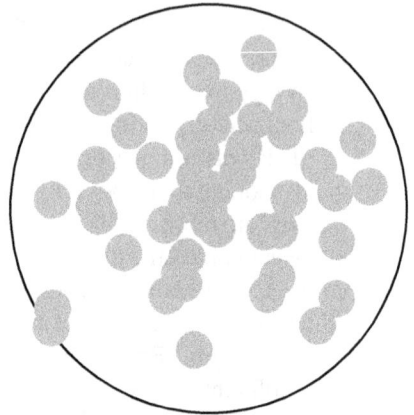

each other wasn't enough. But it's the same problem – you can't 'outcompete' lack of governance with "more love and care" or "more activity". Trying harder is only going to last so long.

The problem was that she asked 'the community' to do something. But the community can't do anything that complex. Keeping the noise level down has so many dimensions – changing the room's interior design, changing how many people sit at a table, changing how events are run, and whatever else we might come up with. Asking 'the community', given that they had no functioning governance system at the community level, had no chance to succeed. It's like a blob of people. Or like a ship that's in pieces. (Besides, Rachel's problem was not the only problem. They also struggled financially. They struggled with participation. Those are all issues that can't be fixed in an afternoon; they point to lack of systems that funnel conversations into action forward.)

What do both stories have in common, the bagel and the blob? They point to organizations that don't have enough of a 'center' to run well and sustainably. They lack agency on the organizational level.

This is the moment to point readers to a highly related and aligned body of work around the Viable Systems Model (VSM)[1], a powerful body of work developed by Stafford Beer. It provides a systematic lens to see

---

[1]Note that the VSM is meant to apply to systems of all sizes, which means it would also apply to the team level. For this book, it's particularly significant on organizational level.

what functions an organization needs to have in place to succeed. I will use the VSM to identify what the bagel and the blob were missing.

Here are the different systems as described in VSM that are required to make any system viable long term:

- System 1 (Operational Units) are the operational components of the organization, each responsible for a specific operation or process. Decisions related to these processes are generally made within the relevant operational unit, as these are the people with the most knowledge and experience about their specific area.

- System 2 (Coordination) is responsible for managing the interactions between different System 1 units, resolving task conflicts, and coordinating activities. Thus, decisions about coordination and task conflict resolution would be made at this level.

- System 3 (Control) is responsible for overseeing the performance of the operational units and managing resources. Therefore, decisions about resource allocation, performance standards, and other management issues would typically be made at this level.

- System 4 (Strategic Planning and Development) is responsible for looking to the future and planning for changes and opportunities in the environment. Strategic decisions about the future direction of the organization would typically be made at this level.

- System 5 (Policy) is the highest level of decision-making in the VSM, responsible for setting the organization's overall purpose, values, and identity.

Some of the difference in terminology in VSM is a bit confusing for a *power-with* context. I am not using the word 'control'; I'm using 'policy' with a different meaning. But those differences aside, VSM is able to contribute in a comprehensive way to understanding what was missing in the 'blob' and the 'bagel'.

Each operational unit is a system (that itself needs all the functions in a fractal way to be viable); the need for alignment exists on all levels.

On an organizational level, the operational units are doing the core work of the organization, often directly working towards the organizational aim. For example, in a company that produces metal parts, that production will be its overarching aim, and we expect it to have teams working in production. While the HR department might not be producing metal parts

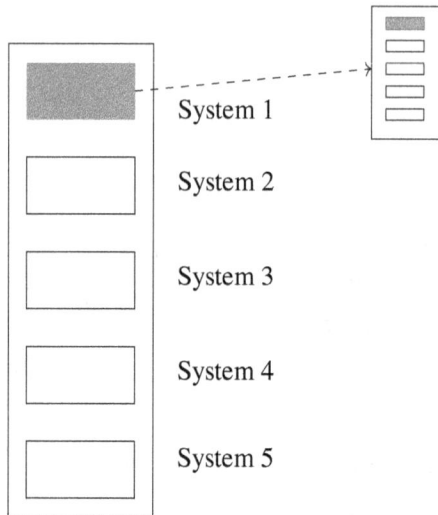

The operational unit in a viable system falls into a system itself

itself, it's still needed to run the whole endeavor because the system needs such a function.

The example of an HR department shows that organizations have new emergent properties that don't exist on a team level. As soon as we have a team of teams, we need to ensure alignment among them.

Even if all work gets done, that still only covers the operational units, System 1. Still, the organization as a whole is left without reliable coordination, performance and resource allocation, strategy and identity, and adaptation – Systems 2 through 5. Those functions need to be included for a system to be effective and viable. If anthropomorphic comparisons help you, only operating on System 1 is like a human with only muscle but no nervous system, brain, digestion, or self-consciousness.

The VSM doesn't prescribe *how* how to realize those functions. It can be via strategies, methods, tools, or roles – the important thing is they have to be filled *somehow*. The combination of strategies is a 'system' because multiple strategies might be used together to fulfill the same system function, even if those strategies seem disparate or unrelated.

New approaches in the self-management world often want to 'unbundle' organizational functions, which means to take functions that are conflated in traditional systems and separate them out more intentionally. An example is that traditional organizations often conflate *coordination* of work with *control*. Yet those two functions could be separated. VSM is a helpful guide when finding the useful 'ingredients' that can be addressed separately and combined in new ways.

The VSM does not explicitly address concepts such as *power-with* or inclusive and participatory decision-making as it's mainly a model for understanding the interplay of systems within an organization that contributes to its ability to adapt and survive in a changing environment.

Interestingly, the VSM has parallels with Prosocial's core design principles, showing us that the different bodies of work seem to point to a more general truth:

- System 1 of the VSM corresponds to the idea of clearly defined boundaries in Ostrom's work, where operational units in the VSM must have clear boundaries to function effectively. We will look at organizational and team-level aims and domains in section 3.1.2.

- Systems 2 and 3 of the VSM align with the principles of participatory decision-making, monitoring, and graduated sanctions in Ostrom's framework, as they involve coordination, control, and decision-making mechanisms within the organization. We will look at those topics in section 3.1.2 and in 3.1.3 on how to divide up operations and decision-making, information flow in section 3.4, and budgeting in section 3.3.5.

- Systems 4 and 5 of the VSM emphasize adaptive governance and self-determination. We will look at strategy in section 3.3 and missions and values in section 3.2.

Let's look at what these systems look like on an organizational level. What does it mean to be a group of groups?

3.1.1   Letting go of responsibility

In self-governed organizations operating in a *power-with* paradigm, responsibility[2] is distributed among its self-managed teams. Systems vary by how much autonomy individuals hold versus groups; for example, in sociocracy, power is typically primarily held by circles (then distributed into roles in secondary steps), while in Holacracy, a lot of autonomy is held by roles. In more free-form systems, some responsibilities may reside

---

[2]Note: self-management in general, and in sociocracy in particular, responsibility includes the corresponding autonomy/authority to make decisions.

with the collective – for example, the board – and some might reside with individuals like the Executive Director, General Manager, or the CEO.

Distributing responsibility to teams pushes decision-making further away than just to another team member – decisions are now made by people on a different team, i.e. a sub-team or even a sub-sub-team! In a linked system (see section 3.1.2), there might still be a connection, but even that fades if there are several organizational levels. For example, in my time as leader of our organization, more than 200 people were involved in about 54 circles, each making decisions. The more teams there are, the more likely a decision will be made without me.

Learning to be a collective of collectives means that we must learn to *let go* of responsibility and trust others. It's about learning where our responsibility as an individual or a team begins *and where it ends*. Recall my definition of *power-with* – necessary for *power-with* – as clarity of what our responsibility is. That includes know what it *isn't*.

Letting go is not easy. It's common for people to love the abstract idea of decentralization and empowering people but freak out at the practice of it. "Yes, we want to let go and give people responsibility to do things but not on *this topic*." In particular, we need to let groups do things in their own way, strictly only caring about whether they reasonably fulfill their responsibilities, regardless of our opinions and preferences on the *how*.

The following is a great example of how hard it is to let go.

> A chapter of a professional organization in Spain decided to move towards self-management. The incoming managing director knew that the projects needed to be solidified because the volunteers were stretched too thin. He designed a structure that distributed authority.
>
> When he proposed the new structure to the board, one of the board members was uncomfortable delegating responsibility – so she wanted to be a member of *all* the circles.
>
> There was pushback. Most board members and the leadership were serious about distributing power, but one board member 'didn't get it.'
>
> A power battle ensued. The situation became unbearable.
>
> Things came to a head: the managing director told the board that "I cannot serve this organization if she is in all circles."
>
> The board member resigned and is now an honorary member of the chapter. It is unknown how this outcome landed on the other board members; my informant and the managing director reported they were happy with the resolution.

This is not a dynamic unique to transitions from hierarchy to self-management. Consider this:

> This is a community that runs by whole-group consensus, meaning all decisions are made by everyone together. Whenever someone suggests working with more distributed decision-making, it's always the same couple that says no. The couple doesn't trust that circles will make decisions that will be bearable to them – their biggest fears are about not having a say in matters of accessibility for people with disabilities – so they undermine every effort at streamlining decision-making, with increasing tensions.
>
> They relax a bit when someone sits down to listen to them and starts building trust with the couple. But by the next day, they have returned to the mindset where they started.

Their trauma and fear leave them stuck on the individual level, and they can't see the detrimental effect on the community. They effectively hold the entire community hostage. Even a very egalitarian organization can be stuck in *power-over* as their power is mis-placed and out of balance compared to the other community members. As long as the couple lives there, the community will remain a 'blob' with limited agency.

There are many reasons for people to hold on to power, but trauma and fear might be the biggest. Likely, they've had the experience of being part of an organization where others had power over them and abused it.

The fear of missing out doesn't have to come from a place of toxic control or fear. It can even come from a place of excitement and passion. This story, *Enthusiastic Teachers*, happened to with client.

> The school had just adopted a circle-based system. The teachers were excited and enthusiastic about the work.
>
> With some worry, the Implementation Circle reported that teachers had formed and populated many more circles than necessary for the barebones operation of the school. We pondered it for a while but then decided that neither of us could detect any unhealthy dynamic, and we were comfortable letting it play out independently.
>
> The issue resolved itself over time when staff dropped out of circles that weren't as meaningful to them and remained part of circles they saw as core. After a while, some circles had folded or merged with other circles, and others were going strong. It all happened organically.

Luckily, there was no lingering tension in this case, so this is a good example of an evolutionary approach to circle structure – form circles where there is energy and see which ones survive. The competition and constraint for attention will ultimately condense the circles to a healthy and appropriate number.

Besides, the personal work of letting go of responsibility requires also trusting that all the parts come together and that we have enough cohesion and alignment to fulfill our overall aim. In our next chapter, we will see reliable ways of dividing up responsibility and decentralizing decisions into semi-autonomous teams that maintain alignment with the overall purpose.

3.1.2   Purpose, aims and domains

Organizational aim

Groups of groups – organizations – consist of all working towards a shared purpose, like a membrane around the organization. It's like the identity of the organization, its raison d'être.

If someone doesn't want the organization to succeed in its purpose, then they're in the wrong organization. If a team is not (at least indirectly) contributing to the overall purpose, it should not exist.

Having an aim   Clarifying an organization's aim is essential to an organization's success – that's why Prosocial specifies "shared identity and purpose" as the first core design principle for successful organizations. It defines what kinds of teams exist and how they work together.

From a multi-level selection perspective, an organization's aim is the unifier at the highest level teams of teams, while a circle's aim is the unifier at the team level. Without the organization's aim, its teams cannot align because they have nothing to align to and will spin their wheels.

I worked with a client who had been in an undefinable struggle for more than a year.

> This was a small organization that saw itself as a learning hub for a learning framework. Its domain included academic research, communities of practice, conferences, and webinars.
>
> Over the last few years, and then more recently, they had run out of steam. Some were contributing a lot; others seemed to lean back. The leadership couldn't put their finger on what was going wrong; it just seemed off.
>
> We worked through a diagnostic process and realized they had been operating with differing perceptions about their aim. Some of

them assumed it was a community of practice [a group that doesn't commit to shared action beyond mutual support] and only showed up for events. Others saw the group as an organization actively moving the learning framework into the world.

In addition, they had never defined whether they saw themselves as hosts or as owners of this particular framework. That made a big difference to them mentally. In one scenario, they would only host conversations with a wide container and many competitive views. In another scenario, they would come from promoting their particular flavor of the framework.

Interestingly, they had operated with an organizational mission but no aim. But the high-in-the-sky statement wasn't providing enough specificity to bring out those nuances that determined what actions they wanted to take.

We could discuss the aim conflict and find a way of holding it that reached everyone's consent. They left the retreat hopeful that their alignment would improve productivity.

In this case, the situation was relatively easy because the organization was small, and the leadership team I worked with saw itself as empowered to make this change.

Imagine how much more difficult of a task this would have been if hundreds of people had been at the meetings! The bigger the organization, the more critical it is to know which group can make these changes.

Changing the organization's aim   An organization not only needs to *have* an organizational aim, but it also needs to be able to *change* it. Organizations need to be able to change over time. We can't predict at its inception what its aim will be years later. We start out with something, learn, and change.

It's like asking a 10-year-old what they want to be when they grow up. They'll have an idea, like a YouTuber, actress, or teacher. But as they learn more about themselves and about how the world works, they need to be able to change their mind.

Being able to change its aim can be a matter of survival for an organization. Let's look at a story to illustrate that, *School Split* from a colleague of mine in Spain.

It was a small and growing school running for 3-4 years. There had been tensions around the school's overall direction for a while.

For some of the teachers and parents, having the school in nature was important. For others, it was more important for the school to be close to the parents' workplaces.

It seemed like an unresolvable conflict. There were five-hour teachers' meetings, tears, and meetings with parents.

They started meeting during summer break to explore different options. People were upset and soon started to believe that 'the other side' was just self-centered.

When they talked, they realized a very fundamental issue: while the conflict was *surfacing* between people, the issue was not between people. It wasn't true that the other side didn't care.' It was simply that they had different needs and visions for the school. Some needed a school close by; others wanted a school in nature.

That's when an amicable separation came up as a possible solution. My colleague facilitated the consent decision to split the group to accommodate both factions.

Both schools were separated by a 30-minute drive between them and kept the same name, just with different place names; they remained friendly and supported each other with shared fundraising events and other projects.

This is a crucial story, not only because it shows the transition from what seems like personal tensions to the realization that having different visions doesn't satisfy anyone and that a split is the best solution. But also because it's impressive when an organization can be aware of itself in this way *and* implement a solution that improves the situation on as high of a level as an organizational split in a self-organized way. I'm sure it was bittersweet to do as any amicable breakup – sad because of the separation, but grateful to set each other free.

Who can change an organization's aim? Just like any decision or activity, it needs to live somewhere. An action will likely only happen if it's assigned to a person or role. A decision will only be made if it's clear who is responsible for making that decision.

Yet, I often see organizations where it is not clear enough who is responsible for its aim. With no place to resolve tensions and make this decision, the only way out is to decide on an all-member group like in the school that split. It can become impossible With groups larger than those in the same room.

Here's a current example where I worry that the lack of clarity might lead to a slow death of the organization in the story *Who Owns the IP?*

The organization is a professional association of a specific communication methodology (let's call it XYZ), incorporated as a nonprofit.

> It was formed in the 1980s by a charismatic and well-loved founder and developer of the communication methodology XYZ. He formally put the stewardship of XYZ into the hands of the nonprofit that now owned the intellectual property (IP). As such, the communication methodology's aim and domain were clear when the professional association was formed: "promoting and practicing XYZ."
>
> Over the decades since then, some practitioners felt like the core of their methodology needed to be updated. They wanted to evolve XYZ and adapt it to current issues. On the other side, the purists wanted to keep XYZ all the same.
>
> Others said that if any changes needed to be made, at least they wanted to guess what the deceased founder *would* have said on those current issues, playing the game of "what would NN say?"
>
> The tensions – and with it, a significant amount of pain – have accumulated over the years. Early signs of desintegration are visible.

Sadly, the way the organization is set up, no one is responsible for deciding what XYZ is. Since no one is empowered and the organization cannot create empowerment to assign it, *no one* can change XYZ. It's like locking oneself out of the house.

Can they just come together and change it? In this example, we're talking about an organization with 800 people, many of whom had personal and treasured relationships with that founder and his legacy. Staying true to the personal interpretation of what the founder would have done was a matter of personal commitment and loyalty. The longer the followers wait, the deeper the rift between the 'sides', and the further the possibility of a solution moves away.

Deciding on XYZ 2.0 *together* is virtually impossible in this situation. A group of 800 people cannot have a meaningful discussion like that, especially with so many nuances and so much painful history in the mix. It's a blob that lacks the agency to make such a nuanced decision. They can discuss the question in online forums but discussing something isn't deciding it.

Not being able to change something so fundamental is like driving a car that cannot steer left or right. It works for a while when driving only forward. But as soon as the first obstacle shows up on the way, then arguing will begin about who is allowed to move the steering wheel. And even a tiny slant in one direction will lead off track over time.

Dividing things up

As we've seen in the above examples, an organization cannot 'act' as a whole. We need to break down the action – and with that, the responsibility – into smaller parts and give it to smaller groups to create a system of actors with agency; that's a division of labor between groups. A team then can create the conditions so aligned action by individuals is possible – division of labor between roles.

It's the decentralization that makes an organization resilient.[3]. Decentralization helps a system distribute power and even regenerate as it adapts and changes its domain distribution as needed, ensuring it can respond effectively to unexpected challenges and shifting priorities.

A good example here is the story of a head of school in Pennsylvania, *Life Saver*.

> The head of school had just begun to distribute domains and decision-making when the pandemic hit. Schools were scrambling – but not this one.
>
> The head of school was sure that a switch to remote schooling in a centralized way would have broken her back. She said, the distributed decision-making "saved her life." Instead of making her a bottleneck to the needed changes, many teams could make changes wherever needed.

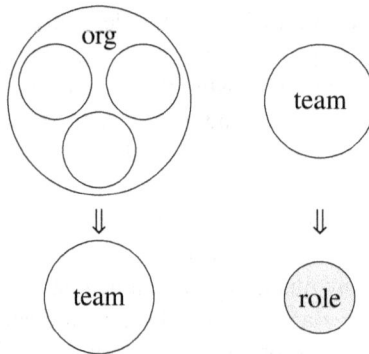

An organization distributes into teams; a team distributes into roles

The approach to divide up an organization's aim into sub-aims is common in all organizations, hierarchical organizations – with departments

---

[3]See Brafman & Beckstrom (2006)

– as well as distributed, *power-with* organizations. Organizations as an entity can't 'do work' but can create units that divide work and guide it.

However, there are significant differences between hierarchical and self-management systems.

Alignment of doing and deciding   In hierarchical settings, *aims* are distributed (= division of labor) but decision-making responsibility isn't. After all, the boss in a hierarchical setting can make/change *any* decision but does hardly any of the work.

By contrast, in self-management, the intention is to have aims *and* corresponding decision-making domains held by the same people – hence the word '*self*-management'. Another word to express that is "polycentric," a word used by Elinor Ostrom to describe systems where decision-making is distributed across multiple smaller centers rather than concentrated in a single central body.

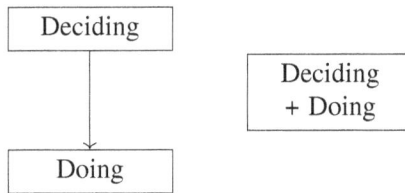

```
 ┌─────────────┐          ┌─────────────┐
 │  Deciding   │          │  Deciding   │
 └──────┬──────┘          │  + Doing    │
        │                 └─────────────┘
        ↓
 ┌─────────────┐
 │   Doing     │
 └─────────────┘
```

Managers managers, workers work. In self-management, the functions merge.

The assumption that those who *do* also *decide* changes the rule set completely because now decisions follow the doing, not the doers follow the deciders.

Rules for placing aims/domains   A centralized/hierarchical system simply operates under the *default* assumption that whoever is higher on the ladder can overrule any decision within the system. Conversely, in decentralized systems like sociocracy and Holacracy, the combination of aims and domains provides to a clearer *rule set on how decision-making responsibility can be placed and reassigned*.

That's a significant and highly underappreciated feature of distributed governance methods. Different from systems where responsibility is assigned at the top by *default*, this system has a simple rule set that is still flexible. Decide the aim and decide how to divide it up, and the organization structures itself according to what needs to get decided and done.

Due to its capacity to change itself, it is self-organizing and autopoietic – "self-making."

Let's compare it with language. A hierarchical or rigid organization is like just learning phrases in another language. All we can say is complete phrases 'I'd like a shower' or 'do you have a room for two,' but we have no idea how to change it if we want a room for three. It's rigid.

Self-governance rules give us grammar for organization so we can build whatever construct. Now, we can form whatever sentence I want to say and build whatever organization I want. Once I understand how to form a circle or a role, I can just do that when/wherever needed, with no central committee that acts as a bottleneck.

The new feature is that sociocracy and Holacracy *have* recursive rule sets even though the specific rule sets might differ. For some systems, power can only be transferred via collective decision-making (= circle consent both for the creation of roles and for selecting people into roles); in Holacracy, the creation of responsibility clusters (roles) is a collective decision while certain individuals can choose who holds an operational role.

The differences in these systems may change the flavor, but like dialects or languages in the same family, they follow almost identical underlying grammar rules.

Decentralization and centralization   So the difference between decentralized decision-making and centralized/hierarchical decision-making is not necessarily how *much* power is decentralized but more whether there is a process to *place* responsibility *intentionally* and *via a collective process*. (I will talk about the polarity between centralization and decentralization in section 3.5.3).

A self-organized organization could *collectively decide* to centralize power in one place. It may be against the spirit, but it's *allowed* by the rule set. As a very simple example, a circle once decided (by consent) to give me, as the leader, a significant decision to decide alone. Someone proposed "let's just allow Ted to decide" and everyone consented. So while the end result *looked* hierarchical – I had the power – it was different from top-down hierarchy. Giving me the power was (1) collectively decided, (2) time-bound with a term, (3) not absolute power because my area of decision-making was very clearly delineated.

That same General Circle could choose by consent to give 100% of organizational power to one person for 15 years and maybe only ask for that overall leader to solicit feedback before making decisions.[4] Again, this is a choice because distributed governance systems have the mechanisms in place to make those choices, while hierarchical organizations are always built the same way.

Self-organization without a rule set There are design patterns that distribute power without a rule set, like some teal organizations (a reference to 'new' forms of organizing in Laloux's *Reinventing Organizations*). They are often role-based but lack a universal rule set that regulates the formation of roles.

How can we ensure the individual roles can act autonomously while keeping the organization aligned? These organizations often operate with a principles/purpose-heavy approach where each team is intently tuned into the organizational aim, using the overall aim as a source of alignment.

This is very flexible, but it *can* mean that these organizations are weak on internal structure with VSM Systems 2-5, unless they have a good way to create processes for those missing functions and informal *power-over*. Given the lack of structure, they often have to make up for their bagel or blob shape with better communication and coordination or have a stronger focus on value alignment to create a comparable level of agency. This works in contexts where commitment and attunement to those principles and values is strong (strong enough), as principles and values are then broadly the *only* source of alignment. (See more comments in section 3.2.4 on values.)

Thus, this approach requires a lot of trust and communication since the teams will rely on making connection and alignment happen. (And it can easily turn out like the bagel structure where all operations are taken care of, but not much collective agency is built on the organizational level.)

Linking Linking is a practice from sociocracy and Holacracy that ensures alignment by making sure that two (or one) people from a circle are *also* a decision-making member of the circle above. Since domains and aims are set locally by consent, the link can make sure that whatever domain is set by the parent circle also works for the subcircle.

The combination of linking with consent balances power between circles because no circle can overpower another circle – the link would

---

[4]In fact, this can be a tactic of transitioning – first acknowledge the power of the existing leader and then, over time, take more and more chunks of responsibility out of their hands to distribute them over time.

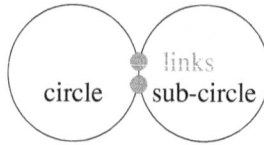

Linking means that one or two people are members of two neighboring circles

simply object. For example, I was part of a Fundraising Circle when it was decided in its parent circle, Resource Circle, that grant writing would be separated from soliciting individual donations. The aim/domain of the subcircle of the Fundraising Circle was changed accordingly. Had the links not been able to consent to this change, it would have been a *power-over* move on Resource Circle's part.

Linking also double-functions as a mechanism for information flow; see section 3.4. In this way, one can imagine an organization like a chain of handshakes between collectives where both have to hold the other's hand to stay aligned. What's important about this is that all the hands connect. If people who want to step out of the *power-over* paradigm simply drop their power and 'let the others pick things up' it will not work. Dropping things on one end doesn't mean the other side will catch it. If the chain of local decisions is interrupted, the ungoverned space provides a breeding ground for power-over and dips in effectiveness.

Note that this system only allows any decision to live in exactly *one* place. That's an intentional feature to avoid duplicating efforts and domain conflicts, but it can make it challenging to chunk organizational decision-making into smaller bits when everything seems connected. (See more comments in 3.5.3.)

Role vs. soul   In role-based systems, individuals are empowered to act on behalf of a collective or an organization.

All organizations separate individuals and their functions from the organization, even hierarchical organizations. It comes with division of labor. For example, if we contact an organization to make a claim in their billing department, we don't contact 'Raki' as a person. Still, we contacted Raki in his function as a billing department representative. In an organization, we don't generally talk to people; we talk to *roles*, and people in roles speak on behalf of a team or an organization, for example, as the spokesperson, rep link, facilitator, or president.

The difference between the person and the role or function has been talked about for a long time; for example, Max Weber, a German sociologist, developed a form of organization with a division of labor, clearly defined hierarchy, detailed rules and regulations, and impersonal relationships. He emphasized the importance of roles and functions in an organization to improve effectiveness.

When we communicate with Raki in the billing department, we're not expecting him to make decisions based on personal feelings or preferences but rather based on the defined aim, accountabilities, and policies of his role. This way, the organization maintains a certain level of consistency and efficiency. This role-based system, especially when more clearly defined and empowered as in self-managed organizations, enhances the capacity for distributed responsibility and autonomous action while still aligning with the collective goals and strategies of the organization. Roles make it possible to interact with an organization in a somewhat predictable way; if there were no roles, we would only be talking to a blob.

Roles also standardize how we interact with people. I don't want to have to be friends with Raki from the billing department for him to process my claim.

Seeing people as their function instead of seeing them as whole people is not unnatural. For example, I remember one of my kids being maybe five. In her preschool, the teachers had changed several times within a short period. When talking about her teachers, she used to call them by their names, as in 'Ms. Lisa wouldn't let me play outside'. But after the third teacher left and yet another new teacher came in, she started referring to them as 'the preschool teacher'. The relationship had always been dual – teacher-student and interpersonal relationship – but without a close interpersonal relationship, the *function* played a more prominent role.

If we compare this with the frame of multi-level selection, functions in the form of *organizational* roles serve the organization's aim (like a 'strategy role'), and *team* roles serve the team's aim, while the 'soul' is serving the *individual* level aim. We are striving for a balanced and integrated approach where the individual can coexist holistically with the team and organizational roles.

Over the last few years, 'bringing your whole self to work' has become much more important. The movement of more authenticity aims not to cut out the rest of the person but to remember that Ms. Lisa is the teacher and a person. And Raki should not have to hide that he's gay while chatting between processing claims.

This section isn't complete without at least a short mention that the assumption of a role vs. soul view can be seen as a rather individualist frame that assumes that a person stripped off their collective identities still exists. In contrast, a mindset based on an ubuntu principle ('I am because we are') emphasizes the interdependence of the individual with its collectives. In the Ubuntu worldview, most notably found in Southern African cultures such as the Zulu and Xhosa, a person is seen as inherently connected to and influenced by their relationships and community; our individual identities are inextricably intertwined with the groups we are part of. Therefore, in an organization embracing the Ubuntu principle, the roles individuals occupy would be viewed not as impersonal functions but as extensions of their collective identity, shaped by and contributing to the communal purpose. This goes back to the question of interdependence and responsibility in section 1.5.3.

But I think roles and an ubuntu mindset are compatible. When I listen to a client or colleague, I might primarily listen with the mindset of the role I'm serving in that moment, but the other roles aren't ignored. All roles and circles are like a web of relationships, so to me, a role is an expression of (one dimension of) the many relationships in the organization.

In Holacracy, the idea is that once we define roles more clearly, we liberate people to be whoever they are *while* filling that function. In sociocracy, the integration of the person and the role are emphasized more, but I think those are just two ways to approach a both-and.

A concrete example of how governance choices can emphasize more or less integration is this: I hold two roles in different circles, A and B. As we're talking in Circle A, I have a tension with a proposal that is based on something in my role in Circle B. Can I object because of something in my *other* role? If the answer is yes, then it's a more integrated but muddy approach to holding roles; if the answer is no, it's a more focused but fragmented approach.

I remember a recent decision in a circle where I held three separate roles in the organization, leading me to different views.

> It was an important decision. The Content Circle, which I led, gathered to discuss the possibility of hiring additional help for localization. We needed someone who could assist speakers of different languages in translating sociocracy materials, providing guidance, and handling technical tasks like obtaining ISBNs and ensuring proper layout for publication on our website. However, it was crucial to acknowledge the financial implications of such a decision.
>
> As the leader of the Content Circle, I naturally advocated allocating more resources to support our localization efforts. As a member of the

> Publishing House Circle responsible for typesetting and book uploads, I welcomed the idea of having dedicated assistance for localizers. Nevertheless, as the leader of the General Circle, which oversees the organization's overall success and sustainability, I needed to recognize the financial constraints we were facing then.
>
> It was a delicate balance between immediate needs and long-term sustainability, held in different hats I was wearing.

Each different perspective adds to the picture; the fact that I was torn between different positions was a feature, not a bug, as the needs of the organization are mirrored in ourselves and each other.

Adaptability I've been emphasizing how the pattern language of distributed responsibility allows us to distribute responsibilities intentionally. The advantage of having such a rule set is also that we can make *changes* in the placement of authority via the *same* rules over time.

Let's take a moment to understand this with an example.

> I talked to an international nonprofit offering support groups and a hotline for people in need. Their staff member told me that they were 'basically self-governing' because all the teams and roles were defined, and the founder mostly 'let everyone do what they wanted.'
>
> She showed me the matrix. All categories of decisions – like financial decisions under $500, or legal decisions concerning the trademark – had a row, about 80 rows in total in this organization of 15 people. For each category, the matrix mentioned who needed to be consulted, how the decision would need to be made (alone or by consensus or consent or majority vote), who would be the decider, and who would need to be informed when the decision was made.
>
> This sounded like a well-run system – but I also asked one question: Who has the power to change those roles and teams if needed?
>
> She was flustered momentarily and explained that those teams had been defined by the founder years ago and had just remained the same.

Self-*management* is the power to manage the work well on a team level. Self-*governance* is the power to decide who decides and how we decide. For a collective of collectives to self-govern, we need to understand who determines who decides what and how we determine that. A system where one person decides who decides is not a *power-with* system.

That is not only a matter of shared power but also a matter of resilience. If an area of decision-making isn't placed in a group's or individual's domain, no action will follow. Remember the story *Who Owns the IP?* where the XYZ organization of 800 people didn't have a way to decide what their framework XYZ even was and how to evolve it over time?

When I realized just how threatening this lack of intentionality was, I worried about my own organization. Would we end up in the same place in a few years when we, as founders, would be gone?

Learning from that experience, I pointed out that in Sociocracy For All, the definition of what sociocracy *is* for us had not been explicitly placed into a circle's domain within our organization and that it needed placement. I had no intention to change anything now, but I wanted to have the 'life insurance' for the organization.

To my great relief, the General Circle decided to hand that domain to the Training Circle. I was relieved for two reasons:

- We now had a way to decide it and were less likely to get stuck. For that, it didn't matter as much to me *who* would hold that domain. What mattered solely was that it *was* held. If the placement is off, it can also be re-assigned. But if *no one* holds it and there is tension, it can never be passed on without a unilateral power grab and drama.

- The second reason was that the General Circle dared to place this domain in a decentralized manner. It was not placed in the board or one of the main circles but instead in a sub-circle of a department circle. The level of trust was encouraging.

Changing domains and aims is a frequent occurrence in role-based/circle-based systems as organizations are constantly evolving.

The story *Pastry Circle*, set in a bakery and cafe, illustrates this.

> The bakery was organized in about a dozen circles. Two of them were the Pastry Circle and the Front Circle. The Pastry Circle – as one would guess – was in charge of making pastry. The Front Circle sold those baked goods and hot drinks at the front desk. The respective domains were distinct and even in separate workspaces within the building. Yet, they ran into a tension that turned out to be about needing more clarity: At the front desk, there was a fridge where the pastries were displayed for sale. The handoff between the Pastry Circle and Front Circle was clear for getting food ready to be sold: Pastry Circle puts items into the fridge, and from then on, it's Front Circle's task to sell them.
>
> While this seems straightforward, there was a gap. The Front

Circle members had to discard of the pastries that had gone past their sell-by date, and they were upset. From their point of view, Pastry Circle was slacking off their job by not taking care of the pastries from beginning to end.

From the Pastry Circle's point of view, things looked very different. For them, they were done with their job as soon as Front Circle had received the pastries.

From a governance angle, this is a clear case: the two circles need to define their domains and handoffs. They have two options: decide that Pastry Circle needs to pick up the pastries after their sell-by date, or they will decide that Front Circle will take care of unsold baked goods. The tension only came up because there was a lack of clarity, mixed with our very human tendency to assume malintent instead of recognizing the lack of governance clarity within the situation.

A placement of responsibility might also need to change because of changes in our environment, as shown in this example.

During the pandemic, my community had to make the hard decision on whether or not (or under what conditions) the shared community building could still be used. Would we all infect each other?

The domain of common house use rested in Common House Circle, which ended up under a huge strain of straddling worries of those people who needed to do their laundry in the common house and the needs of the people who saw it as their right to use the common house in all the usual ways. The circle felt the weight of responsibility.

A few months into the pandemic, they decided in mutual consent that another circle, Community Life Circle, would hold the domain for a while to give the Common House Circle a chance to regroup. The Community Life Circle determined the use policy for the common house for about one year. I was on the Community Life Circle and supported the common house policy, the hardest task the circle ever had to handle. Then, as promised, the domain was returned to the Common House Circle – again via mutual consent.

In this way, the structure determining who decides what is malleable and can adapt, like a glove that grows with the organization.

Specificity I discussed the need for more clarity in section 2.6 on policy and operations. I mentioned that when policies or roles aren't clear, people don't act because they don't have *specific enough* guidance. Recalling responsibility and its important role for *power-with*. How can you be responsible if you don't know what you're responsible for? All our *power-within* and personal work won't make for the fact that what we're responsible for is unclear.

The same is true on the organizational level. Once the organization's aim is clear and specific, acting becomes easier. A group can only be as responsible as it's clear what they are responsible for. When the aim is unclear or too big, collectives struggle. I think it's the most common reason I see them struggle. When our aim is too big, people's minds cannot manifest action and get stuck in high-level discussions instead of doing things. Here's a little story that I call the *Baby Policy* story. It's from a workshop setting, not my organizational life, but it was real and memorable.

It was a workshop and another little exercise to demonstrate consent. I decided to work with a live 'issue' in the room: a baby. A workshop participant had brought their child of about two months.

Before I continue, let me add a comment here. In my life, I have spent countless workshops and conferences with a baby in my arms.

Yet, I'm hard of hearing, which does interfere a bit in in-person workshops when there is too much background noise. Being hard of hearing is a good example of an invisible handicap that requires some group effort to accommodate. So, after checking with the parent in private, I explained to the group that we'd make a 'baby noise policy' to see how we could work with the situation during the workshop.

The aim of this daylong workshop, "learning and experiencing tools from sociocracy,", was written on a poster on the wall. We co-created the noise policy proposal to show picture forming and proposal shaping, a standard sociocracy process to quickly draft a proposal. The proposal said something like when the baby cries, the baby needs to leave the room. We devised a system so it would only sometimes be on the parent to leave with the baby. I divided the group into groups of four and asked them to come to consent on the proposal to practice.

At that moment, one of the participants snapped and proceeded to give a speech expressing their discomfort with this policy, arguing that mainstream culture shuts out babies from public life and policed them. He had even jumped up from his chair to deliver the speech.

I listened to his statement. And I completely agreed with his sentiment. Everything. When he was complete, I told him that.

And then I asked one question: "How does that change what we do in our group, today, with our shared aim of learning and experiencing sociocracy?"

It was like he suddenly deflated, and he responded immediately: "Oh, you mean for *today*? Yeah, that's totally fine!"

It's easy to get pulled into big questions like what's wrong with 'society' or to be pulled back into the painful shadows of the past (like in the Furnace story earlier). Those discussions about the mainstream and the pain of not being heard need space. But for group decision-making, we miss an opportunity to step into our agency whenever we get pulled away from the present moment and the people and issues present. We're thinking so big that we feel paralyzed and powerless.

We can't change the past. We can't 'fix' mainstream on a Saturday morning. Of course, it's essential to understand the bigger context, but working groups are action-oriented, so that's where their leading energy should lie. It's also critical to create spaces where people can express their feelings. That primarily needs to happen in parallel. For collective agency, we need interlinked, manageable pieces that support our focus and presence – "be here now."

It's also helpful to distinguish a lack of clarity from a lack of certainty.

- Lack of clarity relates to clarity or understanding about roles, responsibilities, processes, or decisions. It is usually something to address through good governance. Clear communication, well-defined procedures, explicit roles and responsibilities, and transparent decision-making processes can all help to increase clarity.
- Lack of certainty, on the other hand, refers to situations where the outcome or impact of decisions or actions is unknown or unpredictable. People might struggle with a lack of certainty because if we can't predict the outcome of a decision, we feel the weight of responsibility more.

People might complain about a lack of clarity when really, they are scared of the lack of certainty. They feel the same – uncomfortable, confusing – but they require different solutions.

3.1.3 Leadership

In section 2.6.4, I talked about how leadership in a consent-based circle is a function that makes sure that (1) topics and tasks can surface and (2) the team can act. What's its counterpart on the organizational level? The same principles are guiding here. The leader is to a team, what the center circle is to the organization.

To make sure that all topics can surface and find a place, there is an entity at the center – the General (Company) Circle in Holacracy, the General Circle in sociocracy jargon – that receives and holds the overall aim of the organization and distributes subsets of its authority into subcircles. This makes the system more resilient because *any* topic can be delegated to a circle where it can be resolved. If a new topic obviously belongs to an existing circle's domain, it just gets delegated there. If not – for example, because it doesn't fit neatly into the existing domains – it can still be addressed and resolved by creating a new circle or expanding existing aims/domains to cover the new topic.

This prevents potential gaps in the decision-making process and maintains the integrity of the overall system by continuously evaluating and adjusting the organization's structure as needed. By having a centralized entity responsible for this catch-all function, the organization can maintain coherence and consistency across its various team and domains.

Organizational functions and structure   In many organizations, there is an additional circle like a board, Mission Circle, or Purpose Circle. Jargon can be confusing here, so let's look at this chart.

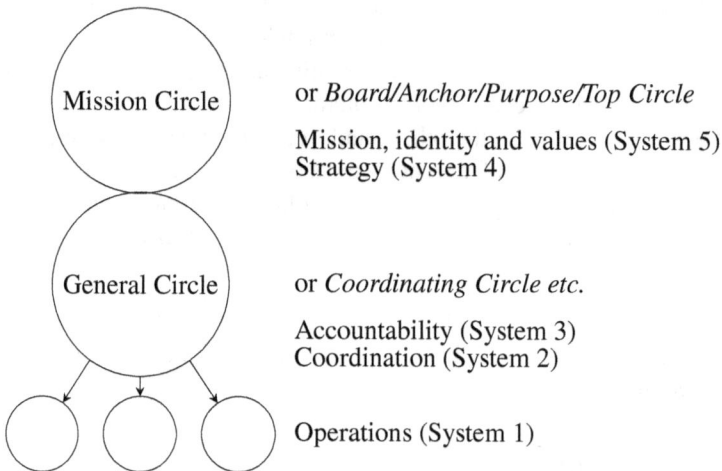

Mission Circle — or *Board/Anchor/Purpose/Top Circle*

Mission, identity and values (System 5)
Strategy (System 4)

General Circle — or *Coordinating Circle etc.*

Accountability (System 3)
Coordination (System 2)

Operations (System 1)

Systems 2-5 are distributed among central circles

This shows *one possible way* to split up the Systems roughly. Remember, VSM's System 1's domain of responsibility is operations, which is taken on by work circles. For Systems 2-5, circle/role-based systems have some diversity in splitting up and allocating or implementing the functions. Some organizations hold more functions in the General Circle and might assign strategy there, and others distribute the functions between a General Circle and a Mission Circle. There is also variety as to whether a circle or a role holds those functions. For example, strategy could be held by a role within the General Circle or in the Mission Circle, or it could be more collectively held. As long as they are held somewhere, all of those options meet VSM's requirements for viable systems.

To identify any systemic issues that may arise, allowing the organization to address challenges proactively is essential to maintaining flexibility and resilience. Just like a circle leader helps a circle to reflect on itself and adjust, a General Circle helps the organization to reflect on itself.

Concerning System 2, the General Circle also serves as a communication hub and a clearing house. It helps to facilitate cross-circle collaboration and ensures that all circles are aligned with the organization's overall aim. As we will see later in section 3.4, the need for information flow is a crucial emergent property of the organizational level. Additionally, the General Circle holds all operations accountable on the highest level.

If an organization doesn't have a Mission Circle (or equivalent), it will need to spread the functions of System 4 and 5 into the General Circle or find another strategy to fulfill the functions. For example, it could define roles or agreed-upon processes or tools for those functions.

Accountability on organizational level   I've already touched on accountability earlier in section 2.6.4. What's more to say here is how accountability works in a consent-based/circle-based system. Suppose a circle sets policy for the circle. In that case, it's everyone's responsibility to comply with those policies – why else would one make and consent to a policy if not because one is convinced that making this policy improves our work?

People get tripped up by the question of who is holding whom accountable. I've already mentioned that each role is accountable to the circle that created it, and all circles are accountable to all other circles' policies. But let's say someone violates policy; who points it out to the violator and stops them? Leaders have to act by default. Unless specified otherwise (for example, in a role) or assigned, leaders will be the ones to reach out to those who don't comply with our rules. The way we hold people accountable is not in a top-down way ('you have to do this because we said so') but more with a vibe of "hey, we made a rule because it's best for us, please follow the rule", or "hey, you promised this, what's in the way?"

That's why, to make sure a General/Company Circle can act in urgent matters on items that have not been placed in a role or circle domain, the General/Company Circle itself needs to have a leader who can act as GC leader act on urgent matters just like we saw in section 2.6.4.

	General Circle	Circle leader
Oversees	department circles	operational roles
Short-term action	(via leader)	make decisions on urgent matters
Long-term action	identify stray topics and delegate them to circles	identify stray operations and delegate them to roles
Chosen by	consent of the department circles	consent of the circle members

A functional comparison of the General Circle and a circle leader

Dispersed leadership and the catch-all   The role of the leader of the General Circle can be tricky. One has to catch all the stray tasks and topics and ensure they have a home while always making sure not to hold on to power but instead to play it back into empowered circles and roles.

I have served in this role for seven years myself and have talked to many leaders in similar positions. The most focused conversation I had a while back was when I talked – and to some extent commiserated – with a nonprofit leader that supports homeless people in the midwest of the USA. She was, just like me then, the leader of the General Circle.

She reflected on how the most challenging part is to play catch-all because it can happen easily that the leader is exposed to a firehose of unassigned domain items that, by default, end up on her desk. In that way, she is carrying a double burden: she has to take care of all of the stray tasks *while* lifting others into the position to take on responsibility in a decentralized fashion. For this position, it is vital to have good boundaries since the position is structurally the last stop for operations.

How well the system works overall shows in what the functional leader does. If there's a high degree of shared responsibility overall, the role melts into almost a formality and only needs occasional attention. If there is less self-responsibility throughout the system and insufficient clarity and structures to integrate the systems to achieve *power-with*, then playing catch-all and empowering others to step into their agency is more work. Or, as my informant put it, "in a decentralized organization, everyone needs to recognize the value of shared leadership. When people are aware of this, it makes the role of the General Circle leader more manageable."

We've already seen an example of that. Remember Brian, who became CEO (the counterpart of the leader of the General Circle) in the story *New CEO?* When he transitioned into leadership, people expected him to change up everything, but he pointed out that he had a say all along in the General Circle. That is an excellent example of shared leadership where the responsibility and care of the organization-level aim had been shared already – and when that is the case, then it hardly matters who plays that role of the CEO.

When people choose hierarchy, they often assume that hierarchy is the *only* way to achieve alignment, clarity, and efficiency because we centralize our common ground (who decides what's true and relevant), our decision-making power, and control. But it's not *hierarchy* that creates the alignment and clarity but *the fact that we have placed responsibility clearly*. Once we understand that, we can have a more intentional design and reach the same level of agency, just without the *power-over* element.

This structure illustrates how *power-over* and leadership can be un-linked, or, said differently, how leadership can go together with *power-with*. This type of leadership is about guidance, attention, and stewardship, not command and control. It doesn't have to mean power is centralized in one person or team. Instead, power is dispersed throughout the organization, and individuals or teams have the autonomy to make decisions within their domains of responsibility. This way, again, leadership becomes a role that serves the organization and its aim rather than a position of dominance over others. Even more, it's in the leader's role to empower others by creating clarity and encouraging people to (re)define roles, aims, and domains so they can claim leadership, thus creating a more dynamic, responsive, and resilient organization.

3.2 Missions and values

When thinking about self-governance, many people are inspired by watching a flock of birds fly together. What if we, as humans, could fly in this beautiful, self-organized manner and effortlessly collaborate to make things happen that are bigger than all of us?

In other words, how can we create an organization where everyone flows together toward the same shared vision while being free to move around and make decisions autonomously?

Birds don't move in a flock without rules. There are simple rules that guide their behavior, just like human governance follows simple rules:

1. Separation: To avoid a collision, each bird tries to maintain a certain distance from others around it.

2. Cohesion: Each bird moves closer to those slightly further away birds, which helps the flock stay together.

3. Alignment: Birds align their direction and speed with the birds nearest to them.

These principles keep everyone together, apart, and aligned – just like simple governance rules do. A simple rule set, applied ongoingly and recursively, can achieve the same effortless collaboration.

However, there's a difference. Humans ask *why* questions. I think if we replaced birds with humans in the same rule set as the flock of birds, they'd likely stop after seconds and ask, "Wait, why are we doing this? And why are we doing it like this? Why can't I come closer? Why do I have to keep my distance? Why are we going in this direction?"

Humans need to know *why* they are doing something because they are self-aware and can question and understand their actions. We're meaning-making creatures. We want to know what the bigger story is that we fit into. (That might be a blessing or a curse!)

That reason, or the higher purpose, of an organization can be codified in the mission and other artifacts and agreements.

- vision statement
- values statement
- theory of change statement
- strategy statement
- mission (purpose) statement
- . . .

There are many different ways of defining these (and even more if we include terms like aims, goals, targets, objectives, and the like). I will not get too involved in exact definitions because any definition I'd give would unnecessarily cause division and confusion. I want to show the fundamental, underlying patterns here instead.

3.2.1   A little detour into semantics

Here is a trick from formal semantics – a formal way of understanding what words, phrases, and sentences mean. I'm not aware of anyone using it in the sphere of governance in this way, but it's useful!

In (formal) semantics, the meaning of a word or phrase is described by imagining all the possible worlds (or situations) where that 'thing' or 'activity' happens or exists. For example, 'dog' refers to all the dogs in the real world plus all the dogs in imaginary worlds.

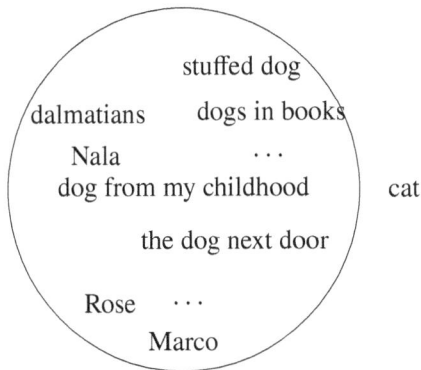

The word dog refers to the set of all dogs, including imaginary ones

When children learn the word *dog*, they will try to grasp what set it applies to. They hear people around them refer to things as *dog*, and they try to match that. If they include too much in the set – and use *dog* for a cow or a cat – they get corrected by other speakers. If they start only calling their own dog Marco *dog*, they have to learn to expand the set of dogs to more entities than Marco The One And Only Dog. Over time, they learn what set of animals the word *dog* applies to, and that's when they understand what *dog* means. It's an alignment task to match words and the corresponding set.

The same works for sentences. The sentence *Tim cut his finger* can refer to many different scenarios, like one where it's bleeding a lot and one where it's not bleeding at all, scenarios where Tim cut it with a knife, and others where Tim got a paper cut. It can be scenarios where he cut his middle finger or his ring finger. If I now say *Tim cut his **ring** finger*, there are fewer options (because we're taking away all the scenarios where he cut any other finger), which means the set of options is smaller.

The more abstract – unspecified – things are, the more possible scenar-

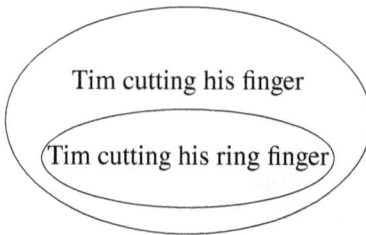

ios are in the set. The more specific we are, the *smaller* the set of possible scenarios.

Specificity helps because then we have a smaller set of options to choose from. If we don't have that, then I don't know which of the many possible options to choose, and I might feel unsure or even paralyzed.

3.2.2   Back to aims

Aim statements work just like that. Just like a child learns to align with everyone else's categorization of what counts as a dog and what doesn't, organizations need to align with each other on what counts as 'successfully carrying out the aim' and what doesn't. Specificity helps here, too. If I give a group of people the instruction to 'make the world a better place,' it's likely that they will argue about how to do that because it's hard to align on something so vague. They will have to do a lot of negotiating until they have alignment between many options. Unless they are pragmatic, pick up some trash on the side of the road, and call it a day, they will likely only start doing something. If, instead, I ask the same group to remove all the trash from the side of the road around the house, that's more actionable.

When we start a team, we should have some sense of what the team should be doing – specific enough to get started. But as we understand better what the work *is* and what its unique questions are, as we understand each other's assumptions, and as the work changes – a complex alignment process – we get more and more clear on the exact set that we want to carry out. It will never be fully clear because we're not specifying every detail but 'clear enough.' That's the work that every parent circle needs to help their child circles do and that every General Circle needs to do for the organization as a whole.

Policies reduce our options in the same way. If you remember how policies are useful constraints (see section 2.6), policies help us eliminate unhelpful behavior from a set. For example, a policy might prescribe work gloves in which case cutting your finger would happen less often because working without gloves is not an allowed action in the set. Of course, an organization can only define the set of allowed actions and implement consequences if someone breaks the agreements, but the intention is to create a rule set of constraints that gives us good outcomes.

3.2.3 The relationship between missions and aims

For an aim, ideally, the alignment is so exact that everything in the set, from the organization's view, is a desirable action. For example, if the aim is *developing educational materials about personal finance*, then I would assume that *anything* I do that's an expression of developing educational materials about personal finance is a desirable activity if it doesn't violate existing policy. Ideally, it's a perfect fit, like a tight glove. The aim says what we do and we do what it says.

I described this principle earlier as *everything is allowed until it's not*; we need to specify: everything within the aim is allowed until it's not.

Missions are different. Since they are high-level, they are a broad set, and they include even things that we are likely not doing in our organization. Let's look at a real-life example. Here's the mission of an organization:

> *Our mission is to create a more caring, respectful, and equitable society by empowering and building resilience and solidarity.*

This sounds like a wonderful organization – but what kind of organization is it? It could be an organization that builds a social media platform. It could also be a community development non-profit organization, or it could be a social-justice-oriented law firm, or a lot of other options. That's how different aims can have the same mission or vice versa; one mission might lead to different aims.

When an organization doesn't define its aim but only its mission, some people might do 'law firm things', and others might be doing 'mutual aid organization things' as everyone fills in their understanding of the mission creatively. There will likely be lots of alignment issues, which, with the human ingredient added, come out as conflicts and paralysis.

The *same aim* can also be associated with *different missions*. Imagine two non-profit organizations. Organization A's mission is to improve literacy rates among children. Organization B's mission is to reduce poverty.

Both organizations might share an aim to *increase access to quality education*, since education is known to address both the mission of *improving literacy* and the mission of *reducing poverty*. So, this same aim (increasing access to quality education) serves two different missions (improving literacy and reducing poverty).

That means the relationship between missions and aims looks like this:

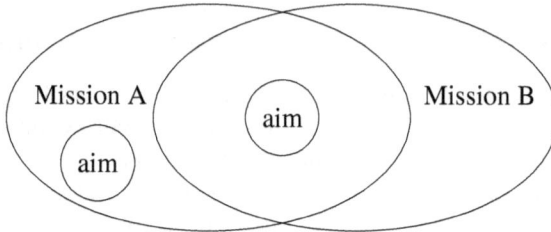

Same mission, different aims. Same aim, different missions

The question is whether the aim could also lie partially outside of the mission. In other words, could we have an aim under a mission where some aim activities are outside of the mission?

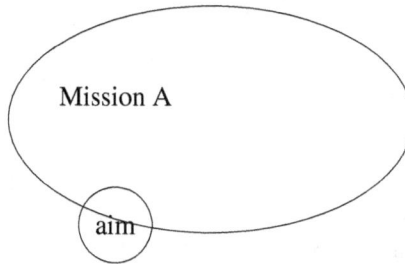

Some aim activities fall outside of the mission

Is this possible? In a properly structured organization, the set of aims should ideally fall *entirely within* the set of the mission. This is because the mission represents the overarching *purpose* or goals of the organization, and the aims are the specific objectives designed to fulfill that mission.

If some aims fall outside of the mission, it may indicate a misalignment in the organization's strategy. Such aims might not contribute towards achieving the organization's mission and could potentially divert resources and focus away from the mission-critical tasks.

Suppose we have a set of aims, half inside and half outside the mission. In that case, it might suggest that the mission is not comprehensive enough to cover all the organization's activities or that some of the aims are irrelevant to the mission. In either case, it could signal that the organization needs to reassess its mission or aims to ensure they're properly aligned.

Why does this matter? Because both of those models are used in organizations, and it's confusing. In one perspective, each project that serves to carry out the overall is fair game because it should automatically align with the mission. In the other perspective, every new project or program needs to be evaluated against the mission and how well it serves to bring that mission to life. In the first scenario, the mission is a guiding star that I think about from time to time when I need a reminder of why we're doing the aim. In the second scenario, we fight out the mission on each decision. And if we don't even distinguish missions from aims (or whatever terms an organization chooses), then it's entirely unclear.

I recommend that each organization have one statement like an aim, as a binding agreement on *what* they're doing together. Additionally, an organization can have an optional higher-level statement that nourishes the people's sense of meaning, belonging, and purpose and provides more guidance on the kinds of activities we want to focus on.

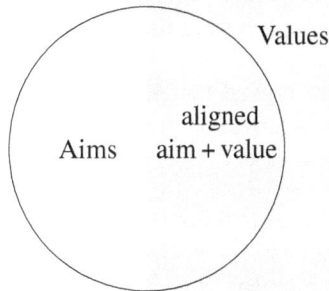

Values and aims intersect

3.2.4 Values

Values are often even wider in scope. For example, if a child learns the word *kindness*, there are a *lot* of possible scenarios where there might be kindness involved and from which a child could deduce what kindness means; it could mean feeding a street dog in Indonesia, or it could mean lending sugar to a neighbor. If I say that in our organization, only kind behavior is allowed, that still is not very specific because it can manifest in many different ways that have nothing to do with our aim or mission.

Aims are binding because they define what's allowed and what isn't. Is that true for values as well? Here's a story on that which I will call *Respect And Care - Value Clash*. It happened in an all-member meeting of a mutual aid organization. The organization brings together people who can support others, e.g. by providing rides, meals or making a simple homepage, with the aim of improving connection and support. The value statement of the organization includes the keywords "respect and care".

> An interaction became awkward. One member had made a comment that suggested that she was seeing the mutual aid network organization as something people could do in their free time after work.
>
> Also in her group was another woman, Cheri, who happened to be unemployed. Cheri was one of the key members, devoted and loyal to the organization. Cheri not only added many volunteer hours in the organization helping other people but also met many of her basic needs, like car repairs through the mutual aid network. For Cheri, the network was a core part of her life, a way of being outside the economic systems that had repeatedly disadvantaged her. Cheri got very upset when the other volunteer, Kathy, dismissed the network as something for wealthy people's extra time. Kathy felt misunderstood, and the situation got heated.
>
> In the debrief, Cheri argued that Kathy "violated the network's values" because her characterization of the network and people's situations "lacked respect and care."

Typically, it would need more to be expelled from the organization. We don't kick people out of organizations when they don't follow our values of "respect" or "care" in every moment. So, values don't seem to be binding.

Besides the vagueness, there's a good reason values should not be binding because sticking to *one* value dogmatically can enable problematic behavior. Extreme respect can slip into blind obedience, and 100% honesty can be dangerous and cruel. Therefore, values cannot be seen as absolute. Not only is strict compliance to "honesty" as a value diffuse, but it is also undesirable without balance.

But if values aren't binding, what are they, and how do they contribute to governance? One significant contribution is as a unifier. As mentioned in section 3.1.2, values can be a source of coherence that holds all the activities and decisions in alignment. For obvious reasons, that works best in situations where there is high value alignment. Some hope that, together with mission alignment, it can serve as the only function to hold the organization together. I have doubts that that is possible in lieu of governance agreements but values are certainly a contributing factor towards alignment, in particular if they are specific enough.

I want to go back to speech acts for a moment because they offer a distinction that is helpful here, too. An aim is a *declarative* speech act – declaring what is a desirable activity in a team or the organization as a whole. A value statement, on the other hand, has two readings:

- The most common reading is an *expressive* speech act where the statement gives voice to a *sentiment* more than a commitment. Approving a value statement is like saying "we so much care about environmental impact!!" together. That can lead to a sense of belonging and integrity and, indirectly, give us a sense of alignment, but it's non-binding for decision-making.

- The other reading is binding and helps us make decisions. It's a *commissive* speech act where the organization 'demands of itself' to stick to the values. We collectively commit to prioritizing one value set over others (within reason). It's like a collective saying: "we want to value environmental impact over affordability."

Let's show the difference with an example. Let's say we have to decide on book packaging materials. It's surprisingly expensive to use non-plastic packaging and work with local printers. So we either keep things affordable by using plastic and working with big international distributors, or we keep things clean but would have to add 30% in price.

Suppose environmental impact is a value we express but *don't* put into a *binding* policy. In that case, we might override it in the name of affordability (or whatever else takes precedence). That doesn't mean values are entirely pointless because they might still affect decisions positively when the values are present in people's minds.

Yes, if we explicitly state that value as a *binding* commitment, the organization would likely go with the more environmentally friendly solution because they've made the guiding principles explicit. Two things help here. One is specificity. The more specific a value or guideline, the more easily people can follow it. Secondly, since there can be tradeoffs for aligning with a value, comparative statements like "we want to value environmental impact *over* affordability" help guide choices. We say what we do but also what we do *less*.

I would argue that a binding statement needs that specificity to be useful; yet, if they have that specificity, they aren't values anymore, but they act more like *strategies* or policies.

3.3 Strategy

A strategy describes what's important but in a much more tangible way than values, but the logic is the same – a strategy is a *self-commitment* for the organization, like a promise. The whole point of a strategy statement is to be specific enough about how we intend to act so we can make choices *between* possible actions. A strategy is a relational term because by choosing one strategy to focus on, there are other things we're *not* focusing on. That can mean allocating resources like money, time, attention, and air time. As a whole, strategies are about bandwidth and finite resources.

So a value set like *we value effectiveness and inclusiveness* is not a strategy because it doesn't provide enough specificity to guide whether that now means I answer the client's email tomorrow and my colleagues today or vice versa. In other words, it doesn't spell out what we *don't* focus on to achieve it.

A metaphor that works for me is a comparison with a human body. All the organs and systems in the organism work together to keep the human alive and thriving, doing human things like building, procreating, eating, and socializing. But that's not the end of it – humans interact with their environment and might have to prioritize their activities. For example, if the human faces a good opportunity for procreation, maybe hunger fades into the background for a few hours. If the human faces a threat, digestion slows down, and all available energy is used in the muscles to escape or fight the threat.

In other words, when the needs of the organization change, then the internal autonomy/alignment needs to be renegotiated. Muscles or digestion? Marketing or customer support? Growth or consolidation?

Without a strategy, the organization as a whole can't respond to its environment in unity. That might be okay early on, and if there's no crucial change in the environment, the system can just bumble along. But if we need to run or stretch, unity matters. Imagine only the legs run away from a threat without the support from the heart and the lungs. It's fatal. In an interdependent system, all parts need to work together. Deciding together how to shift internal resources, that's strategy.

3.3.1 Unity

Strategies are often associated with mandated top-down plans that micromanage their members. 'Don't insult me with a 5-year plan.' People are also quick to point out that planning long-term in this rigid way is bound to fail in a world of complexity and shorter feedback cycles. Just because strategies in overly bureaucratic top-down organizations are rigid and sometimes far from reality, that doesn't mean strategies are inherently like that or have to have unrealistically long terms. Alignment via strategy can be helpful while being agile and effective manner.

Here's an excellent and admirable story about that in *A Recruiting Business Pivots*.

> A recruiting business of several hundred people in North America was in trouble when businesses closed down because of the pandemic. For a recruiting business, that's a killer – they would have a hard time offering services when the whole world stops hiring all at once. Yet, this self-managed business has the policy that no one can be fired, so letting people go was not an option.
>
> My informant, let's call him Ernie, told me they knew they had to change their focus to make it through this new situation. To pivot, they became experts on recruiting staff for nursing homes and contact tracers. They made that year the most successful year in the company's existence.

Without an overarching strategy, this shift in focus wouldn't have happened. So, how can one achieve this level of unity?

In a top-down organization, it's easy. Unity and aligned action is achieved via decisions at the top. Those in the 'lower' parts of the organization don't have much of a choice but to get in line with the strategic direction set further up the ladder. (Of course, people's resentment and lack of willingness can undermine that effort.)

In a decentralized organization, since they cannot be forced, that means the parts of the organization would need to *choose* to cooperate to carry out a strategy.

So, how did this recruiting business do it? Ernie was a key person in this; organizational strategy was in his domain.

> When the pandemic hit, Ernie used an all-company platform to come up with a thematic goal. It was accessible to everyone, and about 30 people were actively involved in hashing out the strategy. It took them three weeks to be clear on what they needed to do.

What I love about their approach is that their response was so immediate. There was no drawn-out strategic planning process. The strategy was defined, and from then on constantly adapted and changed.

What's crucial about this story of the recruiting business is that the sensemaking and development of the strategy was participatory. Everyone could have contributed, and there's a good chance that there were more lurkers than active contributors. If many people are involved in making the strategy, then more people's valuable ideas are included and it's more likely that we already have buy-in even before implementing the strategy.

It had not always been this way. Ernie told me this story from an earlier moment of their transformation.

> At this point, the self-managed part was only a unit of about 120 people in a bigger company still running business as usual. In this hybrid situation of not-yet-transitioning, some people had already taken responsibility as self-starters, and others hadn't quite yet. Ernie himself, from what he told me, felt a strong responsibility and ownership of strategic decisions in the company. He deeply cared, and he had ideas and knew the company well. To share his thinking and have more shared exploration, he repeatedly proposed that the group should spend more time discussing strategy. But the others dismissed it.
>
> This happened on three more occasions until Ernie complained and asked, "Why do you keep bumping off talking about strategy?"
>
> His team was candid with him when they explained. "Ernie, there is no need for us to talk about strategy because you are holding it so tightly anyway."
>
> Ernie was baffled and shocked. He hadn't seen that by holding the topic, he was safeguarding and in a way, keeping the topic away from the others. They didn't feel like their voices were or would be heard. That was the opposite of what Ernie wanted! He cared about strategy, which was exactly why he wanted to talk about it, and it was ironic that his deep care was getting in the way of improving the strategy. He decided to take a step back and let the team come up with a new strategic direction for the company.
>
> In thinking about his story, Ernie also realized that he had been emotionally holding onto the responsibility for the success of the business overall, and he needed to let go. He demoted himself from the lead role and decided to trust the collective intelligence of the team more often.

The more participatory process during the pandemic succeeded in tapping into a broader resource of people's thinking.

Whatever design an organization chooses, a strategy needs to be made on the level it applies to with input from 'lower levels' in a participatory process. Just like operational and policy decisions, strategies can happen on all levels – individual, team, organization, movement. Strategies can have different lengths of time. An organization can have a strategy for a few years or for three months.

Before we move on, let's see how Ernie does strategy, guided by the Three-Horizons Model as formulated by Bill Sharpe 2013.

> One person has the role – in this case, Ernie, and it's a full-time job – to hold strategy in the business. His role is to have conversations with people in top-level roles to engage in dialogue about strategic directions. He curates what he distills from the conversations and shares it with a wider group.
>
> The Horizon Model describes three different timeframes of innovation: Horizon 1 is the present, characterized by business-as-usual activities that keep everything going. Horizon 2 represents the near future, where innovations and disruptions might change the situation, positively or negatively. Horizon 3 represents innovations towards a sustainable, regenerative future. If the current activities were continued without changes, things would slow down over time. That's why, while being in the present and ultimate future, an organization needs to put plans in place to prepare for the future further away.
>
> In his work, Ernie weaves elements of Horizon 1, 2, and 3 thinking, always integrating the views and playing them back into the organization. He co-develops with the people in more abstract roles ('higher' in the organization') the ideas to feed into the roles they are in contact with. The co-development is important for buy-in, and he has regular conversations with all key people in the company.

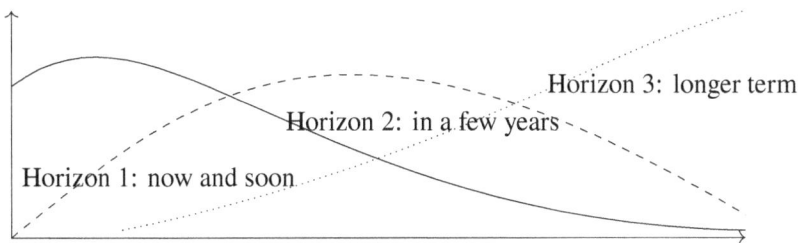

A three-horizons model for strategy

He designed a multi-directional way between his role as the strategy holder and the high-level and mid-level roles. The strategy always stays top of mind, it gets renewed and adapted. If a big change is needed, a short co-development sprint can be called.

This is an organization of 300 people, and it seems to work well. What's appealing about this approach is that strategy becomes emergent and ongoing, not just a once-in-a-while effort that gets forgotten again. An organization can adjust the cycle of conversations in a nimble way. Yet, that only works if the topic of strategy is securely held, either by a role, a team. Attention to strategy needs a place.

Whoever is holding the strategy can then set up a participatory process that considers top-down and bottom-up information, regular reviews, shared sense-making, broad participation, and enough autonomy in balance with alignment.

3.3.2   Strategy as bulk prioritization

Let's say I face a decision to prioritize between two tasks. I can write one more email before the weekend begins. Do I write an email to the unhappy customer or to my unhappy coworker? Let's say I make a decision to take care of the coworker because I like them.

Yet, with a zillion little decisions like that, how can an organization move the needle a little bit toward prioritization of customers?

Recall the distinction between operational and policy decisions: an operational decision is a *one-time* decision on something. A policy decision is to determine a more *general rule* that will apply to similar cases.

If we prioritize individual tasks, we might determine which specific action is more important than others on this week's list. We might make that decision as an operational, one-time decision, based on our sense of urgency and importance; maybe we also make that decision based on personal preferences, or on how much we enjoy the task and how long the person has waited for our response. There's nothing wrong with that – but it's unlikely that everyone's individual actions will form a coherent pattern.

A *strategic* decision is now a *bulk decision on priority*. For example, we might make a strategic decision that *in general*, customer needs are above all else. Then it would follow from it that one would respond first to a client and *then* to a colleague when all customers are satisfied, or only if the colleague's request is directly related to a customer that's waiting. That's how an organization can move the needle via a strategy, single decision by single decision, and across individuals.

The strategy gets communicated like stress (or relaxation) hormones that rush through the body. Now, each body part knows what to do. Increase breathing and decrease digestion. Focus attention. As such, a strategy can be seen as alignment towards a temporary prioritization of activities that *overlays* the activities towards the aim.

Ideally, a strategy should be specific enough to answer many questions about prioritization, just like a policy set should answer many questions about operational decisions. But the same questions of 'enough' that we've talked about earlier in section 2.6 apply here as well. Some people might be fine with an informal sense of strategy or a strategy that only answers some of the operational questions of priorities. Others might be more comfortable if the strategy is spelled out more explicitly and with more specificity. A smaller group will likely have an easier time being on an operational level, while a larger organization might need to define strategies more formally because it's harder to read the shared sense of priorities in a larger group. Many considerations flow into what people are comfortable with as 'aligned enough.'

3.3.3 Strategies and power

In a decentralized organization, each part can act independently and start changes quickly. That's a big plus for reacting to changing circumstances. For example, my organization never once had a meeting about our response to the lockdowns during the pandemic in 2020. All circles responded to it independently without a shared discussion, depending on the work and domain of the particular circle.

Yet, hoping that all the individual pieces will just fall in line magically only works if there is sufficient buy-in and accountability to the strategy. Since no circle can be forced to align their individual decisions with the organization-level strategy, only buy-in can achieve unity. Let's look at another story I'll call *Strategy Circle*. A chapter of an environmental activist organization I supported ran into an issue.

> They had about two dozen circles working on different efforts. They had a social media group, a circle organizing direct nonviolent actions, a circle on internal conflict resolution, a website circle, one for political advocacy, etc. Until then, each circle had simply made its own choices. The Website Circle made the website, the Actions Circle did actions, and so on. Of course, there was cooperation. If Actions Circle planned an action, it would be mentioned on the internal website. Photos from the actions would be given to Social Media Circle for their posts.
>
> But people felt like it was time for a more intentional strategy. What would it be? They could choose to focus their activities on

publicly effective activities. *Or* they could focus on advocacy and lobbying closer to the local government. *Or* they could work a stronger partnership strategy – investing time for relationship building with other activist organizations for stronger alignment between groups.

Of course, there were many opinions on what would be the best idea. It wasn't even so clear if there even *should* be an aligned strategy; maybe there was strength in doing all the things at once? But most chapter members felt worn out and sensed that they had been spinning their wheels without getting anywhere because they had been doing too many things at once, and none of them well.

A Strategy Circle was formed as a subcircle directly under their Anchor Circle (General Circle). The Strategy Circle started working and worked up a theory of change and a strategy full of recommendations for concrete, applicable steps for each circle.

Some people who saw the list were delighted and ready to go.

Others weren't so thrilled. They were dismayed that any one small group of people considered themselves the decision-makers for such a big decision. They didn't want to be told what to do.

This describes really well the issue that many decentralized organizations have, especially those that come from a strong culture of participatory processes. An organization like that can have difficulty rallying everyone under a strategy. Their commitment to their own team can be bigger than their commitment to their organizational aim. This can signify an organization that acts more as a set of teams than an organization.

The sense of each team having to fend for itself – just like the parallel when individuals feel like they have to fend for themselves in a team – can be exacerbated when they perceive *power-over*. As we have seen in previous chapters, a *power-over* situation will decrease the sense of unity and shift the system towards more individualism and dysfunction.

That can be problematic, particularly in decentralized organizations where teams with their own decision-making domains might feel strongly that no one should make decisions in their domain(s) of responsibility. That's what happened in the environmental activist organization where people asked things like: "Why is the Strategy Circle allowed to make so big of a decision on behalf of the organization?!"

That's why it's crucial that the whole chain of decision-making around any overall organizational strategy is made in a *power-with* paradigm that provides legitimacy for both the whole process and for the final output. As soon as this question comes up, it can already be too late – drama ensues, and buy-in drops.

3.3.4 Strategies and emergence

At the same time, any strategy team not only needs to listen well but also leave room for an emergence of strategy. A strategy is therefore partially *prescriptive* and partially *descriptive* – noticing what is coming up. Ernie, in the recruiting business, did that well by constantly weaving the conversation on an ongoing basis.

Strategy teams need to be able to elegantly weave both parts, the prescriptive, centralized strategy and the descriptive, emergent parts that come more bottom-up. Still, if we want something specific to happen, it needs a place. If no one is holding the strategy, then the whole organization is too prone to diffusion of accountability – and no one feels accountable. That means a strategy needs to be held securely in one place.

Having a central place is not at odds with an emergent strategy.

A client recently told me how they saw it: their Mission Circle developed and implemented a strategy that came out of their Theory Of Change. It guided what the organization would focus on in their movement work. They told me that their Mission Circle "infuses the organization with their strategy and Theory Of Change so people don't forget what we are doing and can choose it again, every day." I loved that!

They also follow through by regularly reviewing their progress toward achieving the stated goals in the strategy with necessary adjustments.

The Mission Circle in this organization ran reading groups and visited circles to inspire them. Their path towards their goals was tracked and evaluated. The strategy was not just a piece of paper but a living and actively stewarded process. (It's basically acting as a strategy and mission help desk; see section 3.5.3.)

Here's a nice story about emergence.

A few months ago, I was asked to facilitate a process for a small, forming community. The group of about 12 members wanted to build a project from scratch on previously undeveloped land. While they got to know each other and enjoyed each other's company, they looked for land. They tried and they tried but affordable land zoned in the right way turned out to be even harder than they anticipated. The pandemic made things even harder because the social glue of potluck gatherings was missing. Nothing seemed to move forward, and some members started discussing alternative plans. Could they buy houses on one street and live their community dream that way? Some people were excited by the comparative doability and affordability of that plan. But for others, retrofitting a road built for individual houses was a far cry from the future they had longed for for themselves. When they invited me, they were close to splitting as a group or giving up altogether.

In my pre-conversations with a member of the group, I learned more about the situation, their history, their values, hopes, and dreams. I started to form the opinion inside myself that they should go for the retrofit. Too many things were stacked against them. Better to get a smaller version of your dream than to give up, no? That's how I entered the meeting. In the rounds I facilitated, I asked them to reflect on what they were longing for, why they had originally joined the project, and whether they could live with the retrofit. I wanted to understand how many members would leave the group altogether if I proposed the retrofit. But in listening to each of the members, I tuned into their deep love not only for each other but also for the project in the way they had dreamed it up originally. I realized that they were not ready to say farewell to their plan and that they did have in fact some more energy and grit to keep searching.

With each person I listened to, my mind flipped about 20 times during that round. I got a little stressed because I felt responsible for rescuing them. And I was sure that my rescue would have to be to propose the less desired solution and save whatever was left to save. In my mind, I had been invited to help them do the hard work of letting go. But there was also a nagging feeling that I might be wrong. About halfway into the round, I realized that I had to let go of the pressure of trying to rescue them. I had to open myself up fully and just listen. Tune into where they are and where they want to be. Receive and let the information flow through me to reflect it back to them.

While the last person in the round spoke, a proposal popped up in my head (just in time!). I said, "when I walked in here, I thought I had to help you let go of your original vision. But what I hear is actually something else. Instead of discouragement and burnout, I hear the love for the project and the lasting desire to make this project happen the way you envisioned it. But I also worry because some of you are close to throwing in the towel so I don't want to leave you just with the decision of 'soldiering' on. So here's my proposal: How about we give the group another four months of effort to find a solution for the original plan? But during that time, we don't just wait. We make a punch list of things you still want to try before you're willing to give up and settle for a Plan B."

Their faces lit up. Those who were worn out were relieved to hear that there would be an end to the limbo state. Those who were not ready to give up felt their energy rising for that last push. We did a round on punch list items – what were the things they could still try, or try again? Where hadn't they asked for land, where hadn't they posted, and who in the town administration hadn't they talked to in a while? I asked for consent for my proposal, and each member consented wholeheartedly. Then we went through the punch list and assigned it to circles, and we consented to the land search circle overseeing the process and to call for a meeting once the time limit was over.

Last week, one of the members and I chatted. Here's what happened. One of the punch list items was to give one more lead one more try. That lead was a couple that owned land and wanted to develop it with a community project. Originally, when they had talked, it seemed like a misfit because of their very different approach. But time had passed since, and both sides were now ready to compromise, only to learn that their visions were actually much more compatible than they had originally thought. They decided to merge, and now the development is in planning!

To me, this isn't a story of a facilitator rescuing the group. While I surfaced the proposal, it wasn't mine. Most facilitators or collaborative teams will know these moments. The proposal was no one's. It was in the air. I only made sure it could get a shape that could be approved. Had I followed *my* strategy, I would have missed it. Written-down strategies can have the same effect or distract a group from what's surfacing.

A great practice of listening to emergence can be found in Theory U (Scharmer 2009). The most compelling idea in this context – and a valid criticism that Otto Scharmer shared with me about governance systems like sociocracy – is that we need to listen to the future. Yet, strategies and even policies are always and necessarily a relic of the past. Even if we update them every week, the moment we approve them, they are already in the past, and based on the thinking of the past. Balancing emergence and orientation to an unknown future with our experience and learning from the past is crucial to a successful and adaptable governance model.

Strategic decisions harness the power of an 'idea market' for strategic ideas. With an open strategy, a highly participatory strategy process, and a healthy dose of diversity of ideas, innovation can be fostered very much along the lines of the healthy forms of competition in multi-level selection (Stadler & Hautz 2021 et al.)

3.3.5   Budget

Budgets fit into this discussion because our organizations' budgets are an expression of what we prioritize in terms of our allocation of resources. There are many different ways of addressing budgets in decentralized organizations. In the following paragraphs, I will show the basic budgeting systems I've encountered in organizations.

My assumption for this section is that the organization shares one budget. Other models, like the Haier/Rendanheyi model or in Market-Based Budgeting used at Zappos, make each circle its own profit/loss center. In those cases, the finances don't form one whole but operate more like a market, and the models below don't apply.

A centralized budget   One team sets the budget, for example, the General/Company Circle or a Finance Circle). The centralized approach is simple and provides more unity because this one team has a good overview of all expenses. On the other hand, it is also less participatory. All teams ask the central team for budget approval.

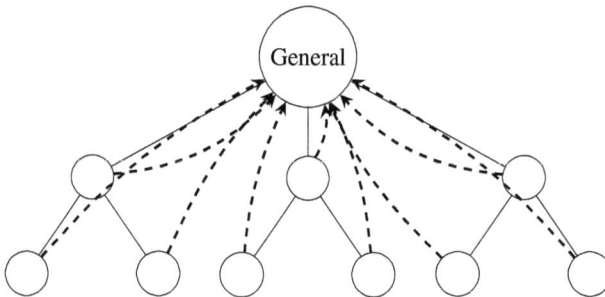

The General Circle as the central fiscal decision-maker

This is most common and doable in smaller organizations; the central team will know what's going on and what's needed.

In larger organizations, all the usual issues with centralization come up in centralized budgeting. It might trigger reactions to the centralized, perceived *power-over* situation (no matter where that team sits in the structure) because the more teams there are, the less each team will be understood in detail by that central team and might get frustrated about not having a chance to influence the budget to a level they want. The central team might feel like their decisions are misinformed because they see budget requests

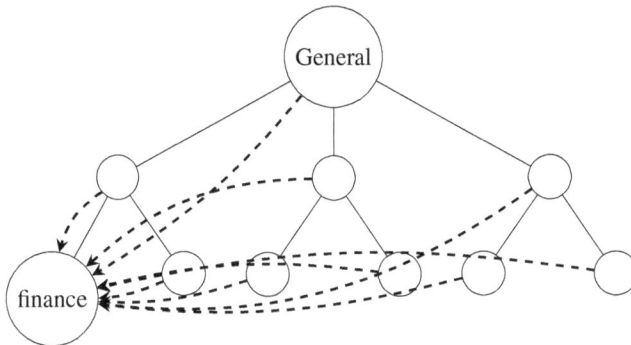

Finance Circle as the central fiscal decision-maker

but don't know enough about the narratives or strategies connected to the numbers.

A variation of the centralized budget is if the whole membership approves the budget. There might be legal requirements to do that, or it may be the organization's preference. I witnessed an interesting dynamic in an organization where the whole membership approves the budget.

> The annual budget meeting happened on a Tuesday evening. About 45 of the 70 members were present.
>
> Each team had submitted its budget, and the Finance Team had aggregated it into a budget proposal. Usually, the General Team vets the budget before coming to the whole membership, but time pressure and last-minute changes had thrown a bit of a monkey wrench into the process.
>
> Teams with significant changes presented their proposed budgets, and members asked questions.
>
> The budget projected too many expenses (by about 3%), so changes needed to be made. The facilitator – a member of the Finance Team – went through the budget line by line and asked for proposals to reduce them. A final proposal with a decision was made by consent of those present.

While this is a good solution, I am aware that some members of teams felt like their budgets had been changed too much on the fly without giving teams a chance to deliberate about the changes and get on the same page as a *collective*, even though of course most team members were present for the whole-member meeting.

This shows that even with an all-member meeting where all individuals come together, the level of *teams* can be skipped, bringing discomfort in those who care about the togetherness and shared reality within teams.

A decentralized budget   In this model, budgeting follows the organization's structure. Each team is responsible for creating its budget, which is then submitted to its parent team or the team directly above it in the structure.

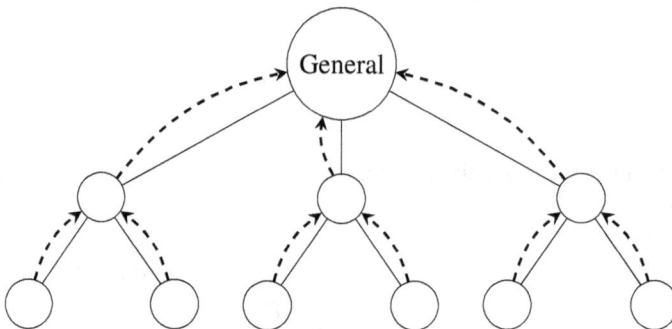

Each team makes their own budget decision and submits the budget 'upward'

Each parent team then reviews the budget requests from its sub-team and has to balance these requests against its operating costs and the overall available resources. This could involve negotiations with its sub-team to adjust their requests, prioritize their needs, or even decline some requests if the budget is insufficient.

At the highest level, the General Circle or General Company Circle (or equivalent) manages the organization's overall budget and makes high-level budgetary decisions. These decisions are informed by the aggregated budget requests that have flowed up from the lower teams.

The specifics of this process can vary depending on the organization's rules and policies. In larger or more complex organizations, a dedicated Finance Circle or similar group might handle budgetary matters across all circles. In such cases, this Finance Circle works closely with all other teams to develop, review, and implement the organization's budget while the final decision is made as described above.

This way of budgeting will emphasize the autonomy and specific context of each team. It will be prone to a situation where the organization shows lack of unity and alignment with a shared strategy.

A downside is that it can also be a lot of work because each team needs financial skills, and financial discussions need to be had in all the teams. This can create a lot of overhead. This way of budgeting can also increase tensions when some teams are comfortable asking for budget increases, and others might be more hesitant – for example, technical units might plan more confidently than marketing or vice versa. Those bigger patterns might be invisible as they get buried in many small decisions.

This system is only as good as the information flow in the organization. Imagine you sit in the General Circle, and a subteam asks for a considerable amount of money, increasing the budget for its parent team when it comes to the General Circle. Should the General Circle increase the team's budget so that the team can increase its subcircle's budget and that subteam can give its subteam what they asked for? The General Circle might still be too far removed from the request to understand.

A client of mine complained about their own situation. They were still young but had implemented a decentralized budget from the beginning. When a subteam wanted to make a new hire, the General Circle wasn't eager to approve such a big increase in the team's budget. So effectively, the General Circle now held the power on whether the hire could be made, despite efforts to decentralize decisions. It also requires more work to make cross-organizational comparisons. How does a $10K expense in Circle A compare to a $10K expense in Circle B? That's a tricky puzzle! Of course, these problems aren't unique to decentralized organizations; what's unique is the challenge of getting on the same page with more people in a decentralized situation.

A decentralized budget will work best if expenses change incrementally without big jumps.

A participatory budget   In this model, members can determine the funding of specific buckets of money. Teams make proposals that are approved by decision-makers. The process has many variations, depending on who the decision-makers are (all employees, all members, all shareholders, etc.), and how the decision is made (majority vote, ranked-choice, consent, other methods).

A participatory budget lies in a tricky middle ground in the polarity between centralization and decentralization. The teams compete with each other even more if it's a voting process like a majority vote.

But who thinks about unity on an organizational level? If the voters are aligned and have shared reality, they can act as the unifier. Still, with larger groups of voters, there will likely not be one conversation, meaning

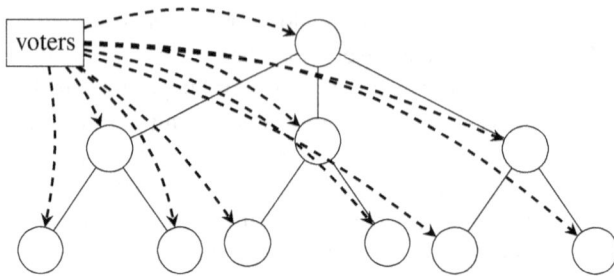

A participatory budget with a voting mechanism

there is no place for collective agency. Depending on the quality of the deliberation and how the organization-level aim is held and owned, this process can be unifying and engaging or disenfranchising and frustrating.

I think it's best placed in organizations where decision-making tends to be highly centralized, and participation in budgeting is a big step toward participation. If there is a highly *power-with* situation, this process might be used in pockets of the organization.

In addition, this way of budgeting shares all the issues from the decentralized budgeting process. It's hard to keep an overview, and decision-makers are far removed from decisions.

Combinations   Combinations of the above strategies are possible. For example, most decisions may be made in a centralized way, but the Research and Development funds are distributed in a participatory budgeting process.

Or the infrastructure expenses are decided centrally while extra funds are distributed decentralized.

A combination we've been using in our organization is to have fiscal circles within the structure that serve as a budgetary stop for all subcircles – it seems like a way to balance how much time is spent on budgetary conversations and focus that energy on a handful of circles – not all but also more than one. The difference is only evident with more layers, i.e. in more complex organizations.

Combinations can design the level of centralization and decentralization intentionally by designing (and re-designing) for the right moment in the organization's evolution. This requires a high level of awareness of the organization's state of centralization and decentralization and what is needed by the organization and its individual units or teams.

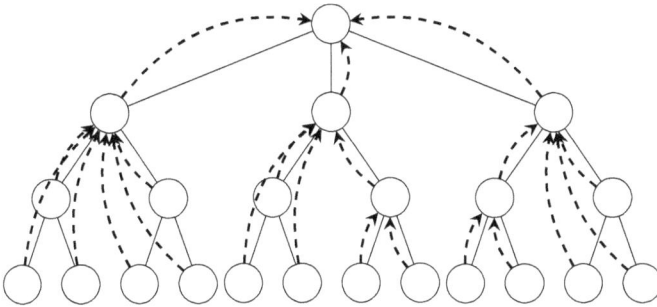

A decentralized budget with interspersed centralized budget nodes

Budgets as unifiers

The problem with budgets is that the financial resources are shared and finite, assuming the organization has one shared pool of resources. As such, the shared budget is a significant unifier. If one group overspends significantly, the overall accessible resources are now diminished for everyone. While decision-making can be decentralized, a shared resource pool ties everyone together.

In the next chapter, we will talk more about information flow, but visualization and structure of financial information become more critical for budgets, as does sense-making of financial information. In my experience, many groups need help understanding budgets, especially in complex organizations. To make good decisions, people have to have common ground on what the information is and what sense they make of the numbers.

Sense-making always carries some uncertainty. Advertising for awareness is a good example. Determining whether advertising for general awareness is worthwhile is not a trivial task. That means if we evaluate the marketing budget, we must come to a shared understanding and sense-making of how we interpret the data and how much money we're willing to spend. The same is true in centralized organizations, but an already difficult decision made with more people will be even more challenging.

Good information flow and a coherent strategy are an excellent foundation for making decisions with buy-in. Those translating a strategy into the budget need to have the courage to say *no* to some things and *yes* to others. Furthermore, it's very common for monetary discussions to trigger hard feelings, making conversations about financial decisions even more tender and difficult. For purpose-driven organizations with more than one bottom line, there's another layer of determining how much the organization wants to invest into their own financial well-being and how much to spend on impact.

Budget transparency requires data gathering, data interpretation, and visualization. Shared decision-making on budgets requires sense-makin, and being on the same page on how to translate strategic decisions into financial decisions. All of it happens within a context of uncertainty, with all the guesses and bets one needs to make for planning for an uncertain future. Also in the mix are the overall chargedness of financial decisions in our society... considering how many skills and actions are needed to plan a decentralized budget *together*, it's not a surprise at all that most budget decisions, even in self-managed organizations, are still made in a centralized or even top-down way!

This huge challenge needs solving if we want to truly decide together. Another way to say it is that to have *power-with* organizations, we need to solve the design puzzle on how to make financial decisions in a participatory and *power-with* way.

I'd like to also talk about DAOs, decentralized autonomous organizations. DAOs hope to govern a shared resource – a treasury – via blockchain technology in a transparent and participatory manner by giving voting rights to every shareholder (= tokenholder) to make decisions, including whether a project can get funded. Its basic principle follows the image above under participatory budgets. For example, DAOs with token-holders as voters often struggle with uninformed voters. In many of these participatory processes, people complain about low engagement rates where the few who engage have a disproportionate weight. It can lead to a tyranny of those with more free time. This is both a governance issue and an issue of information flow. If it took zero effort to be and stay informed, then participatory decision-making would be much easier.

More than just having access to data is required. We also need shared *sense-making* where we interpret what sense we make from the data points. Which ones matter, and what's our guess on how they are connected and dependent? In a VUCA (volatile, uncertain, complex, ambiguous) environment, we can never untangle all causes and effects. And yet, our shared forward motion needs to be based on our best guess of what is happening. That means we need to interpret the data together and get on the same page about our assumptions to experiment. Getting the right people up to date and then in one place to interpret data is an additional logistical challenge.

While DAOs are promising, and I understand the excitement in the movement about new possibilities for organizations, the new opportunities only address a subset of the emergent properties and related issues connected to organizations. Voting mechanisms are still a competitive, individual-based frame. They also need to solve the information gap that we will talk about in the next chapter. DAOs exist not only in shareholder decisions (on-chain) but also in off-chain decisions – these are the decisions that manage the algorithm, effectively deciding *how* on-chain decisions are made. Off-chain decisions are often made by developer teams very similar to traditional core teams. A lot more design work has to go into developing a holistic and well-balanced approach to make good use of this new technology.

Participatory grantmaking

I also want to mention participatory grantmaking here because it's a pattern very similar to budgeting within an organization. The mechanisms of participatory grantmaking can also be used internally by organizations, for example, for funding ideas directly from employees or members.

I'm talking about situations where a grantmaker has funds that they want to give to organizations or groups to carry out projects. It's similar to budgeting because it's (simplified) *one* pot of money that needs to be distributed into a select number of places that all want the money. There is a strong competitive trait to the process because, different from budgeting internally to an organization; the applicants don't share a purpose; they are *only* in competition.

And yet, the decision of how the funds are distributed needs to be made ideally according to some coherent strategy on the side of the grant giver. But either way, it has to be made by *someone somehow*.

I have two real-life stories of innovative grantmakers who have very different approaches. One of them changed the *who* (at least partially) in this equation, and the other changed the *how*. Let's hear them.

The first story I will call *Decentralized Grantgiving* because they have a decentralized approach to grant giving. It's a grant giver with decades of experience and a strong focus on support for grassroots groups. They are convinced that people connected to a community know best how funds could benefit locally, so they decentralized their grant giving early on.

> There are 27 advisory boards. Some are geographically based (on a country or subregional level), and some are thematic, like supporting a particular work. The coordinator of each advisory board is salaried; other participants receive an honorarium. The advisory boards can

pick their own members, but the foundation staff spends a lot of time with potential advisors to get to know them and what they care about to ensure alignment.

The available funds are split up between advisory boards according to a formula, about 100-250K per advisory board. Those advisory boards are not nested, but each is connected to the center staff of about 50 people. The staff provides opportunities for learning and cross-connection so advisors can learn from parallels in other advisors' work and sense-making.

Those advisory boards have hardly any restrictions on how they can be organized or how they make decisions. The grant giver gives them full control of distributing the funds, based entirely on trust.

This is an interesting hybrid. The first distribution of funds to the advisory boards is centralized (via a formula), and it's a decentralized process from then on.

In my interview with the staff member, they mentioned exploring two possible changes. One is that there is a higher demand and more funds, so they are considering growing beyond the 27 advisory boards. However, they have a sense that growth might require more structures to maintain the integrity of the process. For example, they might need to require a more uniform structure within the advisory boards while still granting them full freedom to distribute funds according to their choice.

The second change they are exploring is more decentralization of their staff operations and decision-making. The foundation uses a traditional hierarchy, but they feel drawn to a more distributed way of making decisions that align with the value of 'those closer to the need know best.'

My second story is about a different funder based in the UK. They are very centralized in their basic approach: applicants submit their grant requests, and one central committee decides who is awarded money by a majority vote process – the project with the most votes projects funded.

When Fiona came onto the committee a couple of years ago, she brought ideas from her own organization, which was self-organized with consent, roles, and circles.

One concept that was dear to Fiona was consent. She inspired the committee to change the process slightly. They still voted to determine the level of support for each application. But, at the end, a proposal was made based on those numbers – for example, to accept Proposal A (5 votes), Proposal B (4 votes), Proposal C (4 votes), and Proposal

D (3 votes). That decision on the slate of applicants was then made by consent.

But Fiona wanted a different result. The process still felt competitive overall, and the consent decision at the end made littles difference to that. They tried a few variations, but finally they landed on the following process that they were extremely happy with. The frist step is to come up with an agreed-upon list of criteria, for example a balance between small and big projects.

Then, each committee member goes off and thinks about who they will nominate. "So when we sit in a circle, we do quite a lot of really connecting to each other. We share how we feel, how we felt about the process, the difficulty of the choices, and so on. And then we remind ourselves about our agreements – listening, active listening, understanding that we just have a piece of the puzzle.

And when we say what project we nominate, and we put it in the center. We bring our own perspective as our piece of the puzzle, but we are still really open to the other's perspectives. And then we listen to the why from each one.

Then we do a change round. Everyone can change their nominations.

After that, there is silence. We have a role of what we call the mycelium. That person looks at the nominations – how many nominations there were for an application – but also considers the reasons that were given and how strong they were. So, it's not the facilitator that brings the proposal. The mycelium role is just really someone who is just listening and then makes a proposal. With that proposal, there is a consent/objection round."

Fiona told me how different this process landed on people. "And everyone says that is really incredible. The difference in culture from our process last year to this year is like night and day. The feedback people give us is that it is amazing how the group is completely glued. We really support each other in our differences."

The funder also told the committee that in previous iterations, the committee had been all egos. Now, the opposite happened. Competition faded into the background. The most surprising thing?

"I asked the other committee members, do you remember which applications were your favorites? And we did not."

The last comment, in particular, is fascinating. The collective level took over so well that the group members shed their individual preferences and completely tuned into the collective's preferences, becoming one entity.

Now, imagine we could combine all those building blocks. We could have a decentralized grant giver where advisory boards together decide the ratio of how funds are distributed into each advisory board's domain. Then advisory boards have total freedom to choose, and they follow a process where collective wisdom is harvested to make the final funding decisions.

So much local support and collective could be unlocked when our processes are designed to hold the collective's perspective!

On the other hand, it's also clear that the more participatory and deliberate our decisions are designed to be, the more effort can be needed. How much effort is justified for making these decisions?

3.3.6   A system of many pulls

Whenever I sit down to work, I have a lot of choices. There are projects to work on, things to write, emails to answer, and meetings to plan. The overall aim of an organization points to the set of all allowed and expected activities in the organization. But that still leaves too many choices.

Policies (agreements, agreed-upon workflow, and roles) further add helpful constraints that help us focus on the desired work in the most effective way. Policies are like a helpful filter. Instead of doing *all* or *any* actions in any manner, policies give us guidelines.

Missions, values, and strategies further reduce and qualify what kinds of activities are desired in the organization. Ideally, they give me some hints on what to focus on. Budgets tell us what we can or choose to afford, which further restricts our choices.

If we want to make choices together, we need to create a foundation so the activities and outputs align with the collective's shared priorities and values. Most organizations struggle with having too many options, and that's when alignment helps narrow down the options and align the actions.

But we mustn't forget that those constraints come with a downside – overhead. The more things we define, the more things we have to keep in mind for each decision. Before I do a task, I have to ask myself whether there's a workflow on that. Whenever we make a policy, we have to check whether the new policy is compatible with all other, previous policies.

Not defining things and just giving people autonomy also has its place. Organizations are like a complex choice-limiting game that helps us pick helpful actions to further the aim in an aligned way. Governance is the game by which that happens. The level of how much and deeply we want to constrain is a choice we make together cumulatively each time we make a new decision.

3.4 Information flow

There's a joke my colleague makes about information flow in decentralized organizations. He refers to an intentional community of about 70 people who, for 18 years, used to make all decisions in a centralized way. Meaning: everyone got together once a month in one big group and made decisions.

The community then switched to a decentralized governance system and has been running that way for a good decade. The joke: "before sociocracy, when everyone decided everything together, everyone knew how little we were getting done. Now, in sociocracy, no one knows how *much* we're getting done!"

It's true. I can't tell you how many times someone shoots an email to the whole community about this and that and how it needs to be taken care of, with no idea that a circle is already working on it or has a whole other assessment on whether something needs to be done, and what.

Information flow is central to many things, including strategy and budgets. For example, a decentralized budget requires excellent information flow. I am aware of organizations where the budgeting process is entirely hands-off, and there are no limits to what a team can spend. That's possible for them because they have a live dashboard that lets everyone see the finances and projections in real time with ways to get fully curated financial information. The effort they put into information flow pays off in their ease of budgeting. Since this is a well-resourced company, they are choosing their freedom over a more conservative budgeting approach.

Information in the organization is a commons, a set of resources created by everyone and needed by everyone but often overseen by basically no one. Information flow and its resulting challenges worry me the most about the otherwise welcome rise of decentralized organizations. If we can't solve the information flow puzzle with new methods, technologies, and protocols, we will out-complexify ourselves very soon. People don't operate well when they are overwhelmed by information – and more decentralization certainly doesn't help with that.

As we saw in the sections on *clear enough*, *explored enough*, and *good enough*, we *never* have enough information to make a *fully* informed decision. And even if we knew everything about the current state, we can't predict the future with certainty. Yet, if we want more people to make informed decisions autonomously, then *more people* need to know *more*. This leads to a crunch where people's processing capacity – bandwidth and time – is the bottleneck.

Since decentralized organizations often have more connections between departments and more fluidity in their collaboration, communication can and needs to happen between many different players. It's more complex than hearing from your boss what you need to do next and talking with your coworkers right next to you. In self-management, relevant information originates in many places and needs to be received in many places. It's a many-to-many relationship, and the numbers increase with every team or role because, with every additional role, we have one more receiver for all information from all senders and one more sender potentially holding information for all receivers.

Regarding competition/cooperation – decentralized organizations often struggle with too much autonomy and pluralism in their information flow and too little alignment when everyone does their own thing. We need more robust procedures, training, and standardization for information flow to improve decentralized decision-making.

3.4.1   Being our own PR center

Small organizations might still get away with emails and an all-member meeting here and there. But as soon as we hit a certain number and complexity, we run into information bottlenecks and issues. How soon we hit those issues depends on several factors, like the number of people involved, task interdependence, the complexity of the work, language and cultural differences, etc.

If domains of responsibility and expertise are easy to separate and tasks can largely be carried out independently, it works well. Defined domains help in reducing the amount of 'stray' information because we can contain the amount of information someone needs to know and reduce it to what's needed in the domain. Domains filter information automatically because I only need to track closely what happens in a domain I'm a part of.

But no matter how much we try, with complexity, it gets harder and harder to keep straight what domain lives where. In addition, we want to work *across* silos, so we need to know what is happening in the other teams.

Every role, every team often needs to take care of its own informational service to solve the alignment issue in a decentralized way; every team needs to become its own public relations office. Finding effective ways to keep people informed and the info up to date is a feat. It's not enough to have the information written somewhere. People need to either receive and retain the information or know how to find it – and it needs to occur to them to look for it. They can't know what they don't know.

It's easy to be on the complaining side of this conundrum. Having been on the other, 'guilty' side of it plenty of times, it's clear to me that the responsibility of everyone being informed needs to be on both sides – those *providing* information and those *receiving* information. Not only is it a very time-intensive and skill-heavy endeavor (writing clearly and finding good strategies to inform people), but it is also not a task one can do perfectly. No matter how perfectly we provide information, some people will miss it altogether, miss nuances, or forget the information and where they found it. No matter how perfectly people read all the information provided, sometimes people will fail to convey information accurately and might not make tacit knowledge explicit.

In the meantime, there are ways to create an organization-wide common ground to increase alignment and order. Some artifacts and technologies can support organization-wide information flow.

The table on the next page lists what each organization needs. *Push/pull* refers to who initiates the transfer of information. In a push setting, the sender pushes the information out, like in a newsletter. In a pull setting, the source provides the information, but the recipient accesses the information at their own convenience, e.g. a phone list or a manual.

Organizations don't use separate tools for all these functions; it's even better to cluster them so people don't have to look in six different places. For example, tools like Slack or email can be used for *all* push communications, and a wiki *all* pull information.

But paying attention to each of the different needs is important, including conversations about who should have access permissions to what. The ideal is to be as transparent and forthcoming as possible. Having policies written down for all to see aligns with the Core Design Principle #4 "monitoring of agreed behaviors"; if agreements are written down for all to see, we can increase accountability.

Just like meeting minutes are a written version of a group's common ground, an organization-wide wiki or its counterparts can become the organizational common ground, keeping a record of the information that *should* to be known organization-wide. Of course, that wouldn't capture informal or tacit knowledge, which includes an understanding of work culture, norms, practices, traditions, and unspoken rules, all of which can also be crucial for an organization's functioning. Those need to be written down if just holding them without a written record isn't enough to foster that common ground.

A key challenge in disseminating information within decentralized organizations is the complexity of gathering the data we intend to share. For

Mode	Recipient	Examples
Push	Own Team	Task management system team communication like reminders Role reports
Push	Other Team/Role	Team lead(er) reports from parent team Team delegate reports from subteam
Push	General Membership	Internal newsletters, announcements, memos Sense-making statements (collective common ground) (Onboarding materials)
Pull	Own Team	Meeting minutes Project documents/resources on shared drive
Pull	Other Team/Role	Shared Data/Analytics Budgeting and Financial Reports Legal and Compliance Information
Pull	General Membership	Organization-wide policies & guidelines HR information Knowledge base/wiki

Information Management in Decentralized Organizations. This doesn't include communication to the outside of the organization (e.g., a press release).

instance, creating a regular newsletter that includes reports from various teams necessitates asking these teams and sub-teams to sift through and compile their information. This can feel like a Sisyphean task. The information for another team or the membership that comes from more than one team is many-to-many information – information comes from a variety of places and goes into a variety of places.

A perfect pattern would be to have information flow effortlessly, like hormones in the body, allowing many-to-many communication. Many parts of our bodies affect our hormones, and many parts with appropriate receptors 'read' the messages. For example, a smart tagging or hashtag protocol could mimic hormone receptors. Any team would broadcast a message with a certain tag and receiving teams or individuals could decide to follow certain tags.

Artificial Intelligence (AI) might be even more useful in identifying, and collating and curating information. It may provide relief here in the production, the curation, and the findability of information. AI tools can analyze large volumes of content to identify patterns and relationships and support people trying to understand information. It can generate content targeted to a question. Natural language processing can help us understand user queries and suggest relevant content – that way, we can find information even without knowing the exact location or wording. In a way, our old systems were like index cards where we could only find information when we knew how to find the index card. When we wanted to find a book in the library without knowing the title or the author, we were helpless. Our only chance to find the book we wanted was to ask the librarian whether they remembered the book with the blue cover where the protagonist marries a woman from Iran who then had an accident. With AI, our set of information curation and management tools has increased significantly. Yet, it's also possible that AI will allow us to *produce* more noise, thus increasing the pressure on people's attention and bandwidth again.

The one pattern still needed then would be a way to keep these pieces of information up to date (including version control). Documents that provide information that can be pulled needs to be updated regularly.

Therefore, a smart information management design that considers all these factors is needed to form a solid basis for decision-making in organizations. The success of decentralized organizations hinges on our ability to develop and evolve the patterns of information flow within them.

3.4.2 Feedback

The basic assumption of self-organization in sociocracy is that decisions are more sustainable and have better outcomes if more needs are factored into the decision.

Let's start with a super simple example. Let's say a communications circle decides all circle secretaries must submit one-paragraph meeting summaries after each meeting to store in the organization's logbook. Let's say this decision makes a lot of sense for the circle deciding it, i.e. it is very likely to be good concerning the circle's aim. In short, this is a great example where a decision is within the circle's domain and is a really 'good' decision for its effectiveness.

But let's say this decision was made without feedback from the circle secretaries in other circles, and circle secretaries are dismayed and don't want to comply. Making circle summaries adds extra to their workloads.

Had the Communications Circle asked those affected for input, it would have been much more likely to get good results. It would have smoothened the waves, and it would have surfaced essential information that makes or breaks how the decision can be implemented. So even if a circle doesn't care about courtesy and inclusive decisions, it's simply not *effective* to do things without appropriate feedback because even the best plans in our heads don't work as well without considering input from those affected.

The commitment to feedback and improvement is deeply transformational. See this story, *File Storage Feedback*:

> The Support Circle decided that all circles had to follow a certain file storage system, with nomenclature for files. After two significant leadership transitions, things had gotten out of hand – and no one knew where to find key documents. Support Circle tried its best to get people on board, hear their feedback, and include it. And yet, when they evaluated how well the new system had worked, the circle was dismayed at how mixed the uptake had been. Some people had creatively found their way around the new system by adding folders that did not follow the recommended standard. Other circles had rendered the nomenclature useless by introducing new terms instead of using the recommended ones. What did the circle do with the feedback? Many feelings and interpretations came up: "The others didn't follow our system because they didn't bother to understand it", or "they are undermining our system because they don't care about us."

Some of those interpretations might carry some truth, but in my experience, it's not very helpful to assume bad intentions. If we are committed to learning from the feedback, we can't only walk around with our own judgments. Did the others in the organization know enough to comply with the recommended system as designed? Had the information been presented in a way that could be understood well, given where others were at? The circle was sure that they had. So what was going on?

> In this example, it turned out that the circle had not factored in who would be working with the file system, and it turned out that in this case, two external contractors had supported note-taking. Since they were only contractors, they hadn't been trained or asked for feedback. Since their main task was administrative, other people followed the external administrators' example, assuming the guidelines must have changed. So, there was a very easy explanation for the mess, and none of the judgmental assumptions had been true.

No one was being mean, and no one was undermining anyone. Everyone had just tried to do their best given what they knew.

Whatever happens, it is feedback. For example, even *if* the others had actively undermined the circle's success, that would have been feedback on the sense of cohesion and collaboration or closeness between the teams.

The mantra I keep telling myself is that whatever we observe, it is feedback for *something*. The question is just for what.

Sometimes, we might interpret that our observations tell us about something we don't have a way to change. In the story *File Storage Feedback*, they might come to the conclusion that having contractors do such key work creates too much friction in the shared work. Can Support Circle do anything about that? Maybe yes, maybe no, depending on how decision-making is distributed in the system. Maybe it's part of a bigger issue of how the organization is funded that makes contractor relationships necessary. The Support Circle might give feedback about that situation, which then becomes feedback to those with a say on funding. Or maybe no one in the organization can do much about it.

Within an organization, most often, those who can make change will be our colleagues. Asking them for input will save us a lot of trouble and make decisions better and smoother.

The same is true for those in the wider network of our organization, for example, customers or stakeholders. If customers aren't asked whether they want a certain feature, then our best product development is pointless. In the same way, stakeholders have to be considered. If parents of a private school dislike a new policy, then the policy can be as good as it wants to be, and the school will likely lose families.

3.4.3 Metrics

To maintain an overview of an organization's various activities, many implement metrics. The problem with metrics is that they are often associated with top-down, coercive contexts and utilized to control people.

However, on their own, metrics are merely data that we can choose to collect and interpret. Given the significance of feedback in effective self-organization, metrics, both qualitative and quantitative, are frequently employed to gain insights into the functioning and performance of the organization—just without the power-over framework.

While I cannot determine how representative this is, my impression is that OKRs (Objectives and Key Results) are quite popular in self-management contexts. We use them ourselves. OKRs can be set to establish clear goals and track progress at various levels within the organization. By setting objectives and defining key results, self-managed organizations can align their efforts, prioritize tasks, and monitor their performance without the need for traditional top-down control mechanisms. So, in a way, metrics can be a way to do with *less* control! Metrics can be a source of alignment allowing more comparability, which then allows us to be more autonomous.

In self-managed organizations, OKRs can be set by individual teams, cross-cutting teams, or even by individuals themselves. They can be set bottom-up or top-down. The more participatory and consensual their adoption, the more easily there will be buy-in.

One issue with OKRs is that they may or may not align with the organizational structure. The ideal of cascading OKRs (where one OKR is a sub-OKR of the parent team's ORK) doesn't always work out because success might not fall into neat packages that can be tracked independently. It's simply not always true that OKR1 and OKR2 make OKR3. Assuming so can stifle teams because they have to fit their own metrics into a subset of the higher-level OKRs which can lead them to neglect to focus on their own unique contribution.

OKRs can be defined bottom-up or top-down. In a top-down manner, one big OKR is divided into parts that are taken on by the next-lower teams which can lead to artificial packaging. In a bottom-up manner, OKRs are defined by teams and passed up in the chain. This can lead to mismatches and situations where we're comparing apples and oranges because Team A might count website traffic and Team B might track customer satisfaction, and the two can hardly be compared directly.

Just like with strategy, it's a constant oscillating movement to create autonomy and alignment with reasonable resources and attention.

On the other hand, OKRs can be particularly useful to evaluate the flow *across* departments of an organization. Then it can be an opportunity to have discussions across units about what matters and how the flow between departments can be improved

A story about that comes from the founder of a sociocratic organization in France.

> Their CEO told me that their regular decisions are made in circles and roles. The decision-makers are all 200 people in the organization in their respective roles and circles. Yet, for an annual process, they bring together only the partners – about 30 people – in a process to define OKRs for the coming year.

He admits their process has flaws, as it can be complicated and time-consuming. This constitutes their compromise of what they find useful; in the past, it had included many more people but now decided that the 30 partners will do it.

Following the same pattern of other topics in this book, with a more participatory, bottom-up approach of setting metrics, a challenge, and opportunity is that now more people need to know how to find and track metrics that are meaningful – to make sure they're not just an exercise to tick off boxes. It's essential to balance setting meaningful goals without becoming bogged down by an overemphasis on metrics at the expense of seeing nuances and wider patterns.

3.4.4 Performance and accountability

System 3 in the Viable Systems Model states that there needs to be a function responsible for overseeing the performance of the operational units. This is true also in a self-organized context.

Tracking performance means to compare the expectation with the actual results. In a *power-over* context, the expectations might or might not be explicit, and even explicit agreements are often set top-down. For example, a boss might say that XYZ wasn't good enough, even if there was no stated expectation of how it would be done or if that expectation had been set unilaterally by the boss.

One issue with performance is that even when made in an ideal *power-with* fashion, performance reviews have a strong connotation with *power-over* situations. That means that lots of power dynamics and shadows of the past are to be expected here. In our practice, we make sure to let the person being assessed speak first and last on each topic to give them a chance to self-disclose and stay in full agency for the process. But still, people can have such strong reactions to feedback and evaluations that they often dismiss the desire for feedback altogether.

Another common line of reasoning is that if everyone is a peer, no one is empowered to evaluate anyone's performance. I disagree with that. Instead of implementing performance evaluations by one person, dispersing the process to include more than one perspective is a good idea. The group that works with a person will have useful insights on things that person can improve. Overall, we have to keep in mind that performance is about alignment. There might be behaviors or misunderstandings that lead to a lack of alignment or that undermine performance, and it's in the interest of the organization to create shared reality. In addition, if there are no consequences for violating agreements, alignment will suffer. It is therefore in the interest of the organization to track performance and give feedback when alignment isn't guaranteed.

In a *power-with* context, the agreements that set the expectations forming the backdrop for performance are made collaboratively. Several artifacts can set the context for individual performance evaluations:

- role descriptions
- metrics
- performance and improvement plans
- organizational artifacts like mission, purpose, strategy, value statements, policies

In an ideal state, those agreements are made in a way so the people assessed are decision-makers, or at least had a chance to give feedback. For example, I was a decision-maker in defining the role I was selected for, which means I had a chance to consent or object to expectations that were hardwired into my role. The improvement plan that was generated in my performance review required my consent, and subsequent performance is measured against those agreements.

The more explicit and specific – within reason – those agreements are, the easier it will be to be accountable. Remember 'specific enough' and 'defined enough'? That applies here, too. If a certain behavior or performance is expected, it should be made explicit. Or said differently: everything that is expected should be made explicit, and everything agreed upon should be expected.

If people are a direct part of making agreements, it's more likely that they will have buy-in on those agreements which is often the case in *power-with* contexts. Buy-in is typically not an issue in small teams. But in a bigger organization, there will be more places where autonomous decisions are made that might affect everyone. That means that with a certain organization size, the number of decisions that any given individual member *wasn't* a part of will increase.

Let's look at it: In a 5-people organization, everyone is likely part of every major decision. It's likely that everyone will be accountable for decisions they have made themselves. In an organization with 50 people, each person is likely only part of 10% of decisions and so on. How heavy this effect weighs depends on how much task interdependence there is, i.e. how many of the decisions other teams make directly affect other people's work. So the bigger and more interdependent an organization is, the more it happens that people have to stay accountable to *other teams'* policies and expectations which means that buy-in and accountability might be reduced and needs to be encouraged by giving feedback or enforced.

This is partially also an issue of information flow because the bigger an organization is the harder it will be to know all the guidelines and policies that apply. Therefore, accountability will highly depend on how well the information flow has been tended to.

In either case, a lack of accountability must be factored into the system. There's a central and decentralized approach to accountability. Each team needs to make sure its own policies are respected by everyone else in the organization. And each person and team needs to make sure to track its own people's performance and alignment.

As stated earlier, unless there's a defined role (like a mentor or a peer coach), by default a leader will be in charge of providing feedback about team performance. If an individual doesn't follow the agreements, they risk the group cohesion that allows the team to achieve team-level aims. Agreements alone aren't enough, there has to be accountability. The strategy chosen should match the level of the violation (and not be out of proportion). That's why Prosocial calls core design principle 5 "graduated responding to helpful and unhelpful behavior."

3.4.5   Information flow via a social network

Information flow as a system requires specific attention in a decentralized organization. All other systems depend on the shared common ground- a shared acceptance and mutual knowledge of the same facts on which we can base decisions.

The more connection there is between people, the better information will flow. Avenues for information sharing and connection can also be created in informal contexts. Any organization benefits from more inter-connectedness, both by increasing innovation and better alignment.

- Increasing collaboration and innovation. When individuals from diverse backgrounds and areas of expertise interact, they bring different perspectives, knowledge, and skills to the table, increasing creativity and, therefore, innovation.
- Breaking down silos. Interpersonal connections help break down silos within organizations. Silos can lead to a lack of understanding, duplication of efforts, and missed opportunities for synergy. Individuals can bridge these silos by fostering interpersonal connections, creating a more interconnected and cohesive organization.

It promotes a shared understanding of organizational aims, values, and collective responsibility.

- Knowledge transfer and learning. Interpersonal connections facilitate the flow of information and knowledge within an organization. Through informal conversations, networking events, and interpersonal relationships, employees can share tacit knowledge, experiences, and insights that are not typically documented or easily accessible.

Serendipity, for example, is an undervalued factor for success! Any organization is full of unexplored potential and opportunities that could be acted on if only we knew what others are working on or struggling with.

What are the channels of informal information flow? Here are a few:

- Informal Networks. Informal networks exist outside the formal communication channels and often emerge spontaneously through personal connections, friendships, and common interests. These networks enable the flow of information, knowledge, and social support among employees. They can be formalized through initiatives like Employee Resource Groups (ERGs), which bring together individuals with shared characteristics or interests to foster connections and promote collaboration. They can also increase the sense of belonging and create spaces for psychologically safe conversations.
- Communities of Practice. Communities of practice are groups of individuals who share a common professional interest or expertise within an organization. These communities provide a platform for members to collaborate, share knowledge, and learn from one another. They facilitate the transfer of specialized knowledge, promote innovation, and support ongoing professional development.

3.4.6   Resolving conflict together

Conflict resolution is a topic that belongs everywhere and nowhere. I want to at least touch on conflict resolution, as it's vital to collaboration.

There are two different kinds of conflicts[5] that can arise in teams:

- *Task conflict* refers to disagreements and differences in opinions or approaches related to the tasks, goals, or work processes, and those conflicts or tensions should be resolved via governance protocol, like reviewing a role and its responsibilities.

---

[5]See Grant 2021.

- *Relationship conflict* refers to interpersonal conflicts and tensions among individuals or groups. It typically involves negative emotions and difficulties in communication and collaboration.

The problem with any unresolved conflict is that it inhibits the flow, collaboration, and general effectiveness in organizations. Conflict between people reduces access to information. That's why psychological safety – an environment where people feel safe expressing thoughts without judgment is crucial for resolving conflicts. In this way, conflict resolution and psychological safety are essential for alignment *and* for healthy variety. No wonder it's such a crucial element of effective collaboration!

To illustrate this, let's look at an example.

Rosa worked in a US production company in an early 1980s sociocracy implementation. Born in the 1930s, Rosa was a hard worker but certainly not making waves. She chose to speak last in rounds, and she typically held back. One day, the team was working on a sick leave policy for the company. A proposal had been made, and they did a round of reactions. Rosa spoke last, as usual. When it was her turn, Rosa sat there and didn't say anything for a good solid two minutes. Her face turned red; her breathing was getting shallow. She was tense.

After a few minutes, Rick said, as calmly as he could, *we're really interested in what you have to say. There's no rush.*

After a little while, she spoke and blurted out: *We don't need this policy.* Asked to explain, Rosa laid out a number of shortcomings in the proposal. Given that she worked in administration, she was closest to things, and her insight mattered. They included her input in a modified policy, which got everyone's consent.

That day, something clicked for her. Rick called it her 'baptism of fire'. She finally trusted that the power structure in the company had changed for real. The moment strengthened her belief that her voice did in fact matter and that change was possible. A bit of a complainer before, she was now cheerful and much more positive.

Until then, how many of Rosa's ideas had never seen the light of day? Rosa had taken a risk and was able to contribute to the work. Speaking up meant taking a risk, but it was well-received and supported the group's aim. More trust and connection increase our chances of making better decisions because more information surfaces.

Since conflicts hamper collaboration towards an organization's aim, it's in the organization's interest to support resolving them. Every organization needs effective conflict resolution, which might involve:

- Ombudsperson; mediation or arbitration services.
- Conflict resolution policy defining steps on how to resolve conflicts.
- Internal coaching service.
- Training and workshops.
- Peer mediation programs.
- Regular check-ins and feedback sessions.
- Implementing a formal grievance procedure.

Many strategies address both task and relationship conflicts. The key is creating an environment where people feel safe surfacing issues early before they escalate.

Is conflict resolution even part of governance? In some systems, it is. Some systems see conflict resolution and relationship care as part of the *group's* responsibility, for example, in a governance framework called Organic Organizations (O2) by Target Teal. They use a Care Mode:[6]

> The "Caring Mode" is a moment of the Circle Meeting whose objective is to stimulate the presence and connection between the participants. This Mode should not be used to make changes to the Organizational Structure of the Circle or to engage Partners in their Roles and Responsibilities.

In either case, clear governance helps avoid conflicts in the first place. Just like a lack of clarity in roles creates conflict for individuals, unclear responsibilities between teams can also lead to unhelpful group dynamics. Effective information flow and flexible domain management prevent them.

Ultimately, to hold relationships, the collective level must be held well through governance, relationship stewardship, interpersonal skills, and organizational principles. Structures can support trust and psychological safety, unlocking the full potential of our collaboration.

3.5 Organizational governance choices

There are additional needs for governance on the organizational level.

- Legitimacy. How does an organization as a collective of collectives *choose* a governance system?
- Centralization and decentralization. How do small decisions accumulate into the flavor of a self-governance system?

---

[6]https://github.com/targetteal/o2-pt/blob/master/EN/meta-agreements.md, retrieved June 9 2023.

We've already looked at governance choices on *team* level in section 2.7. While all of those topics carry over to organizations, in this section, I will focus only on what's unique on the level of *organizations*.

Note that I am assuming governance systems that are somewhat formalized. Self-management systems like Semco or the ideas and examples mentioned in Reinventing Organizations by Laloux or Humanocracy by Hamel/Zanini emphasize – and I concur – that a big part of the system is not the system itself but the mindset or principles at play. Yet, practices and specific implementations *also* matter. Here, my main concern is always whether a system can be changed, including whether it can be adapted locally and depending on its context over time.

3.5.1 Who decides the governance system?

I emphasized in section 3.1.2 how important it is that an organization can change the aims and domains of individual units so they can adapt. That means we need a governance system that allows for that and specifies how to do it. Ideally, the same practices for forming/changing aims and domains apply across the whole organization so that groups are formed and changed according to the same pattern.

I know a few organizations with chimera governance systems – e.g., one part is sociocratic, others are hierarchical, or Holacratic. That doesn't work so well because handoffs become unclear and alignment suffers; it's often only a transition phase towards a more steady state where all teams work according to a uniform rule set.

For alignment, there must be one place that decides how the organization is governed. But where? If the organization is small, it can simply propose and adopt a specific model or change it over time. A proposal on governance can simply be worked out and approved by the group.[7]

But what about collectives of collectives? What do we do if the organization is already too big to get everyone into the same room to adopt a governance system together? Who decides then?

The issue here is that the whole game changes. As I've explained earlier, a team differs from an organization in that in an organization, there will be foundational decisions that not everyone can participate in making. That might be fine for decisions more related to parts of the work. But most people see the governance system as something so fundamental that

---

[7]Also see my book *Who Decides Who Decides, 2021*, about how to do that. There, I describe how a group can adopt consent decision-making as a basic decision-making tool, even when it doesn't have a defined and agreed-upon decision-making method.

it should *not* be decided by 'other' people. But if other people shouldn't decide it for everyone, does that mean it has to be decided by everyone together? How do we do that in an organization of 100, 1,000, or 10,000 people?

There are three basic options. This chapter will take a look at each.

- The governance system is put in place by the legal owner, the board, or its counterpart. I will call that a *top-down implementation*.
- There is no formal adoption, and people simply begin to change their practices in a decentralized way as they see fit. I will call that a *bottom-up implementation*.
- There is a form of *power-with* implementation.

Top-down implementations

I call top-down implementations all those implementations where someone (an individual or a group) with formal power decides to implement, and everyone else needs to follow along with the new governance method.

The most typical example is if there is a hierarchical organization that changes its governance towards self-governance. In those cases, the formal leader – owner, board, or founder – makes this decision.

This kind of governance system change typically works when the power situation is clear, like an autocratic king forming a parliament and approving the constitution. While there might be a disagreement, it's clear who needs to go if they aren't in alignment – those at the bottom.

Most successful implementations are in this category. A change team, put in place by the leadership, designs the new system, and the new system gets adopted by the hold leadership. For many, it's the leadership's responsibility to steward a system that works well for the organization, so it's easy to argue that a top-down implementation is an example of good stewardship.

The one question is how well a transition like this can work if the power relationships are entrenched, and the new system is only window dressing. Is a system imposed by the old leadership able to create truly shared power? Can a 'ruler' invite others to share power, or does that mean the system will always be at the former ruler's mercy?

This depends on one crucial factor: who holds the domain of governance post-transition. If, for example, the owner is still holding the power of the governance system, then the new system remains at the mercy of that owner who could decide unilaterally to change it back into a hierarchy.

Yet, if the new system transfers the power to change the governance system in the future into the organization, then the handover is complete.

There are a lot of social-emotional factors to consider here. This next story, *Benevolent Top-down Implementation* is a great example.

> This was a socially oriented funding network organization in the startup phase. The founder, Boris, was well-liked and involved. He had started the organization and held most of the operations. As voices criticized him for taking up too much space, he looked into alternatives.
>
> He was excited about implementing a decentralized, consent-based governance system to share decision-making and responsibility. To ease the process and to get there as soon as possible, Boris developed a proposal that spelled out the basic organizational structure and governance practices. He floated the proposal among his colleagues.
>
> His colleagues were livid that he had 'grabbed' the power of proposing and went into full rebellion mode.
>
> The organization folded soon after because too many people turned away in frustration – partly because of the 'power-over move' and partly because of the drama surrounding the incident that paralyzed the organization.

What happened here? Did Boris make a mistake? And if so, what could he have done instead?

This story shows that the chances of success are much lower in cases when it's unclear where the organization is transitioning *from*. Did Boris have the power to decide the new governance system? It's apparent that people didn't believe so.

But then who did have the power? This organization operated in a form of a power vacuum, and a power vacuum is a difficult place to do *anything*, even more, implement a governance system!

Looking at this story, it's incomplete to begin the story where I did. The real issue happened much earlier when the organization was *started*. It was started with no clear governance structure, which meant there was not enough structure to support *power-with*. It was what I called a blob. That, in turn, meant that, as is commonly the case, whenever there isn't enough structure to support a *power-with* process, then *power-over* and *power-under* take over. Boris' attempt to push for a decision on governance was seen as a *power-over* move. And rejecting his proposal, from where I sit, was a fatal *power-under* move from the side of his colleagues. Instead of saying no or constructively using their natural power, they complained and rebelled, which gave away the power they had.

Due to the lack of structure, they had to fall back on the remaining general pillars of resilience – skills & experience, and trust & relationships, and principles & values. I assume they fell apart because trust wasn't big enough to counter the narrative of the *power-over* move, and the experience wasn't deep enough to understand the governance principles at work.

Governance transitions *can* work well when trust cushions the *power-over* narratives. See the story *Meditation Center Implementation*.

> They ran a meditation center, and their governance could be best described as chaotic.
>
> Eventually, six people formed that wanted to implement a coherent and explicit governance system. After the group studied consent-based, role/circle-based governance, they were ready to implement and decided to adopt it. There had not been any formal process, so they were running by the principle of 'do first apologize later.' The other members were initially stunned and upset, but the group cohesion and trust were good enough to de-escalate the situation.
>
> After introducing the distributed governance system, they formed a General Circle, which then formally adopted the governance system.

So interestingly, this group implemented first in a unilateral decision. Even though it was lateral and not top-down, it was *power-over* in my definition because it was an overreach of their responsibility. But they apologized and acknowledged, and created a formal adoption process after the fact.

There are countless more examples of good processes where people with formal *power-over* power used their power to change governance. We've already seen Emil from the story *Fishbowl to break the power game* early on in this book who implemented top-down in his department with great success. Other clients may have implemented top-down but with much co-determination on the *how* of implementation with others from within the organization. Most of the time, that works.

Bottom-up implementations

Let's go back to Emil's story because his story is both a story of top-down and bottom-up implementation. While writing this book, I received notice that he had been fired from his job. I was shocked.

What had happened? Emil had been the head of the department where he had implemented their 'teal' form of self-management. The experiment ran for about seven years very successfully. He had even been asked to replicate his success in a bigger, related department.

But the departments were not an island but part of a bigger, very hierarchical situation. So when Emil's boss changed, everything became different. Once that boss heard about Emil's advanced experiments with self-management, Emil needed to go.

This reveals a significant danger in self-management efforts that didn't receive a blessing from above – those in power can pull the plug within an instant and undo the progress that took years to build. We can speculate why Emil was fired. Did his boss feel threatened? Was it all just fear? Disbelief that it could work despite the evidence?

Sometimes, it's simply obliviousness. A former head of school told me her heartbreaking story of their self-governance journey. Let's call it *School Board Pulls The Plug*.

> It all began with the student council of a boarding school in the Northeast of the USA. Students had heard about sociocracy and taken training under the radar of the school administration. But over time, when the student council's effectiveness had increased noticeably, the head of school became curious.
>
> Randa, an educator and administrator with a deep and systemic understanding of organizations, quickly saw the potential in circle-based, consent-based governance. The more she learned, the more she loved it. She got her teachers and administration trained and slowly implemented the new governance structure, slowly handing off more and more power.
>
> It wasn't without struggle. Randa was needed in many places, and it took a lot of work to run a school and change its governance simultaneously. Randa knew the implementation was under-resourced. She knew too much depended on her, but she was ready to push through for the school's and the teachers' sake, who soon began to love the new sense of empowerment.
>
> It seemed like they had reached critical mass when the work became too much for Randa – burnout. Randa hoped it was an acceptable moment to leave.
>
> The legal board – which didn't hear much about self-management and didn't get trained – made a hire. Self-management was not part of the process or the qualifications for the new hire.
>
> When the new head of the school came in, self-management was stopped instantly and it was back to command-and-control governance.

For good measure, here's another heartbreaking story that's very similar, *Governance Recommendation Ignored*.

This professional association, incorporated as a nonprofit, had a board, a handful of staff, and a few hundred members.

Historically, the board needed to do a better job of making its work transparent, and people grew impatient. People who wrote to the board didn't get replies, or it took months to hear back. It was unclear to members how people became board members and what they did.

A group of people initiated a process that would propose a new governance system that would be more participatory and inclusive. The initiators asked the board for buy-in on whatever process the governance exploration team would develop.

Here's where the stories of recollection differ in what happened. Some say that the board had allowed the process to make a recommendation. Others say the board promised that whatever recommendation would be worked out would be accepted automatically by the board. Several dozens of thousands of dollars were freed up to compensate people for their time, which was seen as a commitment from the board and management.

The governance redesign effort drew in dozens of people and unleashed a lot of excitement. Along the way, there were value clashes and disagreements within the community, but also alignment and a growing sense of empowerment. A new future seemed possible!

A group made it across the finish line and submitted a formal recommendation – a fully formed governance method – to the board.

There is no clarity of what happened next. But it is certain that the governance change never happened, not even parts of it. The whole process came to nothing, leaving a painful scar in the community.

What do we learn from this? Firstly, it's again the learning that those in power can make or break new governance initiatives. But there's more to learn here. Note that what I'm writing is not a criticism of the failed efforts, just an attempt to contribute to learning and reducing the chance of repetition.

If we look at the process, there might have been a lot of *power-with* in working up the governance recommendation *but* there was not enough *power-with* with the board. If the board – or designated parts of the board – had been more integrated in the process, it would have been easier to make this shift together. Instead, it created an *us vs. them* dynamic with all the symptoms of *power-under* and *power-over* that come with it.

It requires a lot of trust and relationship to transition from a hierarchical system to a *power-with* system in a top-down implementation. The same is true for bottom-up implementations, and if there isn't enough trust, it will likely go down in flames.

Now, this is all easy to say. As a consultant, I often feel conflicted when I support projects that don't have the superior's blessing (yet), and asking about who has the power to determine the governance system is on my checklist for the very first conversation. Putting effort into changing a governance system is only worth it if the deciders are on board. But sometimes the deciders are simply too far above those interested, or it might be that the deciders will want evidence before giving their blessing so that people might work towards visible successes first. Experiments, even those without a formal blessing, can pave the way for bigger changes.

Power-with implementations

Given that our starting point is most likely *power-under* or *power-over* (with no one in charge), is it even possible to implement self-governance in a *power-with* way?

In an ideal form, an implementation needs a place to start from. Typically, there are initiators but that's not enough. Just like a blob can't develop agency, a few rogue actors can't act on behalf of the organization to change its governance. That means the first step is to create a structure that has the responsibility and authority to *make* such a change. That's typically an implementation or change team.

If an organization (or a department) *doesn't* have the power to make this decision, for example, because the mother company forbids it, even the internal self-organization will be inhibited. (Remember Prosocial's Core Design Principle 7, the authority to self-govern, as a success factor!)

For the scope of this book, I'm less interested in the mechanics of implementation but more in the conditions to make it a *power-with* process. In an ideal situation, we can create *power-with* by bridging the current, formal leadership with others that symbolize more of a bottom-up process in one implementation team.

Depending on the size, it can be tricky to determine who should be on that implementation team and who decides that. The struggle can shift from "who is on the implementation team" to "who decides who is on the implementation team." If its inception is considered as too top-down, it will lose legitimacy. The process that finds acceptance by everyone (or most) will depend highly on the organization.

This story, *Self-chosen implementation*, shows a way in which an organization of 150 people was able to change their governance system in a *power-with* manner.

A community of 150 people lived and worked together, running several shared businesses in a big US city. The existing leadership was tired and overwhelmed by complaints. They initiated a research project to explore alternative governance models. The research project group decided sociocracy seemed promising.

A transition team was formed to study sociocracy and make a change plan. They designed a potential organizational structure and transition process, which the leaders supported.

The process was a top-down rollout of identifying leadership for the various levels, which then turned around and identified delegates from the bottom up to complete the transition process.

As the top-down selected leaders and the bottom-up selected delegates interfaced with each other in the newly created circles, there were more minor changes in who was playing which role and how the circles' aims were identified, but the process had enough integrity to hold those kinds of changes. The launch event that put into place those circles was moderated by representatives of the old leadership and the implementation team. The implementation went smoothly.

The big question that comes up in all of these processes is one of legitimacy. Governance, in general, is a big game of legitimacy. Any system that distributes authority relies on the perception and trust that they have the power to distribute power and that they are doing so by appropriate, legitimate processes.

Legitimacy is enabled by our roles in the organization. As mentioned before, Raki doesn't act as a random worker but as Raki-from-the-billing-department when he makes billing decisions. The legitimacy to do that comes from whoever appointed him (like the Billing Circle), which got its authority from the next-higher circle in a nested system. That group, on the other hand, got its legitimacy from somewhere else.

And that's how legitimacy is a trickle-down game where each group is legitimate because of the authority it received from its next-higher entity. But who is the *source* of all this legitimacy?

3.5.2 Legitimacy

Let's start with a story, *Two Entities*, that illustrates the topic of legitimacy.

The story comes from a group in Canada with a complicated multi-entity organization construct. They had maneuvered themselves into a tricky situation and didn't know how to get out of it; at least, that's what they thought. It was a head-spinning issue!

There was 'the community' on one side, a group who wanted to buy into a housing project together. Then, there was a nonprofit with a board and team of professional staff (builders and others) overseeing the building process. To make things more confusing, some of the professionals were at the same time community members. They wanted 'the community' to take more ownership of the process because, after all, those were the people who wanted to live in the community. Then again, the professionals were clear that they wanted to build the project fairly quickly with input but also with a lot of responsibility on the project so it would move faster and more inexpensively. But they had tripped themselves up a little and didn't know how to bring those two entities together. Should the community members become members of the nonprofit? That didn't make sense because the community members were recipients of a service, not builders. Should the nonprofit become a subset of the community? Not everyone was convinced that was a good idea. Should the two entities co-exist with mutual board membership somehow?

While finding out what structure and combination between the two entities would give them what they were hoping for, it became clear to me that that was not our only question. There was a more complicated question underneath: even if they *could* find a way to combine the two entities, who would decide that this would be *the* way?

It was clear that everyone was well-intended. No one questioned the legitimacy of the group that met with me, but they felt insecure about it. Sadly, their situation had no strong founder personality and no other place to draw external authority from. They also didn't have a strong moral argument to prove their legitimacy was grounded in morals. So I looked at option number 3, legitimacy via good process.

I knew returning to the other 40 people in the maze of organizations and relationships was bound to fail. There was no way to include everyone because it's hard to get 40 people on board for any decision that requires reading a dense governance document and weighing the pros and cons of governance choices. They also had a significant number of only loosely connected members, and it would be hard to make a decision look legitimate if no clear super-majority were present for the decision.

Also, because of the complexity, I knew that if they took the decision back to the large group, several months of soul-searching would ensue, and the process to get to this point had already worn them out.

So instead, I asked them how confident they felt that the large group had mandated them to make this decision of adopting a new governance method when they had been formed originally. They all felt strongly that they had been chosen for that purpose. That was some ground to stand on! I felt relieved because, to me, that was solid legitimacy. But some of them still felt awkward about making such a big decision on behalf of the whole organization, including future members. And that's when I decided to use a magic trick of governance.

Reminding them that they had just told me that they felt like they had the mandate to make the decision, I asked them for consent on the following proposal: "we hereby affirm that we have legitimacy to make a decision about governance in XX". Somehow, saying yes to that seemed easy to them because it just reaffirmed the mandate they understood they had been given. Interestingly, they all consented to that proposal without hesitation.

I pointed out to them that this decision would need to stand even if there might be a little bit of quarrel in some corners of the organization and that they would need to be 'legitimacy buddies' to each other. If someone would ever question the legitimacy of the decision, they would need to back each other up and confirm that in fact they *did* have the power to decide 'because that was decided'.

I was aware that we were creating legitimacy out of thin air. They were aware, too – there was some giggling and a little bit of insecure smiling.

Legitimacy is a funny thing. In a way, we had to build the foundation for the next step. We revisited the basic governance proposal they had selected earlier, and then they were happily ready to consent.

We all have a strong sense of what's legitimate, but it can be hard to define. People forget that legitimacy is largely fabricated. That it works when it is accepted. 'The founding fathers' didn't have any more right to form a state on the land than this nonprofit delegation had the power to decide their group's governance structure. But they needed permission to see it that way because they found it hard to claim that power. I had played deus ex machina by affirming them that they had the power to give *themselves* authority.

Recall what I said about declarations in section 2.4.4 on speech acts. Legitimacy often gets created by a declarative, sometimes even with the tell-tale magic word *hereby*, like in "The Corporation is hereby authorized to execute agreements . . . to the fullest extent permitted by law." A statement like that just creates legitimacy out of nowhere, simply by stating it. If someone uses the word *hereby*, then they presuppose that they *have* the power to *grants* someone else (or themselves!) a certain authority.

By-laws often have a phrase that creates legitimacy, and then a Rules and Regulations document that tells how the self-granted authority is acted upon and distributed in the organization. Foundational documents often refer to external (pseudo) sources in an attempt to increase the subjective sense of legitimacy, for example, historical documents, religious texts, or codes like the Hippocratic Code. We've even seen our own governance manual, Many Voices One Song, quoted in other organization's foundational documents ("as stated in. . . ") which is quite funny because my internal reaction is "wait, you can't rely on that, we are also just humans who wrote that."

It's essential to see that the legitimacy game never ends because there is no *absolute* legitimacy. I just wrote this book, relying on others that also just wrote things, based on others. There is no absolute foundation. After all, we're all just visitors on this planet. In my world, an organization can't be owned because we're so interdependent that formal ownership can seem like an arbitrary line we draw between the inside and the outside. Any organization, including start-up businesses, build on knowledge, skills, ideas, resources, and a space that come from somewhere else or are shared 'assets' in the first place. Nothing and no one is truly 'self-made', and that undermines the legitimacy of the concept of absolute legitimacy.

Creating legitimacy

I dove deeper into the concept of legitimacy in the legal sense and learned that there are several ways to acquire or fabricate legitimacy.

- *Descriptive* legitimacy comes into play when an individual or group follows established norms or rules, hence being perceived by others as legitimate. An example would be if a founder formally appoints their son as their successor. Since the founder has the authority to do so and the act is in line with an accepted norm or process, this endows the son with descriptive legitimacy.

- On the other hand, there's *normative* legitimacy, which goes beyond mere adherence to rules. This form of legitimacy assesses whether the group's or individual's authority is morally justifiable. It aligns the exercise of power with ethical standards, societal values, and the organization's goals. Thus, a leadership transition would possess normative legitimacy if, for example, the son was not only appointed by the founder but also demonstrated competence, integrity, and alignment with the organization's values in his new role.

To illustrate these forms of legitimacy, here is a story where a tension escalated to all levels, *Who Can Close The Common House?*

> This story is set in a consent/circle-based living community project during the pandemic. They faced a tricky decision. Who would decide whether or how the shared community building could still be used?
>
> For some, it was obvious that the decision would be, just like all decisions related to the community building, Common House Circle that would hold the decision in its domain. Yet, typically decisions this circle made were limited to choosing what color to paint the guest rooms, so this was out of the ordinary. The unusual situation had led to an unusual amount of decision-making power.
>
> As tasked, Common House Circle issued a Common House use policy during the pandemic.
>
> However, some people were unhappy with the content of the decision, and from there, it escalated. While resisters initially argued that the decision was wrong, they soon argued that the Common House members weren't qualified to make this decision.

Note how the reasoning changed! It's not about the decision anymore but about the legitimacy. If unqualified people make a decision, should it even be followed?

> That line of reasoning didn't get much traction with some other community members, so the resisters of the community Common House policy went to the next level of escalation: they questioned whether the Common House Circle really had the power to make this decision, arguing it was beyond their domain. That, again, didn't go very far because the case was relatively straightforward that Common House Circle decides about, well, the Common House!

Note how they were still questioning the different kinds of legitimacy, now going to descriptive legitimacy.

> Since the resisters were deeply invested in un-doing the decision, they now argued that a governance system that gave a small group the

power to decide a Common House use policy was bad in the first place and shouldn't stay in effect.

Now instead of questioning the decision or the circle's legitimacy, they questioned the governance system as a whole. This incident poked a hole into the legitimacy of the governance system in the community overall – and not just in this organization.

If someone wants to question legitimacy, they almost always can. In their case, someone could have questioned who had been selected in the first place. In the *Two Entities* story, one could question whether I was legitimately making those proposals and whether they were allowed to give themselves the power. The question is not whether legitimacy is waterproof; the question is whether the legitimacy is accepted – or *accepted enough*. Our own sense of legitimacy for ourselves and others is always also a guess of how legitimate it will seem to others.

Vitalik Buterin[8], the co-founder of the blockchain-based platform Ethereum, says, "[l]egitimacy is a pattern of higher-order acceptance. An outcome [...] is legitimate if the people in that social context broadly accept and play their part in enacting that outcome, and each individual person does so because they expect everyone else to do the same."

The concepts of descriptive and normative legitimacy distinguish between how legitimacy is perceived and whether that perception is morally or ethically justified. Another helpful way to see legitimacy is via Max Weber (1919) who distinguishes between three types of legitimacy and authority:

- Traditional Authority: This type of authority is based on long-established customs, traditions, and hereditary rights. People obey traditional authority figures because it's the way things have always been done.
- Charismatic authority is based on the personal qualities, or charisma of an individual leader. People follow charismatic leaders because they are inspired by their personality or vision.
- Rational-Legal Authority: Rational-legal authority is grounded in a system of rules, laws, and institutions. It is the dominant form of authority in modern bureaucratic societies. Legitimacy in rational-legal authority is based on the belief that the authority's actions and decisions are consistent with a legally established framework and set of rules.

Let's see examples of how legitimacy can be created or maintained.

---

[8]Buterin 2021

Legitimacy through external authority   If a group has been formally mandated via an existing process, we can assume they have legitimacy, for example by saying "the elected board formally empowers the governance task force." Another way would be if the founder gives their blessings to a project. We have to find someone to refer to when we say, "xyz said we can adopt this new governance system."

The most common way is when an organization gets incorporated or formed by another organization or person, like the legal owner. The same is true when a group or individual is formally appointed or mandated via existing processes; they are then seen as legitimate because they adhere to established rules or norms.

Here's an example of a founder playing that role:

> I worked with an organization of 15 people that wanted to foster co-leadership and said they operated by co-leadership already but wanted to formalize a more defined *power-with* system.
>
> They also wanted to align their new system with their legal formal structure. Their founder was currently the nonprofit's Executive Director, and everyone loved and admired her.
>
> Despite their insistence that they were operating on equal grounds and all we needed to do was to formalize their informal peer-based system, I soon noticed that everyone looked to *her* on whether this new governance method was okay to adopt. They tried to read the signs of whether she was for real, given that the new system would restrict her power and elevate everyone else's, switching from a classic hierarchy to a *power-with* system.
>
> It was clear that she'd be the source of legitimacy of any new system and that no one would question what she supported. Luckily, the founder always talked affirmatively about the new, *power-with* system, and she was comfortable with her power and using it to *spread* power, so it made the implementation of the new, *power-with* framework easy.

It's more complicated when people aren't comfortable with the power they have. We've already seen this in the company where the CEO leaned back and left the organization to its own devices in the story *Ship With No Mast*. Because he was so hands-off and created a bagel-shaped organization with only operational teams but not organization-level functions, the center couldn't be filled, and the power just sat in the middle, unclaimed.

Legitimacy through a higher moral standard   Sometimes, organizations approve a governance system because they are convinced it is best-suited. That can sound like this: "We are adopting this new governance system because it's the most aligned with our values."

That can happen when an organization has a strong emphasis on collaboration or cooperation or other principles that align well with a governance system they want to adopt. Here's my story about this. It's a second-hand story that someone relayed to me so I hope it's true!

> It was a reconciliation and reparations group that had existed for about two years in Ontario, Canada. It was a group that consisted of indigenous groups and non-indigenous members.
>
> They discussed what kind of governance system they wanted, and many wanted one based on indigenous practices. Yet, some indigenous members were heavily against that because they considered it an act of cultural appropriation.
>
> They then found sociocracy and formed a council that would assess sociocracy as a governance system. That council of the majority indigenous people concluded that sociocracy was close to indigenous practices but could not be seen as an act of appropriation, which led them to give their blessing to adopting sociocracy.

That's an excellent example of a moral ground for adopting a particular governance system. It worked, which means it had enough legitimacy to fit the purpose.

Through 'good' process   Sometimes, there is no external source and no strong (enough) moral ground. We can still create legitimacy by following what is accepted as a 'good process.' An example is that it is commonly accepted if a group elects to change a team by majority vote; for example, if the formal leadership appoints one or more people and the workers get to add worker representatives via a voting mechanism, members would likely accept it as legitimate.

When a formal process like a majority vote is used to determine a course of action, this can be seen as an example of descriptive legitimacy because it follows established norms. If this process is also considered fair, transparent, and reflective of the organization's values, it could contribute to normative legitimacy.

If the process is questionable, legitimacy fades. See this example and see what you think. Was this group in *German Delegation* a legitimate group?

It was a group of German practitioners of a particular methodology in conversation with a professional association.

No German center existed, so the German practitioners were certified via the global center.

This group of six people introduced themselves as the "delegation of practitioners in the German-speaking world". They brought demands from "the German community" towards the international organization about the certification process.

While they explained their claims, it became clear that making agreements with them didn't make much sense. These six Germans weren't elected or chosen by any set process. Therefore, even if agreements would be made with them, it would be unclear to whom these agreements would apply.

They were asked who 'sent' them to talk to the international organization and who they spoke on behalf of. They said they were "elected" which seemed surprising given that there was no known German entity to hold an election. When pressed to say how they were elected, they said, "We tried to ask everyone and no one said no."

Would you consider this group a legitimate group to make a decision?

I understand that this group didn't have a governance system (or defined membership) and, therefore, wasn't able to make any formal decision. 'Lazy consent' – asking everyone to see if anyone says no – only provides a strong form of legitimacy when we have truly gotten a response from everyone and everyone understood what they've been asked. But in this case, it was clear that they had sent a few emails and asked in a few calls and that they were far away from having a formal buy-in from 'the' German-speaking members. It was a set of individuals and not an organized collective. Therefore, there was no shared agency and not enough structure to empower anyone to make decisions on their behalf. This is no one individual's fault, it's a lack of systems in the collective overall. It's also hard to retrofit these structures when a loose community already exists and no structure has emerged or been put in place. A blob doesn't have much agency to improve its clarity of systems.

It's happened to me countless times that potential clients contact me in the middle of these fundamental governance issues, and it's quite common that they can't be helped. The most memorable moment was when a group told me this: "Ted, everyone in the group agrees that we want to hire you to help us with our governance issues, but we don't know how to make the decision". I never heard from them again and the group folded and dispersed a few months later.

Here's another story of lacking legitimacy, but in this one, my judgment was that the lack was self-chosen in a *power-under* way.

> A team of 2 people had been tasked by a foundation to host an online community looking at ways to provide better insurance to digital nomads.
>
> It was an exciting project. They were considering implementing a circle-based, consent-based governance system for subscribers of the insurance project.
>
> When asked who gave them the mandate to explore governance solutions, it turned out that they weren't sure. They had been put in place by the foundation that paid for the exploration, but they didn't see themselves having the power to decide the governance system.
>
> Instead, they wanted 'the members' to decide on the governance system. The problem was that 'the members' was a discord channel with more than a thousand people who talked online. It was clear to me that an unstructured group of a thousand people who don't know each other would never be able to design a governance system. They needed to work with a subset.
>
> The consultant suggested that the staff facilitate the discussion, design and improve, and then propose a governance system. Yet, they were unwilling to do that, saying that the governance system should come from 'the members.' I insisted that this was almost impossible to do. Even if a small group of members found each other in discord and worked on a governance system, then how would it get approved after? For example, what if someone doesn't like their proposal and makes a counterproposal? And even more, how will it be adopted by majority vote? Who will decide how it will be approved?

Most interestingly, they disappeared from the radar. I recently looked them up and noticed they had implemented a hierarchical structure with an executive team. I have no idea how the story continued, but it's curious that there wasn't enough legitimacy for a system of self-governance but enough to institute a centralized power system. I guess the question of legitimacy didn't need to be answered when one just puts a structure on top!

Once we see legitimacy, it's everywhere. It's in the discussions of indigenous rights, arguments between state and federal levels, in international relationships, it's in courts overruling previous rulings, and in fundamental decisions of who gets to set the narrative. Self-management and more self-empowerment of groups cannot be understood without considering the mechanics and psychology of legitimacy.

Who owns the constitution?

In the previous sections, I focused on the legitimacy of making and approving a proposal for a governance change. But as I've pointed out in other sections, *making* a change is not enough – whatever decision we make, it also has to be *changeable in the future*. So the question is, in whose domain is the governance system? Once it is in place, who can change it?

Different frameworks have their own answers. There are systems of self-management where the governance system (constitution) can only be changed externally, or it's put in place and cannot be changed. Just like a static set of aims and domains can stifle innovation and adaptability within an organization, a static governance system might decrease the level of evolution and adaptation an organization can make.

In Holacracy, the constitution can be changed by the *Ratifiers*. Ratifiers are the people who have signed the Holacracy Constitution, agreeing to cede their power to the rules and processes of Holacracy. They are typically the founders, directors, and other high-level executives of the organization. They can amend or repeal the Constitution using whatever authority they relied upon to adopt it, provided any amendments are made in writing.

In sociocracy, the counterpart of the constitution, which we often call the governance agreement, can, in theory, be placed in any domain as the organization sees fit, at least if there are no legal conditions. Most often, it's the Mission Circle or General Circle that holds governance in its domain but I've seen implementations where the governance system itself is held in a department circle. From my viewpoint, I'm not aware of any disadvantages of that as long as it's clear.

In some organizations, it might be that the whole membership needs to ratify the governance agreement. That can create issues because it means that disagreements can spill over into decisions about the governance system, which can divide the organization. Imagine ten people in a group of 100 who want to make a change in governance – for example, give circle leaders significantly more power – and the other 90 disagree. That's a large group of people to have a conversation with on a topic that requires nuance and good listening. Many blobs never have the change to evolve.

But even beyond that, the most worrisome outcome is a situation where the governance system lives nowhere and change requests have no place to be received or considered.

3.5.3 Centralization and decentralization

The subsidiarity principle is a fundamental concept in political and social philosophy. It says that matters should be handled by the smallest, lowest, or least centralized competent authority rather than a higher or more centralized one. Higher-level authorities, such as governments or institutions, should only step in when local or lower-level entities are unable to effectively handle a particular issue or when there are broader common interests at stake that require coordinated action.

In the self-management movement, radical decentralization is celebrated as *the* way to go. And while I think that more decision-making on 'lower' levels of the organization is good, it's also clear from what we've seen so far that decentralization *only* – as an instance of autonomy – would mean to miss the other side of alignment. Decentralization is not wrong but it's only one side and therefore incomplete.

An organization needs to be able to be aligned to have agency so the big unifiers like strategy, budget, aim, mission, information flow, and governance system need to be in place to give the system agency. So *both* are needed, centralization and decentralization.

As I've said in section 3.5.3, in a system that *places* power intentionally and collaboratively, the system can decentralize and centralize power as needed. Many decisions can be made centrally – centering unity – *or* in a decentralized way – emphasizing autonomy, and cumulatively changing culture.

The distribution of power within a decentralized organization is thus reflected in the choices made by its parts, resulting in varying degrees of centralization and decentralization. If a lot of individual domains are centralized, the organization will, overall, have a more centralized feel. If domains are very decentralized with lots of autonomy and trust, it will have a decentralized flavor. Here are some examples:

- A centralized vs. a decentralized budget
- More/less emphasis on central information systems
- Many policy decisions that regulate everyone, fewer operational decisions that leave autonomy
- Declared values vs. a more undefined, open value set
- Central metrics vs. local metrics

Additionally, organizations may experience different dynamics based on whether they are putting emphasis on roles or collectives (teams or circles). In some organizations, roles are used so heavily with so much independent autonomy that it almost feels like a set of individuals working loosely towards a shared aim. In other organizations, where circles are the main emphasis, it can still feel decentralized but with more sense of alignment.

Let me be clear about one difference here. When discussing centralization, I do *not* mean (coercive) top-down hierarchy. We often see centralization in coercive, top-down organizations but that's not the only way to centralize. When I talk about centralization, I talk about chosen centralization where autonomous parts opt into the system willingly for the sake of the group. Here's an example, in *Centralized Pay Rate*.

> A social justice platform had started with largely volunteers. Over time, more and more people took on hours that were paid.
>
> The organization had a strong ethos of autonomy, trust, and self-determination so there was no salary policy. In the absence of an organization-wide policy, every circle was able to determine the pay rate for each role they approved and filled. Budgets were organized and approved by circles so circles were free to set whatever pay rates they considered appropriate.
>
> Over time, people grew uncomfortable and asked for more guidance around determining pay. They *wanted* a centralized system.
>
> Finally, a circle assumed power and created, with feedback, a system. When it was instituted – legitimatized by the General Circle – the dominating sentiment in the organization was relief. While there were individuals here and there who disliked this or that about the new system, overall, people were happy with this level of centralization.

In this story, what's important to see is that the new system was made centrally – and in a way that means top-down – but that it was still chosen. If a circle decides not to follow the system, what would happen?

The question is what happens when, over the years, maybe more and more parts of the organization get centralized in this way; the people who asked for the centralized system might leave over time and new people come in that don't know that it was chosen. Would they experience it as mandated? How much proactive choice can be maintained over time?

There are two crucial factors here. One is the question of how the circle was populated and mandated that made the decision. In a circle-/role-based system, that power to make decisions in the domain of pay rates comes from somewhere. Therefore, there is a consent-based context that provides legitimacy, making it not coercive.

The other factor is that in self-governed organizations, traditionally there is more of a culture of getting feedback from outside of the decision-making team. Yet, that's hard to enforce and depends on people filling linking positions, and overall responsiveness. Each group in a decentralized system continuously needs to maintain its legitimacy by being responsive, productive, and accountable. Participation needs to be lived.

Here's an example, *Outdoor Cats*.

> The community had had a decade of tension about outdoor cats. Opinions were extremely divided – some people hated cats because they pooped into the sandbox and killed birds. Others considered cats beloved members of their family. A circle faced the difficult task of settling the years of tension with a policy.
>
> The circle invited community members for exploration and input. It set up salons for cat lovers to talk to cat haters and surveyed the whole community on the issue. The circle drafted a policy, which was far from perfect, but rather an arbitrary compromise – which was acknowledged. At this point, making *a* decision will be better than no decision and more tension.
>
> The policy set a cap on the number of outdoor cats in the community. And it required that each person who got a new cat had to talk to their neighbors in a direct, in-person conversation, to witness the impact of their decision.
>
> There have been only two new cats in the community since, and no new tension in about 9 years of practice under the new policy.

Note that the policy was made with feedback, and it combined a centralized aspect – the cap – as well as a decentralized strategy – everyone talk to their direct neighbors. I count this story as a solid success story both in how the policy was made and in what the policy said, carefully balancing feedback, centralization, and decentralization into a mix that works.

Help Desks Effective systems often *combine* centralized and decentralized approaches. Let's look at the example of conflict resolution to show the integration of decentralization and centralization for effectiveness:

- **Centralized:** Appointing a central ombudsperson or ombuds circle that anyone can call upon to support conflict resolution as needed.
- **Decentralized:** Ensuring sufficient structures, resources, and skills are in place throughout the organization so that conflict resolution can occur wherever conflict arises. That may involve training individuals to address conflict independently and implementing standardized procedures or processes that anyone can use to engage with and resolve conflicts.

A specific strategy to create hybrid forms of centralization and de-centralization is by forming circles that perform *dual functions*. In my organization, we call these *help desks*. A help desk circle *both* carries out work and supports *other* circles in completing that work themselves. Help Desks can be an effective bridge when neither centralization nor decentral-ization alone can adequately support the organization, and a combination can't be reached otherwise.

To illustrate the concept of a Help Desk circle, let's use the example of combining the centralized function of an ombuds circle with oversight and proactive support for decentralized conflict resolution. The Ombuds Help Desk now has two objectives:

- *Providing* conflict resolution and mediation for roles and circles within the organization.
- Assisting *other* circles in implementing conflict resolution and me-diation themselves.

The Ombuds Help Desk can act on demand as needed, but it can also step back if all circles can handle their issues.

Here's another example: imagine a Webinar Circle that both *hosts* webinars and supports *other* circles in conducting webinars. If another circle, such as the School Development Circle (SDC), wants to host a webinar on the organization's platform, they would contact the Webinar Circle. The Webinar Circle can either take on the task and conduct the webinar as part of its regular operations or act as a Help Desk, supporting the SDC in running the webinar themselves. In this way, the Webinar Circle empowers and assists the SDC, acting as a service provider for webinars.

Help Desks are a good strategy to reconnect topical domains in an organization with regional chapters. Let's say we have a central Website Circle as well as regional chapters. Who holds the initiative if we want to redesign the contact page on the website for the French chapter? Website Circle or the French unit?

Without the concept of help desk circles, the only way to place domains without confusion is to either have a local Website Circle for every language (requiring the commitment of people time and money) or to have all the regional circles' websites done by the central Website Circle (giving local circles only limited agency). With a help desk function, Website Circle can be the team that makes websites by default but can also support those chapters that want to make their own website by providing training and guidance, empowering more of a decentralized stance.

A good Help Desk is findable, clear, and supportive, ensuring that it

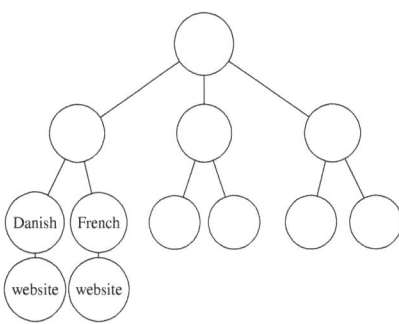

Doubling effort, local autonomy   *Efficient, less local autonomy*

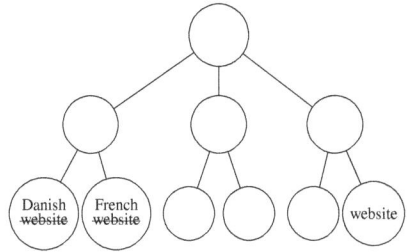

effectively assists work circles within the organization in achieving their
goals. It provides templates, sample workflows, documentation, and other
useful materials to facilitate the work of these circles. A Help Desk can
make direct agreements to clarify domains and operational handoffs, for
example, specifying that English/French Circle needs to maintain the basic
page setup with a footer and header but can change everything else.

These organizational structures require careful thought to identify the
primary responsibility of providing a service (in this case, language-based).
Then, we define all other, secondary relationships as service relationships
– in this case, the website publishing service.

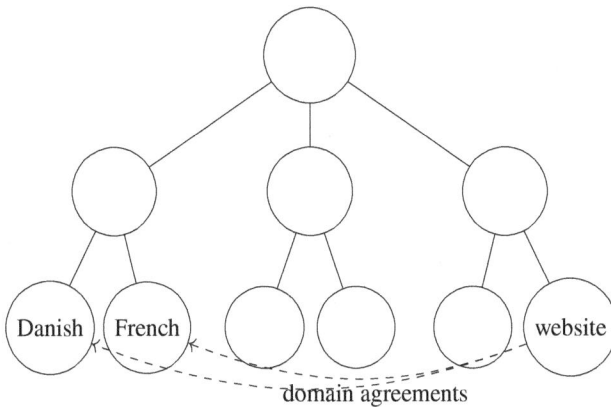

A help desk supports other circles to encourage decentralization and autonomy
in other places

Furthermore, a Help Desk may also serve as an aggregator of data that can help inform the work of various circles within the organization. By collecting and analyzing relevant information, a Help Desk can provide valuable insights that contribute to more informed decision-making and efficient operations across the organization. In this way, a Help Desk offers practical support and is vital in promoting collaboration, knowledge sharing, and overall effectiveness within an organization.

A related pattern, often called a peach pattern (e.g., in Sociocracy 3.0), is a help desk circle system that primarily delivers services to client-facing circles. It's a structure where most energy is in the producing teams (System 1 in VSM), and there's a loosely connected system of help desks on call that support those client-facing teams in different areas. This pattern can be useful if an organization is primarily involved in projects of a more fluid nature because services can be delivered with lots of operational autonomy. It can be low on strategic direction between System 1 and the other Systems.

Multi-perspectives and balance   The level of decentralization and centralization also depends on how much intermixing between roles. Let's contrast an organization with a coarse chunking of roles where every person in the organization holds one operational role that keeps them busy for 40 hours a week. Everyone is a member of one or two teams, but not more. Let's imagine the other extreme, where an organization has a fine-grained use of roles, and every person fills 12-15 roles in several teams. It's clear that between the two different organizations, dynamics around (de)centralization will play out differently.

The good thing about having many roles is that we can hold many perspectives in one decision. Let's imagine the six people making a decision together where everyone holds at least three roles in different corners of the organization. Now, we have 18 unique perspectives in the room – and in reality, even many more – that inform our decisions. That's powerful and yet still manageable. In either case, strength lies in combining perspectives, not in a monoculture of perspectives.

By increasing interconnectedness and alignment, striving for more mixed roles in an ever-changing constellation can make for a strong and resilient organization. It needs to be balanced with the commotion frequent role changes bring and the potential overload to people in many different, changing roles. It can also get chaotic, with people forgetting what has been talked about and where, and ironically, it can hinder information flow because everyone assumes that everyone else got informed somewhere else.

It's a matter of balance again, but a balance that needs to be created by many individual decisions in many places. It's more a pattern that emerges than a strategic decision that can be made centrally. It can still be steered with the appropriate buy-in.

For example, my organization would like to consolidate more roles on fewer people over time; one way to do that is to give new roles to people already in existing paid roles and instead of hiring new people into roles. This cannot be enforced in a system where teams are free to choose how they fill roles, but teams might follow the recommendation out of free choice, thus creating a unified approach by aligned, individual actions.

Roles can invite multi-perspectiveness. One can enhance this approach by defining roles that hold more abstract pieces. For example, one person in a team could hold the Steward Of The Seven Generations role or the Environmental Guard, Affordability Admin, or Value Steward. Yet, cognitive costs – mental overload – will limit how many roles we can hold and consider at once, both as one person and as one group.

Some people strive to have a system where "everyone affected by a decision makes the decision," but it's easy to see how that's impractical. It's unlikely that we'll always get *everyone* into the same room, which is affected by a decision. Our goal should not be to represent *people* but to represent *perspectives*, and feedback is a way to invite input from all affected. It's much easier to interview and consider the data from interviews with 1000 people than to invite 1000 people to make a decision together.

If feedback is taken seriously, it can be a factor of alignment on the organizational level. Suppose we hear feedback from the *inside* of the organization (from other individuals and other teams). In that case, we can hear how well a practice is working for others in the organization, increasing how well the parts and activities fit together. Getting feedback can even be the only unifier in place of shared decision making for alignment.

Organizations that use the so-called advice process limit shared decision-making on the team or organization level and entrust individual roles (or sets of individuals) and simply ask them to get feedback from colleagues to make sure there is alignment with others. The advice process might be codified in an organization to say how many people someone needs to get feedback from (and how) to make it safe enough. This is a way to balance autonomy and alignment, centralization and decentralization, with a different strategy, but too much individual action may raise legitimacy questions.

3.5.4   Side-note: Organization-level membership

In a self-managed organization, one sticky question is the question of general, organizational membership.

What does it mean to be part of an organization? Does it mean one is a worker in one of the groups? Or just a general member? A member of what?

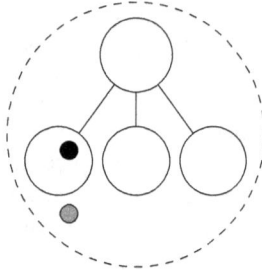

black: team member, grey: organizational member

The organization might have a system where team membership trickles up into organizational membership and that's the only way to be an organizational member. This is typically the case for paid contexts. If someone has a paid role, that makes them part of a team, and therefore part of the company. There might be open questions about contractors or external consultants.

In volunteer organizations and more complex organizations, we might have workers who aren't members, or members who aren't workers.

- Maybe team members are not members of the organization e.g. administrators in a professional organization, or the janitor in a school.
- Maybe an organization member is not a worker, for example, a board member or a supporting member. This can also happen when stakeholders are part of the organizational structure without being workers in the strict sense.

How does one become an organizational member if not via team membership? It could be by signing a value statement, paying a membership fee, opting into a certain system, or joining a slack channel. What level of legitimacy is needed is a policy decision in the organization. It doesn't follow from general principles of self-organization.

Other privileges, like access to information or resources, discounts, or event participation, might come with organization membership. As such, organization membership and team memberships must be looked at separately, and appropriate systems for tracking designed and implemented.

Defining those membranes and the rights and responsibilities of each level is not trivial. One question that often needs to be addressed, for example, is whether a person removed from a team automatically loses organization-level membership. I've seen both – someone who was removed from one team but remained in the organization. But I've also seen cases where it was argued that losing team membership automatically meant losing organization-level membership status.

This is not only a policy question but also a question of logistics, especially in a decentralized system. If a working member leaves the last team they were a part of, do they automatically lose organizational membership? Who would even notice that they are not a team member if all teams decide their team membership autonomously? Do all teams have to track organization-level membership? Keeping those systems up to date takes work when many autonomous players are involved.

Another place where this question comes up is around the onboarding of new members. Who shows them around the organizational systems? Is there a centralized onboarding system held by a Membership Circle, or is it in the individual circle's domain to onboard members to the organization-wide systems?

Being part of a collective and part of an organization that includes that collective is not the same!

3.5.5   Working with a mix of volunteer/staff members

Another dynamic affecting the level of centralization and decentralization is when there is a big power differential between members of the organization. This is very common when there is a mix of staff and volunteers. That has less to do with the fact that only some are paid, but more with the dynamic that paid workers can often spend more time in the organization than volunteers.

So how do those situations affect decentralized organizations that attempt to institute a *power-with* governance?

The main issue is that *power-with* works so much better when all members are on equal footing – equal understanding of the operations, information, and systems. But that's not true when full-time workers are in a team with people who only spend a few hours per month within the organization. The staff people are often involved in many of the operations, while volunteers might only have contact with one department. So it's not a dynamic between volunteers and staff but between less and more involved people.

Using the mental models I've introduced in section 2.2, the issue is that the less involved don't have enough shared common ground with the staff person, which means they will either have to defer to the staff person and just trust them when they make decisions they don't know enough about, or the staff person needs to fill everyone in, taking up a precious meeting time. A shared common ground is an essential starting point for collectively held power.

Sometimes, this is mixed with a power differential, for example, if a minister of a spiritual congregation works full time while volunteers run the rest of the organization. In those cases, the difference in hours is exacerbated by the reputation that comes with being a spiritual leader. In those cases, the laypeople might not say no because they fear losing the affirmation from the beloved leader, which means that shared decisions by consent are not guaranteed if not all objections surface.

In extreme examples, groups can also lack the multi-perspectives in the organization that make decentralized organizations so strong. Volunteers might only know one small part of the organization and not much from 'behind the scenes.'

All those factors contribute to a setup where the capacity for shared power is diminished. There are imperfect ways to mitigate these issues.

- Involve volunteers and invest time and energy to educate them.

  If the power differential is manageable, then the staff people's job is to fill volunteers in and give them a chance to have their own insight. That might mean visualizing financial information, taking time to report extensively, giving volunteers access to survey results to have some unmediated insight into the organization etc.

- Involve volunteers as workers, not as decision-makers.

  Some volunteers simply want to contribute. They want to plant, clean up, serve, and support but not necessarily sit in meetings. In that case, a self-organized organization might not consider the volunteers decision-making workers but 'worker bees' who simply do operations. In this scenario, the organization is a provider of volunteer opportunities, and it means little to volunteers how the organization's workers are organized.

In some cases, more involved volunteers might be asked to join a related circle as a bridge builder. The dynamics will be the same as in the previous point because those hand-picked volunteers will likely still be less informed than staff. Still, they can serve as bridge builders between those volunteers who are only involved in operations and those who also influence decisions. Either way, feedback from volunteers should be invited and considered.

- Include volunteers as decision-makers only where they are involved.

If the volunteers of an organization are motivated to shape the decisions that affect their work, teams can be formed that make decisions autonomously. This can happen with or without staff support, but volunteers here make decisions about the work they understand and are directly affected by. For example, in a congregation, maybe the kids' education program is run by volunteers and therefore, the Education Circle is volunteer only with one staff link.

In those cases, staff will still need to work extra hard to provide infrastructure, for example, by working that volunteer-based circle into the budgeting system or by proactively keeping them informed about policies made by staff that will affect them.

- Volunteers in communities of practice, the staff runs the organization.

I'm adding this pattern because it's not uncommon. In some organizations, volunteers are involved in communities of practice – groups of people who meet to support each other individually, not to accomplish a shared aim around an output that is achieved together. For example, there might be book clubs or discussion groups that are connected to an organization that hosts volunteers. In those cases, quite often, the staff hosts the communities of practice, and volunteers 'receive' the service of having a network of other like-minded volunteers to exchange ideas with or to do activities with.

The hardest dynamic about mixing volunteers and staff is being honest with each other. Too often, staff feels like they have to work extra to lift volunteers onto their level, but that often leads to frustration and overwhelm on the side of the volunteers who feel like the bar is too high to contribute meaningfully and staff who are frustrated when volunteers slow down operations around infrastructure or products and services.

3.6   Chapter summary

As organizations grow beyond a team, they need structure and governance to coordinate across teams and maintain alignment with the overall aim. With that decentralization also comes the issue of knowing who can decide the overarching system of the organization.

Distributing authority and responsibility requires distributing and decentralizing decision-making into semi-autonomous groups *while* holding the organization-level functions. An appropriate balance of decentralization and centralization is needed to simultaneously allow for distributed activity and alignment. In addition, leadership on the organizational level serves as a coordinating hub and catch-all for topics not covered by existing domains, a crucial part of empowering dispersed leadership.

Yet, there are organization-level functions that need to be covered. I'm using The Viable Systems Model as a framework for the functions an organization needs: operations (system 1), coordination (system 2), control/accountability (system 3), strategy (system 4), and policy/identity (system 5). Organizations can implement those functions in various ways.

- Aims define the aligned activities in an organization.
- Missions and values can provide a deeper meaning to the actions by answering the why. Values are not binding.
- A strategy provides a bulk prioritization to guide operational decisions. It overlays activities with temporary priorities based on changing circumstances. Strategies need to balance prescription and emergence.
- Budgeting allocates finite shared resources. Approaches include centralized, decentralized, participatory, or combinations.
- Information flow and shared interpretation are key. In addition, an organization needs to steward its organization-level common ground by designing organization-wide information flow as a basis for all decisions.
- The placement of authority and responsibility comes with a need to know *how* to divide up authority & responsibility. This is encoded in organization-level governance. Unified governance, built on a shared sense of legitimacy. The legitimacy to establish governance often comes from founders, moral authority, or good process, or from a wider government that grants its existence. But legitimacy must be maintained; it's not absolute.

Chapter 4

Beyond one organization

This chapter is about cooperation beyond the organizational level – coalitions or federations between organizations and direct partnerships that enhance collaboration between organizations and movements. This categorization is not as cut and dry as I am making it seem; the reasons for that are that (a) there are no set definitions of these terms, and (b) an alliance beyond one organization may include aspects from several kinds of super-organizational organizing. For example, any organization with a more grassroots-oriented outreach might have a network 'layer' around the organization that includes people who aren't technically members but engage in events or platforms connected to the organization.

A simple and tangible example is that my organization has members. A good number of people attend events like conferences or are former members. They might know each other or contribute to the organization and other people in the network in different ways.

For this chapter, my intention is not to explain how coalitions, inter-organizational collaboration, or movements work. That's done much better in other places; for example, consider how Visa brought together various banks and financial institutions to cooperate and collaborate in developing the Visa payment system (Hock, 2005).

This chapter aims to show the broad strokes of the themes in this book – collective power based on principles of *power-with* outside of top-down hierarchies – and how they apply to collaboration beyond one organization. The basic patterns look like this:

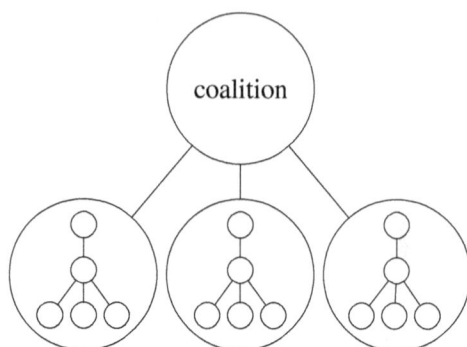

Coalition

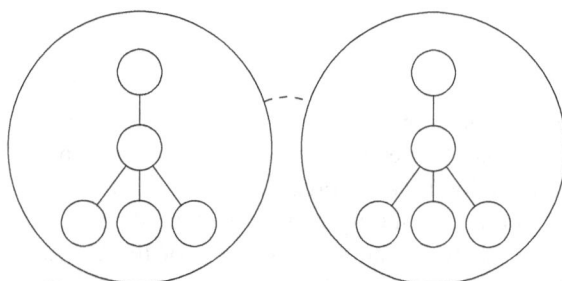

Partnership

4.1 Coalitions

Forming coalitions is in the shared interest of an organization if a coalition together can achieve something that no organization can achieve by itself in terms of impact (e.g., more effective advocacy), access to resources (e.g., pooled funding or shared knowledge) or coordination (e.g., coordination of standards).

Coalitions are collectives of organizations that cooperate around a particular aim. For example, the Climate Action Network (CAN): CAN is a global coalition of over 1,500 organizations worldwide that work together to address climate change. Their shared goal is to promote sustainable development and advocate for policies that reduce greenhouse gas emissions, increase renewable energy use, and mitigate the impacts of climate change.

Another example is the Coalition for Epidemic Preparedness Innovations (CEPI), an alliance that brings together public, private, and philanthropic organizations to accelerate the development of vaccines against emerging infectious diseases. Their shared goal is to prevent future epidemics by funding and coordinating research and development efforts for vaccine candidates.

4.1.1   A coalition of sovereign entities

Organizations are typically sovereign entities. They widely control their resources and processes (within the legal frame). And yet, they need to collaborate. This both-and of independence and interdependence is captured in the last two of Prosocial's core design principles:

- *Authority to self-govern.*

- *Collaborative relations with other groups.*

If we assume that coalitions use the same basic idea of multi-level selection, just one level higher, then the same parameters apply again. Organizations are the individuals that are autonomous actors, and coalitions form the group level. The dynamics will be the same. Organizations compete over funding and market share, clients/customers, and attention. And yet, there are situations where cooperating makes sense.

Again, remember the positive side of autonomy; each member organization is a lab for better approaches to addressing the issues in the topic scope of the coalition. For example, two organizations might each be focused on alternative energy storage solutions that would help the coalition, even when it means that two members are in direct competition. The more variety, the more innovation, the better the ideas that evolve. So, even from the coalition point of view, friendly competition can be constructive. And just like all other polarities of this kind, it's governance and agreements that can reign in competition to a constructive level and foster prosocial, coalition-supporting behavior.

In a collective impact initiative, multiple organizations work towards a common agenda, leveraging their unique strengths and resources. The backbone organization serves as the backbone of this collective effort, providing essential infrastructure and support to enable effective collaboration. The five key conditions for shared success in collective impact are described like this:[1]

---

[1]Turner et al. (2012)

- Common Agenda. All participants have a shared vision for change, including a common understanding of the problem and a joint approach to solving it through agreed-upon actions.

- Shared Measurement. Collecting data and measuring results consistently across all participants ensures efforts remain aligned and participants hold each other accountable.

- Mutually Reinforcing Activities. Participant activities must be differentiated while still being coordinated through a mutually reinforcing action plan.

- Continuous Communication. Consistent and open communication is needed across the many players to build trust, assure mutual objectives, and appreciate common motivation.

- Backbone Support. Creating and managing collective impact requires a separate organization(s) with staff and specific skills to serve as the backbone for the entire initiative and coordinate participating organizations and agencies.

In collective impact initiatives, a backbone organization can be that coordinating entity for more impact, especially in a social or environmental sphere. The backbone organization is like the organ that provides the functions needed by the whole and, therefore, plays a crucial role in facilitating and supporting collaboration among diverse initiative member organizations to address complex social or environmental challenges. Here are the common threads of what backbone organizations do (still from Turner et al 2012) across different collective impact efforts:

1. Guide vision and strategy
2. Support aligned activities
3. Establish shared measurement practices
4. Build public will
5. Advance policy
6. Mobilize funding

Turner and colleagues give an example of a Competitive Workforce (PCW), which "with its partners, has created a common, regionwide workforce data collection and reporting system to track results and improve performance for multiple agencies. To date, approximately 50 public and nonprofit agencies are utilizing the system, and a regional workforce dashboard is being built to aggregate key measures." That's a powerful collaboration effort, adding value to what any individual organization could have done alone.

It takes a lot of time, money and people (and some convincing) for organizations to collaborate in this way because it means potentially abandoning or modifying current activities to 'get in line' with the coalition.

Interestingly, in a *power-over* frame, the dynamics for coalitions differ from the situation in organizations. In a traditional top-down organization, the leadership can impose changes and expect compliance. However, in a coalition of organizations, this approach doesn't work because organizations tend to be sovereign entities. Coalitions operate based on choice and incentives rather than hierarchical authority. This means that coalitions function in a more collaborative and cooperative *power-with* framework already since top-down hierarchy is not an option in the first place. When organizations form a coalition, they unite voluntarily and work towards common goals, recognizing that they cannot impose their will on each other. Instead, they rely on mutual understanding, shared interests, and incentives to foster collaboration and drive collective action.

4.1.2   What makes a good coalition?

Recall the company that only consisted of operational teams and had a power vacuum in the middle that I compared to a bagel. There, I used the Viable System Model (VSM) to identify what they were missing. Now we can do the same again, just one level up. If we imagine individual *organizations* in the place of *teams*, a coalition can easily end up in the same position as the software company – a power vacuum in the middle and lack of essential 'organs' that make the whole thing work and give it agency.

A coalition that is merely a network of organizations that join as equal members with very little governance and structure might work as a connector between members of the member organizations but it will typically be weak in terms of its shared goal and direction.

We can again turn to the VSM to see what they might be missing.

Here are the different systems as described in VSM again, including an exploration of their application to coalition work.

- System 1 (Operational Units): the work towards the coalition's aim. The shared goal is often just a subset of the coalition. For example, a membership organization might work towards climate change awareness locally while the coalition works on climate change awareness globally. The same coalition might have membership organizations that focus on climate change awareness and degrowth so that the coalition only represents a subset of the organizational aim.

Whether a coalition can include System 1 depends on whether the member organizations carry out the operations toward the coalition aim. For example, the coalition wants to lobby in the United Nations while none of the member organizations do that because they are only involved in regional and national efforts. Then, the coalition will need its own operational units to carry out the operations of the coalition level.

- System 2 (Coordination), System 3 (Control/accountability): A coalition needs to coordinate the efforts of the coalition member organizations. In a collective impact scenario, there might be a backbone organization that provides the service of coordination between the members. The same is true for performance and accountability on the coalition level.

- System 4 (Strategic Planning and Development) and System 5 (Policy/Identity and Mission). The coalition needs a way to think strategically for the coalition beyond the interests of the individual coalition members. It also needs to be able to adapt to its environment and change its approach as needed. An advisory board or a backbone organization might be able to play this role.

From a VSM perspective, a backbone organization covers some of the needs in Systems 2 and 3 by offering, among other services:

- Facilitation: The backbone organization facilitates communication, coordination, and collaboration among participating organizations. It helps establish shared goals, coordinates meetings and working groups, and fosters a culture of trust and collective decision-making.

- Data and Measurement: It collects, analyzes, and shares relevant data and information to inform decision-making and track progress toward shared goals. This may involve developing a shared measurement system, monitoring key indicators, and conducting evaluation and learning activities.

- Resource Mobilization: The backbone organization plays a role in mobilizing resources to support the collective effort. This may include securing funding, coordinating in-kind contributions, and facilitating resource sharing among participating organizations.

A backbone organization is often the biggest attractor with the extra resources to steward the coalition as a whole.

Yet, many coalitions are set up without that. In the following, I will highlight some common patterns in coalition work.

4.1.3   Issues

Coalitions and networks often have a weak center, just like the bagel. The main reasons for that are often a lack of shared aim (or vague aims) as well as the fact that coalitions are often chronically underfunded. This means that the coalition cannot build enough structure to function properly, or it only functions on a very low level with low impact.

People who split their time between coalition work and work in their 'home' organization often face tough choices with finite resources – should they invest their time and energy into coalition work or into their 'home' organization? Since the coalition work often has an aim that is broader and therefore less actionable than the organizational aim, the urgent needs of the organization might trump the importance of the coalition work.

Oftentimes, coalitions are also just temporary – often aligned with funding cycles – which contributes to a weaker center because collaborations cannot mature.

Unclear or peripheral aim

As mentioned, the aim of the coalition might either be broad, or it might be specific but rather peripheral to the individual organizations' daily operations. Let's look at two examples that illustrate that.

My organization, Sociocracy For All (SoFA), is part of a coalition with a very broad aim of *supporting systems change*. While that is something SoFA stands behind because it's aligned with our mission and compatible with our aim, it's also broad. Because of the broad scope, there is a big variety of other partner organizations, making it hard to find common ground and mutuality in our daily tasks.

On the other hand, SoFA is part of a coalition that manages certification for sociocratic consultants. While that is very specific and actionable – stewarding the certification process and fostering exchange between the certified consultants – certification for consultants is just a small subset of the organization's operations. The coalition always risks being put on the back burner because so many issues and projects demand SoFA's attention.

To work effectively in a *power-with* way, coalitions can only work when (1) the individual coalition members' needs are met enough to at least partially focus on the coalition's aim and (2) when there is enough governance and agreements to coordinate on the coalition. If that doesn't happen, as usual, it's going to fall into dysfunction or power-over/power-under.

Power dynamics between coalition members

This section doesn't come as a surprise. In systems with not enough governance structure and agreements to hold the coalition and therefore, balance competition, member organizations will be more prone to play power games, sideline each other, or even undermine each other's efforts.

The more substantially the coalition is set up and the more obvious the benefits of collaboration are to the member organizations, the better the coalition will be able to mitigate and reign in competition.

Funding

Funding is a big topic in coalitions. The coordination costs of providing any structure that connects coalition partners need to be supported. That means that coalitions often form around funding sources. Since coalitions often have no revenue stream of their own, funding for coalitions is often grant funding. Another model is to ask all coalition partners to contribute a fee that supports the center.

Each organization as an individual unit depends on its own revenue stream to survive. As with any desired *power-with* situation, the system will lean away from alignment and towards self-centeredness when basic needs aren't met and organizations need to focus on their own efforts to survive.

Even if there is funding for the coalition, for example, with a big grant, member organizations will often compete for those funds because they feed their own organizations' budgets. In short, if there is no funding, the center will be weak, meaning there will be low effectiveness. If there *is* funding, then organizations will still be in selfish mode and compete over it. That changes when enough resources are available on the coalition level that aren't distributed to the organizations but held as 'overhead.' 'Overhead' has a bad reputation, but everything in this book suggests that effective cooperation is only possible with enough resources to steward it.

Shared aim, but no shared domain

While a coalition might have a shared aim, they often don't have a shared domain. This means they might have things they do together but hardly anything they decide about. They don't do operations together, so they have only limited facilities or resources they allocate as a coalition. (That's different if there is funding on the coalition level that doesn't get paid out to the member organizations.)

But here's another interesting aspect. *If* they have something they decide about, it's often resources or operations within the domain of the individual organization's domain. Let's look at an example. Let's say three organizations form a coalition to apply for funding together. They receive the grant and piece together how they split the work among the organizations. To keep it very simple and relatable, let's assume that one coalition partner is tasked with developing standards for the metrics of the coalition, and another organization is tasked with developing an IT platform for those standards. The issue is that developing the IT platform, in a self-organized context, will likely be held in a team within one organization that makes decisions autonomously.

What if the coalition-level people make a decision to change something about the IT platform? This directly rules into the domain of a working team within the coalition-member organization. That works if representatives of the IT Platform Circle are present in the coalition, but oftentimes, it's the organization's leadership that is tasked with making those kinds of agreements on the coalition level. Imagine you work in the IT department of an organization, and all of a sudden, someone tells you that the organization's coalition changed its standards and you need to spend days of work to accommodate their needs. Who wouldn't ask, wait, who are they to tell me to do that? The teams deep within the organization will often be somewhat remote from the coalition aims, leading to a weaker commitment to that level.

Another systemic struggle in coalitions is that there is insufficient overlap in operations to prioritize coalition work. For example, imagine a newly formed coalition of 12 mature organizations that want to work together towards a bigger impact. Let's say some of these organizations offer webinars and other online events as part of their operations. They might all benefit from pooling their events into a shared events calendar but it would take a lot for the member organizations to be willing to give up their webinar teams to leave it to the coalition-appointed team in another organization.

Information flow and infrastructure

As we've seen in the previous chapter, within one organization, there is often more relevant information than people or teams can process and retain. In coalition work, this effect increases significantly. Within a coalition, there is much more going on, and it often happens with much less interconnection because organizations are more siloed than units within the same organization.

For example, while it's already hard for one person to understand the details of one organization, it becomes even harder to understand budget decisions in another organization, even if that might be necessary to understand how coalition funds are spent among the member organizations.

There is also often a lack of unity around infrastructure. Finances, information flow, and task management, as well as cultural or language barriers, make it harder to understand each other and, therefore also weaken the coalition and its ability to collaborate as equals. Strategies that support coalition-building include work around interoperability – standards and tools that allow each member organization to use their own tools – e.g., their own calendar or bookkeeping system – that then can interface or be mapped onto another coalition partner's or the backbone organization's systems. Note that in collective impact initiatives, shared infrastructure, as well as shared metrics, are building blocks to work together.

Let's use a straightforward example. Suppose we have a coalition that wants to list all coalition member events. In that case, either every member organization needs to input their events manually or create and follow a system where member organization events can easily be transferred from the organization's to the coalition's website system, no matter what format it is in. If it's hard to do, it will simply not happen.

There's not only a technical but also a structural barrier. Commonly, the information flow between organizations is only upheld by a handful of organization members, or even just one member – for example, think of a situation where Executive Directors of different organizations come together to form a coalition. Oftentimes, those coalitions highly depend on the personal relationships of the people in the coalition and don't extend to the organization as a whole. That's comparable to an effect I've described earlier, where there is no common ground of mutually shared information between teams if there is just one (or even) two people who report back and forth. That is okay if autonomous teams can work together but less information is always a risk for lack of opportunity and less coherence, meaning negative power dynamics and missed opportunity costs are not far behind. In coalitions, this effect will compound because there's more information and often an even smaller and weaker bottleneck.

Coalition are much easier to dream up than to live effectively, especially when the cross-organizational collaboration isn't funded or taken care of. In the next section, we will see some more hopeful examples.

Coalitions based on incentives

While coalitions can rarely rule into organizations because organizations are sovereign, there is a way to have alignment on a coalition level without coercion.

A template for that is how the ISO standards are made. Since no international entity can rule into national legislation, the only way international standards can be made is by voluntary self-commitments. ISO standards are not legally binding; instead, they serve as guidelines or best practices that organizations can *choose* to follow. Why would organizations do such a thing? To improve their operations, products, or services, demonstrate responsibility, or gain a competitive edge. Again, these commitments are not legally binding, but implementing them benefits the organizations.

Internally, the ISO currently makes decisions through a consensus-based process involving its members, which are national standards bodies from various countries. Each technical Committees, which consist of experts from member countries who have experience and knowledge in a specific field, is responsible for developing standards within its respective field. Within the Technical Committees, there may be several Working Groups focused on specific tasks or sub-topics. Working Groups are composed of experts nominated by member countries, and they prepare drafts for new standards or revisions to existing ones. They make decisions with lots of feedback loops. As far as I understand, the goal is to reach a consensus (that sounds more like consent, as it's emphasized that not everyone needs to be in full agreement) within Technical Committees and Working Groups. At the end, there is a formal voting process at the final stage, the approval stage, with a 2/3 majority vote.

Alignment with ISO standards show that a world based on voluntary self-commitments is possible.

4.2 Interorganizational collaboration

I want to discuss inter-organizational collaboration in *direct* partnerships. While the previous chapter talked about coalitions with a center like a backbone organization, in this section, we will consider collaboration without a center that mediates it. The patterns in this section apply to 1:1 partnerships between organizations and to multi-partner networks of organizations.

Given the complexity of our world with many interdependent issues, no one organization is big enough to solve things on its own. It also doesn't seem viable or wise to build huge super-organizations. Another option is to strengthen the tissue between organizations to improve collaboration in small, nimble ways wherever needed.

Yet, while that seems to make sense, partnerships often confuse decentralized organizations, and that has at least three reasons.

- The first is that it's unclear *who* is connected.
- It's unclear what the partnership looks like.
- Changes in structures can lead to missed connections.

Let's look at the first point. Who partners with whom? We all understand what it means to be 'partners' or 'friends' as one person with another individual. But how is a *group* friends with a *group*? Or a group of groups with a group of groups? Does that mean that everyone is connected to everyone? Or are simply their spokespeople or their boards connected?

Partnership agreements can be made directly on different levels of the organizations, just as a unit or a whole. For example, Organization A may have a *mission*-level partnership with Organization B, but Organization B also has a *team*-level partnership with Organization C. So it's not enough to say we are partners; we have to specify which part of the organization is partnered with which part of the other organization.

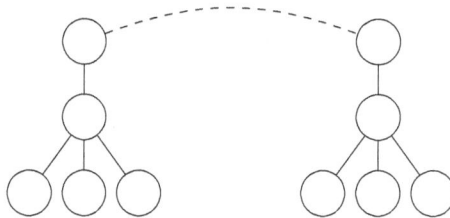

Organization A has a mission-level partnership with Organization B

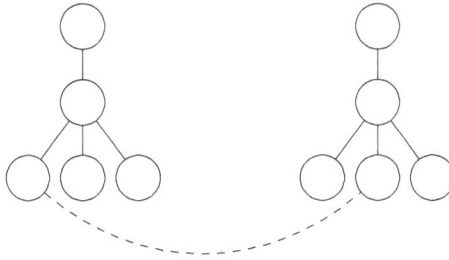

Organization B has a team-level partnership with Organization C

Secondly, it's not clear *what* partnering means. Or does it mean creating complementary interfaces? Or does it mean doing things together? And if so, how much, and how deeply?

Saying 'we're partners' without backing that with action is an empty promise. What does being partners mean? Does it mean we do things together or give each other special benefits? That needs to be defined to fill the partnership with life.

Personal relationships are different from institutional relationships, as illustrated in this next story, *Online Magazine*.

> An online magazine published articles from partner organizations and individuals over the years. The founder of another organization ABC had a good relationship with individuals in the online magazine team, and there was ongoing contact about articles being published via the online magazine. As ABC grew, this relationship grew more into a formal organizational partnership.
>
> With its growth, the internal points of connection changed. The person who held article writing in her role was not the founder anymore. ABC also hired someone for social media and for running conferences. What were *personal* relationships before needed to be transformed into *organizational* relationships.

If we see partnerships independently of individuals but instead as domain elements, they are easier to maintain as they shift over time. That means that if a team that holds a team-level partnership with an external partner forms a subteam, then it might be that the subteam needs to hold that partnership.

In the below example, Team A forms two sub-teams, Aa and Ab. Team Aa is assigned the partnering Team X.

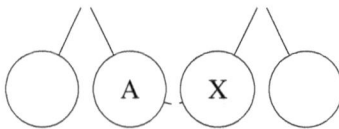

partnership connection before

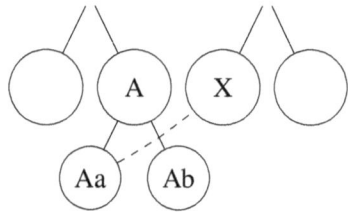

Partnership connection point shifted

Organizational relationships and goals are held locally. That can also make it hard to speak for the organization as a whole and make promises about services or shared activities that are decided elsewhere.

This issue carries over to *all external relationships* that a team within an organization has. That might be suppliers, or other corporations that a team might work with. The structure grows (and shrinks) with the work, and all relationships need to follow those changes.

Wherever cooperation between organizations is desirable – to reach a higher goal or simply to improve the work on an organizational level – we need to create enough structure to make that happen.

It then becomes an issue of interoperability on a governance level. How can we create a governance protocol allowing a shared rule across organizations? A tissue between organizations can form once collaboration protocols are robust and clear. That tissue doesn't form a superorganism but supports the information flow and innovation among the partnering organizations while maintaining autonomy of each.

- A partnership can be for information exchange only. These information-share collaborations help align work with each other, for example, because of special expertise or interdependencies. No decisions over resources are made here. There might be recommendations to the partners for synergistic action – a voluntary self-commitment.
- A partnership can include resource sharing and joint decision-making. In those cases, one partner invites members of the other organization in as decision-makers.

As a metaphor, information exchange is like neighbors chatting in the streets. Yet, if they want to sit down and eat a shared meal together, they need to decide at whose house they will eat it; one must be the host.

The agreements for collaboration either follow the script of the hosting organization, or governance agreements for the collaboration are made together.

In a perfect world, we wouldn't have to re-make those agreements each time. The example on the following page shows a minimalistic set of governance rules to ensure governance interoperability.

A minimum viable governance structure

1. The collaboration consists of _____ for the aim of _____
2. The domain of the collaboration is: _____.
3. The hosting organization is: _____. Connection point: _____.
4. Term (how long this agreement holds): _____
5. Budget allocation (partner/hosting): _____/_____
6. (optional) Each collaborator agrees to the following protocols:

   - governance protocol (this document)
   - conflict resolution playbook (elsewhere)
   - accountability playbook (elsewhere)

7. Who decides what?

   - Every team within the collaboration has a decision-making domain and is the final decision-maker on decisions in that domain.
   - The domain can be modified by mutual consent with the hosting organization.
   - The team can pass decision-making responsibility into a role or a sub-team.
   - *New* team members require *current* members' consent.

8. How do we decide?

   - Policies require consent of all team members in the domain.
   - Consent means having no objection; objections are based on misalignment with the aim.
   - Operational decisions are made by whoever or whichever team holds the decision in their domain.
   - Policy decisions require reviews upon the term end.

9. Meetings and agendas

   - The primary goal of meetings is to support alignment for operational work. Meeting agendas are set by consent.

10. Additional governance agreements will be added as needed. The domain for this protocol is in _____, and its review date is _____.

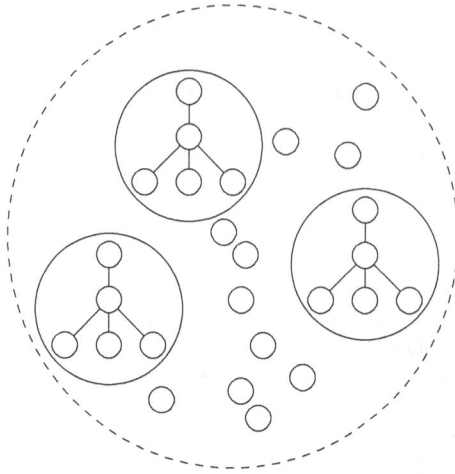

Movement (organizations and individuals)

4.3   Movements, networks and organizations

Movements are a larger-scale form of collective action that typically transcends the boundaries of specific organizations or coalitions. Unlike coalitions, movements often lack a formal center or hierarchical structure. Instead, they are characterized by a decentralized and organic nature, with individuals and groups coming together around a shared cause, vision, or set of values.

Networks are connections among individuals or smaller collectives that may or may not have a shared purpose or mission. While movements are often organized around a certain desire or demand of an external entity like the government, networks can simply exist for mutual benefit.

Networks are on a spectrum of how organized they are. Often, an organization holds and steers a network to provide infrastructure. Just like movements, networks often lack the agency that legitimizes shared action.

In my words, a network is to an organization what a community of practice is to a collective. A network exists predominantly for mutual support, influence, belonging, and shared information, while an organization together provides a product or service. Accordingly, a community of practice is a group of people sharing information and supporting each other but not acting as one unit.

That said, organizations, networks, and movements are part of a continuum without sharp lines and clear definitions, and people name the entities they belong to with little conceptual clarity.

Movements can mobilize a diverse range of individuals and organizations, often spanning different sectors, geographies, and demographics. They are driven by a shared common ground, perspective, and sense of purpose. Participants come together voluntarily and autonomously to advocate for social, political, or cultural change. The members of a movement are often self-identified and might be individuals, teams and organizations. There is no formal membership.

The difference between movements and organizations is that movements harness "the power of organizing without organizations" – the subtitle of the book *Here Comes Everybody* by Clay Shirky. Shirky points out that all organizations struggle with a dilemma first named in 1937 by later Nobel-Prize winner Ronald Coase in "The nature of the firm". To do things, firms – organizations – need to put in coordination effort. That means every action will be associated with transaction costs. If we pool our resources, we can lower transaction costs.

For example, if I work as a freelancer, I have to make my own website. If I team up with someone, we can each cut the time spent on the website. But the more people we add to the firm, the more coordination we have to do, and that equation will shape organizations.

We will get back to what this means for collective organizing. For now, let's acknowledge that putting in the legwork for collective action is costly. As I've laid out in this book, just creating common ground requires time and effort. Shared decision-making adds coordination costs, as do all the artifacts that help us steer together. It's useful only to do things together when there is a benefit.

Now, what does organizing without organizations look like, and what does it have to offer? Can new forms of organizing reduce the transaction costs associated with governance to almost nothing? Shirky makes the argument that this is the case. One of his many great examples is Wikipedia, which builds on volunteer effort to create and improve content, building a huge information commons with lots of volunteer help.

Salim Ismail and others describe A similar concept in the 2014 book Exponential Organizations. The basic idea is that traditional organizations are constrained to building infrastructure – for example, a hotel business to build new and expensive hotels to expand their business. By contrast, a business model that uses people's homes as assets, as does Airbnb, can be expanded at a super-low cost and fast.

One of Shirky's main points is the internet's and social media's role in all this. Using platforms, social media, hashtags, and similar new forms of technological features, people can find each other, share information, collaborate in production, and organize collective actions much more easily than before. Tufekci (2017) points out that for big marches or actions, the long, hard work of organizing in a more organization-like manner now starts after the first action, while before the internet, it was the other way around – that's how easy it has become to get the word out if there's interest.

4.3.1   What movements can do

So what can movements do? Movements often rely on individual action and mass participation to' do things' and bring about change.

What can they do together? As for concrete actions, the speech acts they can perform are limited. Mass movements often make requests. (They would call them demands but they have limited power to enforce them.) But it there's no organization that can pressure critical leverage points in government or institutions, a march on the street has limited power.

Yet, if ten thousand people march together at a protest, they can make a topic more salient. I'd call what they can do a mass collective expressive speech act – expressing desires and discontent or a more beautiful vision but often limited agency to act on it beyond that. It's collectively saying 'we care,' and 'this matters.'

That counts for a lot. Movements and networks can connect people and 'enrich the soil' so new projects and endeavors can grow with those new connections. Some movements turn into political parties or new organizations.

Movements can affect electoral politics and nudge leaders in key positions to change policy or other decisions. The public attention is a threat to those hoping for limited accountability.

Movements can create content and share information in a coordinated way, like Black Lives Matter, or the #MeToo movement.

Another big factor is that large groups of people can undermine the normative legitimacy of those in power by pointing out the lack of moral power. We already know that legitimacy is the currency of governance.

The more structure and cohesion there is, the more agency a movement will have. A movement, as an entity, does not possess agency in the same way as individual actors or organizations do. Instead, it is the individuals and groups within the movement who exercise agency through their shared beliefs, values, and actions. Movements provide a platform and collective space for individuals to come together, mobilize, and work towards a common goal. The agency lies in the collective power, actions, and influence of the individuals within the movement. Collective agency on the movement level is therefore low, instead collective agency will remain on the individual, organization, or coalition level.

We will return to integrating "the movement" and "the organization" in a moment.

4.3.2 What movements struggle with

Movements come with limitations and issues as well. Tufekci (2017) describes many of them alongside stories that illustrate them.

- Movements aren't able to make tactical shifts. To illustrate, she tells the story of a protest in Gezi Park in Turkey. After putting pressure on the government, the government sent a delegation to negotiate. But the protest, lacking leadership and formal processes, wasn't easily able to provide a delegation of the protesters. When that delegation had worked out a deal (to have a national plebiscite) protesters weren't sure what to think and how to respond. Confusion set it. Meetings were held. Some started leaving. As Tufekci puts it: "Ordinary people started appearing less and less in what was a chaotic, time-consuming, and lengthy process that seemed to produce no decisions, no forward momentum, no tactical shifts."

  The movement hadn't been able to change its tune and respond to its changed circumstances, which is a good example of the lack of shared agency that I've talked about throughout this book. Too little governance means too little agency and that's true for movements.

  The same happened for Occupy when their camp was taken out by the police, "it had no decision-making mechanism to help it face this inevitable turn."

- Movements that are leaning in an anti-authoritarian, egalitarian way and operate by consensus in large groups can easily have assemblies that are "burdensome and sometimes tactically disastrous for movements" (p. 99) Tufekci recounts a particularly destructive moment where a block from two people made it impossible to go with an overwhelming majority of voices in favor.

- Movements, because of the way they are set up, often are skewed in participation towards people who have time and means to put in countless volunteer hours, leading to structural bias.

- Movements are prone to power grabs from charismatic leaders. Because social media favors clicks and engagements, leaders might become "de facto spokespersons." Though egos might play a role here, they are not based on bad intentions or selfishness. "These de facto leaders find themselves in a difficult position: they attract much attention that is desirable for moments, but they lack formal recognition of their role as de facto spokespersons."

All of these patterns should look familiar! We have encountered all of them throughout the book as symptoms of too little governance to align and create collective agency.

An interesting question here is why movements choose to organize that way, given the fragility that comes with it. *Why* do they organize that way?

One big reason is that left-leaning movements tend to be disillusioned with government and therefore "[it's easier to] prize 'consensus' than it is to move them forward through tactical shifts" (p. 2015). Tufekci mentions the Tea Party movement that used similar organizing tactics but was more savvy in understanding how to make change by affecting electoral processes, ultimately leading to more impact on policy. "They focused intensely on process – and how to block or shift it to their liking."

From my point of view, there's a big misconception within leftist spaces that conflates two issues: governance and top-down governance. That makes a lot of sense, given that most people only experience governance in its coercive forms. Anti-authoritarian movements reject governance, structures, and anything institutional. One could fill books with stories about how people shied away from setting up institutions for fear of power over and either weakened their movements or led to power-over behaviors through the backdoor because they lacked formal governance structures.

We've already seen an example of that in the story *Who Owns the IP?* on page 133 where a founder of a social framework rejected governance and created an institution that is still weak and unable to make "tactical shifts" or even to maintain its integrity over time.

Throwing out governance only means to give away power – which then leaves the field to others to claim it.

Another misconception that follows from the concepts we've seen in this book so far is that anti-institutional movements overemphasize individual power. That makes sense given that they often don't build institutional power (because of their dismay about governance), which births movements where individuals have a lot of power at the cost of the collective.

The following story, *Local Climate Chapter Aim Conflict*, is a cautionary tale. It shows that the rules about good governance design also have to be kept in mind on a movement level. It's a story about a power vacuum on the movement level that had a devastating effect.

It was a local chapter of a global climate movement, incorporated as its own organization. As an organization, they were loosely connected to the movement, but that movement didn't have an identifiable center. The movement founders had put a set of aim statements in place, and then local chapters got together and saw themselves in relation to that movement. That meant they took the original aim statements and used them as their own, to be enacted locally.

Over the years, tensions had grown in the chapter. Some people thought the approach in the original aim statements wasn't enough. In particular, they found that the original aims had left out the connection between social justice and climate justice, which they saw as critical. In fact, they saw it as so critical that doing climate work without it seems not worth doing (or even detrimental). That's why some people wanted to modify the aim statement by adding a sentence about social justice and its climate-oriented mission.

This local chapter was set up sociocratically, and while it had what they called an Anchor Circle, it was unclear whether that Anchor Circle had the power to change the aim. Some thought the aims couldn't be changed – after all, it was only that set of aims that kept the whole movement together. Others argued that the chapter was its own organization and could change its aim as they pleased.

Were the initiators open to changing the aim statements to include social justice alongside climate justice? It's complicated. They didn't see themselves as the people who could make that call. Plus, what would all the other chapters say if the movement's aims were changed top-down? Coming together and fighting it out in a distributed global movement with hundreds of thousands of members? Impossible.

The question of the movement's aim had fallen into a power vacuum – changing the global aim was not in *anyone's* responsibility.

In the city chapter, which I was connected to, the conflict couldn't be resolved either. The impossible situation puts people on edge. There were tears, there were screaming, hour-long fights, and even threats. It deteriorated as a chapter.

The same happened on a national level. Within national and regional parts of the movement, the tension led to an actual split of those who kept the original set of aims and those who re-wrote them to include social justice. There were now *two* umbrella organizations on the USA level, heavily impeding the whole movement's ability to act. People were confused and frustrated, and many left the movement.

In a perfect world, we could do the internal work *and* work on our organizational aims both with 100% of our energy and attention. In practice, that's impossible, and the intricate balance of what's 'enough' inner work vs. 'production' must be negotiated continuously in every organization. (It goes on the list of the 'enoughs' next to 'connected enough'!) That's hard, and likely succeeds only when all sides are able to hold a both-and mindset. As soon as one side tips into either-or thinking and says things like "you don't care about anti-racism, you only care about climate" (or the flipped statement), the discussion will go sideways. Because organizations indeed have to become anti-oppressive and give it their all to address oppressive behaviors, policies, and practices internally and around them. Given how much pain is involved in any of these topics, it requires even more patience, compassion, and willingness to do the work. That's probably impossible, at least for now. Still, the work is a priority. Suppose the personal and collective lived experience is that people don't care about a group's issues. In that case, it's so easy to hear "I care about the climate" as "I don't care about anti-racism work" even if that's neither said nor intended.

This is a perfect storm for many organizations. They are under-equipped for these conversations, and not experienced enough to hold a both-and topic even if emotions run high. To avoid getting stuck and letting the organization fall into factions, groups need to figure out where to place a conversation so it can be had in the hope of actionable outcomes, and to balance those conservations more intentionally with other priorities.

On the movement initiator's side, I'm guessing it seemed like such a good idea to let people self-organize and copy the original aim statements while letting them decide everything else. It seemed like it gave everyone freedom – but it was a semi-freedom. In particular, the lack of clarity and the absence of a place to decide tied everyone's hands.

One of Prosocial's core design principles is the authority to self-govern. In my assessment, among other factors, this climate movement fell apart because organizations didn't have the authority to self-govern, and the movement level didn't have the legitimacy to change its aims.

Ultimately, if the global movement had decided to keep or update the mission *or* proactively allowed local chapters to write their own mission, there would have been a way out. From my point of view, this movement was bound to die within a few years after it started because of that basic design error of not placing the mission into a designated domain. It's like locking oneself out of the house. As for that movement and its chapters, it remains an unsolvable problem.

4.3.3 Movements interfacing with organizations

Interestingly, neither Shirky nor Tufekci mention much about the organizations that organize big protests and their own governance. Their focus is the advantages and dynamics of "leaderless" or "organization-less" movement and organizing. But I wonder if that leaves crucial issues invisible.

Many movements may present as leaderless but aren't. The coordination of some of the shared assets and infrastructure is still held somewhere – twitter handles, bank accounts, patents – they give legitimacy to speak *as* or *for* the movement. There is a lot of power associated with holding the logins, even if there may be no legal incorporation or an associated bank account. Even if we tell ourselves that 'the movement' is decentralized and leaderless, it's clear that *someone* will hold the access.

Therefore, looking at the many great things that movements and user-generated direct collaboration can do is fascinating and hope-inducing, but who controls the infrastructure?

I imagine those movements like a coral reef that offers many organisms to join and participate in the movement. While that happens independently and with very little cost, it's still true that someone builds and maintains the coral reef structure and with that maintenance comes the power to make changes that shape the movement.

When the infrastructure organization is neglected, that power becomes invisible and will lack intentionality – and likely integrity. What is needed is a more critical exploration of how organizations interface with movements. How do Wikipedia volunteers – who do a lot of the work and contribute to policy decisions – and Wikimedia Foundation staff interact?

Both are needed. Wikimedia Foundation ensures the platform remains operationally stable, legally compliant, and financially viable. There can be tension when decisions made by the Foundation (for instance, software changes or new initiatives) are perceived as infringing upon the autonomy or values of the volunteer community. Such issues are typically addressed through community consultations and discussions, which can sometimes be extensive and heated.

In more abstract terms, movements might excel at System 1 in the Viable Systems Model – the operations. That is true, especially when they employ volunteers or run their operations on assets they don't need to maintain (like Airbnb). Low transaction costs make for operations, for example, we can have a huge number of individual protesters at a march, send lots of emails and postcards to lobby legislation, and created social media content. They might also employ mechanisms for performance control, like Wikipedia quality control, which helps volunteers to self-correct mistakes or misleading statements in Wikipedia articles. Yet, what about Systems 4 and 5? I'm not convinced that the strategic direction, the movement's aim, values statements, and identity can be held in a decentralized manner. Just because hundreds of thousands of people want something, that doesn't mean it turns into constructive action.

The familiar patterns of centralization and decentralization show up again. Who has the power to make changes in governance? Who holds the bank account, can accept donations, and who owns the patent? And what are the best ways to hold those in a centralized way while allowing as much decentralization as safely and constructively as possible?

4.4   Chapter summary

Coalitions are organizations of organizations. Coalitions allow organizations to collaborate towards shared goals. They need coordination (a backbone organization) to be effective.

The tension between centralization and decentralization is present on this level. Direct partnerships between organizations require clear aims, domains, and governance agreements to facilitate collaboration while respecting autonomy. Typically, organizations are typically emphasized more than coalitions, leading to more competition, underfunding, and lack of alignment on the coalition level.

I touched on inter-organizational collaboration. Partnerships struggle with a lack of clarity and protocols to carry over governance interoperability to create coherence on the super-organizational level.

Movements create their own challenges, and I could only highlight the dynamics. Movements harness decentralized participation for social change but are often too decentralized to carry out complex tasks, shift strategy, or depend on organizations to hold the center. They connect people and spread information easily but often lack centralized functions like strategy and identity. Central infrastructure and assets like websites enable movements but concentrate power, requiring intentional stewardship.

Balancing decentralized participation and centralized coordination is key across all forms of inter-organizational collaboration.

Chapter 5

Society and planet

This chapter will touch on a different kind of 'group' and some of its emergent properties – society. I do this not to 'explain' society but to show the interference and interaction between organizations and society. Pertinent topics here are economic, education, and legal systems, so we cover them in the first section.

We will look at how government would need to change to be in alignment with a self-organized world, and we will look at several stories of real-world projects. Then, I will take a look at identities and their impact on organizations. I will end the chapter – and this book – with a fictional description of a more self-organized world.

5.1   Society and organizations

A self-organized organization is not free to choose *everything* about how to work because it's part of a broader system that sets limits to what's possible. Organizations are embedded in the social, legal, and economic system that surrounds them.

Organizations also depend on coordination on a societal level to do what they do. A simple example is that most companies rely on infrastructure like roads. Companies also expect that their future employees will be able to read and write, which they learn in schools that are funded and coordinated on a governmental level.

Organizations are autonomous actors, but they are all unified by laws, regulations, and economic systems that rule 'into' the organizations.

5.1.1 Economic systems for self-organization

One of Prosocial's core design principles to allow for sustainable *power-with* self-governance is a 'fair distribution of contributions and benefits.' In the case of workers in an organization, this often means salaries.

I'm mentioning salaries in this chapter and not in the chapter on teams or organizations because our monetary system can't be separated from society. Even if a team sets salaries for team members together, the remuneration in the form of salaries only makes sense in the context of society. If my organization gave out its own currency with no purchasing power outside of my organization, would anyone work there?

Most workers in organizations work to support their livelihood – resources that are needed to feed and house them as people, not just during work time. The question of how to pay is therefore not only a team or organizational question but also a personal and societal question.

To understand how society affects self-organization in organizations, let's start with a story, *Who Gets The Role?*. It's fictional but not far-fetched at all. Imagine an organization where each team can make hiring decisions in a decentralized hiring practice.

Let's assume that a team hires new members with consent. (The example works in parallel if the team lead makes the decision.)

> There are two members already in the circle who both work 50% and are paid for that part-time role.
>
> There is an opportunity to increase *one* of their contracts to a full-time position (for example because there's a new 50% role that could be clustered with one or the other role). Applicant #1, Jane, just divorced and has to pick up more work to pay for rent. All team members know that she's in dire need of more paid work.
>
> Applicant #2, Destiny, doesn't need the money as she has another freelance job on the side. Yet, it's also clear that she would be better at the role because she has more experience in that particular field.

If the team wants to decide, they must weigh Destiny's experience against Jane's economic needs. Will they choose the one who is better at the role or the one who needs it more? In other words, will they decide for the *individual*'s benefit or the *organization*'s benefit?

I know this is a blatant oversimplification that makes it appear like a false binary. Jane could also get support, catch up on experience, and be better at filling the role. Many other factors are in the picture, like diversity or how well people work together.

My point is that societal factors affect the choices that people make *inside* of organizations and how well they run. The decision of Destiny vs. Jane will likely stir up lasting discomfort (or even resentment) in the team. Although, in an ideal world, we would only look at what's best for the organization, things are more complex.

It must be in the organization's interest to make sure that an organization can decide in the interest of the organization as much as possible. That is much easier if all workers are already in secure living conditions. If some are wealthy and others are barely scraping by, it creates a tension that makes it harder to operate in a *power-with* manner.

Self-organized organizations work the best in as choice-ful a society as possible.

Gerard Endenburg – the developer of the Sociocratic Circle Method underlying sociocracy – even states that there should be a Subsistence Guarantee: "The [Subsistence Guarantee] can be regarded as an equal threshold for everyone's means of subsistence, just as decision-making by consent guarantees the same threshold for each individual in the decision-making process." (p. 43) He draws a parallel between equal consideration in access to salaries and being considered in decision-making. Assuming that all voices are equal in the circle, we also have to ensure all people are economically equal.

Transparent, co-designed remuneration policies

In most organizations, salaries are not transparent and this conversation doesn't even happen. This lack of transparency can lead to disparities in pay, unequal treatment, and a limited understanding of how salaries are determined.

But if everything, including salaries, is self-organized, then an organization needs to be able to talk about money. Would Destiny, Jane, and their team members from the story above have been able to have this conversation? Because such conversations have been avoided for so long, many teams start with very little experience in remuneration models.

Many are used to a defer-and-complain approach where they complain about remuneration but from a safe distance. It's much easier to point fingers than to propose a more viable policy because of the complexity of the topic. That's why, in many contexts, people are unwilling to address pay even when they have the chance to have a say. Or they might be attached to overly competitive systems, as that has been the dominant framework in companies.

An early and inspiring example is the practices at Semco. Semco follows a system called "Open Salaries," which emphasizes transparency and employee participation in determining compensation. It's a combination of transparent salaries, peer setting of remuneration, and a mix of self-appraisal and peer feedback. High-performing employees may receive higher compensation, bonuses, or other rewards based on their contributions and achievements. The performance evaluation is typically conducted through a participatory and multi-perspective approach, including input from peers, supervisors, and subordinates. Semco also has a profit-sharing program in place where a portion of the company's profits is distributed among employees. In addition, employees can negotiate and tailor their compensation packages based on their personal requirements, financial goals, and life circumstances.

Having those conversations is often not trivial for organizations. Here's a good example of that. It's about a company that revamped its salary system. Previously, their remuneration package consisted of a base salary supplemented by bonuses.

The base salary was a fixed amount of money that workers were guaranteed to earn no matter how they performed. The bonus was a variable amount of money that was earned based on performance-related metrics. Here, the base salary had been low and the bonuses high.

> The company engaged in the process of reviewing payment structures. The leadership was willing to switch to a base salary system but employees were against it because they were scared to lose income.
>
> They devised a transitional system where each employee could choose whether they wanted to be paid according to the old or the new system. Most employees chose the new system. After a while, every employee had switched over – and when asked about it, they even said that 'bonuses don't make any sense.'

We can only speculate on why this system might have suited them better. Maybe employees recognized that the old bonus-based system fostered a competitive environment, which contradicted their values of collaboration, teamwork, and collective success? Or maybe just came to perceive the new system as fairer and more equitable among employees. Maybe it provided a stable and consistent income regardless of fluctuations in sales.

I hope that the next few years will bring established and flexible patterns that can serve as a guide in many organizations so that each organization does not have to invent their own. The more practice and experience people have with this topic, the more smoothly new systems will be developed and implemented.

Here's a positive example. A colleague working as a consultant for pay structures in self-managed and traditional organizations told me this story, *Remuneration policy*, about a company in central Europe.

> The company had asked for support in developing a new pay structure for about 600 people. They defined the project and identified the decision-makers first, and then ran a participatory process, inviting workers from the organization to join in a design process around salaries. Some feared that hardly anyone would be willing to be involved – too risky to talk about salaries? But 53 out of the 600 people showed up and 40 were willing to work on the process!
>
> They decided to narrow down the group and ran an election to have a manageable group size. Since diverse voices and perspectives were desired, each of the 40 willing collaborators was allowed to pitch their particular perspectives to give the voters information. Based on that, they elected ten people who served as a work circle with an 'outer circle' of people who gave input during the design process for the remuneration policy.
>
> When the first complete draft was ready, they got feedback from the whole organization. By then, the proposal already had so much buy-in that the final deciders only had a chance to approve the proposal – otherwise, they would have risked big resistance. To ensure alignment, the work circle *and* the deciders decided together by consent and they rolled out the new structure.

This is a story of a process that involved many voices and was run transparently. A uniform remuneration policy was developed that applied to the whole organization in a central way. An additional factor in role/circle and consent-based organizations, however, is that roles are more decentralized than regular remuneration policies assume. Let's look at that issue next.

Roles vs. positions

In role-based systems like sociocracy and Holacracy, the concept of a job becomes more nuanced. Instead of having *one position* (or job), the focus is on the sum of one's roles.

For illustration, let's look at my roles in my organization. Even when I was still the Executive Director (ED) of the nonprofit with about 200 members, I always held more than just that one role. In fact, being ED only occupied me for less than 7% of my time. The rest was a collection of roles in different circles, like managing book sales in Publishing House Circle (ca. 5%), overseeing training as leader of Training Circle (ca. 15%), certain roles in consulting (28%), and a role in budgeting (3%) which was held in Financial Wellbeing Circle. Over the years, I held about 8-10 roles at a time on average (which, as far as I know, seems to be average for role-based organizations).

Roles tend to be fluid, with lots of changes over time. When client work involved me more, I might have been less active in my other roles. When budgeting consumed more of my energy, other roles had to wait. (Even people who don't work in self-organized workplaces are familiar with the effect – we all hold many roles in our lives, and we balance the changing level of involvement over time.)

This is of course not atypical even in traditional organizations, in particular in higher level positions where people might be point person or lead on a project or area; what's different in self-management is the independence of roles from a set position which also affects pay. The position is made up entirely of roles.

Here are some typical questions that come up:

- "Are all roles paid the same? What if half of my roles are valued at a lower pay rate than the other half? Do I have to track how many hours I spend on each role?"
- "If my roles fluctuate, does my pay fluctuate as well? How can I be paid the same every month?"
- "If roles have different pay rates, who decides what the pay rate is? Circles? HR? And on what basis?"
- "If one leaves *all* roles, does one lose one's job?"

While these questions are more of a logistical nature, there are also questions about identity: "What do I write on my business card? Who am I if I don't have one job title? Does this mean I cannot get promoted anymore? How do I explain to future employers what my level was? "

There are two basic approaches, both with pros and cons.

Role-based systems   A role-based system leans heavily on the side of individuals or even sub-individuals (roles). Every worker is paid for the work done in their roles. It's like the gig economy way of working, or like a freelancer, just within a company. The teams are the 'clients'.

Taking myself as an example, I'd have a 7% contract as ED and a 28% contract with Consulting Circle, and so on. I'd get paid however much time I spend in each role, possibly with a cap or just by the hour.

Role-based

Advantages

- It's direct and transparent because people are directly paid for their work.

- Role-based pay clarifies the value of each role in terms of hours or compensation, and it can be seen as fair by the group.

- Circles have a high degree of autonomy and can set pay rates and hire people into roles that suit them and their workload.

- People can tailor to their needs and desires how much they want to work.

Disadvantages

- Can be bureaucratic. Every hour needs to be tracked by role. Every piece of work needs to be assigned to a role so it can be accounted for.

- A culture may emerge where individuals strictly adhere to their designated roles, potentially leading to excessive bureaucracy, because they are not paid for anything outside of what's trackable in their roles.

- Role decisions affect role holders not only personally but also financially. If one person is chosen for a role over another based on their skills, the team needs to deal with a colleague not only not getting the role but also missing out on extra pay.

- Not a lot of stability as salaries fluctuate.

Position-based

Advantages

- Payroll simpler.

- Position-based pay offers teams the freedom to select roles without economic consequences for individuals who are not selected.

- Teams have a choice and can pick people without having to factor in their financial situation.

- Stability for workers in their salaries.

Disadvantages

- Can make team budgeting hard because it's unclear how much time was spent in what team. Even if tracked separately, it's hard to have cost control as a team.

- Can be seen as unfair. What if someone works more or harder and gets paid the same?

- Can make cost control by team harder when workers serve in multiple teams.

Advantages and disadvantages of role-based vs. position-based systems

Position-based (salary-based) systems   A salary-based system clusters all roles together and levels out differences and fluctuations. In essence, a position-based payment system is like a traditional 'job.' From a self-management perspective, it empowers both role holders and fellow team members to exercise full choice in nominating, consenting, or objecting to role assignments.

Again, taking myself as an example, what it would mean is: I am employed with a 100% contract and get paid that. Within my full-time work, I hold different roles and divide up my time accordingly and flexibly.

I'm familiar with an organization that paid people their full salary no matter what roles they were holding. The only requirement was that employees hold one or more roles; if they stepped out of all roles, employees had a 3-months grace period to find themselves a new operational role in the organization. It's like the Universal Basic Income-version of self-management, leaning very heavily on trust.

Organizations are experimenting with blended systems to mitigate the disadvantages of both systems and keep cost control and transparency while also keeping the system transparent and stress-free. Position-based certainly hold advantages because of their simplicity, but many open questions remain. More experimentation will be useful in this field to find solutions and prototypes that can be adopted in various organizations.

5.1.2   Purpose and profit

Organizations are not mere economic entities; they play a significant role in shaping the world around us. In recent years, more and more people have realized that an organization's purpose and impact on society are relevant and that maximizing profit can't be their only raison d'etre. What questions come up around purpose and decentralized organizations in the wider context of society?

An organization's purpose serves as its north star, defining its reason for existence. While financial sustainability is, of course, essential, a singular focus on maximizing profit often fails to inspire individuals to stay committed to the organization – especially if it's someone else's profit.

There are three ways in which purpose matters that I want to highlight.

- Purpose alignment serves the organization. In organizations where members have more autonomy and choice, purpose assumes even greater significance. Because people can choose more freely, alone and together, where to put their energy, purpose alignment is relevant to a decentralized organization's success

- Purpose matters to people on the inside of organizations. People aren't just workers. They have their own sense of meaning. Let's imagine a worker who *doesn't* feel aligned with the organization's purpose and wants to *leave* the organization but can't afford. This creates a disadvantage both for the worker and the organization.

  A purpose-driven, self-managed organization relies on its workers' free choice to work. All the pulls external to the organization interfere with how well the organization can operate. Purpose-driven organizations know that. Some self-managed organizations pay good severance pay to people who leave after a trial period to ensure that only those people who are fully committed stay.

- An organization's purpose matters not only internally but also externally. How the organization's purpose is perceived and how it aligns with society-level needs and values plays a crucial role its reputation. People today are more conscious of the organizations they support, favoring those whose purpose aligns with their values. This alignment between purpose and external perception significantly impacts an organization's success and sustainability.

This is an example of how holding the different levels of *individual – team – organization – beyond one organization* is not about playing one against the others but about an *integration*. If an organization's purpose aligns with my personal purpose, then my personal purpose is served by contributing to the organization, and vice versa. If my purpose positively contributes to society, then it will be a mutually beneficial relationship.

Gerard Endenburg, the founder of the Sociocratic Circle Method, viewed self-governed organizations as owning themselves or completely divorced from the concept of ownership. That way, the organization acts on its mission and aim with as little outside intervention as possible.

Shareholders in a traditional sense, as the owners of a company, have a financial interest in its success and often expect management to focus solely on maximizing profits. This profit-centric mindset incentivizes behaviors and decision-making that may not align with an organization's broader purpose. The problem is that shareholders typically have a *legal right* to receive a portion of the company's profits, typically through dividends, and profits increase the value of their share, giving shareholders larger returns when they cash out. They also have the right to participate in the company's management, either directly or by electing directors who represent their interests. That's at odds with the view of many self-governed organizations that primarily exist for their purpose and are run by the workers.

Pointing fingers at shareholders falls short because our economic system is built around profit and profit maximization. New legal patterns and frameworks are needed to bridge the gap between purpose and financial sustainability and integrate the two. Worker-owned cooperatives, FairShares Commons, Employee Stock Ownership Plans (ESOPs), Multi-Stakeholder Cooperatives, and B Corporations offer examples of how ownership structures can be reimagined.

Currently, there is a misalignment in what organizations should be optimized for, leading to a clash. It seems illogical to carefully and deliberately share power when legal and proprietary power formally remains with a select few. True equality in decision-making cannot be achieved in such a scenario because the legal system doesn't care about how roles are split up internally in the organization. What matters is the legal power. No self-management talk can conceal that.

Traditional hierarchical power structures in organizations, particularly in shareholder-driven companies, can lead to coercive and mono-perspective decision-making and control, reducing the potential for truly collectively held power. Shareholders are not impacted by the organizations' decisions beyond the profits. And even organizations that want to 'do things differently' get worn down over time.[1]

That's why most organizations that enter the path of self-governance also discuss ownership structures. After all, "[e]mployees who think and act like owners don't need a lot of oversight" (Hamel & Zanini).

But getting there is not without hurdles. Here's a story, *Two Brothers*, that illustrates how the two can create tensions.

> Orien had started a software business. This went well and the business grew. As more people got involved, Orien's brother Perez became a co-owner. Orien continued to be very involved operationally and in leadership roles, while Perez's involvement was more peripheral.
>
> Orien had always felt awkward about having all the power as the business owner, so he was curious about more self-management. The more he mentioned it to his employees, the more – cautiously – excited they got until, at some point, there was an expectation of shared power but not a lot of structure to hold it.
>
> The company asked for help in formalizing some of the structure. Orien was ready to share the power and responsibility. He was hopeful.

---

[1]The 'degeneration' hypothesis posits that, over time, many cooperatives tend to succumb to the pressures of the neoliberal, capitalist systems in which they are embedded (Storey, Basterretxea, & Salaman, 2014).

As we explored options, the question of ownership resurfaced with increased urgency. For Orien, there was no charge here. He didn't even think he should own the business alone. He wanted to share everything. In fact, the idea of turning the company into a worker-owned company had crossed his mind multiple times over the years.

Yet, his brother got scared. As an owner, he felt threatened by the idea of sharing power. He didn't believe that people could carry the weight of responsibility.

Those who had suspected that 'the whole power-sharing topic was a scam', felt confirmed. This dynamic deteriorated the self-management effort. It decreased the trust on all three sides – workers, Orien, and Perez.

On a positive note, there are many examples of organizations success-fully transitioning into new forms of ownership, such as cooperatives and FairShares Commons. One IT business, initially a proprietary company, discovered self-management and implemented it. Their next step is to be-come a worker-owned co-op. There are hundreds of stories like that where organizations push toward the next level of collective agency, including ownership.

5.1.3   Legal systems for self-governance

Another system that would need to change to allow for *collective power-with* is the legal system. The legal system is often based on hierarchical structures, with clearly defined roles and lines of responsibility. That makes sense – the legal frame requires clarity. But, a point I've made in this book is that clarity is separate from *power-over*, and one can be *clear* while distributing responsibility, as long as the governance system is clear.

Additionally, in a more distributed leadership system, roles do shift more often and with less formality, which, currently, is hard to reconcile with legal requirements and responsibilities. Legal issues such as liability and accountability can be more complex in a self-governed or distributed leadership system, as there may be less clearly defined lines of responsi-bility. Who signs a contract on behalf of an organization? Who enforces contractual obligations? Who is ultimately responsible?

The same is true for employment laws. New forms of working can create mismatches with current employment laws. For example, employ-ment laws related to discrimination, workplace safety, and labor relations may place specific responsibilities on employers to ensure their employ-ees are treated fairly and safely. In a self-governed, self-managed, or distributed leadership system, these responsibilities may be shared among team members, making it more difficult to determine who is responsible for compliance. Self-management may also challenge traditional employment relationships, as employees may have more autonomy and decision-making power, making it difficult to determine who is employer and who employee.

To illustrate, there are several pairings in my own organization where lines of accountability are difficult to determine. Let's use me and my colleague Carmen as an example. I am a member of a team, where Carmen is the leader, making Carmen my 'supervisor.' Yet, in another team, I am the leader and Carmen is a 'regular' circle member, making *me her* supervisor.

Self-management and self-governance are highly interdependent with the legal system. Deep changes in how we relate to each other at work, at a large scale, would significantly impact our internal and wider economic and the legal systems. Let's have a look at a few examples with more depth.

Legal compliance

The interplay between collective and individual responsibility, as well as the law, is often evident in the function of boards. Boards have a fiduciary responsibility. Traditionally, board members, whether in for-profit or non-profit organizations, are tasked with overseeing the organization's financial health and ensuring that its operations align with the best interests of its shareholders or stakeholders. In this traditional model, board members can be held legally accountable for their decisions and actions, which can have significant consequences for the organization and its stakeholders.

Why is that the case anyway? Let's get a quick glimpse into history. The US incentivized the creation of nonprofit organizations by providing tax benefits for donations to charitable, educational, and religious institutions. As nonprofit organizations grew in number and influence, so did the need for governance and oversight. Board members of nonprofit organizations were entrusted with the fiduciary responsibility to ensure that the organization effectively fulfilled its mission and used its resources in the best interests of the public or the specific community it served.

However, self-governed organizations challenge that conventional board structure. With responsibility and decision-making responsibility distributed more broadly throughout the organization (often involving employees and other stakeholders in strategic planning and oversight), the conventional understanding of centralized fiduciary responsibility and accountability is challenged. This often scares people. They feel the burden and are very uncomfortable giving up power to others to decide autonomously when board members are – in their view – 'responsible for everything.'

Another topic that keeps coming up is the question of staff on the board. In role/circle-based systems, it is common to have staff on the highest circle. People are worried about 'paid people on the board' and the mixing of staff and board because it transcends the traditional binary view of workers on one side and 'oversight' on the other.

Workarounds exist that 'overlay' the real decision-making structure with the legal structure. A strategy called *Committee Of The Whole* can be used where more people are included in a decision than formally required. That way, a group can satisfy the law and add their preferred ways of decision-making.

An organization took an interesting workaround to solve the issue of 'who signs the formal contracts?'

> This was an organization that was a stand-alone chapter of a national organization. In their setup, the national organization has a board and the chapters run without a board and have a lot of freedom. The only agreement between chapters and the national organization is the charter that all regional chapters are required to sign.
>
> As the chapter reorganized into a distributed decision-making system, it was unclear who would sign that charter. Should they all sign or pick one person? And who?
>
> Their General Circle asked themselves who would be the most obvious choice based on operations. Which operational role intersected the most with the national organization? They determined that it was their bookkeeper who herself was not a member of the General Circle but a member of the Finance Circle.

I was impressed with their pragmatic decision to be solely guided by operational questions. It was a choice that defied hierarchical conditioning where those powers are associated with status.

There is already more choice within the legal system than people assume. There is room for creativity that board members are often unwilling to consider. Board members often feel this responsibility as a heavy burden and get scared to do something wrong. It's risky – and often expensive – to leave the beaten paths and craft bylaws that support collective power while being compliant with the wider system. Even legal advisors might recommend more conservative approaches than necessary to minimize potential legal risks, and board members will be hesitant to go against the advice of legal counsel.

It almost seems people are compliant to what they think the system is, engaging in what in German is called 'vorauseilender Gehorsam' – anticipatory obedience. As much as I myself would expect that it's the law that keeps our options limited, it seems that a big part of that is actually our overly obedient minds, replicating unneeded power structures.

Breaking an inability to make a decision at the top level

Another example of workarounds that people get worried about is this: if the regulations say that decisions on the board have to be made by majority vote, does that mean that one *can't* make the decision by consent? It's very common for people to get worried that using consent is not allowed. They forget that one can consider a decision made by consent a supermajority vote (by 100%).

The law often provides default standard bylaws in case organizations don't specify enough how they want to operate. Those regulations then commonly include the phrase "unless specified otherwise". People quickly forget that bylaws are not systems that fall from the sky or as downloads from the internet. These documents are human-made, meaning they can be changed and adapted to accommodate the systems we want to give ourselves. There is more leeway than we think as long as we're clear because clarity is what the law rightly requires.

Clarity is even more vital in crises. Any organization needs to make sure it can decide in *any* situation. The inability to make a decision creates a risk for organizations. For example, let's take an example that we've already heard – a forming school can't decide whether to build a school building close to the city or more in the countryside. Let's assume there is a lot of conflict, and the conflict escalates up to a board level. Now the board *has* to make a decision eventually, or else all operations within the organization eventually come to a halt and the organization dies.

The same could be true for an organization unable to take a legal step or make a financial decision because of an inner dispute. The point is that *not* making a decision might be the worst outcome compared to any other choice. Having agency as an organization means being able to decide, whatever happens.

When I was fourteen, I went on a canoe trip. We were a group of 7 teenagers in one big canoe on a sizable river. The one supervising grownup was in another boat. I remember him passing our canoe and teasing us: "There's an island in the river further ahead," he said, pointing forward with his hand. "It doesn't matter which way you go, but don't crash onto the island."

Easy enough, I thought; we just have to decide which way we go.

I'm embarrassed to report that all I remember was people screaming "go left!", "no, let's go to the right!", and then the sound of the bottom of the canoe hitting the sand. We had, in fact, done exactly what our counselor had feared. We had not made *any* decision and hit the island.

This moment of deep embarrassment stayed with me for a long time, beyond the minutes it took us to get the canoe back on the water. I asked myself, back then, how could it happen that we were so stupid as a collective? We all saw the river bank, we had even been warned, that there was no real difference between left and right, and none of us wanted to hit the sandbank. And yet, we had made the worst choice of all: no choice. (I count that as one of my formative moments growing up. Maybe it turned me into a governance geek because I wanted to avoid that shameful situation going forward.)

Often, unsolvable decisions get passed on upwards. In circle-based systems, if a circle can't decide, it gets escalated to the next-'higher' circles. This chain of playing hot potato would then find its endpoint at the board level (assuming the board is the 'highest' level of the organization). Now a decision *has* to be made.

But if we're all equals and there is no boss at the top, how can we give ourselves a system where we can choose between the left and right of the island no matter what?

Many boards htat seek consensus decision making will have a tiebreaker rule that says that after a certain number of attempts, a majority vote will make a decision. The intention is, of course, to avoid paralysis. However, there are two problems here. The first one is that often, the rule set that says *when* the group switches to majority vote is hard to define. The language often used is "when reasonable effort has been made, including appropriate means like outside facilitation, decision-making shifts to majority vote."

Let's say we are trying to make a decision by consent, and I am the only one with an objection. We talked about the issue for three meetings and then invited a colleague to help us decide. Yet, there is still no solution in sight. Now, someone claims that a reasonable effort has been made, and suggests moving to a majority vote. What will I say if I really care about the issue? I will obviously claim that it's against process because the efforts made have 'not been reasonable enough.' With those vague regulations, we still rely on common ground understanding regarding *when* we would leave consent behind and ignore minority objections.

The second problem is that when we know that, ultimately, any decision can be made via a fall-back majority vote if we simply wait long enough, then how motivated will people be to listen and learn from the objections people bring? Having a majority vote, even as a fall-back easily undermines the shared responsibility laid out in this book.

Systems like these need careful design. The ideal system. . .

1. has a clearly delineated way of when it would be deployed
2. has an outcome within a considerate amount of time
3. is unattractive to use, so that groups will be more likely to use their regular system instead of playing process games against each other

My colleague Jerry Koch-Gonzalez has co-developed a clever system that allows decision-making at all times, but disincentives using that system. It is our fall-back in our own organization. I count the fact that we've never used it as a sign of its success but that also means I don't know how it would play out. Here's the system, in a short version:

Any three Board members or one-third of the Board, whichever is greater, may initiate the resolution process by restating the proposal in question and saying "we invoke the resolution process on proposal X," where X is the proposal that the Board has been unable to decide. If there is any disagreement among those initiating the resolution process, the Board Secretary, by their own judgment, will determine the language of Proposal X. Once the resolution process has been invoked, there is no discussion of whether sufficient effort was made to resolve the proposal.

The Board secretary, or any other Board member, should the secretary fail to act, immediately initiates the random selection of one Board member present, and that Board member is immediately removed from office. A consent process on proposal X is immediately initiated. If consent to approve, withdraw, or amend the proposal is not reached within 30 minutes, this process repeats with a second member removed. This process repeats until consent is reached or until the number of Board members is reduced to three (or the minimum number of Board Members required by government statute if greater than three), whichever comes first. If the number of board members is reduced to three, and still no consent is reached, then the decision shall be made immediately by a majority vote of the remaining members.

The software https://www.randomresult.com/pick.php, shall be used for the random selection of the Board members. If that software is no longer available, the youngest Board member will select another software that uses the same method within 15 minutes of the invocation. If the youngest Board member fails to select and initiate the selection process within 15 minutes, the next youngest shall do so with the same conditions, progressing until the selection has been made. If it is impossible to access a computerized randomizer, then the youngest Board member will select and use a manual method.

When issue X has been resolved and minuted, the number of board members is returned to the previous number, and the previously removed Board members are immediately reinstated as Board members with their original roles and terms, and the decision-making process reverts to consent as stated in the Bylaws and Policies and Procedures.

The decision on proposal X may not be reconsidered for 6 months without consent of the Board. In this case, there will be no recourse to the failure to reach consent.

Given that failure to consent at the BOD is likely to be controversial and painful, if a decision has been made in this manner, then the operational coordinators, or the Board Chair if the General Manager fails to act, will initiate a Restorative Circle (a formal NVC-related process) with the failure to decide by consent as the trigger event.

Honestly, I laughed out loud the first time I read his proposal. I thought it was a joke. It read like a game show and not even a good one! Then I looked at my colleague's face and realized he was serious.

But let's consider it. The advantage of that system is that it leaves no room for vagueness. Every step is designed so there is no wiggle room or place for discussions.

1. It's clear when it gets deployed. All it needs is a defined number of people and the magic words.
2. It is certain to give a solution within the same meeting.
3. Since the process is so unattractive to all involved – and potentially to their disadvantage – it's likely that a board member would only propose it if they saw the organization's well-being in danger. There is not enough incentive to use it for personal gain because it might backfire. No one who cares about an issue (either by proposing or objecting) would choose to engage in a system that includes the possibility that they would be excluded from decision-making. Since no one wants to be the one who gets voted off the island, it is a high incentive to avoid using the fall-back and to better work things out from the get-go. There is a clear rule *and* no one will want to use it until enough people admit that not making a decision at this point is worse than any other outcome.

I don't believe this is the only way to do it, but honestly, as crazy as it sounded to me at first, it's the best one I know. Creativity and experimentation are still needed to find elegant solutions to structural problems that we face in self-management and its wider system.

Legal experts who care about the value system, as well as consultants and practitioners, are currently working on developing and testing these solutions so one needs to reinvent the wheel, and a pool of good practices can be made available to a wider set of organizations in the field. I anticipate there will be more innovation over time, both on the legal side of ways to incorporate and plug into the legal system.

HR (Human Resources)

Human Resources – the part of an organization traditionally overseeing hiring, compensation, training and development, compliance, and workplace safety – has to change in organizations based on collective power. In decentralized organizations, HR responsibilities are distributed across the organization, rather than concentrated in a central HR department. This allows for faster decision-making, greater flexibility, and more employee engagement.

In self-organized organizations, employees are empowered to take ownership of their own development and career growth, and often, the responsibility for managing one's own career rests with the individual. Alternatively, the HR function might offer support and guidance on people's paths.

How centralized or decentralized HR functions will depend on the organization. It can be that teams make hiring decisions, with each team acting as its own recruitment function. The advantage of such a system is that it directly empowers those with an understanding of the work to determine who should be hired for what role and at what pay.

Yet, the disadvantage is that now many places need to have discussions about pay that they might not feel equipped to have; they also need to act as their own Human Resource system. A decentralized approach can dilute expertise and leave people hanging.

That's why it makes sense to have a uniform system that is decided in a participatory but central way. Having that dedicated HR function in a central position can make it easier to maintain legal compliance and adhere to the legal requirements in the given context.

A subtle effect of a more centralized approach is that in a system where one team makes the HR-related or financial decisions, a significant power over something that affects everyone is held in one place. No matter where that place is (at the top, in the center, or somewhere else in the system), it's still a centralized approach and often triggers reactions that are tainted by the shadows of the past that sound like this: "they don't care", "they don't understand" and so on. Even though the system might be based on shared power, it's still one team or department making decisions that can *feel* hierarchical to people. Good information flow, transparency, as well as participatory feedback processes, can take reduce the tension.

There are several other topics within the realm of HR where an organization can choose a more centralized or decentralized path, each with the common advantages and disadvantages of centralization offering more unity, specialization, and consistency while decentralization offers autonomy, more tailored, context-sensitive decisions, and choice.

- Paid Time Off (PTO) policies
  Centralized: Standardized PTO policies applicable to all employees
  Decentralized: Teams or circles determine their own PTO policies

- Conflict resolution
  Centralized: Centralized conflict resolution process
  Decentralized: Teams or circles handle conflict resolution within their own context

- Personal growth and professional development
  Centralized: centrally planned professional development programs for all employees
  Decentralized: Individuals or teams take ownership of their own growth and development

- Recruitment and Hiring
  Centralized: Centralized recruitment and hiring process for all positions
  Decentralized: Teams or circles handle recruitment and hiring

- Performance Management
  Centralized: Standardized performance evaluation processes
  Decentralized: Teams or circles develop their own performance management systems

- Compensation and Benefits
  Centralized: Centralized compensation structure for all employees
  Decentralized: Teams or circles have flexibility in determining compensation and benefits

Depending on size, resources, and culture, each organization needs to find a balance between both sides of the equation. Ideally, the focus shifts from traditional HR towards empowering individuals and teams to make decisions and take responsibility for their work. Instead of enforcing policies, HR professionals will coach others through processes or offer their expertise, such as a Help Desk (as mentioned in 3.5.3), where a central HR role or circle can offer support and some of the services to more decentralized processes. That can improve the quality of the work, and avoid financial or legal risks, or deal with sensitive data. We want to avoid a system where everyone needs to become an expert on everything!

Typically, self-managed organizations also take on performance management in a decentralized way. Again, there might be a centralized support function and deeper support for offering and receiving feedback both for and by individuals and groups.

My personal experience is that self-organized organizations often lack centralized structures in the area of HR. I don't see that as a systemic issue but rather a lack of maturity and attention. Self-managed organizations often emphasize personal responsibility and decentralization, therefore erring slightly too far on that side. However, the functions and needs of HR-related services don't fully disappear in a decentralized, self-organized context, and not holding them with intentionality only means burdening individuals with a high degree of personal responsibility. To hold organizational functions responsibly, the domains for those functions need to be placed intentionally.

For illustration, let's use me as an example in *Personal & Organizational Needs*.

> Within my organization, I found myself in a situation where I felt an appetite to learn more and teach less. I had produced a considerable amount of output and longed for more exploration, stimulation, and companionship in learning. That longing was not directly connected to a particular role I had. It was neither in my role of training lead nor in my role of book sales or Executive Director. It was everywhere. Therefore, it had no designated place in the system.
>
> While we had a practice of doing annual performance reviews for all people in paid roles, that too was primarily focused on my contribution to the organization, not as much on my career path. Should I seek personal growth within the organization or outside of it? Should I even bring it up, or would it be seen as a betrayal of the organization if I decided to seek it outside?

And even if the participants of the performance review can see me as a full human being with needs inside and outside of the organizational purpose, if we come up with an improvement plan of ideas, I can move forward – like signing up for a course in a new domain of learning – it still it likely my responsibility to make that happen. How much can I make it my organization's issue to help me find my path?

I was undecided and held back. The chair of our Mission Circle inspired a conversation about my perceived lack of stimulation and learning in my roles. Sure enough, just talking about that had a catalytic effect on me and resulted in me leaving the role of Executive Director.

Of course, one can make a point that only a content leader of the General Circle makes for a well-run organization. So, therefore, helping people realize they should transition out of a role is in the organization's service. And yet, distinguishing among the well-being of the person ('soul'), the holder of roles, and the circle member is not always easy. Whose responsibility is my well-being?

5.1.4   Education

Most self-managed systems will recruit and welcome people who have been educated in the general education system. What is covered by that education system and what isn't poses an interesting tension for self-management.

In a self-managed organization, *more* people must have *more* general skills to operate well. A self-governing system needs to balance specialization with members having generalist skills and experience in a variety of topics.

- Financial literacy – because more people are involved in budgetary decisions.
- Governance skills – because more people are involved in decision-making.
- Information management – because more people are involved in curating and receiving information.
- Communication skills – self-governance requires more communication and it relies more on better-quality communication.
- Personal development – as shown in this book, a self-managed system heavily relies on people knowing themselves well, and having done their personal work.

Here's a little illustration of what I mean:

> In my organization, the General Circle currently approves the high-level budget as a rolling budget. That means that all eight General Circle members need to understand the budget. Yet, circles also have fiscal power and responsibility since they are their own fiscal units. That means that about twenty circles – ca. fifty people – have to have a budget conversation and, therefore need to understand the budget enough to make an informed decision. That's a lot of people, especially considering that many have never held this kind of responsibility.
>
> It took years for people to step into full responsibility to hold the budget with full individual responsibility.

Besides financial skills, IT skills are another area of tension in some organizations. Obviously, there is a huge variety here; but as long as there are organizations many of whose members have limited IT skills, it's going to be hard to operate at the level required for effective self-governance.

It's easy to dismiss this and to say 'they just have to learn it'. But that's just pushing the responsibility to individuals while ignoring the big question: Given that many people aren't as literate with technology as needed for smooth collaboration, what will we do? How can we provide enough support and training so a critical mass of people feels comfortable enough to master the necessary tools?

Since those skills aren't reliably taught in public education, organizations have to fill those gaps as part of their professional development. This puts more burden on self-governed organizations. We can't build a world based on self-organization and not think about how the education system must work to match the needed skills.

Where does organization-wide responsibility end and where does society-level responsibility begin? Current education addresses some of these topics, like information management and some IT skills. But what about governance skills, for example? Children in the school system spend far more time learning how to stand in line than making group decisions together. We expect people to leave the school system able to read and write – can we also expect them to know their way around *power-with* governance?

I struggle with being so dependent and powerless with regard to the skills with which people walk in the door. When an organization embraces self-governance, they have to provide the training to do it well; on the other hand, hierarchical training comes for free in any formal education setting, putting all organizations outside of the mainstream at a disadvantage.

The organization I co-founded, Sociocracy For All, provides training for governance literacy that 'should' be taught in school instead of being provided by us. In fact, I think some of the content in this book should be taught in school, on par with teachings about nation-state governance.

There are very early signs of change. When I went to school, we were expected to run elections for our class representative. It was a simple majority vote. Nowadays, some lucky European students learn how to select a class representative using a sociocratic selection process, a project funded by the EU. That is a hopeful reminder that what we teach is a choice. It's not that we teach nothing – most schools teach hierarchical processes (the teacher decides) mixed with unstructured group processes (in student groups) work alongside a competitive majority vote (when electing class representatives). Are we intentional about the governance literacy we pass on?

Children are able to pick up these new forms of governance. Children in sociocratic schools – which exist[2] – get a stronger foundation of peer-based governance.

A few years back, one of my children – in second grade of a public school – told me that the teacher had divided up the class into book clubs, each having group-based conversations about different books. My daughter told me that as soon as they were divided into groups, she raised her hand and offered to facilitate in her group. She was musing that her teacher was probably surprised that she knew the word 'facilitate.' I found the story pretty funny and I asked, "please, don't tell me you did rounds?" And my kid responded "Yes, of course!"

I smile at the thought of children walking around having seen rounds for at least a bit of their educational path. Can we imagine a world where the teacher divides the groups and then asks who facilitates each group and where any nine-year-old knows exactly what is expected of them and how to facilitate a meeting that supports group agency and individual empowerment? I can.

There's a lot of work ahead of us but this is one of the easier areas for positive change, and early efforts are happening.

---

[2]For an inspiring documentary, see the movie 'School Circles'. Also see the book *Let's Decide Together* by Hope Wilder that supports teaching children group decision-making by consent.

5.2 Government

Many are curious how patterns of self-organization could be used in state or national government. What would a self-organized country look like?

Before we jump in, I want to comment on one internalized narrative that readers may carry: that hierarchy is necessary for complex civilizations. The standard narrative is that as societies 'progress' and become more complex and wealthy, they automatically become less equal. It states that early humans lived in small, mobile bands that were egalitarian but that settling down and farming led to hierarchies and social classes. The emergence of cities and states further entrenched these hierarchies. Therefore, the narrative goes, progress comes at the cost of human equality and individual autonomy. That's just how it is.

But this is under discussion. Scholars like Graeber and Wengrow challenge the notion that hierarchy is essential to complex civilizations, suggesting that it may be a myth used to rationalize the historical association between development and inequality. They point to archaeological evidence of large-scale collaborative projects in prehistoric societies that seemingly operated without hierarchical structures. It's not about wanting to return to pre-agricultural forms of living. They highlight that hierarchy and complex civilizations do not need to go hand in hand.

A broader spectrum of possibilities exists beyond the simplistic progression from "primitive and free" to "developed and centrally governed." (That narrative has been challenged on both sides – "primitive" societies can be highly hierarchical, coercive, and even abusive; on the other side, beware a "noble savage" narrative of an idyllic, egalitarian society.)

By questioning the automatic connection between hierarchy and societal complexity, we open up space for exploring alternative organizational structures that prioritize equality, autonomy, and collective decision-making. It challenges us to reconsider long-held assumptions and encourages a more nuanced understanding of the relationship between hierarchy, civilization, and the potential for diverse social arrangements.

In this section, I look at some of the experiments already done that question exactly that narrative of hierarchy as a necessary means to coordinate within and among nation-states.

Our democratic systems are based on majority vote. As I've mentioned in section 2.4 on decision making, the fundamental flaws I see in majority vote are that (a) it reduces the possible options/choices that we can vote for and drowns out nuances between them, and (b), it's optimized for individual preferences, not collective well-being.

As I emphasized in this book, I doubt that sets of individuals can make decisions for a group in a *power-with* way because they lack a mechanism to incentivize for the *collective* purpose.

The origin of majority vote in ancient Athens was intended to be deeply egalitarian. Ancient citizens of Athens – wealthy men – were convinced that the principle 'one citizen, one vote' would provide equal opportunity.

Back then, incentivizing for individual advantage might not have been as questionable as I see it now. In smaller groups like the senate in an ancient context, there might have been enough social cohesion and factual interdependence to consider and prioritize the *collective* purpose in decisions at least most of the time. There were likely more interpersonal relationships, more sense of each other's contexts, and more common ground around what's happening in the city. There was very little mobility, so 'doing your own thing' wasn't an option, leading to a stronger sense of interdependence. Yet, it is crucial to recognize that ancient Athenian democracy was not without flaws, and power dynamics and inequalities still existed, particularly with regard to gender, wealth, and citizenship.

In group sizes and contexts that use majority vote today, its competitive aspect takes over because there is less of a shared purpose, lack of proximity, and because of sheer numbers of people.

Conceptually, the difference between 'the majority of voters' and 'the collective' might be subtle, but it matters. A majority vote doesn't reward thinking for the collective's good. It short-cuts collective sense-making. Instead of an organic system of nested entities, each with its collective-level processes, the system goes from individual voters directly to 'the national government' without enough intermediaries. It's like a tree made decisions on the tree level by having each cell vote individually, disregarding what's suitable for the different systems, bark, and branches.

In first-past-the-pole majority voting with a *the winner takes it all* approach, the minority is overpowered by the majority – *power-over*. In a decision-making method based on alignment with the collective purpose, like consent, people might still not get their preference. But if needs are met sufficiently, and the collective level is worth supporting, they may be more likely to *choose* based on the wellbeing of the whole. It would optimize for a *choice* in favor of the benefit of the group, not a forced imposition by the majority of competing individuals. This shift from *power-over* to *power-with* creates an environment where individual and collective interests are integrated instead of being played against each other – but it requires so much more than just a decision-making method. It requires *power-with* and *power-within* on all levels.

5.2.1   Informing formal government

Before we dream big and think about a self-organized world of free people, let's first look at a real story, *Utrechtse Heuvelrug*.[3]

> The Dutch municipality of Utrechtse Heuvelrug, with a population of 50,000, introduced sociocratic organizing methods in 2012. The project started in a phase of deep mistrust between the town government and the citizens.
>
> As a pilot project, in March 2014, after the city council elections, the eight elected political parties came to consent to a new policy program. This program included a significant reduction in budget – a big success. The project also included measures to give citizens a space to meet with councilors and give feedback.
>
> The mayor of Utrechtse Heuvelrug invited a group of citizens in 2012 to explore ways to enhance local governance and improve the communication between citizens and the local administration. The invitation was extended to all citizens, and a team of 15 citizens called the 'bridge builders' volunteered to participate. The bridge builders arranged meetings to understand the needs of everyone involved - civil servants, citizens, and city councilors. They found multiple gaps and miscommunications among all stakeholders, who sought a more effective way of collaborating but were hindered by existing structures, habits, and behaviors.
>
> They did their research and saw the city more in a facilitator role among stakeholders. To tackle the issues, the plan was to gather and utilize available knowledge and information at the beginning of the participation process (open call); then involve *all* stakeholders; prioritize participants' needs over potential solutions, find creative solutions that everyone can consent to; and encourage collective responsibility for agreed-upon solutions. The bridge builders made recommendations for processes bringing citizens and government decisions together:
>
> 1. Decide early on about the level of citizen participation that will be used for a specific policy issue.
> 2. The city council should set and define the boundaries (e.g., budget constraints, delivery time, and other conditions) for any participation process.
> 3. Subsequently, a project group with stakeholders, interest groups,

---

[3]https://www.tandfonline.com/doi/pdf/10.1080/01900692.2016.1263206

and experts should get the assignment to investigate the topic and decide by consent on a solution within those boundaries.

4. Every citizen who is interested can join this project group.

5. Once the project group has presented its solution, the city council only assesses if the solution proposed meets the boundaries defined earlier (see 2). If this is the case, the solution is validated and acted upon. Any other contribution from the city councilors must be in the form of participating in and/or providing information to the project group.

6. If the project group cannot decide by informed consent within the boundaries set, the city council again has the authority to decide on the policy issue being considered.

In 2014, the city council embraced the recommendations of a working group and implemented new practices to increase citizen participation and improve local democracy. These practices include weekly meetings between citizens and councilors to discuss policy issues and biweekly formal meetings where decisions are made by consent, as long as the issue has been previously explored in one of the evening sessions.

It is a great example of how sociocratic principles can 'fill the vacuum' between a town council and its citizens, and enhance participation and trust in a local government.

Before we discuss this example more, I want to bring a second, very different example of improved participation and accountability of the formal government – in Taiwan.

There, it all started with a proposed bill to regulate ride-sharing services in Taiwan.

The question of ride-sharing services sparked a contentious debate between traditional taxi companies and ride-sharing companies. vTaiwan, an online civic participation platform, was launched in response in 2014. (It was inspired by the platform pol.is created by US entrepreneur Colin Megill.)

The vTaiwan platform allowed citizens to participate in the policy-making process by sharing their views and opinions on the proposed legislation. The platform enables citizens to collaborate, deliberate, and vote on various issues related to the bill, such as safety requirements for ride-sharing drivers and allows participants to suggest alternative solutions. The vTaiwan platform proved highly successful, with over 20,000 participants engaged in the policy-making process. The bill was eventually passed with provisions supported by taxi and ride-sharing companies, indicating a successful collaboration between citizens and policymakers. The key idea behind the platform is to foster a more nuanced understanding of collective preferences by identifying overlapping viewpoints and shared concerns. It encourages participants to express their thoughts and engage in dialogue rather than simply casting a single vote.

Since then, the vTaiwan platform has been used to facilitate citizen participation in a range of policy-making processes in Taiwan, and has been recognized as a model for other countries to follow in promoting citizen engagement in the policy-making process.

The policy-making process in Taiwan's vTaiwan platform follows a similar structure to other policy-making processes, just with more public participation in decision-making. The steps involved in the vTaiwan process are as follows:

- Identification: A specific issue is identified and presented to the public for discussion and feedback.
- Public deliberation: Citizens are invited to participate in online forums to express their opinions, discuss the issue, and propose solutions. The algorithm helps to identify patterns without drowning out minority opinions, while minimizing 'nonsense' opinions or unfounded, extreme positions. The algorithms are also set up in a way that rewards convergence. It results in a cluster of opinions that can inform policy – a systemic constellation of needs and opinions.
- Collaborative drafting: A collaborative drafting process occurs when stakeholders and experts collaborate to create a proposed policy or regulation.
- Expert consultation: Experts are invited to provide feedback and recommendations on the proposed policy or regulation.
- Public review: The proposed policy or regulation is available for public review and feedback.
- Revision and finalization: The policy or regulation is revised based on the feedback received during the public review period and finalized.

Throughout the entire process, there is a strong emphasis on transparency. For example, the first step, identifying the issue, is broadcast publicly on the internet.

There are similarities between vTaiwan and Utrechtse Heuvelrug.

While the process in Taiwan includes a high involvement of technology (both for the platform and the broadcasting), it tries to facilitate the connection between citizens and formal government, similarly to the low-tech process in the Dutch municipality. In both cases, the formal government remains in power and increases the information flow both ways, from government to citizens and vice versa. The formal government put both systems in place, albeit due to public pressure.

There are many more examples of efforts to do this with different forms and means of facilitation and participation. For example, sortition-based bodies can act either as decision-makers or make recommendations. Sortition-based systems build on the idea that a lottery avoids the typical issues of competition in elections. It's not the loudest (or wealthiest, or most populistic) voice that makes it into an office but regular people, chosen randomly. Sortitions are often stratified and make sure that members of the group are representative of the larger population in terms of age, gender, socioeconomic background, and other relevant factors. A sortition approach helps ensure that diverse perspectives and experiences are considered in the decision-making process, leading to more inclusive and equitable outcomes.

The problem with sortition-based approaches is that having enough expertise in the system is hard, especially on highly specialized topics. If, for example, you put me on a sortition-based group to task about cyber security, all I could do is rehash what experts have told me – but who do I listen to? I can't form an opinion of my own because I know too little. Therefore, the power shifts towards experts and the question of who gets asked to be an expert.

There are currently a number of sortition-based experiments, like for citizens' assemblies.

> In 2019, the city of Bristol, England, held a citizens' assembly to deliberate on the future of its local government. The assembly was composed of 100 randomly selected citizens, who were tasked with discussing and making recommendations on a range of issues, including the city's budget, housing, and transportation.
>
> The assembly met for ten weekends for six months, and a team of experts facilitated its deliberations. The citizens had the opportunity to hear from various speakers, including elected officials, policy experts, and public members. They were also able to visit different parts of the city and meet with residents.
>
> At the end of the process, the assembly made several recommendations, including increasing the city's investment in affordable housing, creating a new public transportation system, and reforming the city's

budget process. The recommendations were presented to the city council, which is currently considering them.

In this case, the body was not a decision-making body but merely made recommendations to those who decided.

There is a lot of potential in the combination of these different solutions. The three different approaches – more citizen participation in municipal government, large-scale feedback via mapping of perspectives, and sortition-based bodies can also be combined to mitigate their weaknesses while preserving their strengths. For example, citizen assemblies can be combined with a platform-based polling system to create a less corruptible forum with lots of citizen participation.[4]

5.2.2   Replacing formal government

Given those options, what would it take to have a system where the formal government is completely *replaced* with self-organized pods?

To start thinking about this, first, we need to acknowledge that self-management tools typically work for organizations rather than towns or countries. While the original use of the *word* 'sociocracy' was coined by Auguste Comte, a French philosopher and social theorist, in the mid-19th century, hoping for a state governance method, the sociocratic circle method developed by Gerard Endenburg in the 1970ies, which is now referred to as sociocracy and was the basis for most circle/role-based and consent-based systems, was designed for *organizations*.

Why does that matter? There are two crucial differences between the organizations and towns in this way:

1. Self-management systems involve workers in decision-making or create conditions so workers can be the decision-makers. As for the workers in town management, it can work in the same way (and there are experiments with that).[5]

   But towns don't only have *workers* (people hired, in a broad sense) that *work* in town management; they also have *citizens*. It takes a few

---

[4]See https://compdemocracy.org/polis/book/lottery-selected-assemblies/, retrieved June 27 2023.

[5]Like in Slagelse, DK, see https://www.sociocracyforall.org/sociocracy-at-the-workplace-a-case-study-from-a-7500-employees-workplace-mette-aagaard/, offering early anecdotes that give hope that sociocratic town management is good for citizens because decision-making becomes more local, meaning workers in town management can be more responsive to citizens' needs.

thousand workers in town management to run a middle-sized town – but there might be tens of thousands of citizens who spend their days doing things that are unrelated to town management. Their involvement is not via work but merely by living in a place. That means a self-managed system designed for co-workers is at odds with having people who simply live there and need a voice, in their function as citizens, not workers. If work circles make decisions, what 'work circle' would someone be in who doesn't do work in the running of the town?

In addition, citizens form a huge, somewhat amorphous group of citizens. They are not a team or a circle because they don't work together. They don't even meet, and they are part of stratified groups in complex ways.

2. The other difference between organizational governance and governance of citizens is that organizations have aims. What about towns? Constitutions of countries often state sovereignty, territorial integrity, security, economic prosperity – but for what purpose? What is it that all residents of a city or country are actively involved in doing?[6]

Let's compare the concepts with an intentional community, as that's the closest existing parallel to a city. An intentional community of several dozens of people living together in one place can have a specific aim, like forming a community for people over 55 of age, or a community with certain environmental goals. In that case, one can limit membership to everyone who fits that group or behavior. That's impossible in a town – one wouldn't be able to declare a town for only senior citizens or of a certain spiritual interest because that would exclude people. It's also impractical. Imagine, for example, a town specifically designed for gay and lesbian people. What if a resident has a child who grows up, and wants to stay in the community but doesn't fit the criteria?

Communities with aims that include more immutable features than interests are closer to towns in that their aims can't be applied rigidly without becoming very exclusive (in which case the adult child would not be tolerated in the community). But that doesn't seem desirable or feasible. We can't really put any restrictions on our citizens – everyone should be welcome and that means we can't put any other aim or mission onto the

---

[6]Mazzucato 2021 is arguing that countries could embrace a mission, though I would call what she's talking about a high-level strategy, not an aim.

town. (Unless it's only aspirational and not binding but, as we've seen, non-binding expressions are only indirectly relevant in governance.)

So, aims are tricky, but maybe we can simply run with an implicit understanding of the well-being of all residents. Before we think more about this theoretically, let's focus on a real-life application. It is *very* grassroots and *not* invited or facilitated by the formal government: the Inclusive Neighbourhood Children's Parliaments in India. They use the principles of consent and linking and selection processes like in sociocracy (and Holacracy). They have many people involved – easily more than 100,000 people involved in Kerala alone, and it expands into other regions – so there are likely *many* more involved. (There is very limited tracking of the initiative so numbers are only estimates.)

The basic idea is simple: organize children into small groups and let them figure out together how to improve the world around them. Note that this is not a mock process but a group working on real projects.

The topics they are engaged in have a wide range: talking to parents to let their children finish school, child marriages, improvements in the built environment like street lights or bridges, but also farming, and environmental activities. The children's parliaments focus on the United Nations Sustainable Development Goals, both locally with roles for individual children to focus on Minister of Gender Equality, Minister of Climate Action, and other roles. Peer-selected children from a local circle join the next-wider circle, in eleven layers up until a national level.

The project started in the 1970s within the Catholic sphere. Its founder, Edwin Maria John, had read about 'Basic Ecclesial Communities' in Latin America, where local people read scripture and organize around realizing "the Kingdom of God." Edwin was inspired and saw the power of small groups – "where people have a face and an identity." The organization became secular in the 1990s.

Along the way, someone pointed out to Edwin that what they were doing was close to sociocracy. Edwin saw the connection and included consent decision-making as well as the sociocratic selection process in what they now call neighbourhoodization or neighbourocracy.[7]

Its essential principles are:

- The Principle of Smallness: Have a group small enough to hear everyone. For example, a group should not need a microphone. (This is a little like Google's pizza rule which says never have more people in a meeting than can be fed with two boxes of pizza!)

---

[7]John 2021, Mekolo & Buck 2023

- The Principle of Numerical Uniformity (less populated territories can not outpower more populated territories at the representative level; any member can also only represent one circle)
- The Principle of Subsidiarity: Decisions should be made at the lowest level possible.
- The Principle of Recall Scope: Any decision can be evaluated
- The Principle of Convergence: Cultivating a collective identity.

Children's Parliaments span almost every state of India now, covering both rural and urban settings. It has also been used with adults with great success for several decades. People from other countries are now getting trained there and replicating the project in their countries – mostly in Africa and Latin America – and a Provisionary World Children's Parliament has formed to connect the efforts across the planet.[8]

When talking to leaders in the organization, one question always came up for me. What does the local government say about this all? How do these informal forums change the landscape of the formal government? Of course, there isn't just one answer, here are two anecdotes.

> Sometimes and in some areas, formal governments do feel threatened by the neighborhood parliaments. It's known to people that if you want to be heard by the formal government, you need to go through the neighborhood parliaments because they are too powerful to be ignored.

Another story was told to me by Edwin John.

> There were local circles in an area where it was common for men to leave their homes to do seasonal work in other regions for months at a time.
>
> During those times, the local circles continued meeting, just with mostly women. While maintaining discussions and decisions in their circles without the men, women got accustomed to speaking in public and taking on issues on this level. This led to a big influx of female candidates for the elections of the formal government who had won confidence in their capacity to lead and decide.

I'm sure there's a lot more to learn from this project once it's been studied in more detail. I hope that will happen soon. The project deserves the attention.

---

[8]Highly recommended to watch the documentary "Power To The Children" for more information and a great impression of the work done as well as its principles.

Another self-governance effort that needs to be mentioned here is Rojava, also known as the Autonomous Administration of North and East Syria, is a region in northern Syria. It is primarily populated by Kurds but is also home to other ethnic and religious groups. Self-organization is a key principle of the political and social system implemented in Rojava. This approach is based on the ideology of democratic confederalism, which was developed by Abdullah Öcalan, the imprisoned leader of the Kurdistan Workers' Party (PKK). The region is divided into three cantons: Afrin, Jazira, and Kobani, each with its own autonomous administration. These cantons are further divided into smaller administrative units, such as communes and neighborhood councils. They discuss and decide on matters like infrastructure, public services, and local projects.

The system emphasizes local autonomy, direct democracy, and gender equality in grassroots participation and decision-making. Rojava has embraced a system of direct democracy, where decisions are made through popular assemblies and democratic decision-making processes. Public meetings called 'communal assemblies' are held regularly at the neighborhood, village, and district levels, where residents come together to discuss issues, propose solutions, and make collective decisions by consensus (with a supermajority fall-back in some cases). (See Knapp/Ayboga 2016.)

Learning how to make decisions together in a *power-with* fashion is appealing not only to people who want to institute an alternative to the formal government. It also is appealing to people who already work in formal government. In a small town in Essex in the UK, a Parish Council used the selection process in an experiment to select their chair by consent in 2023. Those involved reported that they enjoyed the lack of competition. They also appreciated the structured format, which they found beneficial for this community-level governance.[9]

Here are some first-hand accounts from the Essex experience. I picked ones that most illustrate the non-competitive, *power-with* spirit.

> "Rather than trying to climb up and say why I am so good at this and I want to be the leader, it became people saying, well, actually, I would like this person because, and then they proceeded to say all the positive things they thought about them, which, to me is just so refreshing. And so nourishing, really. And then the consent that happened after listening to everybody else just made it so incredibly different and wonderful, really."

---

[9]See the full interview here: https://youtu.be/JBn4GWRhP4g

"So it gets the right person for the job, whether or not they're someone who would automatically put the hand up. . . . And the biggest differences at the end of that voting process, you don't have anyone who's feeling like they've lost or they're disregarded, you've got – everyone's pretty much happy with what the outcome is. . . . So the last thing I wanted to say was that the atmosphere at the end of the process was very harmonious. I mean, it's like a team. And that's what was missing. For me the whole time I was at the parish council. I fought like hell to get a meeting. And, suddenly, you've got a bunch of people who are even open to even trying that process. And that's what's really magical about the whole thing."

"And the process planted something very special because the chair felt like he had been chosen by everybody. So he's already held."

Parish community members also reflected on this experiment's effect on themselves as a council. They saw themselves as a more collegial unit.

They admit they're still learning, but what they've experienced so far has made them curious to explore how the 'standing orders' – the local requirements on how meetings are held – can be tweaked to allow more consent-based processes.

This chapter wouldn't be complete without the the Iroquois Confederation, as the prime example of what a participatory democracy can look like. It was a political and cultural alliance of six Native American nations: Mohawk, Oneida, Onondaga, Cayuga, Seneca, and Tuscarora. The confederation was established around the 16th century, and it lasted until the American Revolution; it therefore counts as the longest-running democracy.

The governance of the Iroquois Confederation was based on a system of representative democracy, with power shared among the six nations. The central governing body was known as the Grand Council, composed of 50 sachems, or representatives, from each of the six nations. Each nation was represented by a different number of sachems based on their population.

The Grand Council was responsible for making decisions on matters of common interest to the confederation, such as war, peace, and diplomacy with other nations. It also oversaw the election of leaders and the implementation of laws. The meetings of the Grand Council were highly structured and formal, with strict protocols and procedures for discussion and decision-making. Each nation had a designated speaker responsible for presenting their nation's views on a particular matter. When a topic was brought before the council, the sachems would discuss it in detail, giving each speaker equal time to present their arguments. The council operated on a consensus-based decision-making process, aiming to reach a decision agreeable to all parties.

Not only the system but even more the daily practice of the democratic governance is inspiring. Graeber & Wengrow quote an account from 1630 where a Jesuit Priest, Father Le Jeune, comments "There are almost none of them incapable of conversing or reasoning very well, and in good terms, on matters within their knowledge. The councils, held almost every day in the Villages, and on almost all matters, improve their capacity for talking."

The Iroquois Confederation was a sophisticated system of governance emphasizing consensus-building and collective decision-making to promote the common good, remains an inspiration for modern deliberative democracy, in which citizens engage in respectful and informed dialogue to reach common solutions to public problems.

5.2.3   Governance options

In summary, I think it's important to distinguish two different approaches to using participatory and self-governance methods for government:

- One is to add 'bridges' of citizen participation. That is the approach of vTaiwan, the city in the Netherlands, and many other citizen participation projects.
- The other approach is to *replace* government or individual parts of the existing system with new systems. That's the way of the Children's Parliaments and of experiments to use consent decision-making in government bodies.

The sections below are a list of parameters or tensions that need to be considered in order to design *power-with* government.

Citizens vs. experts   Whatever systems we create, we have to consider the fact that our lives and systems need to balance specialization and participation. Any decision needs to work for the people but it also needs to work for the systems, which means experts who understand the systems need to tell citizens what possible impacts or interdependencies are.

Any system that puts decision-making solely into the hands of citizens will likely not handle the complexities of our systems well enough. And we have to keep in mind that we can't be or become experts at everything. We can't even track things that we would understand satisfactorily because our bandwidth is limited. We can't be part of all the things that affect us.

Let's imagine for my own life (you can do the same for yourself), how many circles I would have to be a part of if this vision of including everyone in all matters that affect them were true.

- workplace
- living community/neighborhood
- town-wide matters, maybe also state and federal levels
- my kids' schools (three different schools, in my case)
- the credit union (bank)
- the food co-op and CSA (farm)
- my choir
- professional organization (in my case, of certified consultants)

Suppose one cast a wider net and wanted everything to be owned cooperatively with member involvement. In that case, we'd have to mention my phone contract company, the library, a gym, all insurance companies, including health insurance and car insurance, the local movie theater, and all my cloud-based services. How about the stores where I buy things?

Let's give this a reality check. I'm part of three sociocratic organizations (workplace, community, professional organization), and honestly, I can't even show up consistently in the second and third. I admire people who have the energy to volunteer for their kids' school, as I'm the parent who only reads every other email sent to the parents.

I don't vote in the credit union elections because I don't even know the people on the ballot. My choir is formally sociocratic, but we gladly delegated almost all power to the director because no one had the bandwidth.

We cannot live our lives and be involved in everything that affects us. I do not have a clue about wastewater management, so asking me about it makes no sense, and that's true for a vast majority of topics that governments need to make decisions about. Putting town management into the hands of citizens without expert help is impossible, given the complexity and specialization needed to run our infrastructure.

This is not something a perfect voting mechanism can fix. As I've shown in this book, majority vote inherently incentivizes people to vote based on individual preference, not on what's best for society. For the collective sense-making to inform a collective-level decision, we'd have to have enough shared common ground and subject matter expertise to build our sense-making and therefore our decisions on that.

We rely on others to inform us of decisions outside our direct experience sphere. Including more people in more decisions is impractical and undesirable as the effects of uninformed voters just compound.

While crowd intelligence might work with independent thinkers, people are vulnerable to being swayed by campaigns or stories and, therefore weaken crowd intelligence. Individual opinions, sadly, don't just add up mathematically into one policy, no matter the voting mechanism.

An extreme alternative view is that citizens are too misinformed to qualify for voting. Maybe they shouldn't even be involved? Would an 'epistocracy' (Brennan 2016) where governments consist of experts who have passed some sort of expert test result in more informed and rational decision-making and potentially lead to better policy outcomes? This elitist view is highly questionable as it is likely to come with its own biases because it would run the risk of a monoculture of ideas that lack diversity. Expert knowledge will likely be abstract; those abstract concepts need to be related to the local and specific. The local people are experts on the local level and the unique challenges and opportunities of their region.

The takeaway: decision-making by everyone on everything is neither realistic nor desirable, no matter the tool we use to collect that information.

Centralization and decentralization Given that, should governments just own their power and run the show? No.

Let's review the advantages of centralization and decentralization.

- *Centralization* is in government – the concentration of power and decision-making authority/responsibility in a central governing body. It exists on municipal, state, national, and supernational levels. Governments make laws and regulations and standardized systems that provide a framework to ensure consistency and coordination in infrastructure and policies.

  Standardization, unity, common norms, and practices help a society function. Let's take street traffic as an example. In street traffic, millions of people who don't know each other cooperate daily with surprising accuracy. It works well! Standardization supports interoperability, efficiency, and reliability. Other examples are quality standards that help with safety or technical standards that enforce that electrical plugs work the same.

  Bottomline: centralization is not bad. But full centralization doesn't work – there is too much complexity for a government to cover everything – it may not effectively address the diverse needs and complexities of different regions or communities. It can lead to a lack of local autonomy and decision-making power, resulting in policies that may not be responsive or appropriate for specific contexts. Centralization is also often bent to an advantage of the few who are able to influence the decision making.

- *Decentralization* is in markets and pluralism, in freedom and autonomy. It works the opposite way – we aim to distribute decision-making authority/responsibility and resources across different levels or entities within a society. Everyone can do whatever they want. That empowers individuals, organizations, and communities to make decisions and take actions based on their specific needs and contexts.

  Competition is a fundamental principle in markets. Individuals, organizations, or entities try to access finite resources (like customer attention and funds). Like on the other levels, competition drives innovation, efficiency, and quality as actors strive to offer better products, services, or solutions.

  In contrast to unity and standardization, pluralism helps us recognize and celebrate diverse perspectives, values, beliefs, and identities.

  Bottom line: decentralization is not bad either. But complete decentralization isn't in everyone's interests. It can lead to fragmentation, inconsistency, duplication of efforts, and a lack of coordination across different regions or entities. For example, if we let the town decide to pour its wastewater into the river, it would have a similar effect to how companies treat externalities – "after me, the deluge." From a national, regional, or global perspective, giving towns completely free reign might not provide enough alignment with global-level wellbeing.

Generally, the ideal is to combine both, hoping they can balance and mitigate each other's weaknesses. That is our current system, or at least its attempt to do so by having a market and government.

- Market failure refers to situations where free markets cannot allocate resources efficiently or produce desirable outcomes due to externalities, monopolies, information asymmetry, or public goods. It occurs when pursuing individual self-interests in the market leads to suboptimal societal results.
- Government failure, on the other hand, refers to instances where government intervention or regulation fails to achieve its intended objectives or produces unintended negative consequences. It can

occur due to bureaucratic inefficiency, corruption, inadequate information, or the inability of government policies to address complex societal problems effectively.

Recall how, on the other levels of networks and collectives, governance mediated between the two polarities of cooperation and competition. On the national level, the government plays two roles: mediator *and* unifier, with regulations, policies, and frameworks that (ideally) promote fair competition (like consumer rights) and ensure a level playing field.

Similar to what we've seen within organizations where different domains or topics may benefit from more or less (de)centralization, different sectors, industries, or policy areas may require varying degrees of centralization or decentralization based on their unique characteristics.

What are useful units?   Currently, the highest powers are nation-states. The legal frame is that states are sovereign and have exclusive authority over their territory. The legal framework of state sovereignty means states have the ultimate decision-making authority within their boundaries. This includes enacting and enforcing laws, maintaining security, regulating commerce, and representing their interests in international relations. Nation-states possess the power to determine their governance systems, make policies, and exercise control over their territories.

It's an oversimplification to say that nation-states are the predominant systems. While that's formally true – since nation-states have the power of violence within their defined territories – the reality is that the global landscape is evolving beyond traditional nation-state boundaries. Globalization, advancements in technology, and increased interconnectedness have given rise to various transnational and supranational entities – international and supranational organizations (like the United Nations, or the World Health Organization), Transnational Corporations, big NGOs, and digital networks don't follow the patterns of nation-states. Global issues like climate change and pandemics transcend national borders.

Nation states are not a 'natural' entity. Their existence is largely due to an intentional effort called 'nation-building' to convince people that they belong to a particular country. Nations like Germany or Italy were *deliberate* constructs that were designed. They were initially met with confusion. People identified with their local culture and language, often aligned with a bioregion. Languages differed widely – in Germany, people in the south don't understand people in the north, and that is still true after a century of media production and consumption that produced a somewhat blended 'Standard German'. Instead of often artificial boundaries drawn on a map, bioregions or smart cities would be a much better meaningful entity. Depending on how one counts, there are a few dozen or a few hundred bioregions on the planet, each with their own conditions and interdependencies.

In addition, nation-states are often carry a colonial history. The intention of nations was to build bigger empires with more political power – they are constructs shaped by a world of competition and power-over, and often, and arbitrary borders.

If we think about decision-making domains and where they should best be decided, nation-states are really just one level among others.

In many ways, nation-states are more and more deemphasized towards more cross-connections on whatever 'unit' is useful and necessary. This could be pushed further. For examples, for local economies, natural ecosystems and therefore also our food systems, bioregions are a more appropriate 'unit' to consider than nation-states. That means that, for example, if we want to improve our water quality, instead of having to work across different municipal domains, our government for those entities would follow the natural environment like watersheds. (See more on the internal structure of bioregions in the next section.)

Some units would need to be 'redrawn' away from states towards bioregions. Other units have to scale up into bigger units. For example, the introduction of the Euro zone instead of national currencies came from the realization that markets are so interdependent that a shared currency and shared oversight would make much more sense than local currencies and oversight. Similarly, for the governance of policies around Artificial Intelligence (AI), bioregions don't make a difference; it's an issue that has to be solved on a global scale. The same may be true for international trade, finance, and climate policies.

But what about the education system? And energy systems? Zoning? Local infrastructure? They might be better served on a smaller scale for governance while enhancing information sharing among players on the same level in different locations.

If we had a system where each of the domains is governed on a different level and entirely held there, nation-states might be useful for something. Nation states would just be one among many strata of organization. This might lead to a proliferation of players that need careful alignment and coordination. For example, imagine a project in a university in Belgium. Let's say they receive grant funding that follows EU regulations, but they also have to follow regional and national legislation and need to comply with town and university *and* department regulations. If we add a global government for climate and AI regulations and other levels in between, it would represent real-life complexity and interdependence but also increase bureaucracy and coordination costs.

That's similar to a model that Hansi Freinacht, a key thinker in the area of Metamodernism seems to have in mind.[10] Instead of increasing voter participation, he argues for more collective intelligence (no matter what the specific voting mechanism might be) and less reliance on decentralization of decision-making (subsidiarity). He proposes more of a meshwork system where we intentionally create interdependencies between different entities, even across countries – like Denmark and Sweden giving each other power on decisions the other country to reflect their interdependency. Other examples are policies about water use for rivers that flow through a country before reaching another, like between the USA and Mexico.

I sympathize with the basic idea that, in my words, seems to ask governance to follow the interdependencies that exist in the world. If policies in Denmark affect what happens in Sweden, then that's an interdependency in the real world currently underrepresented in governance.

I wonder if it's necessary to give each other decision-making power. More learning and shared information might be a unifier, even without changing the power structures. For example, cross-connections in most role-based/consent-based systems are typically not represented in giving each other voting power (via linking) but simply as invitations to create one-time, temporary, or standing opportunities to share information that can internally affect the decision-making.

It would be my hope that if those cross/mesh-connections came with choice-based, voluntary commitment out of the willingness to contribute to the supernational level, it might come with more empathy. Interestingly, the case of Utrechtse Heuvelrug (UH) that we looked at earlier includes a comment on how the now consent-enhanced municipality differed in its attitude from other municipalities.

> An interesting example of the UH's city council orchestrator role is how it shaped the city's response to the European refugee crisis, involving a strong rise in the number of refugees and migrants making the journey to the European Union to seek asylum (as of 2015). Repeated requests from the national government to Dutch municipalities to accommodate and host many refugees have unleashed turmoil and

---

[10]Freinacht 2022

> protests among citizens in many cities in The Netherlands. In the UH
> case, however, the city council carefully orchestrated this process, by
> inviting UH's citizens to engage in discussions with councilors and al-
> dermen in several consultation evenings. This resulted in a high level
> of public support and broad political support within the council for its
> formal decisions on how to host and integrate so-called 'newcomers.'
> As a result, the city of UH has been able to accept and host far more
> than its proportional share of refugees in The Netherlands. (Romme
> et al. 2018)

A greater sense of citizen participation – being heard and considered –
might lead to more inclusive decisions between sovereign entities.

5.2.4 A structure for a bioregion

What could the internal structure of a bioregion look like? This section
provides a highly tentative attempt to give pointers to a potential structure.

For the sake of this sketch, I will assume that the operational and policy
decisions will primarily be made by workers in circles, just like working in
town management is a regular job right now, where daily life is not much
different from working for an organization in the private or non-profit sector. A bioregion has a lot of complexity with big departments as we already
know them, like transportation, health, education, and infrastructure.

But as explained above in 5.2.2, a bioregion is not just workers, and
we need to distinguish between between workers and citizens.

We can learn from the experience of intentional communities. They
compare well because they, different from self-organized companies, are
often a blend of *residents who live in the community* and *workers who
contribute to the community work.*

How are residents involved in the governance of decentralized communities? Mainly, connection happens naturally and unplanned via social life.
Yet, many communities also include an all-member meeting in their governance. (Other words are plenary, Full Circle, assembly, General Meeting,
or town hall.) It's important to see how all-member meetings differ from
workers making decisions in decision-making teams.

All-member meetings for various purposes – decision-making on certain issues or simply connection, learning, and exploration.

- **Decision-making.** How many and which kinds of decisions are
  made in the all-member gathering will affect the level of collective
  agency in the community, as illustrated in the story *'The Community Doesn't Care'* in section 3.1 where one member felt that the

community was unable to effectively act with follow-through. If the all-member meeting makes all major decisions, it often reduces the collective agency. If all decisions are made in circles and there are no decisions in the all-member meeting, things move more swiftly.

- **Exploration.** Regarding whether decisions are made in all-member meetings, the assemblies can serve as sounding boards for topics by giving residents a chance to give feedback on decisions made in the team. As established in section 2.3.3, an exploration is crucially different from a decision, but it is easier to include more people in explorations. Various facilitation formats, like the Art Of Hosting, can support exploration with large groups of people.
- **Information and education.** All-member meetings can serve information flow, by offering presentations and Q&A sessions for members.
- **Connection.** All-member meetings can also serve as connection opportunity where people can listen or give each other advice and support. Small groups or 1:1 connection serve belonging and, at least indirectly, collective decision-making.

How can we scale up the functions of an all-member meeting from a community of maybe 100 people into a town or a bioregion?

- We might simply have very large meetings. Similar facilitation formats might accommodate ten thousands of people like fairs or large conferences do now.
- Another option is to learn from Neighboroughcracy and form neighborhood-based gatherings that nest into larger-scale gatherings.
- We might also offer topic-based gatherings, like a gathering for all citizens interested in cyber security or all dairy farmers in a section of the bioregion.
- A combination of all of the options mentioned.

Would these gatherings make decisions? While it is conceivable that they might make decisions on issues (e.g. via a majority vote), an idea more in line with what I've laid out in this book is the following

- Operations related to public activities (infrastructure) are held in work teams made up of workers in those areas.
- Geographically based all-member gatherings happen from a neighborhood to a bioregional (and inter-bioregional level). Hosting those gatherings could be held by a worker-led team in a department we might call Citizen Connections.

- In addition, all operational teams are responsible for hosting gatherings in their domain. The gatherings provide input to the decisions made in worker-led teams. Those are the topic-based gatherings.

The overall structure would look somewhat like this:

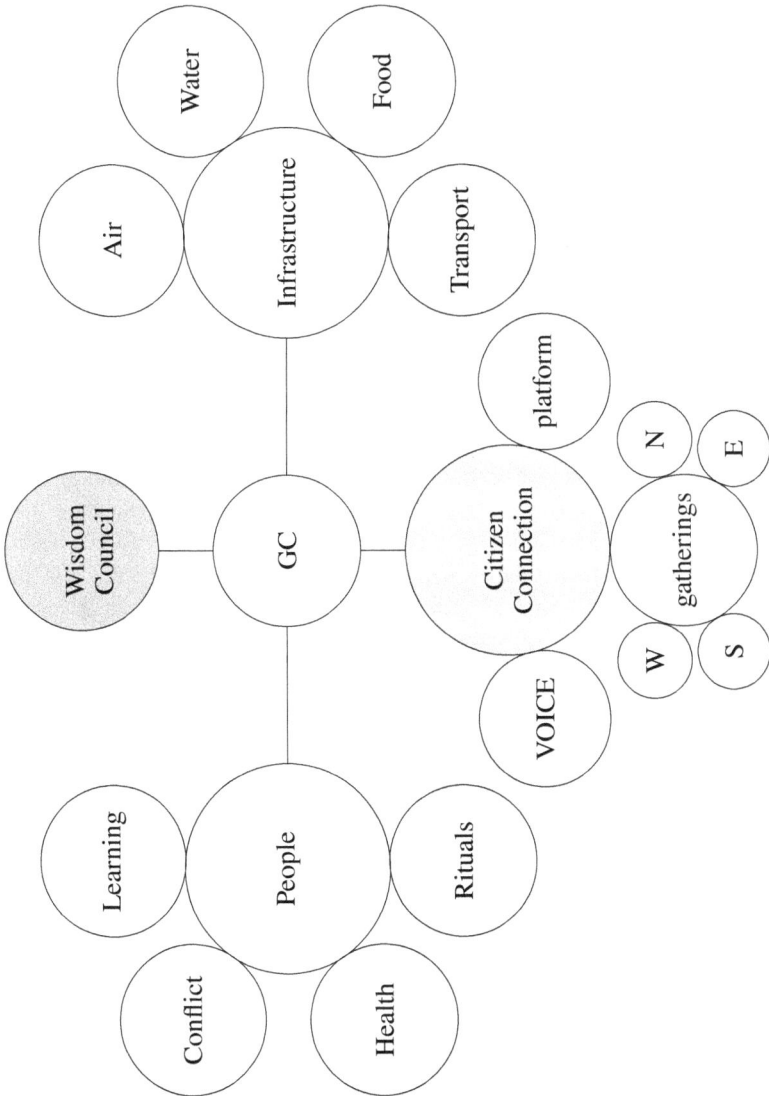

The People and Infrastructure circles are regular work circles, organizing work in a self-organized manner, with subcircles and intentionally
placed domains with the level and depth needed to do the work.

The Gatherings Circle would host local gatherings, most likely with
geographic subcircles (here, as placeholders, north, south, east, west) that
hold a certain area, very much like the neighborhood parliaments. One
distinction might be that the circles we see are not actually the gatherings
but merely the *support bodies* or connection points that *support* local
gatherings with centralized support (like Help Desks in section 3.5.3). An
autonomous bottom-up movement is important here, but wouldn't have to
rule out being met with aligning support in a top-down manner flexibly.

VOICE and Platform could be the circles supporting the centralized
infrastructure services that all gatherings can tap into – a platform similar to Pol.is (as mentioned in section 5.2.1) for nuanced, perspectival,
non-competitive polling. VOICE might stand for *Vocalizing for Organized
Initiative and Community Empowerment* and be a body that supports information flow between citizen efforts and the government (see the fictional
story in 5.5) in a standardized hearing process to make sure spontaneous
marches or protests lead to action in a responsive manner.

The Mission Circle could be a sortition-based circle where randomly
chosen individuals oversee the mission-alignment and make sure the governance system design is good enough for the well-being of the whole. (For
'good enough' governance, see section 5.4.2.) The overall mission and the
foundational governance protocols would be in their domain to make sure
the bioregion has agency even on the highest level. The accountability
mechanisms would need to be spelled out with more detail.

The Mission Circle might also host the connections to other bioregions;
likely there would be direct connections across bioregions, for xample
through a water treatment community of practice that supports sharing of
ideas and concerns with other local water treatment circles.

Budgeting would largely follow a circle-based budget, with the overall
budget overseen by the bioregional General Circle; it might include funds
that are distributed in a participatory budgeting process to include more
citizen participation.

The decision-making processes could be consent in most places, with
an occasional (supermajority) voting process for major decisions, or decisions related to funding new projects.

The below list shows a number of considerations that I see as crucial
in designing larger scale units of self-organization.

- **Information flow.** How could information flow be ensured so citizens and workers can be heard, and there is less distance between government and citizens? How would local gatherings be run? Would it work to have local gatherings for connection and feedback, or would it create too much autonomy in the operational part of the system? On the flip side, will citizens be informed enough to provide useful input? The responsibility for this could be decentralized by putting the responsibility to provide and curate information in each domain while being overseen and generally supported by the Citizen Connections Circle. The same questions also apply to conflict resolution.

- **Private – public.** How would private ventures connect with this system? For example, how would privately owned farming operations or schools feed into the public system? Would organizations be able to join collective impact-like bodies connected to the bioregional government? How many cross-connecting coalitions would break through the silos between departments, and how? For example, would there be a farming program in schools, and where would that be held, in the farming or the education department?

- **Economic systems.** What are the economic systems? For example, would there be a model of universal basic income? What scope might private ownership have?

- **Power distance.** Would citizens feel more empowered or overburdened? Could it work to include more people in volunteer or part-time roles in government to spread the load and reduce the power distance? Would teams be excited to do polling and gatherings to inform their decision-making? What are the blind spots?

- **Super-bioregional connections.** What would be the interconnections with other bioregions or global institutions? Would it be clear what domains need to be held on the bioregional level, and which need to be held on an international level? (See the discussion in section 5.2.3.) Beyond decision-making on higher levels, what would sense-making and information flow among bioregions look like? For example, would bioregions still ignore externalities in other places (e.g. imported rare metals)?

Obviously, there are a lot of open questions here. I hope my impulse can infuse current and future discussions.

5.3   Identities

So far, in this book, I have been treating people in organizations as face-less, context-less workers with more or less a sense of their agency and responsibility. I have not touched on identities and mindsets.

But people aren't just individuals or parts of teams. They are also a part of bigger groups based on their identities, and they run on the big narratives we absorb by living in our cultures.

It's essential to see that identities don't form collectives in a narrow sense. While people sometimes assume that there is a shared goal of *all xyz* people, that's rarely the case. Members of a certain identity are rarely organized in a way that forms agency. That also means that no one can speak on behalf of all women, men, queer people, first-generation immigrants. . . . One can speak *as* a member of an identity but never *for* them. Speaking for a collective requires legitimacy and a process that empowers a person to speak on behalf of a group and an approved message to be asserted.

Even if those identities and narratives aren't collective and don't orig-inate inside organizations, they affect organizations, and organizations themselves impact people within organizations and the narratives on a larger scale. We could be perfect self-managed organizations, and clas-sism, racism, colonialism, and misogyny would still exist, and they would make an imprint on every decision we make in the organization. In addi-tion, the pain the narratives have inflicted on people would still exist, even in a 'perfect' organization.

For teams and organizations, this terrain is incredibly challenging to navigate. Some go down a dangerous path of ignoring identities, hoping to make their impact disappear. They just 'declare' all people as equal. That's unrealistic and harmful, as it dismisses the lived experiences of people who have suffered from various forms of discrimination and systemic injustices. It also hinders the capacity to acknowledge and address these issues within the organization, leading to continued inequality and potential resentment.

Other organizations want to face identities head-on and solve *all* issues and heal *all* of our pain to build 'pure' organizations that don't perpetu-ate *any* unhealthy patterns. Some people even say that nothing is worth doing *until* those forms of oppression are eradicated. This approach can sometimes overshadow the individual's unique experiences, talents, and perspectives, leading to another form of unintentional bias and stereotyp-ing. It also is easy to get paralyzed as an organization.

Others try to do both at the same time – acknowledge and start working on undoing the systems of oppression, *and* do what they do in a new way as much as possible while noticing and undoing the harm that continues to be done, without being purists about it. They know that identities inform, but do not solely define, each individual. To work towards an equitable organization, it is necessary to acknowledge systemic and interpersonal injustices while cultivating a culture that values each person's individuality.

5.3.1   Empowerment patterns

The impact of identities and stories connected to them is everywhere. Here are a few examples.

Let's look at a story where people's race and gender were associated with problematic behavior.

> It was a new group where people didn't know each other well. Most people were in their early thirties, based in the US and UK. They were fairly equally mixed in gender and race.
>
> We were selecting a new facilitator, and the nomination round was regular – a few nominations for this or that person with good reasons. The last person in the nomination round then nominated a Black woman with the reason *I think it would be great for this group to have a female voice to be very present.* In the change round, many changed their nomination to her for the same reason. Reading her body language, I sensed that she was uncomfortable, but I was only an observer in this process, so I just waited to see what would happen.
>
> The current facilitator himself was a strong and verbal proponent of having her become the new facilitator. After the change round, he proposed she fill the role. In the consent round, she objected because she said she wasn't a good facilitator, which kept her from participating well. A reaction round on the objection followed in which a common – and disheartening – dynamic played out. All the men in the group insisted that the best way to empower her was to have her be the facilitator. She, on the other hand, was very clear, and she even said *If you want to empower me and want me to contribute, then don't make me the facilitator. I have a hard time focusing on the content when I facilitate.* When the facilitator proceeded to try to convince her, I finally intervened.

I call this story *Rescuer Pattern*. In Karpman's drama triangle (described in section 1.5), this would be a perfect example of rescuer energy, where – in my reading – the men had felt so good about themselves being *empowerers*

of a (Black) woman that somehow 'needed their help to be heard' that it
became impossible for them even to hear whether their help was productive
or wanted. They were oblivious to it. Or maybe they didn't actually
want to help – or they would have listened to what she needed. Trying
to talk someone into something 'for their own good' is an overreach in
responsibility. But where does encouragement end and overreach begin?

Identities around class, gender, and race seem to invite the drama
triangle dynamics that we need to understand to support a more equal
voice for everyone, including those historically disadvantaged. Here is a
story about class.

> Two founders started a co-op in the medical field. Those two
> founders hired a third person, Felicia, into a part-time position. There
> was a significant age and class difference – Felicia was older and came
> from a working-class background. The two founders were young,
> high-capacity powerhouses from a middle-class background with lots
> of educational privilege. Despite the differences, there was a lot of
> affection, friendship, and respect between the three women. The
> start-up grew, and Felicia quickly became the organization's heart,
> everyone's caretaker, and dearly loved. At the same time, Felicia
> needed a lot of support around the operations of her work. It was
> complex work with a lot of technical background and building the
> road while traveling. That aspect of dynamics could have been better
> – but people were busy building the start-up.
>
> One day, the three founders discussed remuneration in the coop-
> erative, where they disagreed on a core value issue. While the two
> founders wanted a slightly stratified model where some people would
> earn more money than others, Felicia was adamant that the co-op val-
> ues required that everyone be paid the same rate. The founders then
> proposed a proposal, and Felicia objected on the principle of equal pay.
> They talked, explored, and listened, but no common ground could be
> found. Finally, a pragmatic proposal arose: to make this decision by
> majority vote.
>
> Interestingly, Felicia – number-wise in the minority – consented
> with a big sigh of relief. They moved to a vote. As expected, she was
> outnumbered in the vote. The founders felt awful. In their view, they
> had overpowered Felicia. Yet, Felicia accepted the decision without
> visible resentment. Something in her vote against the proposal helped
> her be seen in a way that the conversations hadn't been able to give
> her.

Yet, the overwhelm on the operations side of the work quickly wore Felicia out. Things started to deteriorate. Whenever she needed support, Felicia began to see herself as a second-class member. A particularly tense moment flared up when the young co-op bought a computer for Felicia. They had purchased a Chromebook, which Felicia didn't consider a 'real laptop'. "You bought me only a Chromebook, and that's not a real laptop."

There was a mediation. They made an agreement that Felicia would speak up immediately whenever she perceived something as unfair. Yet, that fundamental tension never went away. Eventually, Felicia left the cooperative.

She left on good terms, however. To my knowledge, Felicia wrote a thank-you letter after she left, in which she thanked the founder for all she had learned in their time together.

It is a story with a lot of facets. We don't know how much both sides contributed to the dynamic. Was the story of being a second-class member a self-fulfilling prophecy, or were the higher-class members oblivious to their own bias? Where does individual responsibility end, and where does organizational responsibility for healing begin?

Of course, there are empowering examples as well. This following story, *Professional Woman Nominates Herself*, for example, I experienced as very gendered and beautifully empowering.

I was asked to pitch sociocracy to a small private college a few years back. They were at the beginning of a big change process around different topics. They agreed to try out a selection process to give them a taste. So we played with the process, choosing a facilitator as if we were an existing group. The guinea pigs were a group of four: two men and two women. I knew they knew each other well.

So we started. After dialing in the qualifications that we considered necessary, it was time for nominations. I asked everyone to think about which person in the group had those qualifications silently and would, therefore, be a good choice. I let them know that it's totally fine to nominate oneself if one has reasons to think one has the qualifications we agreed upon.

We then gathered those nominations for everyone to see. In a round, each circle member spoke and shared their nominations and reasons for the nomination. As you can see below, the men nominated each other, supported by one of the women, and one nomination for the other woman.

Person	original nomination	new nomination
Steven	Matt	
Matt	Steven	
Carol	Mary-Ann	
Mary-Ann	Matt	

Now it got interesting. In another round, the change round, people could change their nominations to reflect their thinking after hearing each other's nominations and reasons. This table gives you a sneak preview, but really *how* it unfolded is the point here.

Person	original nomination	new nomination
Steven	Matt	Matt
Matt	Steven	Matt
Carol	Mary-Ann	Mary-Ann
Mary-Ann	Matt	Mary-Ann

The people in the room were feeling vulnerable already by now – their voices a little scratchy, their faces a little flushed. They had been professional but cordial all day. They were curious but also conditioned by the hierarchical systems that had asked them to be assertive but distant. After the first nomination round, they were already a bit more open, almost tender. Speaking about each other in affirmative, appreciative ways changes the energy in a group.

I explained that these nominations were not expected to all get the same name in the second column. I also explained it wasn't a majority vote. Instead, I asked them to trust me that I'd know what to do if only they stayed with the question of who they thought was a good candidate for the role.

It was completely quiet in the room. Everyone was absorbing what was happening. While this was a fake selection process, people talking about others on the team was certain to get everyone's full attention. Steven stayed with his original nomination. Matt felt empowered by having been nominated to switch his nomination to himself. Carol stayed with her nomination of her female colleague. Now Mary-Ann spoke, and everyone was zooming in on her. She set out to say, "oh I will just stay with my..." And then she stopped. I am sure I held by breath! It took her about three long seconds to continue. And then she sat up in her chair, her whole demeanor changed, and she said with clarity in her voice: "You know what, I think I'd like to nominate myself!"

I celebrated on the inside. The moment was beautiful. We had witnessed her stepping into a completely different game. She had not pushed herself into the spotlight. There wasn't a trace of toxicity in her voice that I could detect. She had simply asserted that she thought she was well qualified for the role. I proposed to select Mary-Ann for the role of our fictional circle. We confirmed that everyone was on board with her filling the role by asking each person for consent.

Earlier in this book, I emphasized the domino effect that if individuals don't take responsibility, then the collective can't take responsibility. So if we want to step into collective agency, we need to support people's agency and their contribution to the group.

How can we support more agency on the individual level? Fortunately, the drama triangle also has a positive, self-responsible version: the empowerment triangle. The Empowerment Dynamic (TED) is a positive alternative to the Drama Triangle, developed by David Emerald. In The Empowerment Triangle, the drama triangle roles are transformed into more constructive and empowering alternatives.

- The Victim turns into a *Creator*: Instead of adopting a helpless, 'poor me' mindset, the individual in the Creator role takes responsibility for their life and actions. They focus on their personal *power-within*, resourcefulness, and resilience to overcome challenges and achieve their goals.

- The Persecutor turns into a *Challenger*: Rather than being aggressive, controlling or blaming for lack of responsibility, the Challenger role provides constructive feedback, encouragement, and support to help the Creator find their agency and responsibility.

- The Rescuer turns into a *Coach*: The Coach replaces the enabling behavior of the Rescuer with a more empowering approach. They facilitate problem-solving without taking on the Victim's responsibility and guide the Creator in discovering their *own* solutions and resources.

Note how the positive roles are all about people's responsibility. The creator doesn't give away agency but holds it themselves. For example, Mary-Ann in the election story, found her creator role when she took agency and put herself forward. The challenger doesn't impede on the creator's responsibility, and the coach doesn't overreach into others' responsibility.

How can we stay in *those* roles? I'm sure there are many answers to that, and more than one strategy is necessary to keep the system balanced. But in my personal experience in observing and participating in groups, I notice that the disempowerment (drama triangle) dynamics come in particular moments when groups are short of resources – time, money, attention, skill, and connection.

I had said in earlier chapters (section 1.5.3) that it takes skills, relationships, structure (and principles) to stay in a *power-with* frame. The same is true not only for personal dynamics around power but also for power dynamics around identities. A system needs sufficient skills in all participants – lots and lots of personal work around gender, race, and class – plus strong relationships, plus a structure that clearly and intentionally distributes power.

Each system needs to lean on *all* of the resources to be strong enough to withstand *power-under* and *power-over*, and that is even more true if working against millennia of patriarchy, xenophobia, and other forms of prejudice and oppression that are internalized and subtle. Since this book is about patterns of governance, I will focus on structures here, but with that, I'm not negating the need for personal work and all other forms of anti-oppression work. It's *all* needed.

With appropriate and intentionally (self-)chosen structures, it's possible to *create conditions* in which these dynamics don't play out as often. This point has been made very eloquently in the essay "The Tyranny Of Structurelessness" by Joy Freeman, noticing how the absence of structure leads to informal power, lack of accountability, exclusion and marginalization, inefficient decision-making, and replication of social hierarchies:

> "... the idea [of a structureless group] becomes a smoke-screen for the strong or the lucky to establish unquestioned hegemony over others. This hegemony can be so easily established because the idea of 'structurelessness' does not prevent the formation of informal structures, only formal ones."

Here's a frequently cited account of the company Valve, which says, "we don't have any management, and nobody 'reports to' anybody else."[11] Former employees describe it as "toxic teams, traumatized workers, opaque management hierarchy" (in Jin 2018).

---

[11]http://dl.pcgamer.com/Valve_Handbook_LowRes.pdf, retrieved June 28 2023.

We've seen many intentionally chosen structures in this book; I want to highlight a few that I've seen effective at keeping toxic dynamics in check:

- Rounds (the practice of speaking one by one until everyone has spoken once). They provide equal opportunity to speak and increase listening. People are less likely to jump to conclusions based on superficial or stereotyping perceptions.

  On the flipside, power dynamics often play out in direct and fast back-and-forths, which are rarely constructive and more prone to cycle into drama triangle roles.

- Small(er) group sizes. In my experience, the behaviors connected to prejudice show up more in bigger groups. Direct, close relationships provide more context and nuances to information, making gaps less likely to be filled in by stereotyping thoughts.

  Conversations in large groups can bring out the worst in people. The issues around miscommunication (with less opportunity to ask for clarification), competitive behavior and less cohesion, and less shared purpose compound turn large groups into a shark tank with less capacity for empathy and connection. The bonds between people get weaker, emphasizing individual interest over the collective interest.

- Clear and explicit decision-making methods. Not all humans are equally equipped to say no; the more clear it is how to say no, the more likely those people will speak up and true alignment can be found. A *yes* is a *yes* only if a *no* is possible and viable.

- A commitment to shared responsibility. Individualizing responsibility (in roles or other forms of clustering responsibility) can trigger drama triangle reactions because people can feel overwhelmed and fall into a Victim stance when they feel alone. Below is a story on that, *Averting A Victim Stance*.

  I was consulting with a congregation of about 30 people. Everyone was a volunteer, just one person was paid half-time, Janine. There had been some history there – in the previous governance system, a lot of the work had been put on Janine because, well, she was the paid person. Janine felt responsible for the same reason, but she also felt resentment.

  When the decision was made to transform into a shared power

self-management system, we had a several-hour meeting to work on aims and domains and the system to change them. We wanted to come up with an initial draft of aims and domains. Sadly, Janine was sick that day, so she couldn't participate. Since I didn't know her, I did not know the dynamics.

When we talked about the aims and domains, it seemed evident to me – simply on a pragmatic level of what kinds of activities typically cluster well – that two of the domains needed to be merged, and Administration would be folded into Communications. I learned that Administration was just held by Janine. As one would expect, she held pride in her work, and the fact that we – I, obliviously – had suggested a merge of domains shocked her. We had a chance to talk with Janine in a group of 12 people, their Mission Circle and General Circle combined (the implementation team).

The tension surfaced in that meeting. Janine spoke up and shared that she felt freaked out about the suggestion to merge. I thanked her for speaking up and reminded her it was a proposal. But I also asked,

"I understand that you feel tender about merging those domains, and it's not working for you. So I understand more, can you tell me your biggest worry?"

"I just feel so overwhelmed with everything. I am worried that I will have even more work. I feel nauseous just thinking about it."

That was a good hint. I guessed that the whole situation felt like it was happening *without* her, making her prone to go into a Victim position where everything was happening *to* her, not *with* her. I picked up on a gender dimension there, too – I tagged her as a woman of a generation who sacrificed herself and deeply attached her sense of worth to that contribution. While that was an extrapolation from her age, her gender, and how she spoke, the risk of entering a full-blown victim dynamic was too big.

Since I was a little slow on my feet trying to wrap my head around the situation, someone used the short silence to speak up and assured Janine that she would get help and that once the circle was formed, it would be "easy to support you and take tasks off you to help with your overwhelm."

The last thing someone in a victim position wants to hear is that their problem is easy to solve. It's a slap in their face and an assault on the little agency they feel. I could tell that Janine was getting ready to dig her heels. So I intervened and emphasized that overwhelm is almost always at an organizational level, not something that can 'just' be fixed. Janine seemed to relax a little.

In Janine's meeting evaluation at the end of the meeting, she seemed peaceful and said "I felt really heard today."

I interpret jumping in an offering to 'help with your overwhelm' as rescuer behavior. When I intervened, I tried to emphasize the *collective* responsibility so Janine would know that she'd have a say and that the responsibility wasn't just put on her.

Power dynamics can't be solved alone. Responsibility has to be renegotiated when we step out of the *power-under/over* game. It's a process. Janine needed to let go and others needed to step up. More governance skills and structures can provide the container in which the interpersonal relationships and relationships to our own agency can shift.

In this way, governance is a huge leverage point to create a robust playing field and an environment where people feel safe to express their true thoughts and be themselves. It is particularly significant regarding having a diverse team, where individuals may come from various backgrounds, cultures, and perspectives.

There's no point in having diverse people on the team if there isn't enough safety for being who we are (see back in section 3.4.6). We need to create inclusive spaces where everyone can contribute authentically. When people don't feel comfortable expressing their views, the potential benefits of diversity, such as increased creativity and improved decision-making, may not be realized.

5.3.2   Counteracting societal patterns

A big question in the field is whether the tools for creating that equal playing field are enough to counteract an unequal world in an affirmative-action way.

Let's take rounds, for example. Whoever speaks first in a round sets the tone for the whole round a little, making it a slightly more powerful position. Another powerful position is to be last, especially when moving towards a decision. So even when talking in rounds where everyone's voice should matter, the order might skew the field.

How can we manage that? If we're all equals, then the best solution is to shuffle and randomize the order from time to time and start with different people to, over time, create some equal(ish) distribution of the power of speaking first or last. This is simple enough. Yet, not everyone agrees with that approach.

Some groups argue that we also need to counteract privilege. Our identities play a role because the way we are perceived and hold ourselves in tone, confidence, style, and the skill to speak compellingly are still present. That's why some say that, for example, young people or working-class people should *always* speak first so they have the freedom to express themselves before getting influenced by others. They argue that this is the only way to create equal power because of how skewed power relations are in society.

In general, those who have grown up with trauma and lack of privilege might have a harder time in a free-for-all environment. That's not *their* own wrong-doing but society's failure. In short, we can't promote systems that promote *power-with* without working towards creating the conditions so people are *actually* on equal footing.

There is a lot of truth to that. If we don't counteract conditioning, we replicate structures of dominance where people with privilege are heard more than others.

On the other hand, this is an excellent example of how the individual, group, group of groups, and societal level are all present in the room at all times.

- If we look at the group level, we want to say "we're all equals" and work with a randomized speaking order.
- If we look at the societal level, counterbalancing lines of oppression seems critical and historically marginalized people should speak first.
- If we look at it from the individual level, we have to consider how each member of a historically marginalized group feels about going first, last, or whenever.

It can be hard to predict what is a supporting or hindering action. For example, some introverts have told me they hate speaking first. Other introverts have told me that they'd rather speak first so they can listen better and stop dreading their upcoming turn to speak. Ideally, we make those agreements locally so people can choose. But can we always ask? And would they always say?

I see no right answer here. The question is what weighs heavier in any particular group – the societal level of the group and individual level? And is there a way to hold them all equally and then decide locally?

5.3.3   Spotting toxic patterns

Here's a problem with the above approach of making those decisions locally. Let's imagine an organization of 40+ people where each person holds several roles in different circles. Now, let's imagine that one worker makes misogynistic, dismissive remarks about another worker. The person making the comments and the person targeted are in a few teams together. It's subtle enough that in each team this person is in, the other members are caught a little off-guard by the comments but don't think much of it. They assume that the comments have to do with a context they are unaware of, maybe from a different team. But the target worker experiences *multiple* aggressions. Where does the targeted worker go for support? No one has coherent insight into the story.

This is a dynamic that I am worried about. The only way to unveil the systemic nature of it is to highlight the *pattern* across circles in some suitable circle. Yet, because likely no one else has an overview of all the different places and the repeating patterns, the burden of proof will have to lie on the targeted person. An identity-based support group can support people by witnessing their concerns and offering individual support.

To make up for the inherent bias, emphasis on self-responsibility has to be held together with the responsibility of the collective to maintain a healthy environment. That means awareness-raising, training, and accountable self-development. Decentralized governance *alone* will fall short.

That is my main criticism of systems that heavily emphasize personal mindset shifts, as they often only emphasize individual responsibility while de-emphasizing collective responsibility. While personal liberation and self-responsibility are necessary for collective agency and responsibility, they are not the only factors needed. We also need governance, skills, and relationships. Without that, personal mindset work solely puts the responsibility on those oppressed and marginalized. We can't just cross our fingers and hope that everyone else will be 'conscious', rather than addressing the root causes of the inequalities and systemic issues.

To create a truly equitable and just society, we need to recognize and address the various dimensions of our lives, including the economic, social, environmental, and historical factors that shape our world. It means going beyond personal mindset shifts and fostering a collective awareness and commitment to dismantling oppressive structures and practices. In doing so, we can work together to create an environment where everyone can thrive and contribute to the well-being of our communities and the planet as a whole.

5.3.4   Collective responsibility for liberation?

Along similar lines, a big question is how much of the organization's energy needs to go towards collective liberation.

An organization may want to manage themselves with a *power-with* framework for efficiency purposes but have no strong intentions of using it as a tool for transformation. Shared power may be part of their governance structure but not a part of their vision, mission, aims, and everyday operations.

Others argue that governance is one piece of a much bigger puzzle. Ignoring the societal injustices and inequalities while celebrating *power-with* governance in a small fraction is like admiring a well-designed room in a house crumbling from neglect and disrepair. It fails to acknowledge the interconnectedness of the larger context and the systemic issues perpetuating inequities.

Effective governance within organizations, they argue, must, therefore go hand in hand with a broader commitment to social justice and addressing structural inequalities.

I feel split on it. On the one hand, it's evident that – even out of pure self-interest alone – an organization that wants to work productively will want to emphasize work towards the shared aim. Since drama, toxic behavior, and double binds (see, for example, the salary discussion on page 248) will distract from that aim, working towards a more just and egalitarian society benefits all *power-with* organizations.

Then again, organizations are formed to achieve organizational aims. As such, it's easy to argue that an organization that exists to provide bookkeeping services should provide bookkeeping services and not spend its days marching in the streets. It goes back again to alignment and balance.

It's again a tension between levels. On the organizational level, it's clear that the organization's aim should be priority #1. On the next-higher level, the organization must care about its wider context. Inclusion and overcoming systemic oppression is the responsibility of all entities on that level.

This shows up in organizations very often in questions of priorities. That might be on a concrete level – like in topic management, where we allocate time and attention to a topic – or in higher-level decisions like budgeting, values, missions, and strategy.

The goal is to manage the polarities and avoid extremes. A both-and is typically possible once the pattern is recognized and explored instead of distributing blame and holding out for perfectionism. My experience is that it's much easier to address the concrete policy question and find an acceptable path than to address the big question – the big question is unanswerable.

An example of zooming in instead is described in the story *Building Trust With A Cis Guy* in section 2.3.2 where a cis guy wasn't trusted to hold a feminist effort and the group around him needed to build trust by finding a short-term way to work together to ease into a collaboration.

5.3.5   Reductionism and context

Whenever we only look at one level or one narrative and identity, no matter what level or identity it is, we will miss important information. Let's take gender as an example.

> I remember a selection process in a small volunteer organization for bioregional organization running sociocratically.
>
> There had been nominations and change rounds, and the facilitator proposed candidates for the different roles. The group's founder, a man in his 50ies, was very active and reliable and an obvious choice for the leader. Many circle members proposed me as the facilitator, given my facilitation experience.
>
> One woman objected to the proposal because now two key roles, leader and facilitator, would be filled by men, which gave too much power to the privileged and would skew our decisions. I felt a mix of confusion and defensiveness. This was just shortly after my gender transition. (And the objector knew that; we had talked about it.)
>
> It was a 'should I laugh or cry' moment for me. I was happy to be counted among the men but also very confused to be mixed into the privilege category. I felt defensive. I had spent 37 years doing all the women's things – giving birth, staying home with several babies, and missing out on a good chunk of my 'career time.' She, on the other hand, was a single woman about my age. It felt simplistic and, honestly, inconsiderate and unfair.

I bet some readers will think: "Well, Ted, you're only telling the stories where you're victimized for being male. You're leaving out the stories in which you *did* have advantages." And that's perfectly right. Ironically, I can't tell you a single story where I got away with something or got extra attention or resources thanks to being male. And why not? Because I didn't notice them. I do not doubt that there have been thousands of those situations in my workplace alone in those last five years.

And yet, there is the sense that her story picked out one strand of truth and ignored many other truths. And that brings us to this section. Once there is a simplified narrative about a dynamic, it can become a lens through which *everything* is interpreted – a reductionist lens that is too simple to be helpful.

Reductionism is an approach to explaining complex phenomena by reducing them to simpler or more fundamental components.

Reductionism leads us away from reality

Reductionist stories, while helpful in understanding systems, are problematic. They often reduce to a simple narrative: good–bad, hero–villain, victim–perpetrator. When a reductionist story arises and gains traction within an organization, it can feel like a storm that blows through the organization and leaves nothing untouched. 'That person is simply a jerk and nothing else, and everyone who defends them is guilty too.'

Let me give examples of what I mean. Here's an example from a client.

> The group was led by a charismatic and beloved leader, Marianna. She had been in leadership for a long time. There was a significant power differential because Marianna held many relevant relationships, particularly with funders. The organization received grants basically because funders knew Marianna. The organization depended highly on those grants, so Marianna was a fixture.
>
> Many of the people who worked in the organization had been protegées of Marianna and – this was a country with high inequality – had social and economic status thanks to the work and, therefore, indirectly, thanks to Marianna.
>
> And yet, Marianna sometimes did things unilaterally. In particular, she had promised that her team would participate in an event with a partner organization. It was a big opportunity but required a lot of preparation on the part of the team. The team felt overloaded at the time, and tensions came up. Who had given Marianna permission to say yes to this when *she* wasn't the one doing the work needed to deliver?
>
> In their anger, some started saying that Marianna was overpowering and dominant.

Others pointed out how much Marianna had done for them.

Yet, the story grew into a judgment that maybe Marianna wasn't the saint they had made her. Did she *actually* care, or was she just doing *her* thing?

The negative story was held firmly by two of the members in particular, and it created a very challenging dynamic. When faced with the allegations, Marianna – who thought of herself as a selfless contributor – was caught off guard. The people accusing her saw that as another proof that she was oblivious to her own power.

Was Marianna a power-hungry leader? Or a selfless empowerer with ambitions for the team?

No matter what 'side' we are on, those reductionist stories are hard to prevent and hard to engage with once people hold them. Confirmation bias – we hear and retain what we want to hear – will ensure that we interpret new facts in that light.

Why do I talk about this in a book about governance? Because prejudices and narrowly held stories prevent people in organizations from seeing reality. Here's why.

- The first reason is that the reductionist story becomes the common ground. New facts are ignored or tweaked to fit the story. The common ground becomes a dangerously distorted version of reality. Organizations that aren't grounded in reality are not as resilient because they may overlook critical information, misjudge risks, and make flawed strategic choices.

- The second reason is that reductionist stories can cause a lot of drama. Reductionist patterns can stick *onto* patterns of oppression and marginalization. Reductionist stories reinforce a *power-over/power-under* story.

- In addition, distortion of people and their perspectives separates them from each other, which makes governance in a *power-with* frame harder.

Therefore, counteracting reductionist stories has to be in the interest of any organization that is based on a *power-with* approach.

The concept of *warm data* (Nora Bateson) is the idea that we lose information when we focus on simple narratives. Talking to each other vulnerably in small groups helps us see more of the nuances and more of the deeper connection of our stories while avoiding the oversimplification of reductionist tendencies. The *power-over/power-under* stories are decentered by adding more context. I think this is why relationships are such a good clue – the more we know about each other, the more we decenter individual aspects of our identities without disregarding them. As in the lines of Pat Parker poem "For The White Person Who Wants To Know How To Be My Friend":

> The first thing you do is to forget that I'm black.
> Second, you must never forget that I'm black.

The vision in this book is to strive for an integration, not a fragmentation of levels. We hold our identities, but we're also individuals, group members, organization members, role holders, friends, and many other things at the same time.

Holding polarities

Ironically, even vilifying reductionism is a reductionist approach. Categorizing and therefore, focusing on some properties while ignoring others isn't all bad. It helps us reduce information to a manageable level. It's a brain-effort-saving way of dealing with the world. Treating every situation as completely new and different would take too long. To help us focus on the essentials, our brain recognizes patterns, tunes out background information, and pays special attention to potential threats. If we couldn't do that, we'd be overwhelmed and incapable of acting. The world would be a firehose of disconnected, mostly irrelevant stimuli.

Remember how children learn the meaning of *dog* by better understanding what creatures fit into the set of dogs and which ones don't. Without an inside or an outside to that set, *'dog'* would have no meaning. While using words might be a simplification, they are still valuable and necessary to communicate.

And there's another vital aspect to this: some simplification is necessary to find common ground. Even though you and I might know a different set of dogs, overlooking that and focussing on the shared albeit simplified meaning of a word means that we can communicate. Imagine a person who finds the language that everyone uses too crude, and they start making up words that they think fit better. Taken to the extreme, it would be impossible to work with that person because we wouldn't understand each other anymore. Differentiation is necessary to an extent, and it needs to be balanced with integration.

Organizations are inherently reductionist. For example, organizational structures are reductionist – no structure can truly represent all the interdependencies and potential places for cross-pollination in an organization. Organizational structures are models that distill the real complexity into something that be drawn and expressed.

But they are helpful. There might be tasks that aren't written down and still get done. Some domains might be hard to separate into distinct circles' domains, but typically, it's still worth doing. All of our governance artifacts are just mental aids to help us understand more quickly who does what and what belongs where, such as when we write role descriptions, domains, agendas, or a memorandum of understanding between two organizations.

Even governance rules are a construct we give ourselves even though reality might be endlessly complex. Are they an oversimplification? Yes. Are they still helpful? Yes!

A lot of what I'm talking about in this book are helpful categorizations: discerning what's part of the topic on the table is a helpful categorization that helps us stay focused so we can act. Having a *shared* sense of understanding what kinds of activities align us with our mission supports our collaboration, as is to be clear on what counts into the accountability of a role and what doesn't. If we don't categorize, then we can't align with each other, and if we can't align with each other, we can't act together. By categorizing and simplifying, we can build *collective* agency.

Again, that doesn't mean that individuals have to compromise or disregard their own idiosyncratic reality. Maybe a good analogy is that we need to be bilingual or polylingual speakers. We need to be able to hold our perceptions and simplified categorizations but also our team's, our organization's, our coalition's, and our identity or society's. We already hold a multi-partial perspective in many areas of our lives, and we can do it more often and more intentionally.

5.4   The planet

5.4.1   Constraints

We live on a finite planet. Resources for everyone, including organizations and countries are abundant but limited.

Therefore, resource constraints are a reality for every collaboration. Clustering and categorizing similar activities into the same category can save resources by creating synergies and pooling of resources.

Remember the difference between operational and policy decisions. Organizations that make all decisions as one-offs have a high degree of differentiation and a low degree of categorization. Yet, with recurring decisions of the same type, it makes a lot of sense to cluster them into one category and treat them the same according to one policy. In appropriate circumstances, this can save time and resources.

Constraints are everywhere. For example, Mission-driven organizations often struggle with holding the polarity between mission and financial sustainability – doing things while being aware of the finiteness of resources. Understandably, if an organization wants to address a big issue, people want to serve that mission. This often leads to arguments in budgeting or in allocation of energy and attention. Out of all the possible things that are needed, which one do we fund or focus on?

He's a real-life example that my organization has struggled with.

> It is Sociocracy For All's aim to make sociocracy accessible, and that includes making it accessible in other languages. Language is a key barrier to accessibility of information – if a sociocracy video is in a language we don't speak, we can't learn from it.
>
> In addition, SoFA's most-spoken language is English because its two founders started out in English, attracting others who were also fluent in English, leading to an organization whose membership predominantly has English as a first, second or third language. (Not everyone speaks English.)
>
> English is not *any* language; it's a language that has been used – and still is used by groups who dominate other groups, strongly associating it with imperialism and colonialism.
>
> To make sociocracy accessible, resources need to be translated and localized (i.e. also changing the content and style to fit the context, like changing examples and the focus.) Localizing content, of course, requires resources – time, attention, and money.
>
> As a mission-driven organization, SoFA 'should' be working hard to localize into *all* languages so that *all* people can have access – because it is impossible to argue that people who speak English are more worthy than speakers of another language.
>
> On the other side, of course, is the resource constraint. The organization cannot afford to localize everything (and localize all non-English content into English and all other languages). This leads to internal tension and discussions.

In my experience, there are subcultures where the mission-driven side has more supporters. If one says, "it's really important to give everyone equal access", all heads nod. In other contexts, it's much more common to lead with the availability of resources, and the statement "we have to make sure it's financially viable" gets the nod. Those absolute statements are universally true. There is no counterargument to "everyone's needs matter." It's true. There's no quantifying it.

There is also no counterargument to "our resources are limited". They are. That's why talking in extremes like that isn't helpful. Those extremes can become reductionist stories that only consider one side. And as soon as that happens, often, the drama begins. One side stands up for equal access and vilifies those who want to limit access "just because" of costs. The other side dismisses the idealists who have 'no idea' how an organization runs sustainably. Some scold, others rescue, or feel victimized.

When emotions are high, middle-of-the-road statements like "let's pay only for those languages where there are at least five members who speak that language" can easily get the dismay of both sides. ("What, what about those who have three members, do they not matter?!" vs. "What?! If we add that many languages, we'll go bankrupt and end up helping no one in any language.") The absolute positions are morally justified, but they do not consider the polarity between ideal and constraint and aren't constructive.

Decision-makers in these situations shouldn't need to compromise. Compromises mean that both sides hold their individual needs and have to cave in to come to a shared way forward. But compromise is often not based on *power-with* but on *power-under*.

A more constructive, *power-with* way it to strive for a process where *both* sides hold *both* poles and together find an acceptable choice to create a cut-off in one particular place. Getting to consent on a solution that meets the needs of the collective in all its polarities is very different from finding a compromise born out of individual interests.

Considering the interplay of autonomy and alignment, denying constraints also means losing out on the innovative edge that comes with overcoming constraints and finding new resources or creative ways of making do with what we have. In the current growth paradigm, while we have gotten better at using our resources more efficiently with better technology, we still use more and more resources all the time.

An organization with the resources to do everything won't be forced to focus and find common ground in shared strategies supporting the collective aim. As such, finite resources can also catalyze unity when the challenge is taken up in a *power-with* manner.

5.4.2 Planetary boundaries

In this book, we've looked at individuals, groups, organizations, coalitions of organizations, and societies. What's the *highest* system in which humans are involved? Our planet is the home for our species and many others.

Just like there are constraints on each of the other levels, our planet is also finite. Fresh water, minerals and other natural resources, capacity to absorb waste and many more constraints limit what is possible on earth. At the same time, everything and everyone on it is interdependent.

That global interdependence is not reflected in governance. While more and more cooperation spans more than the national level, we are largely stuck at the level of nation-states. There is no global government.

As a consequence, there is competition between supra-nationals but insufficient supervision of those powers.

Even more, our current economic and legal systems actively *allow* companies and governments to ignore the impact they inflict where markets aren't self-regulating and governments aren't governing – like increasing inequality – or where governments kick the can down the road – like with final disposal sites for radioactive waste. Those issues simply fall into no one's responsibility.

In economic terms, this is what an externality is. Negative externalities occur when the negative impact of a decision is imposed on a third party who did not participate in the transaction. For example, if a factory pollutes a river, the local community may bear the costs of cleaning up the pollution. The factory can ignore those costs, deciding that it's someone else's problem, and clean-up costs don't have to be factored into the internal decision-making. It is currently legal to refuse responsibility on the organizational level to the wider context if something is classified as an "externality".

The question is, how far away do we define "external"? The river across the street? The pollution in another country? Ecological damage in 100 years? How far away does the impact of a decision need to be so we can safely move forward without consideration of the impact? In other words, when is an impact too far away from our sphere to matter to us? Everything matters, and yet, humans divide and subdivide, categorize and fragment, count things out, and declare them as 'too far away to matter'. Instead of perfect consideration and inclusion, it's the tragedy of the commons on a global scale where some people take the free ride and aren't held accountable.

And there's not only pollution of rivers. We're in a so-called metacrisis

(Schmachtenberger/Hagens 2023) or polycrisis – heading towards several big crises simultaneously – climate and pollution are only some of them. Sadly, they are all connected and easily compound; for example, a drought leads to a refugee crisis, which leads to political destabilization, which leads to the rise of populist leaders, which leads to policies more oriented toward short-term gain, which leads to exacerbated pollution and bigger environmental impact. It doesn't even matter which crisis starts first; they all have a pattern of mutually reinforcing each other.

Unconstrained competition between nations and corporations has led to tragedies of the commons on a global scale - where negative impacts are imposed on third parties not involved in the transactions. Pollution, ecological damage, and wealth inequality can be ignored by individual actors who are not held accountable for these externalities.

That points to the need for a global governance level to regulate global competition and hold global actors accountable. Without oversight and cooperation at the global level, we are likely to continue racing off the cliff of multiple crises.

The world is incredibly complex and interdependent. For me, an image that illustrates that sense of exhaustive interdependence is the idea of Indra's Web. Indra's Web (or net) is a Hindu and Buddhist philosophy metaphor representing the interconnectedness of *all* things in the universe.

The metaphor comes from the ancient Indian epic poem The Mahabharata, in which Indra, the king of the gods, creates a vast net that extends throughout the universe. At each intersection of the net, there is a shiny pearl. Each pearl reflects *all* of the other pearls in the net, creating an infinitely interconnected web of relationships and connections.

The pearls are so shiny that even those pearls further away still shine equally brightly. That's the ideal of equal consideration of everything and full consideration of the interdependence of everything. It's perfection.

That highest, fictional level has no constraints, just like heaven has no walls, and therefore, there also needs to be no competition, and therefore, it needs no governance.

In reality, we can never reach that level. We can *aspire to* that level. I imagine it as a place where there is perfect alignment with our values and all our needs are met. It's a fictional space, of course, but something that has reality as a mental backdrop for our expectations and our longing. As such, the idea has relevance, creating an aspiration, a pull towards doing better.

How far away are we from a governance method that considers *everything*?

In an optimistic read of history, it's fair to say that throughout human history, our governance and management methods *have* become better and better at integrating more and more people. That's Turchin's point in his book *Ultrasociety*. He describes that while building a prehistoric temple might have involved tens of thousands of people, the International Space Station has millions of people cooperating to build it. His point is that because of new technologies, the capacity to have bigger organizations, and new norms & values, our capacity to cooperate with more people has increased. Of course, it's not only about quantity but also quality. With the step from monarchies to democracies, for example, the level of participation has also increased, leading to more *power-with*, albeit very far from perfect.

Our social technologies for governance are getting better. Yet, at the same time, we're navigating dangerous territory between two polarities.

With all those looming issues we're facing, it's easy to long for a powerful leader with the power to implement climate change policies that would fix everything. Let's look at this thought experiment and assume that this may indeed be possible. With all the available resources and one big coordinated effort later, we could work ourselves out of the climate crisis and maybe a few more. But Schmachtenberger reminds us that this would come with huge implications. We could only get there by granting enormous power to one group or person, powerful enough to overrule all other policies in other places. We'd need a global dictatorship – an extreme centralization of power.

We know that centralized, immense power comes with a huge cost. Local contexts get drowned out and overruled. Power abuse is likely. People disengage and protest. Such big power can only be held in place with a significant amount of violence. If we have power, it even changes our brain towards reduced ability to feel empathy or take perspectives. So this amount of power would likely be abused. Overall, it's not a sustainable system – Schmachtenberger calls it the option of *Dystopian control*.

To avoid tyranny, we could look at the other extreme option – *chaotic breakdown*. In that option, we're distributing or decentralizing power much more; we could institute a very local way of decision-making and highly participatory systems. That would likely avoid protests and limit abuse of power, but decentralized approaches are slower and less coherent. We would lose our shared agency because all players would do their own thing. That kind of system wouldn't be able to push through big, transformational changes, even if for the better for the planet. It's hard to accept, but as we have seen, competition between players can rage even if that is to everyone's detriment (called multi-polar traps).

Schmachtenberger argues that there is a third option, which he calls the Third Attractor.[12]. That third option helps us stay clear of the undesirable extremes.

How could we find a middle path with more equal societies, a more sustainable planet, and a more beautiful world? Here are the ingredients he lists[13]:

- A mindset of *Bounded Abundance*.   With the same mindset as the well-known Doughnut Economics (Raworth 2017), bounded abundance refers to a mindset that sees that there *is* abundance but there *aren't* unlimited resources.   Human needs can be met if we acknowledge the boundaries while celebrating and sharing abundance.
- A deep, transformational shift from a competitive to a cooperative mindset. (This is not a contradiction to my points in this book; given that our current system is skewed towards a competitive system, more cooperation would shift us closer to balance.)
- Flexibility and adaptability around uncertainty and complexity. Operating in complexity is a key skill to acquire. (I would count better skills in decision-making, navigating *good enough*, *explored enough* and *clear enough* as well as intentional ways to distribute power for more resilient organizations.)
- Investment in education and technology as a leverage point to solve issues.
- A culture of trust and cooperation. The hope that cooperation is possible – this book is an attempt to spell out what that can look like for teams, organizations and bigger units.

This book is about governance as (and for) the third attractor. It comes about when we are aware of the collective level of the planetary level and its boundaries. While I've been talking about individuals, teams, organizations, coalitions, and their interference with society, the planetary level is the highest. We have a shared need for well-being on that level, including humans, and thus need to learn how to hold the global level as one of the levels.

---

[12]In Search Of The Third Attractor https://www.youtube.com/watch?v=8XCXvzQdcug

[13]as summarized by Michael Haupt in https://roamresearch.com/#/app/MichaelHaupt/page/NYOrVIUY6

scope

full interdependence and consideration of everything

societies   ⟷   planet

⟷   society

⟷

⟷

⟷

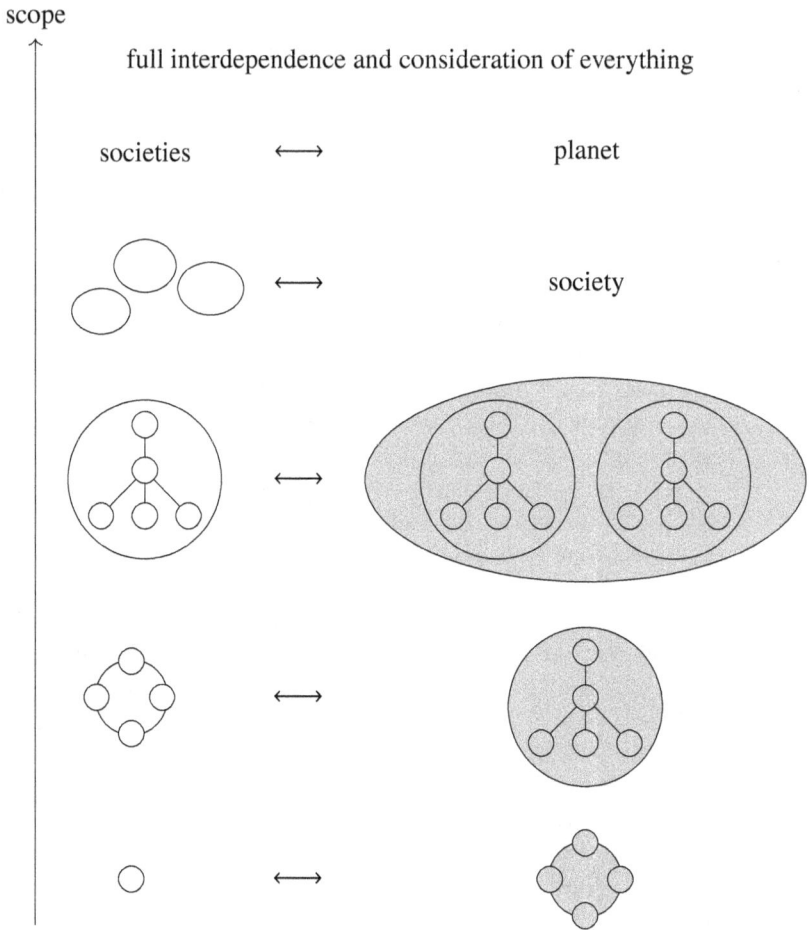

Individual and collective entity on all levels, incl. planetary and ideal level

The reason I care about each and every step in this book is because I believe that *each step along the way is necessary* for a global trajectory that avoids more destruction. Understanding the common ground, the pros and cons of decision-making methods, organizational questions of who decides what, and all the other topics in this book – are all necessary to avoid tyranny on one side and chaos on the other.

Governance is a key leverage in the puzzle. By highlighting governance, I don't mean to say it's the one solution. It's easy to hope for one big, sweeping factor to change the systems in a way that improves everything. The more likely scenario is that it will have to be a set of improvements in many places. One of my favorite quotes from Schmachtenberger is "The solution to all problems is all of the solutions" (Hagens/Schmachtenberger 2023).

Good enough governance

What I am offering in this book is a step towards governance that's *good enough.*

My suggestion is that this might be possible with careful design and more literacy on governance, and questioning some of the entrenched binary assumptions (for example, *participation is good, hierarchy is bad* on one side and on the other side *profit is good and greed is natural*). Instead of hoping for ideal governance, let's find governance systems that are good enough to avoid collapse.

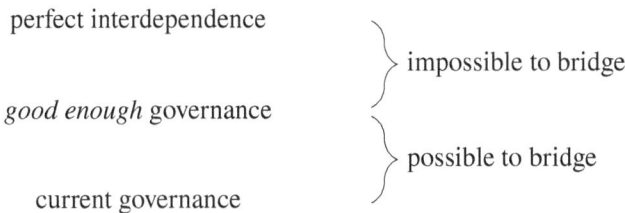

perfect interdependence

impossible to bridge

good enough governance

possible to bridge

current governance

Good enough governance as bridge to bend-not-break

How do we know what's 'good enough' governance?

Just like organizational governance needs to be optimized to sustainably support the organization's aim, intermeshed governance strategies globally need to support the planetary biosphere sustainably – survive and thrive. Therefore, a *good-enough* system of governance tools is a system that puts us on a trajectory that avoids global collapse. And given where we are, it would need to be a governance system that works towards a 'bend, not break' trajectory.

While there will always be unconsidered considerations and unknown unknowns, **better systems should at least consider *enough* of the interdependencies.** Our task for governance systems is to support *more wise* decisions that consider the planetary scale and the generations after us. It's not about finding the perfect system but about piecing together systems that avoid the extremes of chaos and tyranny and move the needle toward survival.

Learning how to make decisions within uncertainty and complexity, managing the polarity of centralization and decentralization, pacing and balancing, integrating our needs between our individual and collective identities – all of those are skills necessary for a future on this planet. There isn't one governance solution, there is just more knowledge and skill to design better practices.

I want to take a short detour into a useful terminology here: wide goals versus narrow goals, as used by Schmachtenberger. With a *narrow* goal, we only focus on a certain subset and ignore most of the interdependencies. We optimize for profit and ignore everything else. That makes things actionable and simple – but it comes at a cost. That's what *cleverness* is – using our intelligence to determine how to benefit from something while ignoring its impact elsewhere.

In an infinitely *wide* goal, we see and consider everything – *wisdom*. He points out that cleverness has to be held in check by wisdom, or the ignored externalities will be too destructive.

How do we inject more wisdom into governance? One way to do that is to include more of the highest human level – the planetary level – in our decision-making. Just like the organizational level can only be considered sufficiently if there is organizational governance, the planetary level can only be considered if there is designated attention to that level.

How do we increase the cooperative mindset on the planetary level?

(More) global governance

A simple answer to holding the planetary perspective in governance is to have global governance. What would need to happen so international agreements like the Paris Agreement – international treaty on climate change – could be binding and enforceable for all countries?

One approach would be replacing current governments with a nested system of bottom-up governance, bioregional or neighborhood style. At the highest level would be a centralized, global responsibility for global alignment on a planetary level. That seems far off from where we are now, and it would require a massive amount of learning and training. A bottom-up chain of *power-with* would need to build on the concepts in this book on all levels. I've been laying out a somewhat purist view of *power-with* approaches. Each chain link would have to be at least *good enough* for the system to hold.

That means people in a global governance system would need to know the steps along the way: how to balance autonomy and alignment on team, organization, coalition, movement and bioregional levels. Enough people need to know enough about it to make it run smoothly and adaptively.

Another, softer approach would be to add global ruling for certain domains, as is done via courts. To my knowledge, the first time this was done was the Nuremberg Trials 1945-1946, where an international community held individuals accountable for "crimes against humanity" in Nazi Germany. Note that this was done in the name of *all* of humanity, not in the name of a nation-state or the allied nations. There was a humanity-level purpose inherent in the endeavor.

Could the same happen for other actions, such as for crimes against nature or future generations? Could it be holding corporations accountable, or nation states? There are now legal cases like Duarte Agostinho and Others v. Portugal and 32 other states[14] of six young Portuguese people who were the first to bring climate change action to the European Court of Human Rights in 2020. Similar lawsuits are happening in Hawaii and Montana. Those supernational courts are another way to enforce action on a super-national level.

Incentivize and support collaboration

Another way is to avoid planetary governance but instead create account-ability to the planetary level – wisdom – via incentives.

Similar to peer-oriented structures, the patterns for inter-organizational work (see section 4.2) allow sovereign actors to collaborate and coordinate. An example of that is how the ISO standards come to be, which I've already described in 4.1.3. Since no international entity can rule into national legislation, the only way international standards can be made is by voluntary self-commitments. ISO standards are not legally binding; instead, they serve as guidelines or best practices that organizations can *choose* to follow.

This example shows that improvements solely on self-commitments are possible. The question is why nations and companies are likely to follow ISO standards. Yet, they don't consistently follow voluntary climate agreements and similar protocols or agreements that ban certain weapons like chemical weapons.

Voluntary self-commitments work when entities benefit from follow-ing the commitments. In the case of organizations following ISO standards,

---

[14]https://youth4climatejustice.org/

they improve their operations, products, or services, demonstrate responsibility, or a competitive edge. What would be the individual advantage of following climate protocols, stronger than just 'wanting to do a good thing'? What would create an economic imperative? Carbon taxes and similar methods are approaches to create an economic imperative that can contribute to change (but might be less reliable than regulations).

Another way to incentivize alignment with global well-being is a big narrative. Narratives have been used throughout history to unify large groups – like followers of religions, nation-states, or movements. Big narratives enable large-scale cooperation and collective action among people who don't know each other. If people believe strongly enough in an idea, they are even willing to give their lives for it. Would they also be willing to dampen their innate competitive drive?

Could the survival of life on earth as we know it be a compelling enough story to change behavior towards "global citizenship"? Are we at the level where, as Daniel Schmachtenberger says, 'winning equals losing' because our competitive behavior causes a level of destruction that will leave no one untouched, no matter how big our bunker and plentiful our provisions are?

This would mean to inject awareness into each and everyone of our decisions, for example, via a process like *The Council of All Beings* as framed by Joanna Macy, where participants take on the roles of various beings from the natural world, such as animals, plants, or ecosystems, and engage in a dialogue or council where they speak from the perspective of these beings.

Some people seem to think so when they say "if we just believe hard enough that things need to change, it will change!" A big wisdom-oriented narrative is critical to global cooperation.

5.5   A story from the future

I want to end with a fictional story. A fictional story of the future.

Let's assume this story happens in a world where all the levels discussed in this book are addressed enough to unlock the next level. On the individual level, people work through their relationship to their own power and become less likely to play drama roles and more likely to be in an empowerment stance. They worked on their inner development tools. They heal from trauma and attachment issues.

On the team level, in this future, everyone learns how to make decisions and communicate clearly and compassionately. People aren't perfect, but decision-making and group dynamics become good enough to support a sense of *power-with*.

Most people master the organizational level in this version of the future. They have an easy time aligning in their roles in their organizations and can cooperate across organizations to strengthen the tissue of collaboration towards initiatives that solve more systemic issues.

Self-organization is supported in this new future. The legal, economic, and educational systems are transformed. Governments include and inter-mesh a municipal, bioregional, and global level.

What would a day in a life of this way of organizing look like? Let's imagine that all domains are held by self-organized groups on particular levels. For example, the wastewater treatment decisions are made by the workers in the plant, and then send links to the regional entity for decisions that can only be made there. Whenever decisions can be made locally, that happens. Whenever local decisions would benefit from regional or even global information flow, there is an exchange to come to a solution that more local groups can then opt into.

> I wake up in the morning in my own room. I don't share a room because I get woken up easily, and sleep matters! One of my house-mates is up already; I can hear them in the shower. I read the local news on my phone. It's a bad habit, I know. But much better than what it used to be when international and national news were predominant. Now I read the local news. It made a big difference in my well-being.
>
> It's a tricky decision to figure out what to read. Of course, I care about other places, but I also know they have ways to figure things out and to get support. Back then, I'd get so anxious in the morning with all the weight from news in other places that I could do nothing about. I prefer global connection meetups where people share directly from their region. Something about hearing it from a real person, even if virtually, helps take it in, and it helps to remember that the stories are connected to real people.
>
> The local news is full of discussions on the new school building. This topic really got everyone's attention. The old one needs to be replaced because there is mold everywhere. The old ways of building – we still deal with the old housing stock all the time. I certainly don't want that for the children. Now there's a big discussion on whether to build one big school or keep the three small schools in their neighborhoods. I scroll through the pros and cons. I can see what

people are thinking in a moderated discussion and visualization tools. Some say neighborhood schools can stay closer to the community's needs and enhance closer friendships with kids close by. It also mixes up the old class divides we inherited from how things used to be. Having one big school building is more efficient and provides better service, especially for those with special needs.

Reading the pros and cons, I'm feeling torn because both sides make sense. But it looks like there's some progress in the discussion. The town-level School Circle asked for input on the community platform. I follow the link and see some of the questions and answers. But I realize it's not how I want to spend my morning. I let it go, trusting that others will be able to make themselves heard and a solution will be found that brings together the advantages of both. The ideas have certainly become better now that more people are being asked to contribute. It's quite relaxing. I don't have to worry about everything. Now that discussions are had with more moderation, I feel more connected to the people around me; it feels more like we're on the same page about what matters.

Time to get up. Today is my community infrastructure day! I opted into a pilot that provides a basic living stipend to everyone who spends one day in community infrastructure. It was clear to me that I wanted to do it. Both sides of the deal seemed interesting to me – I wanted to spend more time understanding the systems that shape my everyday life. And it was time anyway to leave some of my other roles, and I didn't have anything new that was calling for me. The place I chose there is a particularly interesting one, the role center. It's ironic that I got recruited by the very people who connect people with roles in community infrastructure instead of working in community infrastructure directly, but that's okay. It makes sense given my previous experiences.

I ride my bike to the closest coworking center. There is actually another one in walking distance, only 4 minutes actually, but some of my friends work in the other one, so I typically go there. Plus, it gives me a chance to ride my bike – I'd much rather ride somewhere than just go for a bike ride with no destination, which I always plan but never do. Combining two useful things, transportation, and exercise!

I pass the gardens. I'm surprised to see so many people out already. Are these all community infrastructure projects or collective gardens? I'm surprised I don't know. Time to get more involved, I guess!

It's going to be a warm day for late May. I assume that's why people are out early to catch the time before the sun is too intense. I recognize a former colleague from the programming collective. I remember him reducing his contribution there – I have a feeling I now know why he did that; it's weird he didn't share that he'd work in the garden – maybe still an old feeling of pride? That seems silly in a time where everyone is striving for a better mix of roles that combine computer work, physical work, and work with people. Oh well. Old habits take a while to let go.

I hear the chatter and banter between the people in the gardens. I feel a little sting of jealousy. This looks like a tight and fun community. Then I remind myself that I'm biking to a place I literally chose, and that chose me. Fear of missing out is funny. It is a remnant from a time when joyful working was hard to come by. I'm glad I learned how to recognize those thought patterns in one of the life classes. Learning how to talk myself out of feeling like I'm missing out certainly paid off! It almost felt like I grew up a little as a human by feeling more self-responsible or something like that.

As I pass the care center, children are playing in the yard. They are digging a hole in the dirt, and one of the older kids just drags a bucket of water toward the mud bit. This is going to be messy!

In the corner of my eyes, I see a few seniors sitting in the shade. It's been a few years since they combined elder care and preschools. Figuring out the safety concerns and regulations wasn't easy, but everyone saw and wanted the benefits. I remember reading in the local news that the local Care Circle had referred to pilot studies from other bioregions that showed how it could be done – another issue that improved since decision-making became more local and interconnected.

It's fun to think about everything we can do now, and they almost seem to fall into place. It's more like we finally *allowed* them to happen. It was also interesting how it happened. Lots of independent voices were vocal about the change, and then a VOICE effort – Vocalizing for Organized Initiative and Community Empowerment – was formed to funnel the voices into action. They served as the interface between the community members and the local circles holding the affected domains to make change. I've never been involved in one, but a VOICE effort seems much more productive than marching in the streets!

In the corner of the preschool, there's a group of young people sitting in a circle, deep into discussion. I guess they are seven or eight.

I'm surprised not to see an adult there. Looks almost like they are facilitating their own process. Huh, a lot has changed since my kids went to school. I guess they teach group decision-making even earlier now. That makes sense.

In the transition phase, it was tricky to run all the processes and they took a lot of time. We realized that we needed to up our meeting facilitation skills and collaboration skills overall. I used to be involved a lot in that early transition. I'm proud this took so well! There's a good chance, I tell myself, the kids in that circle were taught by someone I taught. That's a motivating thought. How connected everything is! And how sweet that at least some of the fruits of my labor are visible right here in my neighborhood. I pedal a little faster. I wonder what I will learn today that might bear fruits in the community in ten years?

A cyclist sets up to pass me from behind, but instead of passing, the person stays next to me. I look at their faces and recognize Casey.

'Casey! How are you?'

'I'm fine, slow poke.' I smile. Gentle teases are my love language, and of course, Casey remembers.

'Do you want to stop real quick and catch up?', Casey asks.

'No. I am on my way to community infrastructure. First day, I don't want to be late. But you're welcome to message me when you're ready to prioritize time with me again,' I say with some tease in my voice. There's a history there. Casey and I used to be lovers a few years ago until Casey decided to go monogamous for a while and start a family. I was sad to miss her, and I struggled with that decision for a few weeks, maybe because Casey had made it unilaterally, which is hard. I even went to the community empathy center a few times because I wasn't able to unfunk myself somehow. That wasn't Casey's fault, of course. Casey was just making choices that seemed to make sense for that phase of life. I just wish I had been involved somehow. But it's always a good idea to stay in the game, so I'm happy with my invitation combined with the tease.

'That's exciting! You took the deal in the pilot.'

'Yep.'

'I might do that too when Kira turns one, and the paternity phase ends. Ok, good luck, this is my turn! Bye!'

I arrive at the co-working place and find a spot. Since the weather is so nice, I choose a spot near the big window. I log onto the virtual meeting space. The circle lead, Amari, greets me. I recognize her from our first conversation, where we both agreed to this role. We both check in, but I don't have a lot to say. Partially because I already had my chat just now with Casey, and also because I'm just eager to get going. Amari shares her check-in – sick toddler at home, lots of coughing during the night. I remember those days. Being a parent still isn't easy, even with all the new support systems we have built, at least for daytime. Nights are still on parents, and that might never change. I feel sorry for her.

'As for today's meeting, it's going to be quite a first day for you,' Amari shares. 'Are you okay with me sharing the context for about ten minutes, and then we can explore together what this means to you?'

I nod. I appreciate how well she's holding the space. I relax more.

She dives in. 'There is a big question that we don't seem to be able to solve, and it's grown into tension, honestly. The pilot that you're a part of has found more resonance than we expected. About double what we expected, to be precise.'

'That's amazing!'

'Yeah, but we have a hard time adjusting. There is growing worry that we will bloat the community infrastructure when we just accept everyone. As we both know, bloating structure isn't helpful because it becomes ineffective. Originally, there was a worry that we'd pull away people's attention from other parts of the economy, but that actually isn't a current concern anymore. It's really more about how to give meaningful projects to that many people.'

'Excuse me, Amari, I realize I'm new to the discussion, at least this iteration of it. But couldn't one just widen the definition of community infrastructure? For example, parents of sick children could receive help during the night.' I try to package my idea in a joke in case I'd be off base. But my reference doesn't seem to land with Amari. I assume she's too tired. I decide to tune in better.

'Yeah, it's the unsolved tension we had when this whole transition started. Where does community infrastructure end and the more entrepreneurial side of things that some still call the private sector.'

'Like whether vocational education is public infrastructure or needs to be carried by the organizations themselves.'

'Exactly. Now, this whole question of widening the workforce in infrastructure opens that whole can of worms again. People have strong opinions about it. So today's meeting is going to be hot. We decided to have the whole agenda just on that question.' The first attendees of said meeting log onto the meeting.

Once everyone is there, Amari introduces me to the other five circle members. Amari still seems tired, and a little resigned. I am guessing she's worried about today's meeting and what would happen if this fundamental tension cannot be solved.

Everyone checks in as usual. Since my mind is a bit worried about Amari's emotional state, I am curious to hear what she says. She chooses to stick to a bland check-in, almost the same she gave me about being tired. Now I'm even more worried. When people don't share their concerns, that's a big red flag. I thought we had moved beyond this years ago. I notice anxiety crawling up in me.

I am included in all the rounds, but I decide to pass. This is too much complexity and I want to tune in better, also to understand what is so unsolvable that Amari would give up hope.

They talk about the tension. Some operate with a very tight definition of what infrastructure means – roads, bridges, utilities like sewage and waste, and emergency services. (Someone made a side comment that sounds like they'd prefer a society where emergency services are replaced with private insurance, which is an individualistic stand I hadn't heard in a long time, given our more collectively oriented times.) Others count on everything in the well-being economy, like food, communication, even individual transportation, and housing. A small debate gets ignited when someone brings up the question of whether music was a 'public service' or 'extra'. Some see the influx of new workers as a chance to widen the system, and others see it as a threat of tipping into more collectivism at the cost of individual engagement. The music debate causes a quick back and forth, which quickly gets stopped by the facilitator.

'Wait, wait. We all know debate only hardens our opinions and polarizes our views. Let's all take a deep breath and visualize a bioregion where everyone has what they need. I know it's hard to define what basic needs are, but I also know we can figure it out; it's probably not going to be any of the extremes so let's stay with nuances. (He pauses.) Ok, it looks like this issue cannot be solved here; we've been at it for three meetings already. So, I'd like for everyone to consider what might be needed to resolve this issue. What are we missing? We know that there must be a solution that is acceptable given all constraints – there always is. What would it take to find it? Let's do a round.'

'We should have a big community conversation day on the question. This needs wide input.'

'I'd be curious to see how other bioregions came to conclusions on where to draw the line.'

'I like the thought of a community conversation day. I also want to remind us all that whatever solution we find can still be adjusted. We can ease our way into a new distribution slowly and see how far we want to go. There are a few things on the list that are fairly uncontroversial.'

The round continues, and everyone is clear that broader input from a variety of places is the way to go. The hope is that it will inform the decision and, at the same time, increase the buy-in for whatever decision will be taken. One person takes on the task of tapping into the bioregion exchange network on that very question, and two people will get in contact with the community conversation organization team on behalf of this group to feed this question into the standard processes.

After the meeting, Amari and I debrief. Amari's mood seems lighter. I decide to summon all my courage – after all, we don't really know each other well – to ask her:

'Amari, I noticed you seemed to feel heavy before the meeting, and I assumed you felt sad or resigned. Is that true? And if so, I wondered why you chose not to share that in your check-in.'

Amari sighs. 'Yes, you're right. Resigned is a good word for it. You know, those of us more deeply involved in this transition on this level had to hold a lot of responsibility. And not everyone always seems to wish for the best of this transition. There is still a lot of sentiment that maybe it's all too optimistic or naive. It's almost like some *want* the system to fail to prove us wrong. Remember all the discussions about whether people would still do the less appealing jobs when the transition started? Then that wasn't a thing, and all the worrying was just moot. You know, ironically, it's those tensions that make our work the hardest. It's not the real issues we're struggling with, you know? It's the worry about imagined issues that makes this transition hard. I often wonder what it would take to shift that mindset of problem focus into one that wants to succeed. Will it shift with the new generations that grew up differently, or is this desire to suffer a human thing? I think the jury is still out, and the answer will determine whether this new ecosystem can work or not. And honestly, sometimes I worry that the other side might be right or that the self-fulfilling prophecy of failure simply comes true.'

'That's a really big burden to carry. It's basically the same question
we had at the beginning when people didn't believe that even a small
team would be able to self-organize without coercion. Same question,
but this time on a bigger level.'

'Exactly. You know now why I thought you would be a good fit?'

I get to know the rest of the team. I will be working on re-evaluating
the impact measure system for the infrastructure work that helps inform
how resources are spent. It's highly stimulating work, and my mind is
still going through all the difficult questions of the day. I thought I had
left this world when I moved into software. I didn't expect to go back!

The bike ride home is hot, and I feel sticky and uncomfortable as
I arrive home. Time to go for a swim! I chuckle as I walk toward the
pool in my neighborhood. Is this a community necessity or a luxury
item? On the level of neighborhood, the question isn't as pressing. If
the neighborhood wants it and can make it happen, then it happens. It's
a more straightforward approach to the question. There's something
there to learn. But I'm also tired, and I know much more thinking will
happen in community conversations. I decide to stop analyzing. The
cool salt water from the pool helps bring my attention back to what's
around me. I swim a few lengths. As I got out of the water, a thought
hit me. Now that I do the community infrastructure time, I have the
stipend; I don't need to work as much. I could rearrange my schedule,
let go of a few roles in the private sector, and spend more time on
the infrastructure questions. I am free to choose. A mix of emotions
washes through me. There's joy but also fear of not making the best
choices for myself and the community. Am I just addicted to that
sweet feeling of saving the day? What if I fall back into my patterns
of overworking? That's something to explore carefully. I don't want
to burn out, but I also don't want to hold back. When will I ever learn
to strike that balance?

I pass a group of people in a heated discussion. I realize this is
one of those mobile community conversation vans; they brought a
sun umbrella, chairs, and cold lemonade and are engaging people in
conversation. I know from reading about it that their role is to get
people to talk to each other, less to convince them of anything. The
facilitators study the pros and cons of common topics and make sure
the discussions are balanced, no matter who shows up. Sometimes,
they play devil's advocate, but they had to tone that down because it
just upset people. Instead, they gave them more empathy training, and

seemed to do the trick. The signs indicate that this is a discussion about the housing shortage. There still isn't enough housing, and people are getting frustrated with the new system. If more local governments can't ensure appropriate housing, what good is it all? Sometimes, all the issues in the community do seem overwhelming. Some voices are even questioning the leadership and its legitimacy – a warning sign.

I notice how tired my body is from cycling, swimming, and walking. I text Martha as I swing by the farm stand on my way home to coordinate dinner plans. She decided to go to the neighborhood dinner with friends. I bring my groceries home and join her there. The Neighborhood dinner has two meal choices as usual, and I pick the stir fry. It used to be that there was a whole system about how to make sure people only eat there once a day, but it was changed into a less bureaucratic system when it was clear that the overhead was out of proportion given so little abuse.

Then I look for Martha. She's easy to find, I would recognize her laugh from miles away! She is sitting close to the kids' area where her best friend's toddler is stacking play bricks.

It's been a day. Martha is going out with her friends, but I have much to consider. On my way home, I consider swinging by the empathy booth, but I see a line, and it's still too warm to wait outside. Empathy booths count as infrastructure, don't they? Either way, I'm glad people take to them and make good use of that resource. I certainly have, though I also like the AI version of it. But sometimes, talking to an actual human just feels nicer.

At home, I am curious to log into the bioregion exchange network to see what other bioregions are talking about. My world had gotten so blissfully small when I decided to put my energy in my community instead of getting scattered in virtual space. I enter my question and get an overview of the status of the discussion. It also asks whether I want to be connected with someone interested in a related question. But really, I'm too tired to talk right now. And this is more information than I can take in right now. I'll have a look tomorrow.

None of us can write the story in a way that is complete. What we can do is write the story together, with each one of us contributing what we each know. I invite you to continue the story with what you know and I don't.

www.sociocracyforall.org/collective-power

About the author

I grew up in Germany with three siblings and a British father and a mother from the Black Forest in Germany. Originally, I wanted to study literature but that required classes in linguistics, which had me fall in love with linguistics. For ten years, my world consisted of nested structures, constraints, recursion. I wrote my dissertation on the syntax-semantics interface. Just like governance, language consists of interdependent systems between phonetics, morphology, syntax, semantics and pragmatics.

As a postdoc, I moved to Massachusetts in the United States in 2010 and into a cohousing community shortly after. This is where I started to focus on governance. Jerry Koch-Gonzalez and I founded the self-governed member-led non-profit Sociocracy For All which grew to more than 200 people, and gave me the opportunity to interact with hundreds of other organizations to talk about their governance. I'm grateful to those who trusted me enough to let me look 'under the hood' of their systems.

An unexpected point of learning is my family system. With five children and a number of grown-ups, life feels full, meaningful and wonderful with zillions decisions in many places. Via my gender transition, I know a thing or two about alignment with myself and about the societal systems that shape who we are. Explorations of power, groups, social justice, and systems are an every-day occurrence in my life, and I love that.

Gratitude

The names of people and of companies in this book are anonymized as to not to distract from the general lessons they offer. I'd like to thank Adrian Perreau, Alicia Medina, Allan Rhodes, Azuré Keahi, Cecile Green, Charlie Schweik, Cristina Escalante, David Sloan Wilson, Deborah Chang, Donnie Maclurcan, Edwin Jansen, Edwin John, Egon Loke, Emma Back, Eva Rehse, Eva Schonveld, Filipa Pimentel, Gnanasekar Dhanapal, Helena Rau, Joe Garrison, John Buck, Jurriaan Kramer, Max Tite, Mette Aargaard, Nate Whitestone, Nikoline Arns, Nora Plaza, Paul Atkins, Paula Leigh-Doyle, Peter Bullock, Rafaele Joudry, Rea Gill, Richard Heitfeld, Rodger Mattlage, Samantha Slade, Sven Franke, Tom Thomison, Uli Nagel for references, critique, support, stories and proof-reading!

A special mention goes to Philip Grinsted; I prize our thought partnership. I might even be friends with you if we weren't brothers!

Jerry, I'm endlessly grateful to you for sharing your wisdom with me.

References

- Beer, S., (1972). Brain of the Firm; Allen Lane, The Penguin Press, London, Herder and Herder, USA.
- Bohm, S. (1980). Wholeness and the Implicate Order. Routledge.
- Bollier, D. & Helfrich, S. (2019). Free, fair, and alive: The insurgent power of the commons. New Society Publishers.
- Brafman, O., & Beckstrom, R. A. (2006). The starfish and the spider: The unstoppable power of leaderless organizations. Portfolio.
- Bregman, R. (2020). Humankind: A hopeful history. Little, Brown and Company.
- Brown, A. M. (2017). Emergent strategy: Shaping change, changing worlds. AK Press.
- Buck, J. (2014). We the People: Consenting to a Deeper Democracy. Sociocracy.info Press.
- Bunzl, J. (2006). People-Centred Global Governance – Making it Happen. International Simultaneous Policy Organisation.
- Buterin, V. (2021). The Most Important Scarce Resource is Legitimacy. Retrieved June 2023.
  https://vitalik.ca/general/2021/03/23/legitimacy.html
- Emerald, D. (2005). The Power of TED*. Polaris Publishing
- Endenburg, G. (1998). Sociocracy: The organization of decision-making. Eburon.
- Freeman, J. (1972). The Tyranny of Structurelessness. Berkeley Journal of Sociology, 17, 151-164.
- Freinacht, H. (2022). 3 Design Principles for Protopian Governance. https://medium.com/@hanzifreinacht/3-design-principles-for-protopian-governance-bc2bfa7faa9a
- Graeber & Wengrow (2021). The Dawn of Everything: A New History of Humanity. Farrar, Straus and Giroux
- Grant, A. (2021). Think Again. The power of knowing what you

don't know. Viking.

- Hamel, G. & Zanini, M. (2020). Humanocracy: Creating Organizations as Amazing as the People Inside Them. Harvard Business Review Press.
- Harari, Y. (2011). Sapiens: A Brief History of Humankind.
- Hock, D. (2005). One From Many. VISA and the Rise of Chaordic Organization. Berret-Koehler.
- Ismail, S. et al (2014). Exponential Organizations: Why new organizations are ten times better, faster, and cheaper than yours (and what to do about it). Singularity University.
- Jäger, S., Noy, S., & Schoefer, B. (2021). What does codetermination do? NBER Working Paper Series. Retrieved from https://journals.sagepub.com/doi/10.1177/26317877221084714.
- Jin, O. K. (2018). The Nightmare of Valve's self-organizing "utopia". https://medium.com/dunia-media/the-nightmare-of-valves-self-organizing-utopia-6d32d329ecdb
- John, E. M. (2021). Hello, Neighbourocracy! Governance Where Everyone Has A Say. Neighborhood Community Network.
- Johnson, B. (1992). Polarity Management: Identifying and Managing Unsolvable Problems. HRD Press.
- Kahnemann, D. (2011). Thinking, Fast and Slow. Farrar, Straus and Giroux.
- Kaner, S. (1998). The Leader's Guide to Participatory Decision Making. Jossey-Bass.
- Kameda, M. (1991). Information exchange and group decision making: You can lead a group to knowledge, but you can't make it think. In M. A. Hogg & D. Abrams (Eds.), Group motivation: Social psychological perspectives (pp. 45-70). Harvester Wheatsheaf.
- Karpowitz, C., Mendelberg, T., & Shaker, L. (2012). Gender Inequality in Deliberative Participation. *American Political Science Review, 106*(3), 533-547.
- Kaplan, M. F., & Miller, C. E. (1987). Group decision making and normative versus informational influence: Effects of type of issue and assigned decision rule. Journal of Personality and Social Psychology, 53(2), 306-313. doi:10.1037/0022-3514.53.2.306.
- Kerstin, A, Power To The Children. See https://www.powertothe children-film.com/
- Knapp, M, Flach, A. & Aybga, E. (2016), Revolution in Rojava: Democratic Autonomy and Women's Liberation in the Syrian Kurdistan. Pluto Press.

- Laloux, F. (2014). Reinventing Organizations: A Guide to Creating Organizations Inspired by the Next Stage in Human Consciousness. Nelson Parker.
- Mazzucato, M. (2021). Mission Economy. A Moonshot Guide to Changing Capitalism. HarperCollins Publishers.
- Mekolo, Al & Buck, J. (2023). Governance From Below: Can Children Lead the Way? https://leanpub.com/ governancefrombelowchildren
- Nemeth, C. J. (1977). The differential contributions of majority and minority influence. Psychological Review, 84(2), 218-238. doi:10.1037/0033-295X.84.2.218 doi:10.1017/S0003055412000329
- Osorio, M & Shread, C. (2018). School Circles. See https://schoolcirclesfilm.com/.
- Ostrom, E. (1994). Rules, Games, and Common-Pool Resources: The Grammar of Institutions. University of Michigan Press.
- Pentland, A.S. (2012, April). The new science of building great teams. Harvard Business Review. https://hbr.org/2012/04/the-new-science-of-building-great-teams
- Rau, T. & Koch-Gonzalez, J. (2018). Many Voices One Song. Sharing power with sociocracy. Sociocracy For All.
- Rau, T. (2021). Who Decides Who Decides. How to start a group so everyone can have a voice. Sociocracy For All.
- Rau, T. (2023). Decentralization and Centralization in Sociocratic Organizations—Dynamics, Combinations, and Hybrid Solutions, Journal of Nonprofit Innovation: Vol. 3: Iss. 1, Article 8.
- Raworth, K. (2017). Doughnut Economics. Chelsea Green Publishing.
- Romme, A. G. L., Broekgaarden, J., Huijzer, C., Reijmer, A., & van der Eyden, R. A. I. (2018). From competition and collusion to consent-based collaboration: A case study of local democracy. International Journal of Public Administration, 41(3), 246-255. doi: 10.1080/01900692.2016.1263206
- Scharmer, O. (2009). Theory U: Leading from the Future as It Emerges. Berrett-Koehler Publishers.
- Sharpe, B. (2013). Three Horizons: The Patterning of Hope. Triarchy Press Ltd.
- Schmachtenberger, D. and Hagens M. (2023). The Great Simplification (podcast) with Nate Hagens, guest Daniel Schmachtnberger. https://www.thegreatsimplification.com/episode/71-daniel-schmachtenberger

- Senge, P. M. (1990). The fifth discipline: The art and practice of the learning organization. Doubleday/Currency.
- Shirky, C. (2008). Here comes everybody. The power of organizing without organizations. Penguin.
- Smith, J. & Jones, K. (2015). The impact of idea generation on creativity. Journal of Creative Thinking, 27(2), 20-35.
- Snowden, D., & Boone, M. (2007). A leader's framework for decision making [Framework]. Harvard Business Review. https://hbr.org/2007/11/a-leaders-framework-for-decision-making
- Sober, E., & Wilson, D. S. (1998). Unto others: The evolution and psychology of unselfish behavior. Harvard University Press.
- Stadler, Ch., Hautz, L., Matzler, K. and von den Eiche, S.F. (2021), Open Strategy: Mastering Disruption from Outside the C-Suite. The MIT Press.
- Storey, J., Basterretxea, I., & Salaman, G. (2014). Managing and resisting 'degeneration' in employee-owned businesses: A comparative study of two large retailers in Spain and the United Kingdom. Organization, 21(5), 626–644. https://doi.org/10.1177/1350508414537624
- Suarez, C. (2018). The Power Manual. How to master complex power dynamics. New Society Publishers.
- Tuckman, B. W. (1965). Developmental sequence in small groups. Psychological Bulletin, 63(6), 384-399. https://doi.org/10.1037/h0022100
- Tufekci, Z. (2017). Twitter and Tear Gas. The power and fragility of networked protest. Yale University Press.
- Turchin, P. (2016). Ultrasociety: How 10,000 years of war made humans the greatest cooperators on Earth. Beresta Books.
- Turner, S., Merchant, K., Martin, E., & Kania, J. (2012). Understanding the Value of Backbone Organizations in Collective Impact: Part 2. Stanford Social Innovation Review. https://doi.org/10.48558/HHX0-0V21
- Underwood, P. (2000). The Great Hoop of Life: Volume 1: A Traditional Medicine Wheel for Enabling Learning and for Gathering Wisdom. A Tribe of Two Press.
- Vervaeke, J. (2019). Awakening from the meaning crisis. Youtube playlist https://www.youtube.com/playlist?list=PLND1JCRq8Vuh3f0P5qjrSdb5eC1ZfZwWJ
- Weber, M. (1919 [1970]). Politics as a vocation. In: Gerth HH, Mills CW (eds) From Max Weber: Essays in Sociology. London:

Routledge, 77–128.

- Wilder, H. (2021). Let's Decide Together. Practicing Sociocracy With Children. Sociocracy For All.

- Wilson, D. S., Hayes, S. C., Biglan, A., & Embry, D. D. (2019). Prosocial: Using evolutionary science to build productive, equitable, and collaborative groups. New Harbinger Publications.

- Wineman, S. (2003). Power-under: Trauma and nonviolent social change. Self-published.

- Woolley, A. W., Chabris, C. F., Pentland, A., Hashmi, N., & Malone, T. W. (2010). Evidence for a Collective Intelligence Factor in the Performance of Human Groups. Science, 330(6004), 686-688. doi: 10.1126/science.1193147

Stories

'The Community Doesn't Care', 123, 289

A Fork In The Road, 62
Aim Conflict, 130
Averting A Victim Stance, 301

Baby policy, 144
Benevolent Top-down Implementation, 195
Board Member Wants to Be Involved Everywhere, 128
Building Trust With A Cis Guy, 66, 307

Centralized Pay Rate, 212
Citizens Assembly, 275
Claire Doesn't Ask For What She Wants, 70
Cloud Password System, 82
Common House In Pandemic, 143
Couple In Community Blocks Distributed Power, 129

Decentralized Grantgiving, 175
Don't Skip My Item, 57

Emely's Divorce, 36
Emergence, 165
Enthusiastic Teachers, 129

File Storage Feedback, 184

Fishbowl To Break The Power Game, 13
Fishbowl to break the power game, 123, 196
Forest Row, 280
Founder as source of legitimacy, 206
From Bonus To Base Salary, 250
From Secretary to Colleague, 93
Furnace Story, 30, 145

Gender Balance, 67
German Delegation, 208
Glenn's Glasses, 37, 38
Governance Recommendation Ignored, 198

Hard-of-Hearing Note-taker, 75
Holding Strategy Too Tight, 160

I Don't Like Your Facilitation Style, 19
I don't like your facilitation style, 25
Insurance For Nomads, 209

Just Give Me A Minute, 92

Licensing Is Boring, 66
Life Saver, 134
Local Climate Chapter Aim Conflict, 243
Lonnie takes a risk, 17

Many People Need to Understand A Budget, 268
Meditation Center Implementation, 196
Membership Hypotheticals, 95
Multi-perspectives, 140

Neighborhood Parliaments As Threats, 279
Neutral Admin invite, 10
New CEO, 4, 149
Nonprofit With A Matrix, 141

Objecting 11 Months Later, 116
Objections Can Take a While, 92
Oblivious Andrew, 4
Online Magazine, 235
Open Door, 6, 32
Outdoor Cats, 213

Pastry and Front Circle, 142
Paywall Policy, 104
Personal & Organizational Needs, 266
Piñata Candy, 76
Playing Scheduling Riddle, 96
Pleasing Pauline, 20, 54
Power-hungry Leader or Selfless Empowerer?, 308
Professional Woman Nominates Herself, 297
Provisional Consent, 65

Recruiting Business Pivots, 159
Remuneration policy, 251
Rescuer Pattern, 295
Respect And Care - Value Clash, 156
Rosa Speaks up, 191
Runs and Swims, 100

School Board Pulls The Plug, 197
School Split, 131
Second-class Employee, 296
Self-chosen implementation, 200
Shift Scheduler, 105
Ship With No Mast, 121, 206
SoFA board, 8, 31
Standing Aside In A House Sale, 78
Standing aside in a House Sale, 18
Strategy Circle, 163

Ted Decides, 79
Ted Learns To Follow Rounds, 59
The $10 Puzzle, 107
This Little Light Of Ours, 35
Two brothers, 256
Two Entities, 201, 205

Utrechtse Heuvelrug, 272

vTaiwan, 273

Which Kid Gets Which Room?, 76
Who Can Close The Common House?, 204
Who Gets The Role?, 248, 306
Who Owns the IP?, 133, 242
Who Signs The Contracts?, 259
Women Empowerment via Neighborhood Parliaments, 279

www.ingramcontent.com/pod-product-compliance
Lightning Source LLC
Chambersburg PA
CBHW070053030426
42335CB00016B/1877